Born in England in 1916, Eric Bentley became an American citizen in 1948 and in 1998 was inducted into the (American) Theatre Hall of Fame. By that time he was an established playwright, scholar and critic, and today (2008) nine of his plays are in print in a three-volume set under the titles Rallying Cries, *The Kleist Variations* and *Monstrous Martyrdoms*, the best known of the plays being *Lord Alfred's Lover* and *Are You Now Or Have You Ever Been*. He is the editor of the works of Brecht in the Grove Press edition, and the translator of two Brecht plays published by Penguin, *The Caucasian Chalk Circle* and *The Good Woman of Setzuan*. His two books on Brecht are today available in the single volume *Bentley on Brecht*. His critical books include *The Playwright as Thinker*, *Thinking about the Playwright*, *What is Theatre?* and *The Life of the Drama*.

Contemporary ... Provocative ... Outrageous ...
Prophetic ... Groundbreaking ... Funny ... Disturbing ...
Different ... Moving ... Revolutionary ... Inspiring ...
Subversive ... Life-changing ...

What makes a modern classic?

At Penguin Classics our mission has always been to make the best
books ever written available to everyone. And that also means
constantly redefining and refreshing exactly what makes a 'classic'.
That's where Modern Classics come in. Since 1961 they have been an
organic, ever-growing and ever-evolving list of books from the last
hundred (or so) years that we believe will continue to be read over and
over again.

They could be books that have inspired political dissent, such as
Animal Farm. Some, like *Lolita* or *A Clockwork Orange*, may have
caused shock and outrage. Many have led to great films, from *In Cold
Blood* to *One Flew Over the Cuckoo's Nest*. They have broken down
barriers – whether social, sexual, or, in the case of *Ulysses*, the
boundaries of language itself. And they might – like *Goldfinger* or
Scoop – just be pure classic escapism. Whatever the reason, Penguin
Modern Classics continue to inspire, entertain and enlighten millions
of readers everywhere.

'No publisher has had more influence on reading habits than Penguin'
Independent

'Penguins provided a crash course in world literature'
Guardian

The best books ever written

P E N G U I N ⊕ C L A S S I C S

SINCE 1946

Find out more at www.penguinclassics.com

PENGUIN MODERN CLASSICS

THE HOUSE OF BERNARDA ALBA AND OTHER PLAYS

BLOOD WEDDING/ YERMA/ THE HOUSE OF BERNARDA ALBA

FEDERICO GARCIA LORCA

'Lorca was the epitome of Romantic Spain' Seamus Heaney, *Daily Telegraph*

The revolutionary genius of Spanish theatre, Lorca brought vivid and tragic poetry to the stage with these three powerful dramas. In *The House of Bernarda Alba*, a tyrannical matriarch rules over her house and five daughters, cruelly crushing their hopes and needs. The other plays here also portray female characters whose desires are tragically and violently frustrated: a woman's longing for a child in *Yerma*, and a bride's yearning for her lover in *Blood Wedding*. All appeal for freedom and sexual equality, and are also passionate defences of the imagination: in Christopher Maurer's words, 'poetic drama unsurpassed by any writer of our time'.

Translated by Michael Dewell and Carmen Zapata

Edited with an Introduction by Christopher Maurer

The Theory
of the Modern Stage

From Artaud to Zola:
An introduction to modern theatre and drama

Edited by
ERIC BENTLEY

PENGUIN BOOKS

PENGUIN CLASSICS

Published by the Penguin Group
Penguin Books Ltd, 80 Strand, London WC2R ORL, England
Penguin Group (USA) Inc., 375 Hudson Street, New York, New York 10014, USA
Penguin Group (Canada), 90 Eglinton Avenue East, Suite 700, Toronto, Ontario, Canada M4P 2Y3
(a division of Pearson Penguin Canada Inc.)
Penguin Ireland, 25 St Stephen's Green, Dublin 2, Ireland (a division of Penguin Books Ltd)
Penguin Group (Australia), 250 Camberwell Road, Camberwell,
Victoria 3124, Australia (a division of Pearson Australia Group Pty Ltd)
Penguin Books India Pvt Ltd, 11 Community Centre,
Panchsheel Park, New Delhi – 110 017, India
Penguin Group (NZ), 67 Apollo Drive, Rosedale, North Shore 0632, New Zealand
(a division of Pearson New Zealand Ltd)
Penguin Books (South Africa) (Pty) Ltd, 24 Sturdee Avenue, Rosebank, Johannesburg 2196, South Africa

Penguin Books Ltd, Registered Offices: 80 Strand, London WC2R ORL, England

www.penguin.com

First published in Pelican Books 1968
Reprinted with revisions 1976
Reprinted in Penguin Books 1990
Reprinted with corrections, a new postscript and a revised index 1992
Published in Penguin Modern Classics 2008
004

Selection, Preface and commentary copyright © Eric Bentley, 1968, 1976
All rights reserved

The moral right of the editor has been asserted

Printed in England by Clays Ltd, St Ives plc

978-0-141-18918-5

www.greenpenguin.co.uk

MIX
Paper from
responsible sources
FSC
www.fsc.org FSC™ C018179

Penguin Books is committed to a sustainable
future for our business, our readers and our planet.
This book is made from Forest Stewardship
Council™ certified paper.

ALWAYS LEARNING   **PEARSON**

For

HALLIE FLANAGAN DAVIS

creator of the first people's theatre
in the new world

Contents

7

CONTENTS

Preface (1968)

THE reader of a book such as this, or even the bookshop browser who has not yet decided whether to buy it, deserves to be told what he may expect – what the editor intended to offer and what the editor knew he was not offering.

What *is* 'the theory of the modern stage'? Let me break the question into three. What (in the book) is theory? What, modern? And what, the stage?

It is always easier to lead off with a denial. 'Theory' is not criticism: this book (I could tell myself early in my own planning) must not be a collection either of theatre reviews or of articles on plays or playwrights. My concern must be with general principles. With the word 'modern' I had alternatives: the kind of drama we all call modern can be traced back, and often has been, to the middle of the eighteenth century, but generally we are thinking of Ibsen and after. For reasons of space I certainly had to think as we generally do, though I am glad to say that there is a good deal of referring back to the eighteenth century by the authors I have selected. The term 'the stage' takes in forms of art not treated here, such as music hall and perhaps the circus (though the latter really has no stage), and is sometimes used to exclude an art that *is* treated here – the drama. Some people, even when they have finished reading this book, will say it should have been called *The Theory of the Drama*. I myself would plead, however, that no book of pure dramatic theory would give such prominence to, say, Stanislavsky or Gordon Craig. Yet the word 'theatre' (*The Theory of the Theatre*) would probably mislead in just the opposite direction. I like to think that the term 'the Stage' still suggests the inseparable union of theatre and drama. And so this book is entitled: *The Theory of the Modern Stage*.

It also has a subtitle: 'An Introduction to Modern Theatre and Drama', the second half of which merely removes any vestigial ambiguities in the main title. The unremarkable word Introduction found its way in only after my thinking about the book had gone through several stages.

A person who is invited to edit a book on a given subject assumes, does he not, that the subject exists? Publishers must know what they are doing when they issue invitations! And after all one has

9

heard of 'the theory of the modern stage' or something very like it. *Ergo*, there must be such a thing.

A person like myself who has even lived a good part of his life with 'the thing', and with all the phrases used to describe 'it', such as 'theory of the modern stage', is all the more apt to suppose, first, that the thing is very much *there* and, second, that he very certainly knows what it is. Yet, when the moment comes, one wonders.

There is a situation which we would like to be able to say exists, or which, at any rate, the rationalist within us would like to say exists. I would call it the foursquare situation. If life, if history, were foursquare, everything would be what it was, everything would be in its proper place, and classification would be as satisfactory as it sounds. For example, Émile Zola would be Naturalism, and Naturalism would be Émile Zola, and no discrepancy between theory and practice would be permitted. The novels would exemplify the essays, and the essays would summarize the novels.

Now Émile Zola is only a relatively difficult case. At least he did have the grace to subscribe to an Ism, and to define it with considerable lucidity and eloquence. What of artists who are scarcely theorists at all? What of artists who are bad theorists? What of artists who are bad writers?

It might be thought that bad writers would not come within the compass of a book like this in any case. Not so. The theatre arts are not all verbal: some of the theatre's artists must be permitted to be bad writers. They can be overlooked then! says the newcomer to this scene. Not so, neither! What they are fumbling to say may be very good; and it may be significant that it was said, or half-said, by them in particular; and even if it is not very good, it may be important in the future because it has been influential in the past. Is there a scandal in this last criterion? Shall I be told that, if we are talking of mere historical *weight*, I might as well have confined this study to the commercial theatre, and presented the views of C. B. Cochran, Hugh Beaumont, David Merrick and such? No, I think certain standards are built into the very notion of a book like this. That is why I did not bother to mention them when defining 'modern theatre'. It was, is, and will be pretty clear that my understanding of what modern theatre is diverges from that of the average ticket buyer in the West End or on Broadway. When I say that influence is important *per se*, I mean, for example, the influence of Richard Wagner's writing. They are not writings

I admire. They are simply writings I cannot deny the influence, the historic role, of. Therefore something had to be done about them in this book.

I put it thus circumspectly, for no excerpt from the works of Wagner appears in this book, except by way of quotation in an essay by Arthur Symons. The schoolboy in each of us would insist that, since Richard Wagner had theories, he must somewhere have given the definitive account of what they were, preferably in very clear summary form, moving briskly along from A to B to C. One can then set down his A's, B's and C's parallel to, say, Ibsen's, and compare the views of Wagner and Ibsen. But Ibsen did not care to theorize, and Wagner, who did, wrote prose which I, and not I alone, find rather unreadable, whether in German or English. Should I set my readers the task of ploughing through it anyway? I cannot believe they actually would. Symons sums up Wagner better than Wagner ever did, and is readable: that is why his work, and not the *Meister's*, is used here.

Something similar has to be said for Wagner's disciple, Adolphe Appia. There is the same bad prose and the same predilection for grandiose categories and high abstractions. Mr Lee Simonson brings Appia down to earth but so gently and lovingly that the Swiss designer's most ardent admirers can only be ingratiated by what Mr Simonson has written in the chapter included here.

Ibsen, as I say, did not theorize at all. The theory of Ibsenism was only something he occasionally read about, invariably with surprise and sometimes with fury. And the non-schoolboy in us is bound to admit there is something profoundly *satisfactory* about such a tightlipped author, about an artist who explains himself through his art alone. The absence from the present pages of Ibsen, Chekhov and Strindberg implies no disrespect. On the contrary, I respect the reticence of the two of them who were reticent – Ibsen and Chekhov. On the latter I would like to add that the passages usually quoted from him about his plays would hardly be in place here. They are of interest, like everything he wrote, but Chekhov is as secretive about his art and its essential principles as Shakespeare or Mozart. As for Strindberg, he assayed dramatic theory, as he assayed everything else, but only in the preface to *Miss Julie* does he show much theoretical grasp. There were two reasons for not printing that preface here. First, Naturalism is represented, and perhaps better, by Zola. Second, the famous preface is very widely available both in editions of *Miss Julie* and in anthologies of criticism and theory.

In short, 'it would have been nice' to take the great dramatists and have each explain in turn how his art 'works'. In our day, all artists are asked to do that sort of thing all the time on radio and television. But the great ones of the past have not always done it, even in books, and when they have done it, they have not always done it well. Hence, the great figures are represented here by their own work only when their own work provides the best representation for them. It is to be hoped that my table of contents becomes more understandable in the light of this statement.

The book can only, of course, be an Introduction – I return to this word. The schoolboy in us wishes to tell the bookseller: Give me a book that contains all I need to know about modern dramatic theory. True, a person may not *need* to know very much in this field — he may even not need to know anything of it. But granted that he wishes to enter the field at all, and to be glad afterwards that he has, I would say that the best purpose the book can serve is *really* as an introduction – to a subject far larger than itself. What a Bernard Shaw thought about theatre and drama *cannot* be compressed, even by him, into a few pages. To have read the adroit Symons on Wagner is not to have comprehended Wagnerism but only to have made its acquaintance. It would be a disservice to education to pretend that this is not so. And of course education has often performed such disservices – many a Frenchman thinks he knows all philosophy after a brief flirtation with selections from selected philosophers at the *lycée*. Such is the little learning that is a dangerous thing. Education should not bring to students self-contained and seemingly self-sufficient excerpts – excerpts that seem not to be excerpts, and which aim at removing the need for further reading, rather than creating such a need. Introductions should introduce. Such thoughts, at any rate, governed my choices in making this book. I did not wish to pretend to be taking the reader everywhere, to be covering all the ground with him, but rather to provide him with glimpses of the ground from different vantage points, in different lights, through different binoculars. Even where my authors may be dictatorial and absolute, one dictator is here cancelled out by another, and thus the absolute becomes relative. If someone were to describe the book as 'merely a bundle of hints' I should not be dismayed, except by the word *merely*.

If it is important that I should not claim to do more than introduce, it is equally important that this be done with the thoroughness it properly requires. Some anthologies do not meet this condition because the selections are too brief. One gets an author's conclusions without the argument by which the conclusions are reached, and this is not in the least educational. Just the opposite. By that method we train mere quiz kids, students who can cite Aristotle's 'unities' but have not the slightest idea what, in full, and in sequence, Aristotle said about them.

I have chosen such lengthy extracts for this book that – the space available being limited – I could not include very many extracts. This was the price that had to be paid. Granted that the book is purely introductory in aim, it is a price, surely, well worth paying. I have not appointed my ten makers of modern theatre THE ten makers of modern theatre, or my five historians THE five chroniclers of modern theatre.

To return to the question whether one really knows what the phrase 'theory of the modern stage' means. I have said that theory is a matter of general principles. Does the modern stage *have* principles? It would be easy, certainly, to imagine any art proceeding on principles in a way in which it really doesn't. School textbooks are full of such false imaginings. They teach that an Expressionist is one who, before painting a picture, looks through the fourteen points which are Expressionism and works all fourteen of them into his design. If my readers are not more sophisticated than this before they read this book, I hope they will be afterwards.

The proposition that theory is a matter of general principles might mean various things. Again I will start with a denial. I did not presuppose that the modern theatre was like a Church, agreed on a particular set of principles. But neither did I see a mere medley of personal differences of opinion. I started from a sense that there existed a main tradition, generally called Realism, and that there had been many revolts against it. I think it is fairly easy to place each figure represented here on one side or the other of the fence.

If I have avoided a chronological order which might have clarified this matter of tradition somewhat, it is because I saw in it a danger of a false progressivism. A well-known academic course in New York was called The March of Drama. That kind of rhetoric had body in Zola's time; now it rings hollow. I would not wish to present either our Realism or any of the proposed alternatives as that to which all Creation has moved. The names of my ten principal figures are given in alphabetical order.

Although the two main traditions of the modern stage will be repeatedly brought to the reader's attention, and although other large themes will recur here and there in the book, I have not picked the excerpts to prove a thesis, nor have I fought beyond a certain point with the fact that the word *theory* is a loose word. This is no place for the study of the theory of theory. Let me say in the simplest terms what my procedure was.

Realizing that I would be limited to a few figures, I made choices which are hardly personal, but correspond to a kind of consensus. That Richard Wagner is important in the history of theatre is not your opinion or mine, there is a consensus about it, one might almost say it is a fact. For Part One I chose ten names (a good round number) that seemed to have attained a similar status, making sure that I got the right chronological span – the mid nineteenth century to the mid twentieth – and sufficient variety. As to exactly what topics would come up, I let the principals, or their best expositors, speak for themselves, placing the emphasis where they themselves wished to place it. Part One imparts, I think, some sense of artists legislating reality into being. Shelley, in his notorious phrase about 'unacknowledged legislators' was not wholly wrong – he was certainly not talking about nothing. Many things become so because they are said to be so, like *credit* in our economic system. That is why, on occasion, the wildest fantasy can become the flintiest reality, and a crackpot's theory may become solid history. Where would the history of religion be if this last proposition were not true?

But in part, even what the artists, the makers, say early on is only generalization upon what has already occurred. So there is a natural overlap between the first and second part of this book, for Part Two is almost wholly devoted to generalizations. Here the great precursor is Aristotle, who made such generalizations in his *Poetics*, and only by a notorious blunder was it for a long time assumed that what he intended was a manifesto, a prophecy, or a permanent book of rules.

If I believed the modern stage had had its Aristotle, Part Two of this book would be wholly given over to his *Poetics*. For lack of such a document, one picks out a few dozen pages of comment from many, many thousands. There *is* much brilliant commentary, but I had (I thought) to resist the temptation to exhibit brilliance, as also the temptation to 'work in' this or that distinguished name. In Part Two, the point was not to feature the work of any particular man as such, but only to find writing in which many of the threads of Part One were brought together. Say what we will in favour of concreteness and particularity, what we all want to do in the end is: generalize. We want to move on from the particular to the universal, from fact to truth. Let me hasten to add that I by no means consider that this transition is actually effected in Part Two. Only that, in our efforts to effect it, some assistance is given. My choices were made with that, and only that, in mind.

Unlike the choices of Part One, they are personal choices, for there was now no consensus to go by. My reasoning was along these lines. The modern Aristotle would not be a metaphysician but a historian. The 'over-view' we are after is a historical over-view. Not to belabour the word *realistic*, I would say that what we require from a historian is a certain critical realism. In saying this I show, no doubt, the bias that has led to my including in Part Two excerpts by Lukács, Hauser, Brandes, Rolland and Tocqueville. Which is as it should be. If parts of this Preface have sounded like an apologia, I am happy if it ends up, instead, as merely an explanation.

ERIC BENTLEY

Acknowledgements (1968)

FOR permission to publish items in this anthology, acknowledgement is made to the following: for 'The Ideas of Adolphe Appia' from *The Stage is Set* by Lee Simonson to Theatre Arts Books, New York (copyright 1932 by Harcourt, Brace & Co., copyright renewed 1960 by Lee Simonson. Copyright © 1963 by Theatre Arts Books, New York); for 'The Theatre of Cruelty: Two Manifestos' from Antonin Artaud's *The Theatre and its Double*, translated by Mary Caroline Richards, to Grove Press Inc. and Calder & Boyars Ltd; for 'The Street Scene' and 'On Experimental Theatre' from *Brecht on Theatre* by Bertolt Brecht, translated by John Willett, copyright © 1957, 1963 and 1964 by Suhrkamp Verlag, Frankfurt am Main, translation and notes © 1964 by John Willett to Hill and Wang Inc. and Methuen & Co. Ltd; for 'Helene Weigel: On a Great German Actress' and 'Weigel's Descent into Fame' by Bertolt Brecht, translated by John Berger and Anna Bostock, to the translators; for 'The Art of the Theatre: The First Dialogue' from *On the Art of the Theatre* by E. Gordon Craig to William Heinemann Ltd and Theatre Arts Books (All Rights Reserved, copyright 1956 by Theatre Arts Books); for 'A Theory of the Stage' from *Plays, Acting and Music* by Arthur Symons to Jonathan Cape Ltd; for 'The Ideas of Richard Wagner' and 'A New Art of the Stage' from *Studies in Seven Arts* by Arthur Symons, copyright 1925, by E. P. Dutton & Co. Inc., renewal 1953 by Miss Mona Hill, to the publishers; for 'Obsessed by Theatre', Paul Goodman's review of Antonin Artaud's 'The Theatre and its Double', from *The Nation*, to the author; for 'Spoken Action' by Luigi Pirandello, translated by Fabrizio Melano, to the sons of Luigi Pirandello and the translator; for the Appendix to 'The Quintessence of Ibsenism' and 'A Dramatic Realist to his Critics' by George Bernard Shaw to The Society of Authors; for David Magarshack's adaptation of his Introduction to *Stanislavsky on the Art of the Stage* (© 1961 by David Magarshack) to the author, Faber & Faber Ltd, and Hill & Wang Inc.; for 'A People's Theatre', from *Plays and Controversies*, by W. B. Yeats, to The Macmillan Company (copyright 1924 by The Macmillan Company, renewed 1952 by Bertha Georgie Yeats); for an extract from *Naturalism in the Theatre* by Émile Zola, translated by Albert Bermel, to the translator; for Brandes's in-

17

augural lecture, translated by Professor Evert Sprinchorn, to the translator; for 'Origins of Domestic Drama', from *The Social History of Art* by Arnold Hauser, translated in collaboration with the author by Stanley Godman, to Routledge & Kegan Paul Ltd, and to Alfred A. Knopf Inc., publishers of *The Social History of Art*, Vintage Edition, by Arnold Hauser; for an extract from *Sociology of Modern Drama* by George Lukács and 'To Begin' by Otto Brahm, translated by Lee Baxandall, to the translator; for an extract from *The People's Theatre* by Romain Rolland, translated by Barrett H. Clark, to George Allen & Unwin Ltd.

I owe a special debt to friends and colleagues who undertook to make translations 'on spec', that is, before publication of this book was contracted for: Lee Baxandall, Albert Bermel, Fabrizio Melano and Evert Sprinchorn.

I have to acknowledge very much assistance in getting material copied and checking on various data from David Beams and Hugo Schmidt.

One contribution was an outright gift from the copyright owner, the ever-generous John Gassner.

Finally, this volume stands in quite a special relation to Toby Cole. Herself the editor of *Playwrights on Playwriting* and other standard works in the field, she has been both agent and friend to the editor of *The Theory of the Modern Stage*.

E.B.

Ideas are to drama what counterpoint is to music; nothing in themselves but the *sine qua non* for everything.

FRIEDRICH HEBBEL

Without theory, practice is only routine imposed by habit.

LOUIS PASTEUR

Our word *theory*, which we use in connexion with reasoning and which comes from the same Greek word as *theatre*, means really looking fixedly at, contemplation; it is very near in meaning to our *imagination*.

JANE HARRISON

PART ONE

Ten Makers of Modern Theatre

Adolphe Appia

ADOLPHE APPIA, 1862–1928, in figuring out how Wagner should be staged, made himself a pioneer of modern staging in general. Primarily a designer, he also wrote on the theory of theatre. His own writings are not drawn on here, for reasons explained in the editor's preface. What follows seemed to the editor to make a better case for Appia's scheme of things than Appia himself ever made, and it has the additional interest of being written by an eminent designer of the American theatre, Lee Simonson, 1888–1967. It consists of a chapter from his book, *The Stage is Set* (1932)*. It should be added that Appia's own writings, unavailable in English at the time his reputation was made, have more recently been finding their way into print. In book form, the first item was *The Work of Living Art* and *Man is the Measure of All Things*, edited by Barnard Hewitt and translated by H. D. Albright†: and it was soon followed by *Music and the Art of the Theatre*, edited by Barnard Hewitt, translated by Robert W. Corrigan and Mary Douglas Dirks‡. Less than book-length items had been published in English earlier. Perhaps the most notable of these is: 'Living Art or Still Life?', translated by S. A. Rhodes, in *The Theatre Annual 1943* (New York).

* Re-issued by Theatre Arts Books, New York, 1963.
† Coral Gables: University of Miami Press, 1960.
‡ Coral Gables: University of Miami Press, 1962.

The Ideas of Adolphe Appia

LEE SIMONSON

I. MUSIC AS LAWGIVER

To Appia, a passionate Wagnerite, as to Pater, music was the ideal art to whose condition all the other arts aspired. He found in Wagner's music-dramas of the Nibelung's hoard the key to the scenic artist's liberation. As a philosopher Appia longed for the consolation of the Absolute and found it in a new kind of operatic score, a novel cohesion of music and dialogue; once its secrets had been penetrated, its musical intervals, tonalities, and rhythms deeply felt, these could supply an unerring clue to their scenic interpretation, determining not only the form of the stage-setting itself but the movements of actors within it down to the smallest detail of stage business and the fluctuations of light that illuminated them. As an artist Appia found release in music because its emphasis was emotional rather than factual and so supplied a norm which an artist could approximate until his settings were equally expressive. Stage pictures were to be freed from the necessity of reproducing backgrounds of action; they were to be transfigured until every element in them embodied the emotions that it was to arouse as an integral part of its form, its colour, and its total design. *Ausdruckskraft* – the force of expression, expressiveness – was one of Appia's favourite terms, and became the corner-stone on which most of the later doctrines of theatrical expressionism were reared. 'Music finds its ultimate justification in our hearts,' he wrote, using that traditional term to summarize the emotional core of our being, 'and this occurs so directly, that its expression is thereby impalpably hallowed. When stage pictures take on spatial forms dictated by the rhythms of music they are not arbitrary but on the contrary have the quality of being inevitable.'

27

The theories that elucidated the basic aesthetic principles of modern stage design, analysed its fundamental technical problems, outlined their solution, and formed a charter of freedom under which scene-designers still practise, appeared in two volumes under two quasimusical titles: *La Mise en Scène du Drame Wagnérien* (*The Staging of Wagnerian Music-drama*) and *Die Musik und die Inscenierung* (*Music and Stage-Setting*). The first was published in Paris in 1895 as an inconspicuous brochure of fifty-one pages, the second as a full-sized volume, translated from a French script, in Munich in 1899. Neither was ever widely enough read to warrant reprinting, nor has either ever been translated,* a fact which immensely aided Gordon Craig in imposing himself as a prophet on the English and American theatre. Both the book and the booklet are now so difficult to procure that they have become collector's items. But their influence was immediately felt, for Appia was that rare combination, a creative artist of exceptional imagination and at the same time a rigorously logical theorist. Many of his ideas are blurred by an appallingly clumsy German translation, which, like most philosophical German, straddles ideas, so that catching their meaning becomes rather like trying to hold a greased pig running between one's legs. Fortunately *Music and Stage-Setting* contained eighteen illustrations of projected settings for Wagner's operas, which embodied Appia's aesthetic principles with such finality that they became a revelation of a totally new kind of stage-setting and stage lighting, then as strange as the outlines of a newly discovered continent at dawn and now so familiar. These drawings revealed a unity and a simplicity that could be made an inherent part of stage-settings in a way that no one had hitherto conceived, Wagner least of all. Practitioners of stage-craft were converted by a set of illustrations to a gospel which most of them never read.

There is in Appia much of the *Schwärmerei* typical of German music, and at times a mouth-filling grandiloquence, a bewildering mixture of philosophic concepts such as 'inner

* No longer true today. See the headnote preceding this excerpt. E.B.

reality' and the transcendentalism of German metaphysics, expressed in romantic and mystic imagery (also typically Teutonic) used to beatify Art, Nature, and the Poet. Art is an inner something, eternal, ultimate, hidden behind appearance, another *Ding an sich*, which only a particular kind of poet, like Wagner the creator of music-drama, can clothe with meaning. The demands of Music become a kind of categorical imperative which, if obeyed, will lead to the universal laws of the universal work of art:

The loftiest expression of the Eternal in Man can only be reborn and forever renew itself in the lap of Music. In return Music demands that we have implicit faith in her. . . . This book was written in the service of Music and for such a mistress no experiment is irrelevant, no labour too great. . . . In order to express the inner reality underlying all phenomena the poet renounces any attempt to reproduce their fortuitous aspects; and once this act of renunciation has taken place the complete work of art arises. . . . Then Wagner appeared. At the same time that his music-dramas revealed a purely expressive form of art, they also confirmed, what we had hitherto dimly sensed, the omnipotent power of music. . . .

Music and music alone can coordinate all the elements of scenic presentation into a completely harmonious whole in a way which is utterly beyond the capacity of our unaided imagination. Without music the possibility of such harmony does not exist and therefore cannot be discovered. . . .

Music-drama will become the focus for all our highest artistic accomplishments and will concentrate them like rays of light converging through a lens.

Such prophecies and pronunciamentos resound through Appia's theories, at times with Wagnerian sonority. There are times also when his theories seem the scenario for another music-drama in which the artist-hero, guided by the goddess of Music, will wrest a treasure from its crabbed guardians, not a cursed treasure but a beneficent one whose magic touch is capable of transfiguring not only the artist but the theatre and all the world. Two thirds of *Music and Stage-Setting* are devoted to a lengthy speculation on the future of music-drama. Appia accepts Bayreuth as the ultimate expression of German culture, indulges in an elaborate analysis of French culture, shows how German music can arouse the religious nature of French musicians, how the French artist's sensitiveness to essential form can wean Germans from their instinctive dependence on realism. At Bayreuth, in an international poet's Elysium, the two nations are to conduct jointly a presumably endless cycle of music-dramas which will carry Wagner's original inspiration to the expressionistic heights implicit in his music.

At the same time Appia shows a thoroughly Gallic capacity for objective analysis, which he uses to explain the aesthetic problems of the scene-designer and the technical means available for solving them. Here with amazing directness and clarity he dissects the plastic elements of the stage picture. In doing so he anticipates in detail the present technical basis of stage lighting and outlines precisely the way it has since been used, not only as an indispensable means of unifying stage settings, by suggesting mood and atmosphere, but also as a method of emphasizing the dramatic values of a performance and heightening our emotional response to them. The first 120 pages of Appia's volume are nothing less than the textbook of modern stage-craft that gave it both a new method of approaching its problems and a new solution.

2. THE PLASTIC ELEMENTS

The aesthetic problem of scenic design, as Appia made plain, is a plastic one. The designer's task is to relate forms in space, some of which are static, some of which are mobile. The stage itself is an enclosed space. Organization must be actually three-dimensional. Therefore the canons of pictorial art are valueless. The painted illusion of the third dimension, valid in the painted picture where it can evoke both space and mass, is immediately negated when it is set on a stage where the third dimension is real.

The plastic elements involved in scenic design, as Appia analysed them, are four: perpendicular painted scenery, the horizontal floor, the moving actor, and the lighted space in which they are confined. The aesthetic problem, as he pointed out, is a single one: How are these four elements to be combined so as to produce an indubitable unity? For, like the Duke of Saxe-Meiningen, he was aware that the plastic elements of a production remained irretrievably at odds if left to themselves. Looking at the stages about him he saw that the scene-painter of his day merely snipped his original picture into so many pieces which he stood about the stage, and then expected the actor to find his way among them as best he could. The painted back-drop was the only part of an ensemble of painted scenery that was not a ludicrous compromise. Naturally the scene-painter was interested, being a painter, in presenting as many stretches of unbroken canvas as possible. Their centre of interest was about midway between the top of the stage and the stage floor at a point where, according to the line of sight of most of the audience, they attained their maximum pictorial effect. But the actor works on the stage floor at a point where painted decorations are least effective as painting. So long as the emphasis of stage setting is on painted decoration, the inanimate picture is no more than a coloured illustration into which the text, animated by the actor, is brought. The two collide, they never meet nor establish any interaction of the slightest dramatic value, whereas, in Appia's phrase, they should be fused.

'Living feet tread these boards and their every step makes us aware of how meaningless and inadequate our settings are.' The better the scenery is as painting, the worse it is as a stage setting; the more completely it creates an illusion of the third dimension by the pictorial conventions of painting, the more completely an actually three-dimensional actor destroys that illusion by every movement he makes. 'For no movement on the actor's part can be brought into vital relation with objects painted on a piece of canvas.' Painted decorations are not only at odds with the actor but also with the light that illuminates them. 'Light and vertical painted surfaces nullify rather than reinforce each other. . . . There is an irreconcilable conflict between these two scenic elements. For the perpendicular, painted flat in order to be seen, needs to be set so as to catch a maximum amount of light.' The more brilliantly it is lighted, the more apparent the lack of unity between it and the actor becomes. 'If the setting is so placed as to refract some of the light thrown on it its importance as a painted picture is diminished to that extent.'

For Appia there was no possibility of compromise by keeping actors away from perspective back-drops where doors reached only to their elbows, or by warning them not to lean on flimsy canvas cut-outs down stage. He denied painted simulation of the third dimension a place in the theatre with a finality that gave his analysis the air of a revolutionary manifesto. He was the first to banish the scenic painter and his painted architecture from the modern stage. To Appia the actor was *massgebend* – the unit of measurement. Unity could be created only by relating every part of a setting to him. He was three-dimensional, therefore the entire setting would have to be made consistently three-dimensional. The stage setting could have no true aesthetic organization unless it was coherently plastic throughout. Appia's importance as a theorist is due to the consistency and the practicability of the methods he outlined for achieving this result.

One began to set a stage not in mid-air on hanging back-drops, but on the stage floor where the actor moved and worked. It should be broken up into levels, hummocks, slopes, and planes that supported and enhanced his movements. And these were again not to be isolated – a wooden platform draped with canvas here, a block or rock there, planted on a bare board floor, a 'chaise-longue made of grass mats'. The stage floor was to be a completely fused, plastic unit. Appia in this connexion thinks in terms of sculpture. In order to make a model of a stage floor as he described it one would have to use clay. He considered the entire space occupied by a stage setting as a sculpturesque unit. The solidity achieved by setting wings at right angles to each other to imitate the corner of a building seemed to him feebly mechanical. He conceived much freer stage compositions where the entire area could be modelled as a balance of asymmetrical, spatial forms, a composition in three dimensions, that merged imperceptibly with the confining planes that bounded the setting as a whole.

Appia expressed in dogmatic form much of what the Duke of Saxe-Meiningen had demonstrated pragmatically. But in promulgating his theory of a stage setting he completed its unification by insisting on the plasticity of light itself, which no one before him had conceived. He demonstrated in detail, both as a theorist and as a draftsman, how stage lighting could be used and controlled so as to establish a completely unified three-dimensional world on the stage. Appia distinguishes carefully between light that is empty, diffuse radiance, a medium in which things become visible, as fish do in a bowl of water, and concentrated light striking an object in a way that defines its essential form. Diffused light produces blank visibility, in which we recognize objects without emotion. But the light that is blocked by an object and casts shadows has a sculpturesque quality that by the vehemence of its definition, by the balance of light and shade, can carve an object before our eyes. It is capable of arousing us emotionally because it can so emphasize and accent forms as to give them new force and meaning. In Appia's theories, as well as in his drawings, the light which in paintings had already been called dramatic was for the first time brought into the theatre, where its dramatic values could be utilized. Chiaroscuro, so controlled as to reveal essential or significant form, with which painters had been preoccupied for three centuries, became, as Appia described it, an expressive medium for the scene-designer. The light that is important in the theatre, Appia declares, is the light that casts shadows. It alone defines and reveals. The unifying power of light creates the desired fusion that can make stage floor, scenery, and actor one.

Light is the most important plastic medium on the stage. . . . Without its unifying power our eyes would be able to perceive what objects were but not what they expressed. . . . What can give us

this sublime unity which is capable of uplifting us? Light! . . .
Light and light alone, quite apart from its subsidiary importance in
illuminating a dark stage, has the greatest plastic power, for it is
subject to a minimum of conventions and so is able to reveal
vividly in its most expressive form the eternally fluctuating appearance of a phenomenal world.

The light and shade of Rembrandt, Piranesi, Daumier, and
Meryon was finally brought into the theatre as an interpretative medium, not splashed on a back-drop, as romantic
scene-painters had used it, but as an ambient medium
actually filling space and possessing actual volume; it was
an impalpable bond which fused the actor, wherever and
however he moved, with everything around him. The plastic
unity of the stage picture was made continuous.

If one looks at reproductions of stage settings before Appia
– and the history of stage setting might almost be divided by
B.A. as history in general is divided by B.C. – they are filled
with even radiance; everything is of equal importance. The
stage is like a photograph of a toy theatre; the actors might
be cardboard dolls. In Appia's drawings for the first time the
stage is a microcosm of the world. It seems to move from
'morn to noon, from noon to dewy eve,' and on through all
the watches of the night. And the actors in it seem living
beings who move as we do from sunlight or moonlight into
shadow. Beneath their feet there is not a floor but the surface
of the earth, over their heads not a back-drop but the
heavens as we see them, enveloping and remote. There is
depth here that seems hewn and distance that recedes infinitely farther than the painted lines converging at a mathematical vanishing point. In attacking the conventions of
scene-painting Appia created an ultimate convention. For
the transparent trickery of painted illusions of form he substituted the illusion of space built up by the transfiguration
that light, directed and controlled, can give to the transient
structures of the stage-carpenter. The third dimension,
incessant preoccupation of the Occidental mind for four
centuries, defined by metaphysicians, explored by scientists,
simulated by painters, was re-created in terms of the theatre,

made actual. The stage more completely than ever before became a world that we could vicariously inhabit; stage settings acquired a new reality. The light in Appia's first drawings, if one compares them to the designs that had preceded his, seems the night and morning of a First Day.

3. LIGHT AS THE SCENE-PAINTER

Light was to Appia the supreme scene-painter. 'The poet-musician,' he declared, 'paints his picture with light.' Although at one moment Appia announces that his book is dedicated to the service of the goddess of music, at another he says: 'It is precisely the misuse of stage lighting with all its far-reaching consequences which has been the chief reason for writing this book in the first place. . . .'

Only light and music can express 'the inner nature of all appearance'. Even if their relative importance in music-drama is not always the same, their effect is very similar. Both require an object to whose purely superficial aspect they can give creative form. The poet provides the object for music, the actor, in the stage setting, that for light.

In the manipulations of light Appia found the same freedom that, in his eyes, music gave the poet. Light controlled and directed was the counterpart of a musical score; its flexibility, fluidity, and shifting emphasis provided the same opportunity for evoking the emotional values of a performance rather than the factual ones. As music released the mood of a scene, projecting the deepest emotional meaning of an event as well as its apparent action, so the fluctuating intensities of light could transfigure an object and clothe it with all its emotional implications.

Light with its infinite capacity for varying nuances was valuable to Appia for its power of suggestion, which has become for us the distinguishing mark of everything artistic. He points out how in *Das Rheingold* one can give the impression of water through the sensation of depth by keeping the stage dim, filling the scene with 'a vague obscurity' where contours are not defined. For *Die Walküre* the open air will be felt only if the summit of a mountain detaches itself clearly against misty distances. The flames of the *Feuerzauber* are not to be continued an instant beyond the time allotted to them in the score. Their intensity will be emphasized by contrasting them with 'a limpid night sky vaguely pierced by stars'. The light in Mime's cavern, which is illuminated by his forge, is to have an entirely different quality: 'The general feeling given will be one of oppression and a lack of light. The proportions of the setting will contribute to this sense of oppressive weight. Reflections of spurts of flame will intermittently illuminate now this detail of the setting, now that one; and the setting itself, in blocking the source of light, will cast shadows that produce an ensemble chaotic in effect of which, it goes without saying, the personages in the scene will be a part.' The *Waldweben* in *Siegfried* is to be accompanied by a wavering play of fluttering sunlight and leaf shadows. The forest is to be made with the barest indication of a few tree trunks and branches. Siegfried will seem to be in a forest because he is tinged in the vaguely green suffusion of light filtering through leaves and bespattered with an occasional sun-spot. The audience will then see a wood even though it does not see all the trees.

The flexibility of stage lighting, as Appia envisaged it, relates it fundamentally to every movement that an actor makes; the whole setting by fluctuations of light and shade moves with him and follows the shifting dramatic emphasis of a particular scene or sequence of scenes. Appia shows how, in the first act of *Siegfried*, Mime and Siegfried are to be alternately in light and shadow as their respective roles become more or less important. And he points out also that any portion of a setting – a building, a tree, the background of a room – can actually be brought forth or wiped out as its dramatic importance in the scene increases or diminishes.

4. LIGHT AS INTERPRETER

Light in Appia's hands became a guiding principle for the designer, enabling him to give to a setting as the audience sees it the same reality that it is supposed to have for the actors in it. In an appendix to *Music and Stage-Setting* he shows in detail how the control of stage lighting makes this possible for a production of *Tristan and Isolde*.

Act II: As Isolde enters she sees only two things: the burning torch set as a signal for Tristan and enveloping darkness. She does not see the castle park, the luminous distance of the night For her it is only horrible emptiness that separates her from Tristan. Only the torch remains irrefutably just what it is: a signal separating her from the man she loves. Finally she extinguishes it. Time stands still. Time, space, the echoes of the natural world, the threatening torch – everything is wiped out. Nothing exists, for Tristan is in her arms.

How is this to be scenically realized so that the spectator, without resorting to logical reasoning, without conscious mental effort, identifies himself unreservedly with the inner meaning of these events?

At the rise of the curtain a large torch, stage centre. The stage is bright enough so that one can recognize the actors clearly but not bright enough to dim the torch's flare. The forms that bound the stage are barely visible. A few barely perceptible lines indicate trees.

By degrees the eye grows accustomed to the scene. Gradually it becomes aware of the more or less distinct mass of a building adjoining the terrace. During the entire first scene Isolde and Brangäne remain on this terrace, and between them and the foreground one senses a declivity but one cannot determine its precise character. When Isolde extinguishes the torch the setting is shrouded in a half-light in which the eye loses itself.

Isolde is submerged in this whispering darkness as she rushes to Tristan. During the first ecstasy of their meeting they remain on the terrace. At its climax they approach [the audience]. By almost imperceptible degrees they leave the terrace and by a barely visible flight of steps reach a sort of platform near the foreground. Then, as their desire appeases itself somewhat and only one idea unites them, as we grow more and more aware of the Death of

Time, they finally reach the extreme foreground, where – we notice it for the first time – a bench awaits them. The tone of the whole secret, shadowy space surrounding them grows even more uniform; the forms of the terrace and the castle are submerged, even the different levels of the stage floor are hardly perceptible.

Whether because of the contrast of deepened darkness induced by extinguishing the torch, or perhaps because our eye has followed the path that Tristan and Isolde have just trod – however that may be, in any case we feel how softly they are cradled by every object about them. During Brangäne's song the light grows still dimmer; the bodily forms of the people themselves no longer have a distinct outline. Then (page 162, first *ff*, of the orchestra) suddenly a pale glimmer of light strikes the right side of stage rear: King Mark and his men-át-arms break in. Slowly the cold colourless light of day increases. The eye begins to recognize the main outlines of the stage setting and its colour begins to register in all its harshness. Then as Tristan with the greatest effort at self-mastery realizes that he is after all among the living, he challenges Melot to a duel.

In the setting, cold in colour, hard as bone, only one spot is shaded from the dawning day and remains soft and shadowy, the bench at the foot of the terrace.

This was written in 1899!

I know of no single document in the theatre's history that reveals more completely the role that creative imagination plays in staging a play nor one that demonstrates better how inevitably the imagination of a creative artist is specific and concrete. The passage, as well as its continuation and the similar analyses that follow it for the production of the *Ring of the Nibelung*, are the measure of Appia's genius. In comparison Craig's dark hints and his windy pretensions show him, more than ever, to be an inflated talent. Appia can himself be windy in prognosticating the future of German and French music. But once he focuses upon the theatre he is the master and the master craftsman, completely aware of his methods and materials, certain of how they can be organized, certain too of their effect to the last detail. The semi-obscurity of this second act of Tristan is dictated by a vision where, as in the words of the stage-manager of Mons, all is clarity and light.

The chiaroscuro of Appia's drawings is shadowy like Craig's; its misty envelopments, its dissolving silhouettes and vaporous distances, are characteristically romantic. But this picturesque atmosphere is made an integral part of stage pictures that, instead of dwarfing the actor, are directly related to him as a human being. Despite the shadowy shapes around him the actor remains the centre of our interest, the focus of dramatic emphasis. Appia's stage pictures are not conceived as effects into which the actor is put; they spring from the actor and are complete expressions of his assumed personality and passions. Appia, designing for the opera, evolved a type of stage setting so compact, so directly related to the emotional flux of drama, that he anticipated the development of scenic design in the theatre. Craig, designing for the theatre of the future, made settings so emptily grandiose that they have no future place except in grand opera. Appia staged even fewer productions than Craig did. His contacts with the actual theatre were less frequent. But his sense of the theatre was so concrete, so technically true, that his drawings, like his stage-directions, were capable of being translated to a stage as soon as he had made them.

Light fluctuates in Appia's drawings as it does on the stage of a theatre; it fluctuates on stage settings today as it did in Appia's drawings, and gives to canvas forms just such simplifications of mass and outline as Appia indicated. At one moment or another the lighting of any modern production, whether Jones's *Richard III* or Geddes's *Hamlet*, Reinhardt's *Danton's Death* or Jessner's *Othello* (and I could add the names of a hundred others that I have seen as well as my own), are dramatized with light and shadow in ways that repeat, however much they may amplify, Appia's original methods and effects – the same use of shadows to dignify and to envelop form, to translate emotion into atmospheric moods, to define by suggesting. The modern stage is filled with the light that was always to be seen on land and sea but never in the theatre until Appia brought it there. Craig's belated attempt to emphasize the actor with light against an ambiguous neutral screen, the declaration of Arthur Kahane, Reinhardt's assistant, in 1919, 'Lighting is the real source of decoration, its single aim being only to bring the important into light and leave the unimportant in shadow,' do nothing more than paraphrase the ideas and the doctrines of Adolphe Appia.

Appia's light-plot is now an accepted part of every modern production. It parallels the plot of a play and is a visual comment upon it as continuous as a musical score. It is separately rehearsed, memorized by the stage-electrician, and is part of the stage-manager's prompt-book. The fewest of its changes are dictated by actual stage-directions, such as the extinguishing of a torch; the vast majority are an accompaniment to action and aim to emphasize the atmospheric qualities of a stage setting in a way that can project variations of dramatic mood and thereby intensify the emotional reaction of an audience.

Appia's supreme intuition was his recognition that light can play as directly upon our emotions as music does. We are more immediately affected by our sensitiveness to variations of light in the theatre than we are by our sensations of colour, shape, or sound. Our emotional reaction to light is more rapid than to any other theatrical means of expression, possibly because no other sensory stimulus moves with the speed of light, possibly because, our earliest inherited fear being a fear of the dark, we inherit with it a primitive worship of the sun. The association between light and joy, between sorrow and darkness, is deeply rooted and tinges the imagery of almost every literature and every religion. It shows itself in such common couplings as 'merry and bright', 'sad and gloomy'. How much less lonely we feel walking along a country road in a pitch-black night when the distant yellow patch of a farm-house window punctures the darkness! The flare of a camp-fire in a black pine forest at night cheers us even though we are not near enough to warm our hands at it. The warmth of the sun or of a flame does of course play a large share in provoking the feeling of elation that light gives us. But the quality of light itself can suggest this warmth effectively enough to arouse almost the same mood of comfort and release, as when, after a dingy day of rain and mist, sunlight strikes our window-curtains and dapples the floor of our room.

Between these two extremes of flaming sun and darkness an immense range of emotion fluctuates almost instantly in response to variations in the intensity of light. The key of our emotions can be set, the quality of our response dictated, almost at the rise of the curtain by the degree and quality of light that pervades a scene. It requires many more moments for the words of the players or their actions to accumulate momentum and to gather enough import for them to awaken as intense and direct an emotional response. And as the action progresses our emotions can be similarly played upon. It was the singular limitation of Appia's temperament that he could find no basis for the interpretation of drama except that dictated by the tempo and timbre of a musical score. His imagination could be stimulated in no other way. But in indicating both theoretically and graphically the complete mobility of stage lighting he has made it possible for any play to be accompanied by a light-score that is almost as directly expressive as a musical accompaniment and can be made as integrally a part of drama as music was in Wagner's music-dramas.

5. LIGHT ORCHESTRATED

The amazingly concrete quality of Appia's vision is again made apparent by the fact that he predicted the present technical set-up of our stage lighting systems. With nothing more to guide him than the rudimentary systems of his day he understood their inadequacy. He divided light-sources on the stage into two systems – diffused or general light, which merely flooded the stage with an even radiance, called flood-lighting today, and focused, mobile light, now known as spot-lighting. It was this almost neglected source of light which Appia pointed to as the important one.

Without doubt, as soon as scenery is no longer painted canvas set up in parallel rows, all lighting apparatus will be used in a radically different fashion from what it is today, but the basis of the construction will not change greatly. The mobile [spot-light] apparatus will be utilized to create plastic light and its mechanical perfection will have to be made the object of the most careful study. In conjunction with the more or less stationary flood-lighting apparatus, screens of varying degrees of opacity will be used; their purpose will be to soften the oversharp definition of light thrown by lamps on parts of the setting or on actors in close proximity to any particular light-source. But the major portion of the spot-lighting apparatus will be used to break up light and diversify its direction in every way possible. These lamps will be . . . of the greatest importance in maintaining the expressive effect of the total stage picture.

The development of stage-lighting apparatus has followed Appia's prediction. For a while lamps were moved on bridges above the stage and literally followed the action of a play. But the spot-light has been perfected so that it can be equally mobile while its source remains fixed. Lenses of varying sizes – six or eight inches giving a varying maximum spread in combination with electric lamps of 250, 500 or 1,000 watts – are focused to cover overlapping areas or concentrated into a 'spot' the size of a face. Each is controlled by a separate dimmer that regulates its intensity over a range of a hundred fixed points varying from full to out. For a modern production as many as a hundred such spot-lights may be in use, each covering a particular area of the stage floor, hundreds of shafts of light criss-crossing from iron stanchions at each side of the stage, from one or more pipes overhead, casting funnels of light of different colours and intensity which the actor walks into or out of. They are in continual flux, ebbing and flowing, merging and separating, but always slowly and subtly enough so that there is never a jump by which a spectator can become directly aware of the changes that are imperceptibly taking place before his eyes. He feels their effect before he realizes that the changes have occurred.

A light-plot of this sort is separately rehearsed and is then known as a light-rehearsal. For a large production a rehearsal often takes several days of consecutive work that is an important part of a designer's job. Conducting a light-rehearsal is very like conducting an orchestra. Every lamp is a separate instrument carrying its own thread of symphonic effect, now carrying a theme, now supporting it. A certain proportion of these lamps is directed at scenery, part is concentrated on actors' faces. Appia insisted that the 'plastic power of light' was as important for the actor as for the set. He inveighed against the flattening effect of footlights on actors' faces and ascribed the overloading of make-up to the fact that an even brilliance from below wiped out all expression from human features, whereas focused light could model faces and carve expression into them like a sculptor. 'But,' he adds, 'light will not be used merely to strengthen or to weaken the modelling of a face; rather it will serve to unite it or to isolate it from the scenic background, in a natural way, depending on whether the role of a particular actor dominates a scene or is subordinate to it.'

At a light-rehearsal Appia's assertion holds true. Diffused light that merely shows a setting is, as he said, a simple matter. Plastic lighting that dramatizes its meaning is all-important and a matter of complex adjustments. 'The difference in intensity between the two kinds of light must be great enough in order to make shadows perceptible; above this minimum an infinite variety of relationship is possible.' It is this infinite variety, this continually shifting balance between light-sources, which occupy hours of experiment at light-rehearsals.

6. LIGHT AS SCENE-BUILDER

Appia even envisaged one of the most recent developments of stage lighting – the projected scenery that Craig was astounded to discover at Copenhagen.

Light can be coloured, either by its own quality or by coloured glass slides; it can project pictures, of every degree of intensity, varying from the faintest blurred tonalities to the sharpest defini-tion. Although both diffused and concentrated [spot] lights need an object to focus on, they do not change its character; the former makes it more or less perceptible, the latter more or less expressive. Coloured light in itself changes the colour of pigments that reflect it, and by means of projected pictures or combinations of coloured light can create a milieu on the stage or even actual things that before the light was projected did not exist.

Light became for Appia not only a scene-painter but a scene-builder.

The stage setting will no longer be as now a combination of right-angled flats . . . but will rather be arranged for a specific purpose, a combination of varying planes extending into space. This principle gives colour an entirely new meaning; it no longer needs to embody any specific thing on a flat stretch of canvas or to create a factitious reality; it becomes 'colour in space', capable of reconciling and combining all the elements of a setting into a simplified whole. . . .

These continually changing combinations of colour and form, changing in relation to each other and also to the rest of the stage-setting, provide opportunities for an infinite variety of plastic combinations. They are the palette of the poet-musician.

They are the palette and the chisel of scene-designers today. Appia's vision has made even the third dimension itself completely flexible on the stage. Space is no longer absolute. Distance, as far as the eye of the spectator is con-cerned, can be created as effectively by the different intensi-ties of intersecting volumes of light as by actual spacing measured in feet. An actor stepping from a brilliant funnel of light into half-shadow may recede far more perceptibly than if he walked fifteen feet up stage through even radiance. The sky beyond the platform of Elsinore can be infinitely remote although it may be almost within reach of Hamlet's outstretched hand at the rampart's rim. Light can contract the deepest stage or extend a shallow one. The heaviest piece of scenery appears flimsy until it is reinforced with shadows that suggest its mass and weight and veil the actual material of its linen surface. A designer knows how quickly at light-rehearsal a flood of light from the wrong source can literally blow a setting to pieces, flatten out the heaviest column; an electrician's mistake in bringing on a single extra lamp during a performance can be as disastrous.

For a production of *Don Juan* I made a cathedral of a single column, the silver grille of a *reja*, and a black backdrop. The light had to strike the column principally from stage right, and his supposed funeral, which Don Juan had come to witness, was supposed to take place off stage right so that he faced the principal light-source. The opposite side of the column was left in shadow in order to exaggerate its mass, for, heavy as it was, it was only half the scale of a cathedral pier. Enough light had to be concentrated at the base of the column to illuminate the principal scenes of the act; too much would have destroyed the column's solidity. Just enough light had to spill on to the silver grille to make it gleam, but none could spill too far beyond it, for there was no more than six or eight feet between it and the black backdrop. Even then one sensed the shallowness of this space until I shot a ray of light angled downward, from a point out of sight overhead, so that it seemed a ray coming from an unseen cathedral window. The brilliance of this light-ray was such that by the time the spectator's eye had penetrated it it was slightly dazzled; he could no longer tell whether he was looking into six feet of depth or sixty.

The silhouettes of factories seen through the railroad viaduct in *Liliom* (Theatre Guild production, New York, 1921) were not more than eight or ten feet back of its opening. The trees on the gauzes of the park scene in the same play were no more than four or five feet apart. Nothing but the balance of light-planes gave them depth and distance and kept them in place so that they seemed hundreds of feet away. It is comparatively easy to light actors to the exclusion of their surroundings, even when they move through a dozen positions in as many minutes, and in the process distort the setting; it is a simple matter to light a setting and obliterate the actors in it. The designer's incessant problem is to keep both in the right relation throughout the course of a play. Nothing but the complex manipulation of light makes a satisfactory solution possible. No scene painted or built through scenic design is completed until it is finally lighted. The designer is today more dependent on the electric filament than he ever was on the brush.

The lighting of the last act of *Elizabeth the Queen* (Theatre Guild production, New York, 1930) can serve to illustrate how not only the building and painting of a stage setting but even its costuming can be designed almost entirely for their values when lighted. The germ of the scene was the lighting of its final moment: Elizabeth, after Essex had descended the trap-door to his death, was to be seen rigid on her throne-chair, like a bronze statue, staring forever at her fate. Over her head the light was to catch two royal-red banners so that they hung like bloody fangs in the glow of dawn striking through turret windows. Accordingly Elizabeth's gown was made of a copper cloth. But as its metallic brilliance was to be seen only for a final tableau, it was covered with black chiffon stitched to it with a design of black and gold thread almost imperceptible except as its glints gave a sense of encrustation. During most of the act the black film dulled the fabric so that it took no light from Lynn Fontanne's face. The room was an empty cylinder; four narrow windows in an ascending line suggested the spiral ascent of a tower. It was painted in greys and blue, for the turret was to be shadowy with the breath of approaching death. But a fine spatter of dull-red paint was spread on just the portion of the wall behind the throne-chair, invisible until caught by the final light of dawn. The banners overhead were completely lost in shadow at the top of the set. A single candle placed on a chest motivated the general light of the scene. The chest was placed near the trap-door where Essex was to ascend. There were only two areas of light – one around the throne, the other between the chest and the trap-door, at first dim, as no important action took place there for the first part of the act. In each area the light was kept off the walls, raised just high enough to catch the actors' heads. The rest of the stage was in half-shadow.

When the players came on to do a scene from *The Merry Wives*, they emerged from the shadow only by accident, for they were nothing more than a momentary foil to the queen's mood as she paced back and forth waiting. When the trap-door opened and Essex entered, the lights on it were increased, but the change was imperceptible because none of the added light struck the walls; its slightly increased intensity could not be seen except on Essex's face. During the final colloquy the light grew dimmer everywhere except in the small space where Essex and the queen played their farewell. Just before they parted the blue of night through the windows began to fade to the pink of dawn. As Essex descended, the added light vanished with him, leaving nothing more than a flickering candle. A faint tinge of cold blue light stole up the walls. The light through the slits of windows became brighter, almost red. And as Elizabeth straightened in her chair the first shaft of warm morning sunlight struck full upon her, turning her to bronze and at the same time plucking the banners out of the shadow, turning them into bloody fangs that seemed to drip over the queen's head as the curtain fell.

7. LEGACY

Such a bit of stage lighting is a fraction of Appia's legacy to the modern stage. I do not imply that the designers of this generation read an out-of-print German volume and then rushed into the theatre to apply its precepts. They were already in the air, already being projected by spot-lights, already part of a modern tradition and its technique. Modern designers accepted a torch without knowing who lighted it; our experiments amplified Appia's theories almost before we knew his name, had seen his drawings, or had heard a quotation from his published work. Appia's first two volumes contain the germinal ideas that have sprouted, almost without exception, into the theories of modern stage-craft that we listened to – the necessity of visualizing the mood and atmosphere of a play, the value of presentation as opposed to representation, the importance of suggestion completed in the mind of the spectator, the effectiveness of an actor stabbed by a spot-light in a great dim space, the significance of a 'space stage', and the more abstract forms of scenic art.

It was Appia who first said:

Our stage is a vista into the unknown, into boundless space, and this space for which our souls long in order that our imagination can be submerged in it, is given no added value by making our settings part of the structure of the whole theatre building. . . . The Greeks identified the scene of the play with the boundaries of the theatre; we, less fortunate, have extended it beyond that limit. Our drama, thrust into a boundless realm of the imagination, and our roofed-over amphitheatres, into which we are packed, are related only by a proscenium arch; everything beyond it is fictitious, tentative, and bears every evidence of being without any justification except as part of a particular performance.

It was Appia who first emphasized the distinction between the aesthetic values of classic formality and those of modern scenic illusion.

The antique stage was unlike ours, not a hole through which the public was shown in a constricted space the combined effect of an infinite variety of media. Antique drama was the event, the act itself, not a spectacle.

The passage of which these statements are a part gave the cue which prompted our present efforts to dislodge the proscenium arch and to unite the audience with the play by making the stage a part of the auditorium.

It was also Appia who, as a theorist, first insisted on the dominant importance of the director as a dictator controlling every element of theatrical production.

The man we call director today, whose job consists in merely arranging completed stage sets, will, in poetic [music] drama, play the role of a despotic drill-master who will have to understand how much preliminary study stage setting requires, utilize every element of scenic production in order to create an artistic synthesis, reanimate everything under his control at the expense of the actor, who must eventually be dominated. Whatever he does will to a great extent depend upon his individual taste: he must work both as an experimenter and as a poet, play with his scenic materials but at the same time be careful not to create a purely personal formula.

Only an artist and an artist of the first rank can accomplish such a task. He will have to test his own imagination conscientiously in order to free it from every stereotype, above all from anything influenced by the fashion of the moment. But his principal effort as a director will be to convince the individual members of his acting company that only the arduous subjection of their personalities to the unity of the production will create an important result. He will be very like the leader of an orchestra; his effect will be a similarly magnetic one.

This conception of a master artist in the theatre is Craig's 'Master of Drama' and, with Appia's contempt for the scene-painter, supplied the theme for Craig's first dialogues on the art of the theatre and most of their subsequent variations.

The art of the theatre today finds its full freedom within the boundaries of Appia's original concepts in a stage setting that is completely plastic – plastic in the sense of being infinitely malleable, plastic also in the sense of being consistently three-dimensional. More recent experiments in production continue to play with our sensations of space and our emotional reactions to projections, either actual or implied, of the third dimension. We accept the dynamic relations of a three-dimensional actor moving through a third dimension, whether constructed or indicated, as the greatest aid that can be given to the expressiveness of a play in performance. Light itself has come to have the character of a form in space. The illumination focused and projected through the lens of a modern spot-light is a funnel of light that has the shape of a cone. Its outlines, when sharply focused, are often discernible and are often made part of the pictorial pattern of a stage setting. At one extreme, we make stage space absolute, the stage setting purely architectonic, and depend entirely on the movements of actors, singly or in mass, to create the stage picture. Light then acquires, in our eyes, a classic purity of definition. At the other extreme the stage becomes murkily romantic and the dynamics of light is used to create the illusion of an actual extension of the space played in; it is extended until it seems infinite and is filled with every possible combination of shadowy masses related by atmospheric planes that have every degree of opacity.

Like every other form of scenic effect, modern stage lighting is an illusion. It too deceives the eye. But completely controlled, in the way that Appia indicated, it is the most subtle form of deception yet discovered. It is tactile in effect. The modern stage setting is thereby given unity by evading a conflict between illusions of different kinds. Even at its most vaporous moments a modern setting is three-dimensional, continually relates the actor to the space in which he moves, is an extension of his body as well as a symbolic projection of his state of mind. Our emotional reactions to drama when acted are intensified by an aesthetic emphasis upon extension in space, either reproduced or suggested, expressing dynamic patterns of human beings in action, who move through fluctuating planes of light; and these in turn create a dynamic interplay of contours and forms.

The aesthetics of modern stage setting, like the aesthetics of modern art in general, accepts tactile value as the supreme value and the basis of significant form. In the frame of the theatre, as in the picture-frame, we can find no other test of expressiveness. The modern art of theatrical production, 'the art of the theatre', was completely organized, as a medium of expression, when the doctrines that Appia outlined and illustrated were added to the technique of rehearsal and presentation established by the Duke of Saxe-Meiningen's experiments. The unity thus established remains an aesthetic norm. Most of what we call innovation or experiment is a variation of Appia's ideas, deduced from his original premises – the refinements of acting evolved by Stanislavsky, the refinement in the control of electric lighting now being perfected by electrical engineers.

Antonin Artaud

ANTONIN ARTAUD, 1896–1948, was an outstanding member of the French theatrical *avant-garde* between the two World Wars. He shared the hostility to all naturalism and realism of many of his elders (such as Craig and Appia) but made these men seem quite old-fashioned by his very twentieth-century vehemence and primitivism. As the creator of the idea of a Theatre of Cruelty, Artaud has influenced artists as divergent as Jean-Louis Barrault, Peter Brook, and Julian and Judith Beck. It is partly because Paul Goodman (1911–72) has been associated with the Becks that his brief 'Anti-Artaud' is printed here. It first appeared in *The Nation*, 29 November 1958. The two manifestos are taken from *The Theatre and its Double* (1938) by Antonin Artaud, translated by M. C. Richards.* The first manifesto was first published in the *Nouvelle Revue Française*, 1 October 1932; the second was published as a booklet in 1933 by Editions Denoël. Incidentally, Artaud's manifestos shed light on the phenomenon which Mr Martin Esslin has called 'the theatre of the absurd'. (The editor would have represented this phenomenon separately had there been any brief essay that seemed to cover the ground. As things are, the reader is referred to Mr Esslin's book, *The Theatre of the Absurd*.†)

* Published by Calder & Boyars, 1958, and Grove Press, New York, 1958.

† Doubleday Anchor Books, 1961; Eyre & Spottiswoode, 1962; enlarged edition Penguin Books, 1968.

The Theatre of Cruelty

ANTONIN ARTAUD

Translated by Mary Caroline Richards

First Manifesto

WE cannot go on prostituting the idea of theatre whose only value is in its excruciating, magical relation to reality and danger.

Put in this way, the question of the theatre ought to arouse general attention, the implication being that theatre, through its physical aspect, since it requires *expression in space* (the only real expression, in fact), allows the magical means of art and speech to be exercised organically and altogether, like renewed exorcisms. The upshot of all this is that theatre will not be given its specific powers of action until it is given its language.

That is to say: instead of continuing to rely upon texts considered definitive and sacred, it is essential to put an end to the subjugation of the theatre to the text, and to recover the notion of a kind of unique language half-way between gesture and thought.

This language cannot be defined except by its possibilities for dynamic expression in space as opposed to the expressive possibilities of spoken dialogue. And what the theatre can still take over from speech are its possibilities for extension beyond words, for development in space, for dissociative and vibratory action upon the sensibility. This is the hour of intonations, of a word's particular pronunciation. Here too intervenes (besides the auditory language of sounds) the visual language of objects, movements, attitudes, and gestures, but on condition that their meanings, their physiognomies, their combinations be carried to the point of becoming signs, making a kind of alphabet out of these signs. Once aware of this language in space, language of sounds, cries, lights, onomatopoeia, the theatre must organize it into veritable hieroglyphs, with the help of characters and objects, and make use of their symbolism and interconnexions in relation to all organs and on all levels.

The question, then, for the theatre, is to create a metaphysics of speech, gesture and expression, in order to rescue it from its servitude to psychology and 'human interest'. But all this can be of no use unless behind such an effort there is some kind of real metaphysical inclination, an appeal to certain unhabitual ideas, which by their very nature cannot be limited or even formally depicted. These ideas which touch on Creation, Becoming, and Chaos, are all of a cosmic order and furnish a primary notion of a domain from which the theatre is now entirely alien. They are able to create a kind of passionate equation between Man, Society, Nature, and Objects.

It is not, moreover, a question of bringing metaphysical ideas directly onto the stage, but of creating what you might call temptations, indraughts of air around these ideas. And humour with its anarchy, poetry with its symbolism and its images, furnish a basic notion of ways to channel the temptation of these ideas.

We must speak now about the uniquely material side of this language – that is, about all the ways and means it has of acting upon the sensibility.

It would be meaningless to say that it includes music, dance, pantomime, or mimicry. Obviously it uses movement, harmonies, rhythms, but only to the point that they can concur in a sort of central expression without advantage for any one particular art. This does not at all mean that it does not use ordinary actions, ordinary passions, but like a springboard uses them in the same way that HUMOUR AS DESTRUCTION can serve to reconcile the corrosive nature of laughter to the habits of reason.

But by an altogether Oriental means of expression, this objective and concrete language of the theatre can fascinate and ensnare the organs. It flows into the sensibility. Abandoning Occidental usages of speech, it turns words into incantations. It extends the voice. It utilizes the vibrations and qualities of the voice. It wildly tramples rhythms underfoot. It pile-drives sounds. It seeks to exalt, to benumb, to charm, to arrest the sensibility. It liberates a new lyricism of gesture which, by its precipitation or its amplitude in the air, ends by surpassing the lyricism of words. It ultimately breaks away from the intellectual subjugation of the language, by conveying the sense of a new and deeper intellectuality which hides itself beneath the gestures and signs, raised to the dignity of particular exorcisms.

For all this magnetism, all this poetry, and all these direct means of spellbinding would be nothing if they were not used to put the spirit physically on the track of something else, if the true theatre could not give us the sense of a creation of which we possess only one face, but which is completed on other levels.

And it is of little importance whether these other levels are really conquered by the mind or not, i.e., by the intelligence; it would diminish them, and that has neither interest nor sense. What is important is that, by positive means, the sensitivity is put in a state of deepened and keener perception, and this is the very object of the magic and the rites of which the theatre is only a reflection.

TECHNIQUE

It is a question then of making the theatre, in the proper sense of the word, a function; something as localized and as precise as the circulation of the blood in the arteries or the apparently chaotic development of dream images in the brain, and this is to be accomplished by a thorough involvement, a genuine enslavement of the attention.

The theatre will never find itself again – i.e., constitute a means of true illusion – except by furnishing the spectator with the truthful precipitates of dreams, in which his taste for crime, his erotic obsessions, his savagery, his chimeras, his utopian sense of life and matter, even his cannibalism, pour out, on a level not counterfeit and illusory, but interior.

57

In other terms, the theatre must pursue by all its means a reassertion not only of all the aspects of the objective and descriptive external world, but of the internal world, that is, of man considered metaphysically. It is only thus, we believe, that we shall be able to speak again in the theatre about the rights of the imagination. Neither humour, nor poetry, nor imagination means anything unless, by an anarchistic destruction generating a prodigious flight of forms which will constitute the whole spectacle, they succeed in organically reinvolving man, his ideas about reality, and his poetic place in reality.

To consider the theatre as a second-hand psychological or moral function, and to believe that dreams themselves have only a substitute function, is to diminish the profound poetic bearing of dreams as well as of the theatre. If the theatre, like dreams, is bloody and inhuman, it is, more than just that, to manifest and unforgettably root within us the idea of a perpetual conflict, a spasm in which life is continually lacerated, in which everything in creation rises up and exerts itself against our appointed rank; it is in order to perpetuate in a concrete and immediate way the metaphysical ideas of certain Fables whose very atrocity and energy suffice to show their origin and continuity in essential principles.

This being so, one sees that, by its proximity to principles which transfer their energy to it poetically, this naked language of the theatre (not a virtual but a real language) must permit, by its use of man's nervous magnetism, the transgression of the ordinary limits of art and speech, in order to realize actively, that is to say magically, *in real terms*, a kind of total creation in which man must reassume his place between dream and events.

THE THEMES

It is not a matter of boring the public to death with transcendent cosmic preoccupations. That there may be profound keys to thought and action with which to interpret the whole spectacle does not in general concern the spectator, who is simply not interested. But still they must be there; and that concerns us.

*

THE SPECTACLE: Every spectacle will contain a physical and objective element, perceptible to all. Cries, groans, apparitions, surprises, theatricalities of all kinds, magic beauty of costumes taken from certain ritual models; resplendent lighting, incantational beauty of voices, the charms of harmony, rare notes of music, colours of objects, physical rhythm of movements whose crescendo and decrescendo will accord exactly with the pulsation of movements familiar to everyone, concrete appearances of new and surprising objects, masks, effigies yards high, sudden changes of light, the physical action of light which arouses sensations of heat and cold, etc.

THE MISE EN SCÈNE: The typical language of the theatre will be constituted around the *mise en scène* considered not simply as the degree of refraction of a text upon the stage, but as the point of departure for all theatrical creation. And it is in the use and handling of this language that the old duality between author and director will be dissolved, replaced by a sort of unique Creator upon whom will devolve the double responsibility of the spectacle and the plot.

THE LANGUAGE OF THE STAGE: It is not a question of suppressing the spoken language, but of giving words approximately the importance they have in dreams.

Meanwhile new means of recording this language must be found, whether these means belong to musical transcription or to some kind of code.

As for ordinary objects, or even the human body, raised to the dignity of signs, it is evident that one can draw one's inspiration from hieroglyphic characters, not only in order to record these signs in a readable fashion which permits them to be reproduced at will, but in order to compose on the stage precise and immediately readable symbols.

On the other hand, this code language and musical transcription will be valuable as a means of transcribing voices.

Since it is fundamental to this language to make a particular use of intonations, these intonations will constitute a kind of harmonic balance, a secondary deformation of speech which must be reproducible at will.

Similarly the ten thousand and one expressions of the face caught in the form of masks can be labelled and catalogued, so they may eventually participate directly and symbolically in this concrete language of the stage, independently of their particular psychological use.

Moreover, these symbolical gestures, masks, and attitudes, these individual or group movements whose innumerable meanings constitute an important part of the concrete language of the theatre, evocative gestures, emotive or arbitrary attitudes, excited pounding out of rhythms and sounds, will be doubled, will be multiplied by reflections, as it were, of the gestures and attitudes consisting of the mass of all the impulsive gestures, all the abortive attitudes, all the lapses of mind and tongue, by which are revealed what might be called the impotences of speech, and in which is a prodigious wealth of expressions, to which we shall not fail to have recourse on occasion.

There is, besides, a concrete idea of music in which the sounds make their entrance like characters, where harmonies are coupled together and lose themslves in the precise entrances of words.

From one means of expression to another, correspondences and levels of development are created – even light can have a precise intellectual meaning.

MUSICAL INSTRUMENTS: They will be treated as objects and as part of the set.

Also, the need to act directly and profoundly upon the sensibility through the organs invites research, from the point of view of sound, into qualities and vibrations of absolutely new sounds, qualities which present-day musical instruments do not possess and which require the revival of ancient and forgotten instruments or the invention of new ones. Research is also required, apart from music, into instruments and appliances which, based upon special combinations or new alloys of metal, can attain a new range and compass, producing sounds or noises that are unbearably piercing.

LIGHTS, LIGHTING: The lighting equipment now in use in theatres is no longer adequate. The particular action of light upon the mind, the effects of all kinds of luminous vibration must be investigated, along with new ways of spreading the light waves, in sheets, in fusillades of fiery arrows. The colour gamut of the equipment now in use is to be revised from beginning to end. In order to produce the qualities of particular musical tones, light must recover an element of thinness, density, and opaqueness, with a view to producing the sensations of heat, cold, anger, fear, etc.

COSTUMES: Where costumes are concerned, modern dress will be avoided as much as possible without at the same time assuming a uniform theatrical costuming that would be the same for every play – not from a fetishist and superstitious reverence for the past, but because it seems absolutely evident that certain age-old costumes, of ritual intent, though they existed at a given moment of time, preserve a beauty and a revelational appearance from their closeness to the traditions that gave them birth.

THE STAGE – THE AUDITORIUM: We abolish the stage and the auditorium and replace them by a single site, without partition or barrier of any kind, which will become the theatre of the action. A direct communication will be re-established between the spectator and the spectacle, between the actor and the spectator, from the fact that the spectator, placed in the middle of the action, is engulfed and physically affected by it. This envelopment results, in part, from the very configuration of the room itself.

Thus, abandoning the architecture of present-day theatre, we shall take some hangar or barn, which we shall have reconstructed according to processes which have culminated in the architecture of certain churches or holy places, and of certain temples in Tibet.

In the interior of this construction special proportions of height and depth will prevail. The hall will be enclosed by four walls, without any kind of ornament, and the public will be seated in the middle of the room, on the ground floor, on mobile chairs which will allow them to follow the spectacle which will take place all around them. In effect, the absence of a stage in the usual sense of the word will provide for the deployment of the action in the four corners of the room. Particular positions will be reserved for actors and action at the four cardinal points of the room. The scenes will be played in front of whitewashed wall-backgrounds designed to absorb the light. In addition, galleries overhead will run around the periphery of the hall as in certain primitive paintings. These galleries will permit the actors, whenever the action makes it necessary, to be pursued from one point in the room to another, and the action to be deployed on all levels and in all perspectives of height and depth. A cry uttered at one end of the room can be transmitted from mouth to mouth with amplifications and successive modulations all the way to the other. The action will unfold, will extend its trajectory from level to level, point to point; paroxysms will suddenly burst forth, will flare up like fires in different spots. And to speak of the spectacle's character as true illusion or of the direct and immediate influence of the action on the spectator will not be hollow words. For this diffusion of action over an immense space will oblige the lighting of a scene and the varied lighting of a performance to fall upon the public as much as upon the actors – and to the several simultaneous actions or several phases of an identical action in which the characters, swarming over each other like bees, will endure all the onslaughts of the situations and the external assaults of the tempestuous elements, will correspond the physical means of lighting, of producing thunder or wind, whose repercussions the spectator will undergo.

However, a central position will be reserved which, without serving, properly speaking, as a stage, will permit the bulk of the action to be concentrated and brought to a climax whenever necessary.

OBJECTS – MASKS – ACCESSORIES: Manikins, enormous masks, objects of strange proportions will appear with the same sanction as verbal images, will enforce the concrete aspect of every image and every expression – with the corollary that all objects requiring a stereotyped physical representation will be discarded or disguised.

THE SET: There will not be any set. This function will be sufficiently undertaken by hieroglyphic characters, ritual costumes, manikins ten feet high representing the beard of King Lear in the storm, musical instruments tall as men, objects of unknown shape and purpose.

IMMEDIACY: But, people will say, a theatre so divorced from life, from facts, from immediate interests. . . . From the present and its events, yes! From whatever preoccupations have any of that profundity which is the prerogative of some men, no! In the *Zohar*, the story of Rabbi Simeon who burns like fire is as immediate as fire itself.

WORKS: We shall not act a written play, but we shall make attempts at direct staging, around themes, facts, or known works. The very nature and disposition of the room suggest this treatment, and there is no theme, however vast, that can be denied us.

SPECTACLE: There is an idea of integral spectacles which must be regenerated. The problem is to make space speak, to feed and furnish it; like mines laid in a wall of rock which all of a sudden turns into geysers and bouquets of stone.

THE ACTOR: The actor is both an element of first importance, since it is upon the effectiveness of his work that the success of the spectacle depends, and a kind of passive and neutral element, since he is rigorously denied all personal initiative. It is a domain in which there is no precise rule; and between the actor of whom is required the mere quality of a sob and the actor who must deliver an oration with all his personal qualities of persuasiveness, there is the whole margin which separates a man from an instrument.

THE INTERPRETATION: The spectacle will be calculated from one end to the other, like a code (*un langage*). Thus there will be no lost movements, all movements will obey a rhythm; and each character being merely a type, his gesticulation, physiognomy, and costume will appear like so many rays of light.

THE CINEMA: To the crude visualization of what is, the theatre through poetry opposes images of what is not. However, from the point of view of action, one cannot compare a cinematic image which, however poetic it may be, is limited by the film, to a theatrical image which obeys all the exigencies of life.

CRUELTY: Without an element of cruelty at the root of every spectacle, the theatre is not possible. In our present state of degeneration it is through the skin that metaphysics must be made to re-enter our minds.

THE PUBLIC: First of all this theatre must exist.

THE PROGRAMME: We shall stage, without regard for text:

1. An adaptation of a work from the time of Shakespeare, a work entirely consistent with our present troubled state of mind, whether one of the apocryphal plays of Shakespeare, such as *Arden of Feversham*, or an entirely different play from the same period.

2. The play of extreme poetic freedom by Leon-Paul Fargue.

3. An extract from the *Zohar*, The Story of Rabbi Simeon,

which has the ever present violence and force of a conflagration.

4. The story of Bluebeard reconstructed according to the historical records and with a new idea of eroticism and cruelty.

5. The Fall of Jerusalem, according to the Bible and history; with the blood-red colour that trickles from it and the people's feeling of abandon and panic visible even in the light; and on the other hand the metaphysical disputes of the prophets, the frightful intellectual agitation they create and the repercussions of which physically affect the King, the Temple, the People, and Events themselves.

6. A Tale by the Marquis de Sade, in which the eroticism will be transposed, allegorically mounted and figured, to create a violent exteriorization of cruelty, and a dissimulation of the remainder.

7. One or more romantic melodramas in which the improbability will become an active and concrete element of poetry.

8. Büchner's *Woyzeck*, in a spirit of reaction against our principles and as an example of what can be drawn from a formal text in terms of the stage.

9. Works from the Elizabethan theatre stripped of their text and retaining only the accoutrements of period, situations, characters, and action.

Second Manifesto

ADMITTEDLY or not, conscious or unconscious, the poetic state, a transcendent experience of life, is what the public is fundamentally seeking through love, crime, drugs, war, or insurrection.

The Theatre of Cruelty has been created in order to restore to the theatre a passionate and convulsive conception of life, and it is in this sense of violent rigour and extreme condensation of scenic elements that the cruelty on which it is based must be understood.

This cruelty, which will be bloody when necessary but not systematically so, can thus be identified with a kind of severe moral purity which is not afraid to pay life the price it must be paid.

I. FROM THE POINT OF VIEW OF CONTENT

that is, of the subjects and themes to be treated:

The Theatre of Cruelty will choose subjects and themes corresponding to the agitation and unrest characteristic of our epoch.

It does not intend to leave the task of distributing the Myths of man and modern life entirely to the movies. But it will do it in its own way: that is, by resisting the economic, utilitarian, and technical streamlining of the world, it will again bring into fashion the great preoccupations and great essential passions which the modern theatre has hidden under the patina of the pseudo-civilized man.

These themes will be cosmic, universal, and interpreted according to the most ancient texts drawn from old Mexican, Hindu, Judaic, and Iranian cosmogonies.

Renouncing psychological man, with his well-dissected character and feelings, and social man, submissive to laws and misshapen by religions and precepts, the Theatre of Cruelty will address itself only to total man.

And it will cause not only the recto but the verso of the

mind to play its part; the reality of imagination and dreams will appear there on equal footing with life.

Furthermore, great social upheavals, conflicts between peoples and races, natural forces, interventions of chance, and the magnetism of fatality will manifest themselves either indirectly, in the movement and gestures of characters enlarged to the statures of gods, heroes, or monsters, in mythical dimensions, or directly, in material forms obtained by new scientific means.

These gods or heroes, these monsters, these natural and cosmic forces will be interpreted according to images from the most ancient sacred texts and old cosmogonies.

2. FROM THE POINT OF VIEW OF FORM

Besides this need for the theatre to steep itself in the springs of an eternally passionate and sensuous poetry available to even the most backward and inattentive portions of the public, a poetry realized by a return to the primitive Myths, we shall require of the *mise en scène* and not of the text the task of materializing these old conflicts and above all of giving them *immediacy*; i.e., these themes will be borne directly into the theatre and materialized in movements, expressions, and gestures before trickling away in words.

Thus we shall renounce the theatrical superstition of the text and the dictatorship of the writer.

And thus we rejoin the ancient popular drama, sensed and experienced directly by the mind without the deformation of language and the barrier of speech.

We intend to base the theatre upon spectacle before everything else, and we shall introduce into the spectacle a new notion of space utilized on all possible levels and in all degrees of perspective in depth and height, and within this notion a specific idea of time will be added to that of movement.

In a given time, to the greatest possible number of movements, we will join the greatest possible number of physical images and meanings attached to those movements.

The images and movements employed will not be there solely for the external pleasure of eye or ear, but for that more secret and profitable one of the spirit.

Thus, theatre space will be utilized not only in its dimensions and volume but, so to speak, *in its undersides* (*dans ses dessous*).

The overlapping of images and movements will culminate, through the collusion of objects, silences, shouts, and rhythms, or in a genuine physical language with signs, not words, as its root.

For it must be understood that in this quantity of movements and images, arranged for a given length of time, we include both silence and rhythm as well as a certain physical vibration and commotion, composed of objects and gestures really made and really put to use. And it can be said that the spirit of the most ancient hieroglyphs will preside at the creation of this pure theatrical language.

Every popular audience has always loved direct expressions and images; articulate speech, explicit verbal expressions will enter in all the clear and sharply elucidated parts of the action, the parts where life is resting and consciousness intervenes.

But in addition to this logical sense, words will be construed in an incantational, truly magical sense – for their shape and their sensuous emanations, not only for their meaning.

For these exciting appearances of monsters, debauches of heroes and gods, plastic revelations of forces, explosive interjections of a poetry and humour poised to disorganize and pulverize appearances, according to the anarchistic principle of all genuine poetry – these appearances will not exercise their true magic except in an atmosphere of hypnotic suggestion in which the mind is affected by a direct pressure upon the senses.

Whereas, in the digestive theatre of today, the nerves, that is to say a certain physiological sensitivity, are deliberately left aside, abandoned to the individual anarchy of the spectator, the Theatre of Cruelty intends to reassert all the time-tested magical means of capturing the sensibility.

These means, which consist of intensities of colours, lights, or sounds, which utilize vibration, tremors, repetition, whether of a musical rhythm or a spoken phrase, special tones or a general diffusion of light, can obtain their full effect only by the use of *dissonances*.

But instead of limiting these dissonances to the orbit of a single sense, we shall cause them to overlap from one sense to the other, from a colour to a noise, a word to a light, a fluttering gesture to a flat tonality of sound, etc.

So composed and so constructed, the spectacle will be extended, by elimination of the stage, to the entire hall of the theatre and will scale the walls from the ground up on light catwalks, will physically envelop the spectator and immerse him in a constant bath of light, images, movements, and noises. The set will consist of the characters themselves, enlarged to the stature of gigantic manikins, and of landscapes of moving lights playing on objects and masks in perpetual interchange.

And just as there will be no unoccupied point in space, there will be neither respite nor vacancy in the spectator's mind or sensibility. That is, between life and the theatre there will be no distinct division, but instead a continuity. Anyone who has watched a scene of any movie being filmed will understand exactly what we mean.

We want to have at our disposal, for a theatre spectacle, the same material means which, in lights, extras, resources of all kinds, are daily squandered by companies on whom everything that is active and magical in such a deployment is forever lost.

*

The first spectacle of the Theatre of Cruelty will be entitled:

THE CONQUEST OF MEXICO

It will stage events, not men. Men will come in their turn with their psychology and their passions, but they will be taken as the emanation of certain forces and understood in the light of the events and historical fatality in which they have played their role.

This subject has been chosen:

1. Because of its immediacy and all the allusions it permits to problems of vital interest for Europe and the world.

From the historical point of view, *The Conquest of Mexico* poses the question of colonization. It revives in a brutal and implacable way the ever active fatuousness of Europe. It permits her idea of her own superiority to be deflated. It contrasts Christianity with much older religions. It corrects the false conceptions the Occident has somehow formed concerning paganism and certain natural religions, and it underlines with burning emotion the splendour and forever immediate poetry of the old metaphysical sources on which these religions are built.

2. By broaching the alarmingly immediate question of colonization and the right one continent thinks it has to enslave another, this subject questions the real superiority of certain races over others and shows the inmost filiation that binds the genius of a race to particular forms of civilization. It contrasts the tyrannical anarchy of the colonizers to the profound moral harmony of the as yet uncolonized.

Further, by contrast with the disorder of the European monarchy of the time, based upon the crudest and most unjust material principles, it illuminates the organic hierarchy of the Aztec monarchy established on indisputable spiritual principles.

From the social point of view, it shows the peacefulness of a society which knew how to feed all its members and in which the Revolution had been accomplished from the very beginnings.

Out of this clash of moral disorder and Catholic monarchy with pagan order, the subject can set off unheard-of explosions of forces and images, sown here and there with brutal dialogues. Men battling hand to hand, bearing within themselves, like stigmata, the most opposed ideas.

The moral grounds and the immediacy of interest of such

THE THEATRE OF CRUELTY

a spectacle being sufficiently stressed, let us emphasize the value as *spectacle* of the conflicts it will set upon the stage.

There are first of all the inner struggles of Montezuma, the divided king concerning whose motivations history has been unable to enlighten us.

His struggles and his symbolic discussion with the visual myths of astrology will be shown in an objective pictorial fashion.

Then, besides Montezuma, there are the crowd, the different social strata, the revolt of the people against destiny as represented by Montezuma, the clamouring of the unbelievers, the quibbling of the philosophers and priests, the lamentations of the poets, the treachery of the merchants and the bourgeoisie, the duplicity and profligacy of the women.

The spirit of the crowds, the breath of events will travel in material waves over the spectacle, fixing here and there certain lines of force, and on these waves the dwindling, rebellious, or despairing consciousness of individuals will float like straws.

Theatrically, the problem is to determine and harmonize these lines of force, to concentrate them and extract suggestive melodies from them.

These images, movements, dances, rites, these fragmented melodies and sudden turns of dialogue will be carefully recorded and described as far as possible with words, especially for the portions of the spectacle not in dialogue, the principle here being to record in codes, as on a musical score, what cannot be described in words.

Here now is the structure of the spectacle according to the order in which it will unfold.*

* This fuller development of Artaud's *The Conquest of Mexico* was not included in the French edition of *Le Théâtre et son double*; it was first published in *La Nef*, March–April 1950, where the whole text was called 'Potlatch of mighty hosts for their mighty guests.'

Act One

Warning Signs

A tableau of Mexico in anticipation, with its cities, its countrysides, its caves of troglodytes, its Mayan ruins.

Objects evoking on a grand scale certain Spanish ex-votos and those bizarre landscapes that are enclosed in bottles or under glass bells.

Similarly the cities, monuments, countryside, forest, ruins and caves will be evoked – their appearance, disappearance, their form in relief – by means of lighting. The musical or pictorial means of emphasizing their forms, of catching their sharpness will be devised in the spirit of a secret lyricism, invisible to the spectator, and which will correspond to the inspiration of a poetry overflowing with whispers and suggestions.

Everything trembles and groans, like a shop-window in a hurricane. A landscape which senses the coming storm; objects, music, stuffs, lost dresses, shadows of wild horses pass through the air like distant meteors, like lightning on the horizon brimming with mirages as the wind pitches wildly along the ground in a lighting prophesying torrential, violent storms. Then the lighting begins to change, and to the bawling conversations, the disputes between all the echoes of the population, respond the mute, concentrated, terrorized meetings of Montezuma with his formally assembled priests, with the signs of the zodiac, the austere forms of the firmament.

For Cortez, a *mise en scène* of sea and tiny battered ships, and Cortez and his men larger than the ships and firm as rocks.

Act Two

Confession

Mexico seen this time by Cortez.

Silence concerning all his secret struggles; apparent stagnation and everywhere magic, magic of a motionless, unheard-of spectacle, with cities like ramparts of light, palaces on canals of stagnant water, a heavy melody.

Then suddenly, on a single sharp and piercing note, heads crown the walls.

Then a muffled rumbling full of threats, an impression of terrible solemnity, holes in the crowds like pockets of calm in tornado: Montezuma advances all alone toward Cortez.

Act Three

Convulsions

At every level of the country, revolt.

At every level of Montezuma's consciousness, revolt.

Battleground in the mind of Montezuma, who debates with destiny.

Magic, magical *mise en scène* evoking the Gods.

Montezuma cuts the living space, rips it open like the sex of a woman in order to cause the invisible to spring forth.

The stage wall is stuffed unevenly with heads, throats; cracked, oddly broken melodies, and responses to these melodies, appear like stumps. Montezuma himself seems split in two, divided; with some parts of himself in half-light, others dazzling; with many hands coming out of his dress, with expressions painted on his body like a multiple portrait of consciousness, but from within the consciousness of Montezuma all the questions pass forth into the crowd.

The Zodiac, which formerly roared with all its beasts in the head of Montezuma, turns into a group of human passions made incarnate by the learned heads of the official spokesmen, brilliant at disputation – a group of secret plays during which the crowd, despite the circumstances, does not forget to sneer.

However, the real warriors make their sabres whine, whetting them on the houses. Flying ships cross a Pacific of purplish indigo, laden with the riches of fugitives, and in the other direction contraband weapons arrive on other flying vessels.

An emaciated man eats soup as fast as he can, with a presentiment that the siege is approaching the city, and as the rebellion breaks out, the stage space is gorged with a brawling mosaic where sometimes men, sometimes compact troops tightly pressed together, limb to limb, clash frenetically. Space is stuffed with whirling gestures, horrible faces, dying eyes, clenched fists, manes, breastplates, and from all levels of the scene fall limbs, breastplates, heads, stomachs like a hailstorm bombarding the earth with supernatural explosions.

Act Four

Abdication

The abdication of Montezuma results in a strange and almost malevolent loss of assurance on the part of Cortez and his fighters. A specific discord arises over the discovery of treasure, seen like illusions in the corners of the stage. (This will be done with mirrors.)

Lights and sounds produce an impression of dissolving, unravelling, spreading, and squashing – like watery fruits splashing on the ground. Strange couples appear, Spaniard with Indian, horribly enlarged, swollen and black, swaying back and forth like carts about to overturn. Several Hernando Cortez's enter at the same time, signifying that there is no longer any leader. In some places, Indians massacre Spaniards; while in front of a statue whose head is revolving in time to music, Cortez, arms dangling, seems to dream. Treasons go unpunished, shapes swarm about, never exceeding a certain height in the air.

This unrest and the threat of a revolt on the part of the conquered will be expressed in ten thousand ways. And in this collapse and disintegration of the brutal force which has worn itself out (having nothing more to devour) will be delineated the first inkling of a passionate romance.

Weapons abandoned, emotions of lust now make their appearance. Not the dramatic passions of so many battles, but calculated feelings, a plot cleverly hatched, in which, for the first time in the spectacle, a woman's head will be manifested.

And as a consequence of all this, it is also the time of miasmas, of diseases.

On every expressive level appear, like muted flowerings: sounds, words, poisonous blooms which burst close to the ground. And, at the same time, a religious exhalation bends men's heads, fearful sounds seem to bray out, clear as the capricious flourishes of the sea upon a vast expanse of sand, of a cliff slashed by rocks. These are the funeral rites of Montezuma. A stamping, a murmur. The crowd of natives whose steps sound like a scorpion's jaws. Then, eddies in the path of the miasmas, enormous heads with noses swollen with the stink – and nothing, nothing but immense Spaniards on crutches. And like a tidal wave, like the sharp burst of a storm, like the whipping of rain on the sea, the revolt which carries off the whole crowd in groups, with the body of the dead Montezuma tossed on their heads like a ship. And the sharp spasms of the battle, the foam of heads of the cornered Spaniards who are squashed like blood against the ramparts that are turning green again.

Obsessed by Theatre

PAUL GOODMAN

ARTAUD's little book on the theatre is by a man in love and banking everything on his love. He wills this love to give a meaning to life and he wills by this love to counterattack in the society where he is desperate. What he says is often wrong-headed and he often contradicts himself, but he also sees and says important truths with bright simplicity. 'I will do what I have dreamed or I will do nothing' – naturally this comes to doing very little; yet since his death the passion of his dream has moved and conquered theatre people. 'He was the only one of our time who understood the nature and greatness of theatre,' they say of this confused little book (I am quoting Julian Beck). Now if here for a few paragraphs I try to distinguish the true and false voices of this explosion, it is not to diminish the idol of the theatre people; his passion is more important than sound sense; but it is to help simplify their discussions, in order that that passion can be more effectual.

Everywhere Artaud betrays the attitudes and prejudices of a puritan, self-depriving and with a nausea for ordinary food. I should guess that he clung precariously to his sanity by warding off fantasies of cannibalism and other things he thought depraved. When the theatre broke through this shell and provided him a real excitement, he inevitably thought of it as totally destructive and hellish; it had raped him. The theatre, he says, is 'the exteriorization of a depth of latent cruelty by means of which all the perverse possibilities of the mind are localized'.

He is wearing blinders. He does not seem to conceive of the more ordinary neurotic or simply unhappy man to whom the magic of the work of art is its impossible perfection, its promise of paradise. And for the happy there is no art: 'Where simplicity and order reign, there can be no theatre.'

So he famously derives the theatre from the last stages of the Plague, when 'the dregs of the population, immunized by their frenzied greed, pillage the riches they know will

76

serve no purpose or profit. At that moment the theatre is born, i.e., an immediate gratuitousness provoking acts without use or profit.' He goes on to quote St Augustine's horror of the theatre's poison. And he ends with a rhapsody on Ford's *Whore*, whose content seems to him to be the plague itself. All this is brilliantly told, with good oral savagery; it may be only a partial view of theatre, but it is a hot one that could give birth to fine works.

*

Alas! as he thinks it, he becomes frightened of his love, and he begins to reiterate a tediously moralistic theory of illusion and catharsis, false in itself and in direct contradiction to the best things he has to say elsewhere. The action, he reiterates, is only on the stage, it is 'virtual' not actual, it develops an illusory world like alchemy; its aim is to 'drain abscesses collectively'. He seems to think that this symbolic action is the primitive theatre magic, but the very point of the primitive magic is that it is not virtual, it makes the grass grow and the sun come back; the primitive is not afraid of the forces he unleashes.

Artaud's theory of draining the abscesses seems to look like the Greek view of catharsis, but there is a crucial difference: for when it had purged the passions, the Greek play restored its audience to a pretty good community, further strengthened by the religious rite that the play also was, that sowed the corn with the dismembered limbs. But Artaud's play would purge the audience of such vital vices as they have and let them down into the very world from which there is no escape but the asylum. Just so, Artaud is beguiled by the wonderful combination in the Balinese theatre of objective and accurate complexity with trance and indeed witchcraft; but he astonishingly does not see that this is possible because it rises in and still rests in the village, its everyday way of life, and its gamelan. Artaud makes the fantastic remark that the Balinese dances 'victoriously demonstrate the absolute preponderance of the *metteur en scène*' – there is a delusion of grandeur indeed!

Artaud betrays little humour, but his view of comedy brings him to the same dilemma, the fear of total destruction. Comedy, he says, is 'the essential liberation, the destruction of all reality in the mind'. No, *not* all. Comedy deflates the sense precisely so that the underlying lubricity and malice may bubble to the surface. Artaud always thinks the bottom will drop out and that through the theatre one is 'confronted with the absolute'. But it is not the absolute but always a risky next moment that is very real.

But let us start again on a positive tack, and see where Artaud is strong. Artaud is great when he insists that theatre, like any art, is an action in the sense of a physical cause; it is not a mirroring or portrayal that can be absorbed by the spectator and interpreted according to his own predilections. It is not a fantasy. He rightly compares it to psychoanalysis: 'I propose to bring back into theatre the elementary magical idea, taken up by psychoanalysis, which consists in effecting the patient's cure by *making* him assume the apparent and exterior attitudes.' Let me say this my own way: the moment of communication we are after is not that in which a structure of symbols passes from the system in one head to the system in another, when people 'understand one another' and 'learn something'. The semanticists, the language-reformers, the mathematicians of feedback do not give us what we are after; the interesting moment is when one is physiologically touched and one's system is deranged and must reform to cope with the surprise. This Artaud wants to say and does say.

●

It is in the context of theatre as effectual action that Artaud comes to his celebrated assault on literary plays, his refusal to use text to direct from. It is not that he means to attack speech as such, for he understands perfectly that speech is a physical action, it has intonation, it is continuous with outcries and natural signals. He wants, he says beautifully, 'to manipulate speech like a solid object, one which overturns and disturbs things, in the air first of all'. And his remarks on breathing in the essay on Affective Athleticism are solid gold; for the breathing of anger or some other affect has far more theatrical value than the verbalizing or confabulation about it, which can certainly profitably be diminished.

But there is an aspect of the action of speech that he quite neglects and that makes his attack far too sweeping. Words have inter-personal effect, they get under the skin, and not only by their tone but especially by their syntax and style: the mood, voice and person of sentences, the coordination and subordination of clauses. The personalities of men are largely their speech habits, and in the drama of personalities the thing-language that Artaud is after is not sufficient; we need text, but a text not of ideas and thoughts, but of syntactical relations. Artaud polemically condemns Racine as literary, but he surely knew that Racine's theatre did not depend on the content of those speeches, but on the clash of personalities in them, and especially on the *coup de théâtre* of the sudden entrances and the carefully prepared big scenes. *Coup de théâtre* is theatre as action. If the old slow preparation makes us impatient, the fault may be ours.

Artaud neglects these obvious things because he has, I am afraid, one basically wrong idea: he says that the art of theatre aims at utilizing a space and the things in the space; and therefore he makes quite absolute claims for the *mise en scène*. But this is too general; for the theatre-relation is that someone looks at and is affected by, not a space with things and sounds, but persons behaving in their places. Theatre is actors acting on us. So the chief thing is neither interpreting the text nor the *mise en scène*, but the blocking-and-timing (conceived as one space-time solid): it is the directedness of the points of view, the confrontation of personalities, the on-going process of the plot. Artaud was misled, perhaps, by his experience of cinema, where the one who makes the montage, the so-called 'editor', is paramount, for what we experience is the flow of pictures. But for the blocking-and-timing of theatre we need, as is traditional, the collaboration of three: the actor, the director and the dramatic poet.

Bertolt Brecht

BERTOLT BRECHT, 1898–1956, the principal German dramatist of his time, wrote more extensively on the theory of theatre than perhaps any other playwright who ever lived: his theoretical writings have come out as a seven-volume set in German and even at that are not complete. Two of the present selections have been taken from the one-volume selection published in English, *Brecht on Theatre*.* To Mr John Willett's notes following these two selections need only be added that 'The Street Scene' appeared in English before even the German was published, namely, as translated by Eric Bentley in the *Sewanee Review*, Summer 1949. The third selection is from *Helene Weigel, Actress*, a volume of pictures and comments, published in Leipzig and kept in print for a while, in its English version, by *Tulane Drama Review*. (It is of interest to compare Brecht's portrait of the modern actress with Pirandello's on p. 158 and Shaw's on p. 200.)

* Methuen, 1964; Hill & Wang, 1964.

The Street Scene

A Basic Model for an Epic Theatre

BERTOLT BRECHT

Translated by John Willett

In the decade and a half that followed the World War a comparatively new way of acting was tried out in a number of German theatres. Its qualities of clear description and reporting and its use of choruses and projections as a means of commentary earned it the name of 'epic'. The actor used a somewhat complex technique to detach himself from the character portrayed; he forced the spectator to look at the play's situations from such an angle that they necessarily became subject to his criticism. Supporters of this epic theatre argued that the new subject-matter, the highly involved incidents of the class war in its acutest and most terrible stage, would be mastered more easily by such a method, since it would thereby become possible to portray social processes as seen in their causal relationships. But the result of these experiments was that aesthetics found itself up against a whole series of substantial difficulties.

It is comparatively easy to set up a basic model for epic theatre. For practical experiments I usually picked as my example of completely simple, 'natural' epic theatre an incident such as can be seen at any street corner: an eyewitness demonstrating to a collection of people how a traffic accident took place. The bystanders may not have observed what happened, or they may simply not agree with him, may 'see things a different way'; the point is that the demonstrator acts the behaviour of driver or victim or both in such a way that the bystanders are able to form an opinion about the accident.

Such an example of the most primitive type of epic theatre seems easy to understand. Yet experience has shown that it presents astounding difficulties to the reader or listener as soon as he is asked to see the implications of treating this kind of street corner demonstration as a basic form of major theatre, theatre for a scientific age. What this means of course is that the epic theatre may appear richer, more intricate and complex in every particular, yet to be major theatre it need at bottom only contain the same elements as a street-corner demonstration of this sort; nor could it any longer be termed epic theatre if any of the main elements of the street-corner demonstration were lacking. Until this is understood it is impossible really to understand what follows. Until one understands the novelty, unfamiliarity and direct challenge to the critical faculties of the suggestion that street-corner demonstration of this sort can serve as a satisfactory basic model of major theatre one cannot really understand what follows.

Consider: the incident is clearly very far from what we mean by an artistic one. The demonstrator need not be an artist. The capacities he needs to achieve his aim are in effect universal. Suppose he cannot carry out some particular movement as quickly as the victim he is imitating; all he need do is to explain that *he* moves three times as fast, and the demonstration neither suffers in essentials nor loses its point. On the contrary it is important that he should not be too perfect. His demonstration would be spoilt if the by-standers' attention were drawn to his powers of transformation. He has to avoid presenting himself in such a way that someone calls out 'What a lifelike portrayal of a chauffeur!' He must not 'cast a spell' over anyone. He should not transport people from normality to 'higher realms'. He need not dispose of any special powers of suggestion.

It is most important that one of the main features of the ordinary theatre should be excluded from our street scene: the engendering of illusion. The street demonstrator's performance is essentially repetitive. The event has taken place; what you are seeing now is a repeat. If the scene in the theatre follows the street scene in this respect then the theatre will stop pretending not to be theatre, just as the street-corner demonstration admits it is a demonstration (and does not pretend to be the actual event). The element of rehearsal in the acting and of learning by heart in the text, the whole machinery and the whole process of preparation: it all becomes plainly apparent. What room is left for experience? Is the reality portrayed still experienced in any sense?

The street scene determines what kind of experience is to be prepared for the spectator. There is no question but that the street-corner demonstrator has been through an 'experience', but he is not out to make his demonstration serve as an 'experience' for the audience. Even the experience of the driver and the victim is only partially communicated by him, and he by no means tries to turn it into an enjoyable experience for the spectator, however lifelike he may make his demonstration. The demonstration would become no less valid if he did not reproduce the fear caused by the accident; on the contrary it would lose validity if he did. He is not interested in creating pure emotions. It is important to understand that a theatre which follows his lead in this respect undergoes a positive change of function.

One essential element of the street scene must also be present in the theatrical scene if this is to qualify as epic, namely that the demonstration should have a socially practical significance. Whether our street demonstrator is out to show that one attitude on the part of driver or pedestrian makes an accident inevitable where another would not, or whether he is demonstrating with a view to fixing the responsibility, his demonstration has a practical purpose, intervenes socially.

The demonstrator's purpose determines how thoroughly he has to imitate. Our demonstrator need not imitate every aspect of his characters' behaviour, but only so much as gives a picture. Generally the theatre scene will give much fuller pictures, corresponding to its more extensive range of interest. How do street scene and theatre scene link up here? To take a point of detail, the victim's voice may have played no immediate part in the accident. Eye-witnesses may disagree as to whether a cry heard ('Look out!') came from the victim or from someone else, and this may give our demonstrator a motive for imitating the voice. The question can be settled by demonstrating whether the voice was an old man's or a woman's, or merely whether it was high or low. Again, the answer may depend on whether it was that of an educated person or not. Loud or soft may play a great part, as the driver could be correspondingly more or less guilty. A whole series of characteristics of the victim ask to be portrayed. Was he absent-minded? Was his attention distracted? If so, by what? What, on the evidence of his behaviour, could have made him liable to be distracted by just that circumstance and no other? etc., etc. It can be seen that our street-corner demonstration provides opportunities for a pretty rich and varied portrayal of human types. Yet a theatre which tries to restrict its essential elements to those provided by our street scene will have to acknowledge certain limits to imitation. It must be able to justify any outlay in terms of its purpose.*

* We often come across demonstrations of an everyday sort which are more thorough imitations than our street-corner accident demands. Generally they are comic ones. Our next-door neighbour may decide to 'take off' the rapacious behaviour of our common landlord. Such an imitation is often rich and full of variety. Closer examination will show however that even so apparently complex an imitation concentrates on one specific side of the landlord's behaviour. The imitation is summary or selective, deliberately leaving out those occasions where the landlord strikes our neighbour as 'perfectly sensible', though such occasions of course occur. He is far from giving a rounded picture, for that would have no comic impact at all. The street scene, perforce adopting a wider angle of vision, at this point lands in difficulties which must not be underestimated. It has to be just as successful in promoting criticism, but the incidents in question are far more complex. It must promote positive as well as negative criticism, and as part of a single process. You have to understand what is involved in winning the audience's approval by means of a critical approach. Here again we have a precedent in our street scene, i.e. in any demonstration of an everyday sort. Next-door neighbour and street demonstrator can reproduce their subject's 'sensible' or his 'senseless' behaviour alike, by submitting it for an opinion. When it crops up in the course of events, however (when a man switches from being sensible to being senseless, or the other way round), then they usually need some form of commentary in order to change the angle of their portrayal. Hence, as already mentioned, certain difficulties for the theatre scene. These cannot be dealt with here.

The demonstration may for instance be dominated by the question of compensation for the victim, etc. The driver risks being sacked from his job, losing his licence, going to prison; the victim risks a heavy hospital bill, loss of job, permanent disfigurement, possibly unfitness for work. This is the area within which the demonstrator builds up his characters. The victim may have had a companion; the driver may have had his girl sitting alongside him. That would bring out the social element better and allow the characters to be more fully drawn.

Another essential element in the street scene is that the demonstrator should derive his characters entirely from their actions. He imitates their actions and so allows conclusions to be drawn about them. A theatre that follows him in this will be largely breaking with the orthodox theatre's habit of basing the actions on the characters and having the former exempted from criticism by presenting them as an unavoidable consequence deriving by natural law from the characters who perform them. To the street demonstrator the character of the man being demonstrated remains a quantity that need not be completely defined. Within certain limits he may be like this or like that; it doesn't matter. What the demonstrator is concerned with are his accident-prone and accident-proof qualities.* The theatrical scene may show more fully-defined individuals. But it must then be in a position to treat their individuality as a special case and outline the field within which, once more, its most socially relevant effects are produced. Our street demonstrator's possibilities of demonstration are narrowly restricted (indeed, we chose this model so that the limits should be as narrow as possible). If the essential elements of the theatrical scene are limited to those of the street scene then its greater richness must be an enrichment only. The question of border-line cases becomes acute.

Let us take a specific detail. Can our street demonstrator,

* The same situation will be produced by all those people whose characters fulfil the conditions laid down by him and show the features that he imitates.

say, ever become entitled to use an excited tone of voice in repeating the driver's statement that he has been exhausted by too long a spell of work? (In theory this is no more possible than for a returning messenger to start telling his fellow-countrymen of his talk with the king with the words 'I saw the bearded king'.) It can only be possible, let alone un-avoidable, if one imagines a street-corner situation where such excitement, specifically about this aspect of the affair, plays a particular part. (In the instance above this would be so if the king had sworn never to cut his beard off until . . . etc.) We have to find a point of view for our demonstrator that allows him to submit this excitement to criticism. Only if he adopts a quite definite point of view can he be entitled to imitate the driver's excited voice; e.g. if he blames drivers as such for doing too little to reduce their hours of work. ('Look at him. Doesn't even belong to a union, but gets worked up soon enough when an accident happens. "Ten hours I've been at the wheel." ')

Before it can get as far as this, i.e. be able to suggest a point of view to the actor, the theatre needs to take a number of steps. By widening its field of vision and showing the driver in other situations besides that of the accident the theatre in no way exceeds its model; it merely creates a further situation on the same pattern. One can imagine a scene of the same kind as the street scene which provides a well-argued demon-stration showing how such emotions as the driver's develop, or another which involves making comparisons between tones of voice. In order not to exceed the model scene the theatre only has to develop a technique for submitting emo-tions to the spectator's criticism. Of course this does not mean that the spectator must be barred on principle from sharing certain emotions that are put before him; none the less to communicate emotions is only one particular form (phase, consequence) of criticism. The theatre's demonstrator, the actor, must apply a technique which will let him reproduce the tone of the subject demonstrated with a certain reserve, with detachment (so that the spectator can say: 'He's getting excited – in vain, too late, at last. . . .' etc.). In short, the actor must remain a demonstrator; he must present the person demonstrated as a stranger, he must not suppress the '*he* did that, *he* said that' element in his performance. He must not go so far as to be wholly transformed into the person demonstrated.

One essential element of the street scene lies in the natural attitude adopted by the demonstrator, which is two-fold; he is always taking two situations into account. He behaves naturally as a demonstrator, and he lets the subject of the demonstration behave naturally too. He never forgets, nor does he allow it to be forgotten, that he is not the subject but the demonstrator. That is to say, what the audience sees is not a fusion between demonstrator and subject, not some third, independent, uncontradictory entity with isolated features of (a) demonstrator and (b) subject, such as the orthodox theatre puts before us in its productions.* The feelings and opinions of demonstrator and demonstrated are not merged into one.

We now come to one of those elements that are peculiar to the epic theatre, the so-called A-effect (alienation effect). What is involved here is, briefly, a technique of taking the human social incidents to be portrayed and labelling them as something striking, something that calls for explanation, is not to be taken for granted, not just natural. The object of this 'effect' is to allow the spectator to criticize constructively from a social point of view. Can we show that this A-effect is significant for our street demonstrator?

We can picture what happens if he fails to make use of it. The following situation could occur. One of the spectators might say: 'But if the victim stepped off the kerb with his right foot, as you showed him doing. . . .' The demonstrator might interrupt saying: 'I showed him stepping off with his left foot.' By arguing which foot he really stepped off with in his demonstration, and, even more, how the victim himself acted, the demonstration can be so transformed that the A-effect occurs. The demonstrator achieves it by paying exact attention this time to his movements, executing them

* Most clearly worked out by Stanislavsky.

carefully, probably in slow motion; in this way he alienates the little subincident, emphasizes its importance, makes it worthy of notice. And so the epic theatre's alienation effect proves to have its uses for our street demonstrator too, in other words it is also to be found in this small everyday scene of natural street-corner theatre, which has little to do with art. The direct changeover from representation to commentary that is so characteristic of the epic theatre is still more easily recognized as one element of any street demonstration. Wherever he feels he can the demonstrator breaks off his imitation in order to give explanations. The epic theatre's choruses and documentary projections, the direct addressing of the audience by its actors, are at bottom just this.

It will have been observed, not without astonishment I hope, that I have not named any strictly artistic elements as characterizing our street scene and, with it, that of the epic theatre. The street demonstrator can carry out a successful demonstration with no greater abilities than, in effect, anybody has. What about the epic theatre's value as art?

The epic theatre wants to establish its basic model at the street corner, i.e. to return to the very simplest 'natural' theatre, a social enterprise whose origins, means and ends are practical and earthly. The model works without any need of programmatic theatrical phrases like 'the urge to self-expression', 'making a part one's own', 'spiritual experience', 'the play instinct', 'the story-teller's art', etc. Does that mean that the epic theatre isn't concerned with art?

It might be as well to begin by putting the question differently, thus: can we make use of artistic abilities for the purposes of our street scene? Obviously yes. Even the street-corner demonstration includes artistic elements. Artistic abilities in some small degree are to be found in any man. It does no harm to remember this when one is confronted with great art. Undoubtedly what we call artistic abilities can be exercised at any time within the limits imposed by our street scene model. They will function as artistic abilities even though they do not exceed these limits (for instance, when there is meant to be no complete transformation of demonstrator into subject). And, true enough, the epic theatre is an extremely artistic affair, hardly thinkable without artists and virtuosity, imagination, humour and fellow-feeling; it cannot be practised without all these and much else too. It has got to be entertaining, it has got to be instructive. How then can art be developed out of the elements of the street scene, without adding any or leaving any out? How does it evolve into the theatrical scene with its fabricated story, its trained actors, its lofty style of speaking, its make-up, its team performance by a number of players? Do we need to add to our elements in order to move on from the 'natural' demonstration to the 'artificial'?

Is it not true that the additions which we must make to our model in order to arrive at epic theatre are of a fundamental kind? A brief examination will show that they are not. Take the *story*. There was nothing fabricated about our street accident. Nor does the orthodox theatre deal only in fabrications; think for instance of the historical play. None the less a story can be performed at the street corner too. Our demonstrator may at any time be in a position to say: 'The driver was guilty, because it all happened the way I showed you. He wouldn't be guilty if it had happened the way I'm going to show you now.' And he can fabricate an incident and demonstrate it. Or take the fact that the text is learnt by heart. As a witness in a court case the demonstrator may have written down the subject's exact words, learnt them by heart and rehearsed them; in that case he too is performing a text he has learned. Or take a rehearsed programme by several players: it doesn't always have to be artistic purposes that bring about a demonstration of this sort; one need only think of the French police technique of making the chief figures in any criminal case re-enact certain crucial situations before a police audience. Or take making-up. Minor changes in appearance – ruffling one's hair, for instance – can occur at any time within the framework of the non-artistic type of demonstration. Nor is make-up itself used solely for theatrical purposes. In the street scene the driver's moustache may be particularly significant. It may have

influenced the testimony of the possible girl companion suggested earlier. This can be represented by our demonstrator
making the driver stroke an imaginary moustache when
prompting his companion's evidence. In this way the demonstrator can do a good deal to discredit her as a witness.
Moving on to the use of a real moustache in the theatre,
however, is not an entirely easy transition, and the same
difficulty occurs with respect to *costumes*. Our demonstrator
may under given circumstances put on the driver's cap – for
instance if he wants to show that he was drunk: (he had it on
crooked) – but he can only do so conditionally, under these
circumstances; (see what was said about borderline cases
earlier). However, where there is a demonstration by several
demonstrators of the kind referred to above we can have
costume so that the various characters can be distinguished.
This again is only a limited use of costume. There must be
no question of creating an illusion that the demonstrators
really are these characters. (The epic theatre can counteract
this illusion by especially exaggerated costume or by gar-
ments that are somehow marked out as objects for display.)
Moreover we can suggest another model as a substitute for
ours on this point: the kind of street demonstration given by
hawkers. To sell their neckties these people will portray a
badly-dressed and a well-dressed man; with a few props and
technical tricks they can perform significant little scenes
where they submit essentially to the same restrictions as
apply to the demonstrator in our street scene: (they will
pick up tie, hat, stick, gloves and give certain significant
imitations of a man of the world, and the whole time they
will refer to him as '*he*'!) With hawkers we also find *verse*
being used within the same framework as that of our basic
model. They use firm irregular rhythms to sell braces and
newspapers alike.

Reflecting along these lines we see that our basic model
will work. The elements of natural and of artificial epic
theatre are the same. Our street-corner theatre is primitive;
origins, aims and methods of its performance are close to
home. But there is no doubt that it is a meaningful phenom-

enon with a clear social function that dominates all its elements. The performance's origins lie in an incident that can be judged one way or another, that may repeat itself in different forms and is not finished but is bound to have consequences, so that this judgement has some significance. The object of the performance is to make it easier to give an opinion on the incident. Its means correspond to that. The epic theatre is a highly skilled theatre with complex contents and far-reaching social objectives. In setting up the street scene as a basic model for it we pass on the clear social function and give the epic theatre criteria by which to decide whether an incident is meaningful or not. The basic model has a practical significance. As producer and actors work to build up a performance involving many difficult questions – technical problems, social ones – it allows them to check whether the social function of the whole apparatus is still clearly intact.

['Die Strassenszene, Grundmodell eines epischen Theaters', from *Versuche 10*, 1950]

NOTE: Originally stated to have been written in 1940, but now ascribed by Werner Hecht to June 1938. This is an elaboration of a poem 'Über alltägliches Theater' which is supposed to have been written in 1930 and is included as one of the 'Gedichte aus dem Messingkauf' in *Theaterarbeit*, *Versuche 14* and *Gedichte 3*. The notion of the man at the street corner miming an accident is already developed at length there, and it also occurs in the following undated scheme (*Schriften zum Theater 4*, pp. 51-2):

EXERCISES FOR ACTING SCHOOLS

    (a) Conjuring tricks, including attitude of spectators.
    (b) For women: folding and putting away linen. Same for men.
    (c) For men: varying attitudes of smokers. Same for women.
    (d) Cat playing with a hank of thread.
    (e) Exercises in observation.
    (f) Exercises in imitation.
    (g) How to take notes. Noting of gestures, tones of voice.
    (h) Exercises in imagination. Three men throwing dice for their life. One loses. Then: they all lose.
    (i) Dramatizing an epic. Passages from the Bible.

(k) For everybody: repeated exercises in production. Essential to show one's colleagues.

(l) Exercises in temperament. Situation: two women calmly folding linen. They feign a wild and jealous quarrel for the benefit of their husbands; the husbands are in the next room.

(m) They come to blows as they fold their linen in silence.

(n) Game (l) turns serious.

(o) Quick-change competition. Behind a screen, open.

(p) Modifying an imitation, simply described so that others can put it into effect.

(q) Rhythmical (verse-) speaking with tap-dance.

(r) Eating with outsize knife and fork. Very small knife and fork.

(s) Dialogue with gramophone: recorded sentences, free answers.

(t) Search for 'nodal points'.

(u) Characterization of a fellow-actor.

(v) Improvisation of incidents. Running through scenes in the style of a report, no text.

(w) The street accident. Laying down limits of justifiable imitation.

(x) Variations: a dog went into the kitchen. [A traditional song.]

(y) Memorizing first impressions of a part.

On Experimental Theatre

BERTOLT BRECHT

Translated by John Willett

FOR at least two generations the serious European drama has been passing through a period of experiment. So far the various experiments conducted have not led to any definite and clearly established result, nor is the period itself over. In my view these experiments were pursued along two lines which occasionally intersected but can none the less be followed separately. They are defined by the two functions of *entertainment* and *instruction*: that is to say that the theatre organized experiments to increase its ability to amuse, and others which were intended to raise its value as education.

[Brecht then lists experiments from Antoine on, designed to increase the theatre's capacity to entertain, and singles out Vakhtanghov and the constructivist Meyerhold – who 'took over from the asiatic theatre certain dance-like forms and created a whole choreography for the drama' – Reinhardt, with his open-air productions of *Faust, Jedermann* and *Midsummer Night's Dream*, and his seating of actors among the audience in Büchner's *Danton's Death*; Okhlopkov, and the elaboration of crowd scenes by Stanislavsky, Reinhardt and Jessner. But 'on the whole the theatre has not been brought up to modern technological standards'.

The second line he sees as pursued primarily by the playwrights, instancing Ibsen, Tolstoy, Strindberg, Gorki, Tchekov, Hauptmann, Shaw, Georg Kaiser and Eugene O'Neill, and mentioning his own *Threepenny Opera* as 'a parable type plus ideology-busting'. Piscator's theatre was 'the most radical' of all such attempts. 'I took part in all his experiments, and every single one was aimed to increase the theatre's value as education.']

These discoveries [he goes on] have not yet been taken up by the international theatre; this electrification of the stage has been virtually forgotten; the whole ingenious machinery is rusting up, and grass is growing over it. Why is that?

The breakdown of this eminently political theatre must be attributed to political causes. The increase in the theatre's value as political education clashed with the growth of political reaction. But for the moment we shall restrict ourselves to seeing how its crisis developed in aesthetic terms.

Piscator's experiments began by causing complete theatrical chaos. While they turned the stage into a machine-room, the auditorium became a public meeting. Piscator saw the theatre as a parliament, the audience as a legislative body. To this parliament were submitted in plastic form all the great public questions that needed an answer. Instead of a Deputy speaking about certain intolerable social conditions there was an artistic copy of these conditions. It was the stage's ambition to supply images, statistics, slogans which would enable its parliament, the audience, to reach political decisions. Piscator's stage was not indifferent to applause, but it preferred a discussion. It didn't want only to provide its spectator with an experience but also to squeeze from him a practical decision to intervene actively in life. Every means was justified which helped to secure this. The technical side of the stage became extremely complicated. Piscator's stage manager had before him a book that was as different from that of Reinhardt's stage manager as the score of a Stravinsky opera is from a lute-player's part. The mechanism on the stage weighed so much that the stage of the Nollendorftheater had to be reinforced with steel and concrete supports; so much machinery was hung from the dome that it began to give way. Aesthetic considerations were entirely subject to political. Away with painted scenery if a film could be shown that had been taken on the spot and had the stamp of documentary realism. Up with painted cartoons, if the artist (e.g. George Grosz) had something to say to the parliamentary audience. Piscator was even ready to do wholly without actors. When the former German Emperor had his lawyers protest at Piscator's plan to let an actor portray him on his stage, Piscator just asked if the Emperor wouldn't be willing to appear in person; he even offered him a contract. In short, the end was such a vast and important one that all means seemed justified. And the plays themselves were prepared in much the same way as the performance. A whole staff of playwrights worked together on a single play, and their work was supported and checked by a staff of experts, historians, economists, statisticians.

Piscator's experiments broke nearly all the conventions. They intervened to transform the playwright's creative methods, the actor's style of representation, and the work of the stage designer. *They were striving towards an entirely new social function for the theatre.*

Bourgeois revolutionary aesthetics, founded by such great figures of the Enlightenment as *Diderot* and *Lessing*, defines the theatre as a place of entertainment and instruction. During the Enlightenment, a period which saw the start of a tremendous upsurge of the European theatre, there was no conflict between these two things. Pure amusement, provoked even by objects of tragedy, struck men like Diderot as utterly hollow and unworthy unless it added something to the spectators' knowledge, while elements of instruction, in artistic form of course, seemed in no wise to detract from the amusement; in these men's view they gave depth to it.

If we now look at the theatre of our day we shall find an increasingly marked conflict between the two elements which go to make it up, together with its plays – entertainment and instruction. Today there is an opposition here. That 'assimilation of art to science' which gave naturalism its social influence undoubtedly hamstrung some major artistic capacities, notably the imagination, the sense of play and the element of pure poetry. Its artistic aspects were clearly harmed by its instructive side.

The expressionism of the postwar period showed the World as Will and Idea and led to a special kind of solipsism. It was the theatre's answer to the great crisis of society, just as the doctrines of Mach were philosophy's. It represented art's revolt against life: here the world existed purely as a vision, strangely distorted, a monster conjured up by perturbed souls. Expressionism vastly enriched the theatre's means of expression and brought aesthetic gains that still have to be fully exploited, but it proved quite incapable of shedding light on the world as an object of human activity. The theatre's educative value collapsed.

In Piscator's productions or in *The Threepenny Opera* the educative elements were so to speak *built in*: they were not an organic consequence of the whole, but stood in contradiction to it; they broke up the flow of the play and its incidents, they prevented empathy, they acted as a cold douche for those whose sympathies were becoming involved. I hope that the moralizing parts of *The Threepenny Opera* and the educative songs are reasonably entertaining, but it is certain that the entertainment in question is different from what one gets from the more orthodox scenes. The play has a double nature. Instruction and entertainment conflict openly. With Piscator it was the actor and the machinery that openly conflicted.

This is quite apart from the fact that such productions split the audience into at least two mutually hostile social groups, and thus put a stop to any common experience of art. The fact is a political one. Enjoyment of learning depends on the class situation. Artistic appreciation depends on one's political attitude, which can accordingly be stimulated and adopted. But even if we restrict ourselves to the section of the audience which agreed politically we see the sharpening of the conflict between ability to entertain and educative value. Here is a new and quite specific kind of learning, and it can no longer be reconciled with a specific old kind of entertainment. At one (later) stage of the experiments the result of any fresh increase in educative value was an immediate decrease in ability to entertain. ('This isn't theatre, it's secondary-school stuff.') Conversely, emotional acting's effects on the nerves were a continual menace to the production's educative value. (It often helped the educational effect to have bad actors instead of good ones.) In other words, the greater the grip on the audience's nerves, the less chance there was of its learning.

The more we induced the audience to identify its own experiences and feelings with the production, the less it learned; and the more there was to learn, the less the artistic enjoyment.

Here was a crisis: half a century's experiments, conducted in nearly every civilized country, had won the theatre brand-new fields of subject-matter and types of problem, and made it a factor of marked social importance. At the same time they had brought the theatre to a point where any further development of the intellectual, social (political) experience must wreck the artistic experience. And yet, without further development of the former, the latter occurred less and less often. A technical apparatus and a style of acting had been evolved which could do more to stimulate illusions than to give experiences, more to intoxicate than to elevate, more to deceive than to illumine.

What was the good of a constructivist stage if it was socially unconstructive; of the finest lighting equipment if it lit nothing but childish and twisted representations of the world; of a suggestive style of acting if it only served to tell us that A was B? What use was the whole box of tricks if all it could do was to offer artificial surrogates for real experience? Why this eternal ventilating of problems that were always left unsolved? This titillation not only of the nerves but of the brain? We couldn't leave it at that.

The development tended towards a fusion of the two functions, instruction and entertainment. If such preoccupations were to have any social meaning, then they must eventually enable the theatre to project a picture of the world by artistic means: models of men's life together such as could help the spectator to understand his social environment and both rationally and emotionally to master it.

[Brecht goes on, in terms that anticipate the Short Organum and perhaps reflect his work on the first version of *Galileo*, to lament man's failure to understand the laws governing his life in society. His knowledge of these has not kept pace with his scientific knowledge, so that 'nowadays nearly every new discovery is greeted with a shout of triumph which transforms itself into a shout of fear'. (Cf. the long speech in Scene 14 of *Galileo*.) But art ought to be able to give 'a workable picture of the world'.

As it is, he argues, art gets its effects more by empathy than by accuracy. He attacks empathy on the same grounds as before, and describes the attempt to stave it off by methods of 'alienation'. This technique was developed at the Theater am Schiffbauerdamm in Berlin with 'the most talented of the younger generation of actors. . . Weigel, Peter Lorre, Oskar Homolka, (Carola) Neher and Busch', and also with amateur groups, workers' choruses, etc.]

This all represented a continuation of previous experiments, in particular of Piscator's theatre. Already in his last experiments the logical development of the technical apparatus had at last allowed the machinery to be mastered and led to a beautiful simplicity of performance. The socalled *epic* style of production which we developed at the Schiffbauerdamm Theater proved its artistic merits relatively soon, and the *non-aristotelian school of playwriting* tackled the large-scale treatment of large-scale social objects. There was some prospect of changing the choreographic and grouping aspects of Meyerhold's school from artifice into art, of transforming the Stanislavsky school's naturalistic elements into realism. Speech was related to gestics; both everyday language and verse speaking were shaped according to the so-called *gestic principle*. A complete revolution took place in stage design. By a free manipulation of Piscator's principles it became possible to design a setting that was both instructive and beautiful. Symbolism and illusion could be more or less dispensed with, and the *Neher principle* of building the set according to the requirements established at the actors' rehearsals allowed the designer to profit by the actors' performance and influence it in turn. The playwright could work out his experiments in uninterrupted collaboration with actor and stage designer; he could influence and be influenced. At the same time the painter and the composer regained their independence, and were able to express their view of the theme by their own artistic means. The integrated work of art (or 'Gesamtkunstwerk') appeared before the spectator as a bundle of separate elements.

From the start the *classical repertoire* supplied the basis of many of these experiments. The artistic means of alienation made possible a broad approach to the living works of dramatists of other periods. Thanks to them such valuable old plays could be performed without either jarring modernization or museum-like methods, and in an entertaining and instructive way.

It plainly has a particularly good effect on the contemporary amateur theatre (worker, student and child actors) when it is no longer forced to work by hypnosis. It seems conceivable that a line may be drawn between the playing of amateur actors and professional without one of the theatre's basic functions having to be sacrificed.

Such very different ways of acting as those of, say, the Vakhtangov or Okhlopkov companies and the workers' groups can be reconciled on this new foundation. The variegated experiments of half a century seem to have acquired a basis that allows them to be exploited.

None the less these experiments are not so easy to describe, and I am forced here simply to state our belief that we can indeed encourage artistic understanding on the basis of alienation. This is not very surprising, as the theatre of past periods also, technically speaking, achieved results with alienation effects – for instance the Chinese theatre, the Spanish classical theatre, the popular theatre of Brueghel's day and the Elizabethan theatre.

So is this new style of production *the* new style; is it a complete and comprehensible technique, the final result of every experiment? Answer: no. It is a way, the one that *we* have followed. The effort must be continued. The problem holds for all art, and it is a vast one. The solution here aimed at is only *one* of the conceivable solutions to the problem, which can be expressed so: How can the theatre be both instructive and entertaining? How can it be divorced from spiritual dope traffic and turned from a home of illusions to a home of experiences? How can the unfree, ignorant man of our century, with his thirst for freedom and his hunger for knowledge, how can the tortured and heroic, abused and ingenious, changeable and world-changing man of this great and ghastly century obtain his own theatre which will help him to master the world and himself?

> ['Über experimentelles Theater', from *Theater der Zeit*, East Berlin, 1959, No. 4. Also *Schriften zum Theater 3*, pp. 79–106. Two long passages have been summarized to save repetition of Brecht's arguments.]

Helene Weigel

BERTOLT BRECHT

Translated by John Berger and Anna Bostock

I. ON A GREAT GERMAN ACTRESS

DESCRIBE her!

She is of small stature, regular and robust. Her head is large and well-shaped. Her face narrow, soft, with a high, somewhat raised forehead and strong lips. Her voice is rich and dark, and pleasant even in sharpness or in a scream. Her movements are definite and soft.

What is her character?

She is good-natured, gruff, courageous and reliable. She is unpopular.

What is her acting like?

When she acted the maidservant in a Greek play – the maidservant who has to report the death of her mistress – she cried 'Dead, Dead' off-stage in a completely emotionless, piercing voice. 'Jocasta is dead'. It was utterly without lamentation, yet so definite and irresistible that the bare fact of Jocasta's death was more effective at that moment than any sorrow could have been. She did not, then, abandon her voice to horror, but she did so abandon her face; for she showed, by means of white make-up, the effect that death has on those present. Her report that Jocasta had fallen by her own hand as if struck by a bolt admitted little pity for the suicide, but admitted the power of the bolt, so that even the most sentimental onlooker was forced to realize that something decisive had happened which called on his intelligence. Amazed, she described in one clear sentence the dying woman's raving and apparent loss of reason. By the tone of her 'And how she ended, we know it not', a tone that allowed of no misunderstanding, she made it clear that she would give no further information concerning that death: a sign of sparse yet undeviating respect. Now as she walked down the short staircase, her strides were so big that her small figure seemed to be travelling an immense distance from the uninhabited place of horror to the people on the lower stage. And as she held her arms high in formal lament she seemed to be begging for pity on herself, witness of the disaster. And it was then with her loud 'Lament now' that she challenged any earlier, less justified wailing.

What kind of success did she enjoy?

A modest one, except with the connoisseurs. Most of the others were anxious to identify themselves with the feelings of the characters, and did not take part in the intellectual decisions of the play. Thus the momentous decision of which she was the harbinger had almost no effect on them; they saw her only as a vehicle for more and more feeling.

2. WEIGEL'S DESCENT INTO FAME

(from the third night of the *Messingkauf*)

I do not propose to record here how she perfected her art until she was able, not only to make people cry when she cried and laugh when she laughed, but also to make them cry when she laughed and laugh when she cried. I propose to record only what happened afterwards.

For when she had mastered her art and when she wanted to apply it in front of the greatest audience – the people – to the greatest subjects, those that concern the people, she lost her standing and her descent began. As soon as she began to play the first of her new characters – this was an old woman of the working people – she played it in such a way that one could see exactly how the old woman did some things which were against her own interests and some which were to her advantage. It was then that the audience, which was not composed of workers, began to get restless. The fine, well-equipped theatres closed their doors to her and when she appeared in halls in the suburbs, the few connoisseurs who followed her there, though they did not deny her art, thought that it was applied to inferior subjects. And so the rumour spread everywhere was: you are left quite cold. The workers came in crowds, welcomed her heartily and thought her first-rate, but being more occupied with the subject matter, they made little fuss of her. Having learnt with so much effort to guide the attention of her audience to great subjects, that is to say to the struggle of the oppressed against the oppressors, she now had to learn – and it was not easy – to let that attention move away from her, the actress, to the content: to what was enacted. And this was precisely her great achievement.

Many artists make their audience blind and deaf to the world with their superb skill. Weigel's achievement was that she now made the audience see more and hear more than just herself. For she demonstrated not only one but many arts. She showed, for instance, how goodness and wisdom are arts that can and must be learnt. Yet never did she set out to show her own greatness, but always the greatness of those whom she portrayed. She was embarrassed when someone said once to flatter her: you did not act that working class mother, you were that mother. No, she said quickly, I acted her and it must have been her you liked, not me. And indeed when for example she played a fisher-woman who loses her son in the civil war and then goes herself to fight the generals, she made every moment into an historic moment, every speech into a famous speech by an historic character. And at the same time everything was done quite naturally and simply. It was this simplicity and naturalness that distinguished the new historic characters from the old ones. When she was asked how she was able to make the oppressed in revolt appear so noble, she replied: by the closest observation. She knew not only how to make people feel, but also how to make them think, and the thoughts which she stimulated were a true pleasure for them, sometimes violent, sometimes gentle. Here I speak of the workers who came to watch her acting. The theatre experts stayed away and policemen came instead. The truth to which she lent her voice and her explicitness alerted the law, which is there to fight justice. After performances she often found herself now in a police cell. At this time the house-painter came to power and she was forced to flee the country. She knew no other language except the one which no one else knew as she did. And so she played, a few rare times, with small worker companies after only a few rehearsals, to other exiles; otherwise she was busy with housework and bringing up her children in a small fisherman's cottage far from any theatre. Her desire to play to many had brought her to where she could play only to a very few. When she now appeared on the stage, she did so only in plays which showed the horrors of that time and their causes. Perhaps the persecuted who heard her forgot their own troubles, but they never forgot the causes. And always, they left the hall made stronger for their fight. This was because Weigel showed them her own wisdom and her own goodness. She perfected her art more and more, she carried it, ever-increasing, to ever-deepening depths. Thus when she had quite given up and lost her first fame, her second began, her fame at ground level, the fame that was made from the esteem of a few persecuted human beings. She was in good heart: it was her aim to be praised by the ones on the ground, to be praised by as many as possible, but by a few if more was impossible.

E. Gordon Craig

E. GORDON CRAIG, 1872–1966, was one of the most controversial figures of the modern theatre. He has been admired by eminent men from Yeats to Jean-Louis Barrault, and he has been severely taken to task by Bernard Shaw and, more systematically, by Mr Lee Simonson in the latter's book *The Stage is Set*. Like Appia, his spiritual brother, he was a designer and should perhaps first be approached through his designs. The manifesto 'The Art of the Theatre' is today a chapter in the book *The Art of the Theatre*,* but was originally (1905) a separate booklet. Like most of Craig's writing, it not only states Craig's ideas but gives an unmistakable impression of a ferment and a personality. In order that the reader may learn what Gordon Craig, in his day, could mean to people, Arthur Symons's (1865–1945) response to him, dating back in part to *The Monthly Review*, June 1902, is indicated in his piece, 'A New Art of the Stage' (later included in *Studies in Seven Arts*).

* Heinemann, London, 1911; Theatre Arts Books, New York, 1956.

The Art of the Theatre

E. GORDON CRAIG

An Expert and a Playgoer are conversing

STAGE-DIRECTOR: You have now been over the theatre with me, and have seen its general construction, together with the stage, the machinery for manipulating the scenes, the apparatus for lighting, and the hundred other things, and have also heard what I have had to say of the theatre as a machine; let us rest here in the auditorium, and talk a while of the theatre and of its art. Tell me, do you know what is the Art of the Theatre?

PLAYGOER: To me it seems that Acting is the Art of the Theatre.

STAGE-DIRECTOR: Is a part, then, equal to a whole?

PLAYGOER: No, of course not. Do you, then, mean that the play is the Art of the Theatre?

STAGE-DIRECTOR: A play is a work of literature, is it not? Tell me, then, how one art can possibly be another?

PLAYGOER: Well, then, if you tell me that the Art of the Theatre is neither the acting nor the play, then I must come to the conclusion that it is the scenery and the dancing. Yet I cannot think you will tell me this is so.

STAGE-DIRECTOR: No; the Art of the Theatre is neither acting nor the play, it is not scene nor dance, but it consists of all the elements of which these things are composed: action, which is the very spirit of acting; words, which are the body of the play; line and colour, which are the very heart of the scene; rhythm, which is the very essence of dance.

PLAYGOER: Action, words, line, colour, rhythm! And which of these is all-important to the art?

STAGE-DIRECTOR: One is no more important than the

other, no more than one colour is more important to a painter than another, or one note more important than another to a musician. In one respect, perhaps, action is the most valuable part. Action bears the same relation to the Art of the Theatre as drawing does to painting, and melody does to music. The Art of the Theatre has sprung from action – movement – dance.

PLAYGOER: I always was led to suppose that it had sprung from speech, and that the poet was the father of the theatre.

STAGE-DIRECTOR: This is the common belief, but consider it for a moment. The poet's imagination finds voice in words, beautifully chosen; he then either recites or sings these words to us, and all is done. That poetry, sung or recited, is for our ears, and, through them, for our imagination. It will not help the matter if the poet shall add gesture to his recitation or to his song; in fact, it will spoil all.

PLAYGOER: Yes, that is clear to me. I quite understand that the addition of gesture to a perfect lyric poem can but produce an inharmonious result. But would you apply the same argument to dramatic poetry?

STAGE-DIRECTOR: Certainly I would. Remember I speak of a dramatic poem, not of a drama. The two things are separate things. A dramatic poem is to be read. A drama is not to be read, but to be seen upon the stage. Therefore gesture is a necessity to a drama, and it is useless to a dramatic poem. It is absurd to talk of these two things, gesture and poetry, as having anything to do with one another. And now, just as you must not confound the dramatic poem with the drama, neither must you confound the dramatic poet with the dramatist. The first writes for the reader, or listener, the second writes for the audience of a theatre. Do you know who was the father of the dramatist?

PLAYGOER: No, I do not know, but I suppose he was the dramatic poet.

STAGE-DIRECTOR: You are wrong. The father of the

dramatist was the dancer. And now tell me from what material the dramatist made his first piece?

PLAYGOER: I suppose he used words in the same way as the lyric poet.

STAGE-DIRECTOR: Again you are wrong, and that is what every one else supposes who has not learnt the nature of dramatic art. No; the dramatist made his first piece by using action, words, line, colour, and rhythm, and making his appeal to our eyes and ears by a dexterous use of these five factors.

PLAYGOER: And what is the difference between this work of the first dramatists and that of the modern dramatists?

STAGE-DIRECTOR: The first dramatists were children of the theatre. The modern dramatists are not. The first dramatist understood what the modern dramatist does not yet understand. He knew that when he and his fellows appeared in front of them the audience would be more eager to *see* what he would do than to *hear* what he might *say*. He knew that the eye is more swiftly and powerfully appealed to than any other sense; that it is without question the keenest sense of the body of man. The first thing which he encountered on appearing before them was many pairs of eyes, eager and hungry. Even the men and women sitting so far from him that they would not always be able to hear what he might say seemed quite close to him by reason of the piercing keenness of their questioning eyes. To these, and all, he spoke either in poetry or prose, but always in action: in poetic action which is dance, or in prose action which is gesture.

PLAYGOER: I am very interested, go on, go on.

STAGE-DIRECTOR: No – rather let us pull up and examine our ground. I have said that the first dramatist was the dancer's son, that is to say, the child of the theatre, not the child of the poet. And I have just said that the modern dramatic poet is the child of the poet, and knows only how to reach the ears of his listeners, nothing else. And yet in spite of this does not the modern audience still go to the theatre as of old to see things, and not to hear things?

Indeed, modern audiences insist on looking and having their eyes satisfied in spite of the call from the poet that they shall use their ears only. And now do not misunderstand me. I am not saying or hinting that the poet is a bad writer of plays, or that he has a bad influence upon the theatre. I only wish you to understand that the poet is not of the theatre, has never come from the theatre, and cannot be of the theatre, and that only the dramatist among writers has any birth-claim to the theatre – and that a very slight one. But to continue. My point is this, that the people still flock to *see*, not to hear, plays. But what does that prove? Only that the audiences have not altered. They are there with their thousand pairs of eyes, just the same as of old. And this is all the more extraordinary because the playwrights and the plays have altered. No longer is a play a balance of actions, words, dance, and scene, but it is either all words or all scene. Shakespeare's plays, for instance, are a very different thing to the less modern miracle and mystery plays, which were made entirely for the theatre. *Hamlet* has not the nature of a stage representation. *Hamlet* and the other plays of Shakespeare have so vast and so complete a form when read, that they can but lose heavily when presented to us after having undergone stage treatment. That they were acted in Shakespeare's day proves nothing. I will tell you, on the other hand, what at that period was made for the theatre – the Masques – the Pageants – these were light and beautiful examples of the Art of the Theatre. Had the plays been made to be seen, we should find them incomplete when we read them. Now, no one will say that they find *Hamlet* dull or incomplete when they read it, yet there are many who will feel sorry after witnessing a performance of the play, saying, 'No, that is not Shakespeare's *Hamlet*.' When no further addition can be made so as to better a work of art, it can be spoken of as 'finished' – it is complete. *Hamlet* was finished – was complete – when Shakespeare wrote the last word of his blank verse, and for us to add to it by gesture, scene, costume, or dance, is to hint that it is incomplete and needs these additions.

PLAYGOER: Then do you mean to say *Hamlet* should never be performed?

STAGE-DIRECTOR: To what purpose would it be if I replied 'Yes'? *Hamlet* will go on being performed for some time yet, and the duty of the interpreters is to put their best work at its service. But, as I have said, the theatre must not forever rely upon having a play to perform, but must in time perform pieces of its own art.

PLAYGOER: And a piece for the theatre, is that, then, incomplete when printed in a book or recited?

STAGE-DIRECTOR: Yes – and incomplete anywhere except on the boards of a theatre. It must needs be unsatisfying, artless, when read or merely heard, because it is incomplete without its action, its colour, its line and its rhythm in movement and in scene.

PLAYGOER: This interests me, but it dazzles me at the same time.

STAGE-DIRECTOR: Is that, perhaps, because it is a little new? Tell me what it is especially that dazzles you.

PLAYGOER: Well, first of all, the fact that I have never stopped to consider of what the art of the theatre consisted – to many of us it is just an amusement.

STAGE-DIRECTOR: And to you?

PLAYGOER: Oh, to me it has always been a fascination, half amusement and half intellectual exercise. The show has always amused me; the playing of the players has often instructed me.

STAGE-DIRECTOR: In fact, a sort of incomplete satisfaction. That is the natural result of seeing and hearing something imperfect.

PLAYGOER: But I have seen some few plays which seemed to satisfy me.

STAGE-DIRECTOR: If you have been entirely satisfied by something obviously mediocre, may it not be that you were searching for something less than mediocre, and you found that which was just a little better than you expected? Some people go to the theatre, nowadays, expecting to be bored. This is natural, for they have been taught to look for tiresome things. When you tell me you have been satisfied at a modern theatre, you prove that it is not only the art which has degenerated, but that a proportion of the audience has degenerated also. But do not let this depress you. I once knew a man whose life was so occupied, he never heard music other than that of the street organ. It was to him the ideal of what music should be. Still, as you know, there is better music in the world – in fact, barrel-organ music is very bad music; and if you were for once to see an actual piece of theatrical art, you would never again tolerate what is to-day being thrust upon you in place of theatrical art. The reason why you are not given a work of art on the stage is not because the public does not want it, not because there are not excellent craftsmen in the theatre who could prepare it for you, but because the theatre lacks the artist – the artist of the theatre, mind you, not the painter, poet, musician. The many excellent craftsmen whom I have mentioned are, all of them, more or less helpless to change the situation. They are forced to supply what the managers of the theatre demand, but they do so most willingly. The advent of the artist in the theatre world will change all this. He will slowly but surely gather around him these better craftsmen of whom I speak, and together they will give new life to the art of the theatre.

PLAYGOER: But for the others?

STAGE-DIRECTOR: The others? The modern theatre is full of these others, these untrained and untalented craftsmen. But I will say one thing for them. I believe they are unconscious of their inability. It is not ignorance on their part, it is innocence. Yet if these same men once realized that they were craftsmen, and would train as such – I do not speak only of the stage-carpenters, electricians, wigmakers, costumiers, scene-painters, and actors (indeed, these are in many ways the best and most willing craftsmen) – I speak chiefly of the stage-director.

If the stage-director was to technically train himself for his task of interpreting the plays of the dramatist – in time, and by a gradual development he would again recover the ground lost to the theatre, and finally would restore the Art of the Theatre to its home by means of his own creative genius.

PLAYGOER: Then you place the stage-director before the actors?

STAGE-DIRECTOR: Yes; the relation of the stage-director to the actor is precisely the same as that of the conductor to his orchestra, or of the publisher to his printer.

PLAYGOER: And you consider that the stage-director is a craftsman and not an artist?

STAGE-DIRECTOR: When he interprets the plays of the dramatist by means of his actors, his scene-painters, and his other craftsman, then he is a craftsmen – a master craftsman; when he will have mastered the uses of actions, words, line, colour, and rhythm, then he may become an artist. Then we shall no longer need the assistance of the playwright – for our art will then be self-reliant.

PLAYGOER: Is your belief in a Renaissance of the art based on your belief in the Renaissance of the stage-director?

STAGE-DIRECTOR: Yes, certainly, most certainly. Did you for an instant think that I have a contempt for the stage-director? Rather have I a contempt for any man who fails in the whole duty of the stage-director.

PLAYGOER: What are his duties?

STAGE-DIRECTOR: What is his craft? I will tell you. His work as interpreter of the play of the dramatist is something like this: he takes the copy of the play from the hands of the dramatist and promises faithfully to interpret it as indicated in the text (remember I am speaking only of the very best of stage-directors). He then reads the play, and during the first reading the entire colour, tone, movement, and rhythm that the work must assume comes clearly before him. As for the stage directions, descriptions of the scenes, etc., with which the author may interlard his copy, these are not to be considered by him, for if he is master of his craft he can learn nothing from them.

PLAYGOER: I do not quite understand you. Do you mean that when a playwright has taken the trouble to describe the scene in which his men and women are to move and talk, that the stage-director is to take no notice of such directions – in fact, to disregard them?

STAGE-DIRECTOR: It makes no difference whether he regards or disregards them. What he must see to is that he makes his action and scene match the verse or the prose, the beauty of it, the sense of it. Whatever picture the dramatist may wish us to know of, he will describe his scene during the progress of the conversation between the characters. Take for instance, the first scene in *Hamlet*. It begins:

BER: Who's there?
FRAN: Nay, answer me; stand and unfold yourself.
BER: Long live the king!
FRAN: Bernardo?
BER: He.
FRAN: You come most carefully upon your hour.
BER: 'Tis now struck twelve; get thee to bed, Francisco.
FRAN: For this relief much thanks, 'tis bitter cold,
    And I am sick at heart.
BER: Have you had quiet guard?
FRAN: Not a mouse stirring.
BER: Well, good night.
    If you do meet Horatio and Marcellus,
    The rivals of my watch, bid them make haste.

That is enough to guide the stage-director. He gathers from it that it is twelve o'clock at night, that it is in the open air, that the guard of some castle is being changed, that it is very cold, very quiet, and very dark. Any additional 'stage directions' by the dramatist are trivialities.

PLAYGOER: Then you do not think that an author should

write any stage directions whatever, and you seem to consider it an offence on his part if he does so?

STAGE-DIRECTOR: Well, is it not an offence to the men of the theatre?

PLAYGOER: In what way?

STAGE-DIRECTOR: First tell me the greatest offence an actor can give to a dramatist.

PLAYGOER: To play his part badly?

STAGE-DIRECTOR: No, that may merely prove the actor to be a bad craftsman.

PLAYGOER: Tell me, then.

STAGE-DIRECTOR: The greatest offence an actor can give to a dramatist is to cut out words or lines in his play, or to insert what is known as a 'gag'. It is an offence to poach on what is the sole property of the playwright. It is not usual to 'gag' in Shakespeare, and when it is done it does not go uncensured.

PLAYGOER: But what has this to do with the stage directions of the playwright, and in what way does the playwright offend the theatre when he dictates these stage directions?

STAGE-DIRECTOR: He offends in that he poaches on their preserves. If to gag or cut the poet's lines is an offence, so is it an offence to tamper with the art of the stage-director.

PLAYGOER: Then is all the stage direction of the world's plays worthless?

STAGE-DIRECTOR: Not to the reader, but to the stage-director and to the actor – yes.

PLAYGOER: But Shakespeare –

STAGE-DIRECTOR: Shakespeare seldom directs the stage-manager. Go through *Hamlet, Romeo and Juliet, King Lear, Othello*, any of the masterpieces, and except in some of the historical plays which contain descriptions of possessions, etc., what do you find? How are the scenes described in *Hamlet*?

PLAYGOER: My copy shows a clear description. It has 'Act I, scene i. Elsinore. A platform before the Castle.'

STAGE-DIRECTOR: You are looking at a late edition with additions by a certain Mr Malone, but Shakespeare wrote nothing of the kind. His words are 'Actus primus. Scæna prima.' . . . And now let us look at *Romeo and Juliet*. What does your book say?

PLAYGOER: It says: 'Act I, scene i. Verona. A public place.'

STAGE-DIRECTOR: And the second scene?

PLAYGOER: It says: 'Scene ii. A street.'

STAGE-DIRECTOR: And the third scene?

PLAYGOER: It says: 'Scene iii. A room in Capulet's house.'

STAGE-DIRECTOR: And now, would you like to hear what scene directions Shakespeare actually wrote for this play?

PLAYGOER: Yes.

STAGE-DIRECTOR: He wrote: 'Actus primus. Scæna prima.' And not another word as to act or scene throughout the whole play. And now for *King Lear*.

PLAYGOER: No, it is enough. I see now. Evidently Shakespeare relied upon the intelligence of the stage-men to complete their scene from his indication. . . . But is this the same in regard to the actions? Does not Shakespeare place some descriptions through *Hamlet*, such as 'Hamlet leaps into Ophelia's grave,' 'Laertes grapples with him,' and later, 'The attendants part them, and they come out of the grave'?

STAGE-DIRECTOR: No, not one word. All the stage directions from the first to the last, are the tame inventions of sundry editors, Mr Malone, Mr Capell, Theobald and others, and they have committed an indiscretion in tampering with the play, for which we, the men of the theatre, have to suffer.

PLAYGOER: How is that?

STAGE-DIRECTOR: Why, supposing any of us reading Shakespeare shall see in our mind's eye some other combination of movements contrary to the 'instructions' of these gentlemen, and suppose we represent our ideas on the stage, we are instantly taken to task by some knowing one, who accuses us of altering the directions of Shakespeare – nay more, of altering his very intentions.

PLAYGOER: But do not the 'knowing ones', as you call them, know that Shakespeare wrote no stage directions?

STAGE-DIRECTOR: One can only guess that to be the case, to judge from their indiscreet criticisms. Anyhow, what I wanted to show you was that our greatest modern poet realized that to add stage directions was first of all unnecessary, and secondly, tasteless. We can therefore be sure that Shakespeare at any rate realized what was the work of the theatre craftsman – the stage-manager, and that it was part of the stage-manager's task to invent the scenes in which the play was to be set.

PLAYGOER: Yes, and you were telling me what each part consisted of.

STAGE-DIRECTOR: Quite so. And now that we have disposed of the error that the author's directions are of any use, we can continue to speak of the way the stage-manager sets to work to interpret faithfully the play of the dramatist. I have said that he swears to follow the text faithfully, and that his first work is to read the play through and get the great impression; and in reading, as I have said, begins to see the whole colour, rhythm, action of the thing. He then puts the play aside for some time, and in his mind's eye mixes his palette (to use a painter's expression) with the colours which the impression of the play has called up. Therefore, on sitting down a second time to read through the play, he is surrounded by an atmosphere which he proposes to test. At the end of the second reading he will find that his more definite impressions have received clear and unmistakable corroboration, and that some of his impressions which were less positive have disappeared. He will then make a note of these. It is possible that he will even now commence to suggest, in line and colour, some of the scenes and ideas which are filling his head, but this is more likely to be delayed until he has re-read the play at least a dozen times.

PLAYGOER: But I thought the stage-manager always left that part of the play – the scene designing – to the scene painter?

STAGE-DIRECTOR: So he does, generally. First blunder of the modern theatre.

PLAYGOER: How is it a blunder?

STAGE-DIRECTOR: This way: *A* has written a play which *B* promises to interpret faithfully. In so delicate a matter as the interpretation of so elusive a thing as the spirit of a play, which, do you think, will be the surest way to preserve the unity of that spirit? Will it be best if *B* does all the work by himself? or will it do to give the work into the hands of *C, D,* and *E,* each of whom see or think differently from *B* or *A*?

PLAYGOER: Of course the former would be best. But is it possible for one man to do the work of three men?

STAGE-DIRECTOR: That is the only way the work can be done, if unity, the one thing vital to a work of art, is to be obtained.

PLAYGOER: So, then, the stage-manager does not call in a scene painter and ask him to design a scene, but he designs one himself?

STAGE-DIRECTOR: Certainly. And remember he does not merely sit down and draw a pretty or historically accurate design, with enough doors and windows in picturesque places, but he first of all chooses certain colours which seem to him to be in harmony with the spirit of the play, rejecting other colours as out of tune. He then weaves into a pattern certain objects – an arch, a fountain, a balcony, a bed – using the chosen object as the centre of his design. Then he adds to this all the objects which are mentioned in the play, and which are necessary to be seen. To these he adds, one by one, each character which appears in the play, and gradually each movement of each character, and each costume. He is as likely as not to make several mistakes in his pattern. If so, he must, as it were, unpick the design, and rectify the blunder even if he has to go right back to the beginning and start the pattern all over again—or he may even have to begin a new pattern. At any rate, slowly, harmoniously, must the whole design develop, so that the eye of the beholder shall be satisfied. While this pattern for the eye is being devised, the designer is being guided as much by the sound of the verse or prose as by the sense or spirit. And shortly all is prepared, and the actual work can be commenced.

PLAYGOER: What actual work? It seems to me that the stage-manager has already been doing a good deal of what may be called actual work.

STAGE-DIRECTOR: Well, perhaps; but the difficulties have but commenced. By the actual work I mean the work which needs skilled labour, such as the actual painting of the huge spaces of canvas for the scenes, and the actual making of the costumes.

PLAYGOER: You are not going to tell me that the stage-manager actually paints his own scenes and cuts his own costumes, and sews them together?

STAGE-DIRECTOR: No, I will not say that he does so in every case and for every play, but he must have done so at one time or another during his apprenticeship, or must have closely studied all the technical points of these complicated crafts. Then will he be able to guide the skilled craftsmen in their different departments. And when the actual making of the scenes and costumes has commenced, the parts are distributed to the different actors, who learn the words before a single rehearsal takes place. (This, as you may guess, is not the custom, but it is what should be seen to by a stage-director such as I describe.) Meantime, the scenes and costumes are almost ready. I will not tell you the amount of interesting but laborious work it entails to prepare the play up to this point. But even when once the scenes are placed upon the stage, and the costumes upon the actors, the difficulty of the work is still great.

PLAYGOER: The stage-director's work is not finished then?

STAGE-DIRECTOR: Finished! What do you mean?

PLAYGOER: Well, I thought now that the scenes and

costumes were all seen to, the actors and actresses would do the rest.

STAGE-DIRECTOR: No, the stage-manager's most interesting work is now beginning. His scene is set and his characters are clothed. He has, in short, a kind of dream picture in front of him. He clears the stage of all but the one, two, or more characters who are to commence the play, and he begins the scheme of lighting these figures and the scene.

PLAYGOER: What, is not this branch left to the discretion of the master electrician and his men?*

STAGE-DIRECTOR: The doing of it is left to them, but the manner of doing it is the business of the stage-manager. Being, as I have said, a man of some intelligence and training, he has devised a special way of lighting his scene for this play, just as he has devised a special way of painting the scene and costuming the figures. If the word 'harmony' held no significance for him, he would of course leave it to the first comer.

PLAYGOER: Then do you actually mean that he has made so close a study of nature that he can direct his electricians how to make it appear as if the sun were shining at such and such an altitude, or as if the moonlight were flooding the interior of the room with such and such an intensity?

STAGE-DIRECTOR: No, I should not like to suggest that, because the reproduction of nature's lights is not what my stage-manager ever attempts. Neither should he attempt such an impossibility. Not to *reproduce* nature, but to *suggest* some of her most beautiful and most living ways – that is what my stage-manager shall attempt. The other thing proclaims an overbearing assumption of omnipotence. A stage-manager may well aim to be an artist, but it ill becomes him to attempt celestial honours. This attitude he can avoid by never trying to imprison or copy nature, for nature will be neither imprisoned nor allow any man to copy her with any success.

* 'Why waste time talking to so stupid a man as this "Playgoer"?' asked a charming lady – and would not wait for an answer. The reply is obvious: one does not talk to wise people – one listens to them.

PLAYGOER: Then in what way does he set to work? What guides him in his task of lighting the scene and costumes which we are speaking about?

STAGE-DIRECTOR: What guides him? Why, the scene and the costumes, and the verse and the prose, and the sense of the play. All these things, as I told you, have now been brought into harmony, the one with the other – all goes smoothly – what simpler, then, that it should so continue, and that the manager should be the only one to know how to preserve this harmony which he has commenced to create?

PLAYGOER: Will you tell me some more about the actual way of lighting the scene and the actors?

STAGE-DIRECTOR: Certainly. What do you want to know?

PLAYGOER: Well, will you tell me why they put lights all along the floor of the stage – footlights they call them, I believe?

STAGE-DIRECTOR: Yes, footlights.

PLAYGOER: Well, why are they put on the ground?

STAGE-DIRECTOR: It is one of the questions which has puzzled all the theatre reform gentlemen, and none has been able to find an answer, for the simple reason that there is no answer. There never was an answer, there never will be an answer. The only thing to do is to re-move all the footlights out of all the theatres as quickly as possible and say nothing about it. It is one of those queer things which nobody can explain, and at which children are always surprised. Little Nancy Lake, in 1812, went to Drury Lane Theatre, and her father tells us that she also was astonished at the footlights. Said she:

> 'And there's a row of lamps, my eye!
> How they do blaze – I wonder why
> They keep them on the ground.'
> – *Rejected Addresses*

That was in 1812! and we are still wondering.

PLAYGOER: A friend of mine – an actor – once told me that

if there were no footlights all the faces of the actors would look dirty.

STAGE-DIRECTOR: That was the remark of a man who did not understand that in place of the footlights another method of lighting the faces and figures could be adopted. It is this simple kind of thing which never occurs to those people who will not devote a little time to even a slight study of the other branches of the craft.

PLAYGOER: Do not the actors study the other crafts of the theatre?

STAGE-DIRECTOR: As a rule – no, and in some ways it is opposed to the very life of an actor. If an actor of intelligence were to devote much time to the study of all the branches of the theatrical art he would gradually cease to act, and would end by becoming a stage-manager – so absorbing is the whole art in comparison with the single craft of acting.

PLAYGOER: My friend the actor also added that if the footlights were removed the audience would not be able to see the expression of his face.

STAGE-DIRECTOR: Had Henry Irving or Eleanora Duse said so, the remark would have had some meaning. The ordinary actor's face is either violently expressive or violently inexpressive, that it would be a blessing if the theatres were not only without footlights but without any lights at all. By the way, an excellent theory of the origin of the footlights is advanced by M. Ludovic Celler in *Les Décors, les costumes et la mise-en-scène au XVII siècle*. The usual way of lighting the stage was by means of large chandeliers, circular or triangular, which were suspended above the heads of the actors and the audience; and M. Celler is of the opinion that the system of footlights owes its origin to the small plain theatres which could not afford to have chandeliers, and therefore placed tallow candles on the floor in front of the stage. I believe this theory to be correct, for common sense could not have dictated such an artistic blunder; whereas the box-office receipts may easily have done so. Remember how little artistic virtue is in the box-office! When we have time I will tell you some things about this powerful usurper of the theatrical throne – the box-office. But let us return to a more serious and a more interesting topic than this lack of expression and this foot-light matter. We had passed in review the different tasks of the stage-manager – scene, costume, lighting – and we had come to the most interesting part, that of the manip-ulation of the figures in all their movements and speeches. You expressed astonishment that the acting – that is to say, the speaking and actions of the actors – was not left to the actors to arrange for themselves. But consider for an in-stant the nature of this work. Would you have that which has already grown into a certain unified pattern, suddenly spoiled by the addition of something accidental?

PLAYGOER: How do you mean? I understand what you suggest, but will you not show me more exactly how the actor can spoil the pattern?

STAGE-DIRECTOR: *Unconsciously* spoil it, mind you! I do not for an instant mean that it is his wish to be out of harmony with his surroundings, but he does so through innocence. Some actors have the right instincts in this matter, and some have none whatever. But even those whose instincts are most keen cannot remain in the pattern, cannot be harmonious, without following the directions of the stage-manager.

PLAYGOER: Then you do not even permit the leading actor and actress to move and act as their instincts and reason dictate?

STAGE-DIRECTOR: No, rather must they be the very first to follow the direction of the stage-manager, so often do they become the very centre of the pattern – the very heart of the emotional design.

PLAYGOER: And is that understood and appreciated by them?

STAGE-DIRECTOR: Yes, but only when they realize and appreciate at the same time that the play, and the right and just interpretation of the play, is the all-important thing in the modern theatre. Let me illustrate this point to you. The play to be presented is *Romeo and Juliet*. We have studied the play, prepared scene and costume, lighted both, and now our rehearsals for the actors commence. The first movement of the great crowd of unruly citizens of Verona, fighting, swearing, killing each other, appals us. It horrifies us that in this white little city of roses and song and love there should dwell this amazing and detestable hate which is ready to burst out at the very church doors or in the middle of the May festival, or under the windows of the house of a newly born girl. Quickly following on this picture, and even while we remember the ugliness which larded both faces of Capulet and Montague, there comes strolling down the road the son of Montague, our Romeo, who is soon to be lover and the loved of his Juliet. Therefore, whoever is chosen to move and speak as Romeo must move and speak as part and parcel of the design – this design which I have already pointed out to you as having a definite form. He must move across our sight in a certain way, passing to a certain point, in a certain light, his head at a certain angle, his eyes, his feet, his whole body in tune with the play, and not (as is often the case) in tune with his own thoughts only, and these out of harmony with the play. For his thoughts (beautiful as they may chance to be) may not match the spirit or the pattern which has been so carefully prepared by the director.

PLAYGOER: Would you have the stage-manager control the movements of whoever might be impersonating the character of Romeo, even if he were a fine actor?

STAGE-DIRECTOR: Most certainly; and the finer the actor the finer his intelligence and taste, and therefore the more easily controlled. In fact, I am speaking in particular of a theatre wherein all the actors are men of refinement and the manager a man of peculiar accomplishments.

PLAYGOER: But are you not asking these intelligent actors almost to become puppets?

STAGE-DIRECTOR: A sensitive question! which one would expect from an actor who felt uncertain about his powers. A puppet is at present only a doll, delightful enough for a puppet show. But for a theatre we need more than a doll. Yet that is the feeling which some actors have about their relationship with the stage-manager. They feel they are having their strings pulled, and resent it, and show they feel hurt – insulted.

PLAYGOER: I can understand that.

STAGE-DIRECTOR: And cannot you also understand that they should be willing to be controlled? Consider for a moment the relationship of the men on a ship, and you will understand what I consider to be the relationship of men in a theatre. Who are the workers on a ship?

PLAYGOER: A ship? Why, there is the captain, the commander, the first, second and third lieutenants, the navigation officer, and so on, and the crew.

STAGE-DIRECTOR: Well, and what is it that guides the ship?

PLAYGOER: The rudder?

STAGE-DIRECTOR: Yes, and what else?

PLAYGOER: The steersman who holds the wheel of the rudder.

STAGE-DIRECTOR: And who else?

PLAYGOER: The man who controls the steersman.

STAGE-DIRECTOR: And who is that?

PLAYGOER: The navigation officer.

STAGE-DIRECTOR: And who controls the navigation officer?

PLAYGOER: The captain.

STAGE-DIRECTOR: And are any orders which do not come from the captain, or by his authority, obeyed?

PLAYGOER: No, they should not be.

STAGE-DIRECTOR: And can the ship steer its course in safety without the captain?

PLAYGOER: It is not usual.

STAGE-DIRECTOR: And do the crew obey the captain and his officers?

PLAYGOER: Yes, as a rule.

STAGE-DIRECTOR: Willingly?

PLAYGOER: Yes.

STAGE-DIRECTOR: And is that not called discipline?

PLAYGOER: Yes.

STAGE-DIRECTOR: And discipline – what is that the result of?

PLAYGOER: The proper and willing subjection to rules and principles.

STAGE-DIRECTOR: And the first of those principles is obedience, is it not?

PLAYGOER: It is.

STAGE-DIRECTOR: Very well, then. It will not be difficult for you to understand that a theatre in which so many hundred persons are engaged at work is in many respects like a ship, and demands like management. And it will not be difficult for you to see how the slightest sign of disobedience would be disastrous. Mutiny has been well anticipated in the navy, but not in the theatre. The navy has taken care to define, in clear and unmistakable voice, that the captain of the vessel is the king, and a despotic ruler into the bargain. Mutiny on a ship is dealt with by a court-martial, and is put down by very severe punishment, by imprisonment, or by dismissal from the service.

PLAYGOER: But you are not going to suggest such a possibility for the theatre?

STAGE-DIRECTOR: The theatre, unlike the ship, is not made for purposes of war, and so for some unaccountable reason discipline is not held to be of such vital importance, whereas it is of as much importance as in any branch of service. But what I wish to show you is that until discipline is understood in a theatre to be willing and reliant obedience to the manager or captain no supreme achievement can be accomplished.

PLAYGOER: But are not the actors, scene-men, and the rest all willing workers?

STAGE-DIRECTOR: Why, my dear friend, there never were such glorious natured people as these men and women of the theatre. They are enthusiastically willing, but sometimes their judgement is at fault, and they become as willing to be unruly as to be obedient, and as willing to lower the standard as to raise it. As for nailing the flag to the mast – this is seldom dreamed of – for *compromise* and the vicious doctrine of compromise with the enemy is preached by the officers of the theatrical navy. Our enemies are vulgar display, the lower public opinion, and ignorance. To these our 'officers' wish us to knuckle under. What the theatre people have not yet quite comprehended is *the value of a high standard and the value of a director who abides by it.*

PLAYGOER: And that director, why should he not be an actor or a scene-painter?

STAGE-DIRECTOR: Do you pick your leader from the ranks, exalt him to be captain, and then let him handle the guns and the ropes? No; the director of a theatre must be a man apart from any of the crafts. He must be a man who knows but no longer handles the ropes.

PLAYGOER: But I believe it is a fact that many well-known leaders in the theatres have been actors and stage-managers at the same time?

STAGE-DIRECTOR: Yes, that is so. But you will not find it easy to assure me that no mutiny was heard of under their rule. Right away from all this question of positions there is the question of the art, the work. If an actor assumes the management of the stage, and if he is a better actor than his fellows, a natural instinct will lead him to make himself the centre of everything. He will feel that unless he does so the work will appear thin and unsatisfying. He will pay less heed to the play than he will to his own part, and he will, in fact, gradually cease to look upon the work as a whole. And this is not good for the work. This is not the way a work of art is to be produced in the theatre.

PLAYGOER: But might it not be possible to find a great actor who would be so great an artist that as manager he would never do as you say, but who would always handle himself as actor, just the same as he handles the rest of the material?

STAGE-DIRECTOR: All things are possible, but, firstly, it is against the nature of an actor to do as you suggest; secondly, it is against the nature of the stage-manager to perform; and thirdly, it is against all nature that a man can be in two places at once. Now, the place of the actor is on the stage, in a certain position, ready by means of his brains to give suggestions of certain emotions, surrounded by certain scenes and people; and it is the place of the stage-manager to be in front of this, that he may view it as a whole. So that you see even if we found our perfect actor who was our perfect stage-manager, he could not be in two places at the same time. Of course we have sometimes seen the conductor of a small orchestra playing the part of the first violin, but not from choice, and not to a satisfactory issue; neither is it the practice in large orchestras.

PLAYGOER: I understand, then, that you would allow no one to rule on the stage except the stage-manager?

STAGE-DIRECTOR: The nature of the work permits nothing else.

PLAYGOER: Not even the playwright?

STAGE-DIRECTOR: Only when the playwright has practised and studied the crafts of acting, scene-painting, costume, lighting, and dance, not otherwise. But playwrights, who have not been cradled in the theatre, generally know little of these crafts. Goethe, whose love for the theatre remained ever fresh and beautiful, was in many ways one of the greatest of stage-directors. But, when he linked himself to the Weimar theatre, he forgot to do what the great musician who followed him remembered. Goethe permitted an authority in the theatre higher than himself, that is to say, the owner of the theatre. Wagner was careful to possess himself of his theatre, and become a sort of feudal baron in his castle.

PLAYGOER: Was Goethe's failure as a theatre director due to this fact?

STAGE-DIRECTOR: Obviously, for had Goethe held the keys of the doors that impudent little poodle would never have got as far as its dressing-room; the leading lady would never have made the theatre and herself immortally ridiculous; and Weimar would have been saved the tradition of having perpetrated the most shocking blunder which ever occurred inside a theatre.

PLAYGOER: The traditions of most theatres certainly do not seem to show that the artist is held in much respect on the stage.

STAGE-DIRECTOR: Well, it would be easy to say a number of hard things about the theatre and its ignorance of art. But one does not hit a thing which is down, unless, perhaps, with the hope that the shock may cause it to leap to its feet again. And our Western theatre is very much down. The East still boasts a theatre. Ours here in the West is on its last legs. But I look for a Renaissance.

PLAYGOER: How will that come?

STAGE-DIRECTOR: Through the advent of a man who shall contain in him all the qualities which go to make up a master of the theatre, and through the reform of the theatre as an instrument. When that is accomplished, when the theatre has become a masterpiece of mechanism, when it had invented a technique, it will without any effort develop a *creative art* of its own. But the whole question of the development of the craft into a self-reliant and creative art would take too long to go thoroughly into at present. There are already some theatre men at work on the building of the theatres; some are reforming the acting, some the scenery. And all of this must be of some small value. But the very first thing to be realized is that little or no result can come from the reforming of a single craft of the theatre without at the same time, in the same theatre, reforming all the other crafts. *The whole renaissance of the Art of the Theatre depends upon the extent that this is realized.* The Art of the Theatre, as I have already told you, is divided up into so many crafts: acting, scene, costume, lighting, carpentering, singing, dancing, etc., that it must be realized at the commencement that ENTIRE, not PART reform is needed; and it must be realized that *one* part, one craft, has a *direct* bearing upon each of the other crafts in the theatre, and that no result can come from fitful, uneven reform, but only from a systematic progression. Therefore,

THE THEORY OF THE MODERN STAGE

the reform of the Art of the Theatre is possible to those men alone who have studied and practised all the crafts of the theatre.

PLAYGOER: That is to say, your ideal stage-manager.

STAGE-DIRECTOR: Yes. You will remember that at the commencement of our conversation I told you my belief in the Renaissance of the Art of the Theatre was based in my belief in the Renaissance of the stage-director, and that when he had understood the right use of actors, scene, costume, lighting, and dance, and by means of these had mastered the craft of interpretation, he would then gradually acquire the mastery of action, line, colour, rhythm, and words, this last strength developing out of all the rest. ... Then I said the Art of the Theatre would have won back its rights, and its work would stand self-reliant as a creative art, and no longer as an interpretative craft.

PLAYGOER: Yes, and at the time I did not quite understand what you meant, and though I can now understand your drift, I do not quite in my mind's eye see the stage without its poet.

STAGE-DIRECTOR: What? Shall anything be lacking when the poet shall no longer write for the theatre?

PLAYGOER: The play will be lacking.

STAGE-DIRECTOR: Are you sure of that?

PLAYGOER: Well, the play will certainly not exist if the poet or playwright is not there to write it.

STAGE-DIRECTOR: There will not be any play in the sense in which you use the word.

PLAYGOER: But you propose to present something to the audience, and I presume before you are able to present them with that something you must have it in your possession.

STAGE-DIRECTOR: Certainly; you could not have made a surer remark. Where you are at fault is to take for granted, as if it were a law for the Medes and Persians, that that *something* must be made of words.

PLAYGOER: Well, what is this something which is not words, but for presentation to the audience?

STAGE-DIRECTOR: First tell me, is not an idea something?

PLAYGOER: Yes, but it lacks form.

STAGE-DIRECTOR: Well, but is it not permissible to give an idea whatever form the artist chooses?

PLAYGOER: Yes.

STAGE-DIRECTOR: And is it an unpardonable crime for the theatrical artist to use some different material to the poet's?

PLAYGOER: No.

STAGE-DIRECTOR: Then we are permitted to attempt to give form to an idea in whatever material we can find or invent, provided it is not a material which should be put to a better use?

PLAYGOER: Yes.

STAGE-DIRECTOR: Very good; follow what I have to say for the next few minutes, and then go home and think about it for a while. Since you have granted all I asked you to permit, I am now going to tell you out of what material an artist of the theatre of the future will create his masterpieces. Out of ACTION, SCENE, and VOICE. Is it not very simple?

And when I say *action*, I mean both gesture and dancing, the prose and poetry of action.

When I say *scene*, I mean all which comes before the eye, such as the lighting, costume, as well as the scenery.

When I say *voice*, I mean the spoken word or the word which is sung, in contradiction to the word which is read, for the word written to be spoken and the word written to be read are two entirely different things.

And now, though I have but repeated what I told you at the beginning of our conversation, I am delighted to see that you no longer look so puzzled.

A New Art of the Stage

ARTHUR SYMONS

I

IN the remarkable experiments of Mr Gordon Craig, I seem
to see the suggestion of a new art of the stage, an art no longer
realistic, but conventional, no longer imitative, but symbolical. In Mr Craig's staging there is the incalculable element, the element that comes of itself, and cannot be coaxed
into coming. But in what is incalculable there may be equal
parts of inspiration and of accident. How much, in Mr Craig's
staging, is inspiration, how much is accident? That is, after
all, the important question.

Mr Craig, it is certain, has a genius for line, for novel
effects of line. His line is entirely his own; he works in squares
and straight lines, hardly ever in curves. He drapes the stage
into a square with cloths; he divides these cloths by vertical
lines, carrying the eye straight up to an immense height,
fixing it into a rigid attention. He sets squares of pattern and
structure on the stage; he forms his groups into irregular
squares, and sets them moving in straight lines, which double
on themselves like the two arms of a compass; he puts square
patterns on the dresses, and drapes the arms with ribbons
that hang to the ground, and make almost a square of the
body when the arms are held out at right angles. He prefers
gestures that have no curves in them; the arms held straight
up, or straight forward, or straight out sideways. He likes the
act of kneeling, in which the body is bent into a sharp angle;
he likes a sudden spring to the feet, with the arms held
straight up. He links his groups by an arrangement of poles
and ribbons, something in the manner of maypole; each
figure is held to the centre by a tightly stretched line like the
spoke of a wheel. Even when, as in this case, the pattern
forms into a circle, the circle is segmented by straight lines.

138

This severe treatment of line gives breadth and dignity to what might otherwise be merely fantastic. Mr Craig is happiest when he can play at children's games with his figures, as in almost the whole of *The Masque of Love*.* When he is entirely his own master, not dependent on any kind of reality, he invents really like a child, and his fairy-tale comes right, because it is not tied by any grown-up logic. Then his living design is like an arabesque within strict limits, held in from wandering and losing itself by those square lines which rim it implacably round.

Then, again, his effects are produced simply. Most of the costumes in *The Masque of Love* were made of sacking, stitched roughly together. Under the cunning handling of the light, they gave you any illusion you pleased, and the beggars of the masque were not more appropriately clothed than the kings and queens. All had dignity, all reposed the eye.

The aim of modern staging is to intensify the reality of things, to give you the illusion of an actual room, or meadow, or mountain. We have arrived at a great skill in giving this crude illusion of reality. Our stage painters can imitate anything, but what they cannot give us is the emotion which the playwright, if he is an artist, wishes to indicate by means of his scene. It is the very closeness of the imitation which makes our minds unable to accept it. The eye rebounds, so to speak, from this canvas as real as wood, this wood as real as water, this water which is actual water. Mr Craig aims at taking us beyond reality; he replaces the pattern of the thing itself by the pattern which that thing evokes in his mind, the symbol of the thing. As, in conventional art, the artist unpicks the structure of the rose to build up a mental image of the rose, in some formal pattern which his brain makes over again, like a new creation from the beginning, a new organism, so, in this new convention of the stage, a plain cloth, modulated by light, can stand for space or for limit, may be the tight walls of a tent or the sky and the clouds. The eye loses itself among these severe, precise, and yet mysterious

* A reference to the production of the masque from Purcell's *Dioclesian* in 1901. E.B.

lines and surfaces; the mind is easily at home in them; it accepts them as readily as it accepts the convention by which, in a poetical play, men speak in verse rather than in prose.

Success, of course, in this form of art lies in the perfecting of its emotional expressiveness. Even yet Mr Craig has not done much more, perhaps, than indicate what may be done with the material which he finds in his hands. For instance, the obvious criticism upon his mounting of *Acis and Galatea** is, that he has mounted a pastoral, and put nothing pastoral into his mounting. And this criticism is partly just. Yet there are parts, especially the end of Act I, where he has perfectly achieved the rendering of pastoral feeling according to his own convention. The tent is there with its square walls, not a glimpse of meadow or sky comes into the severe design, and yet, as the nymphs in their straight dresses and straight ribbons lie back laughing on the ground, and the children, with their little modern brown straw hats, toss paper roses among them, and the coloured balloons (which you may buy in the street for a penny) are tossed into the air, carrying the eye upward, as if it saw the wind chasing the clouds, you feel the actual sensation of a pastoral scene, of country joy, of the spring and the open air, as no trickle of real water in a trough, no sheaves of real corn among painted trees, no imitation of a flushed sky on canvas, could trick you into feeling it. The imagination has been caught; a suggestion has been given which strikes straight to the 'nerves of delight'; and be sure those nerves, that imagination, will do the rest, better, more effectually, than the deliberate assent of the eyes to an imitation of natural appearances.

Take again some of those drawings of stage scenery which we have not yet been able to see realized, the decoration for Hofmannsthal's *Elektra* and *Venice Preserved*, and for *Hamlet* and for *The Masque of London*. Everywhere a wild and exquisite scenic imagination builds up shadowy structures which seem to have arisen by some strange hazard, and to the sound of an unfamiliar music, and which are often literally

* A reference to the production of Handel's *Acis and Galatea* in 1902. E.B.

like music in the cadences of their design. All have dignity, remoteness, vastness; a sense of mystery, an actual emotion in their lines and faint colours. There is poetry in this bare prose framework of stage properties, a quality of grace which is almost evasive, and seems to point out new possibilities of drama, as it provides new, scarcely hoped for, possibilities to the dramatist.

Take for instance, *The Masque of London*. It is Piranesi, and it is London of today, seen in lineal vision, and it is a design, not merely on paper, but built up definitely between the wings of the stage. It is a vast scaffolding, rising out of ruins, and ascending to toppling heights; all its crazy shapes seem to lean over in the air, and at intervals a little weary being climbs with obscure patience. In one of the *Hamlet* drawings we see the room in the castle at Elsinore into which Ophelia is to come with her bewildered singing; and the room waits, tall, vague, exquisitely still and strange, a ghostly room, prepared for beauty and madness. There is another room, with tall doors and windows and abrupt pools of light on the floor; and another, with its significant shadows, its two enigmatic figures, in which a drama of Maeterlinck might find its own atmosphere awaiting it. And in yet another all is gesture; walls, half-opened doors, half-seen windows, the huddled people at a doorway, and a tall figure of a woman raised up in the foreground, who seems to motion to them vehemently. Colour cooperates with line in effects of rich and yet delicate vagueness; there are always the long, straight lines, the sense of height and space, the bare surfaces, the subtle, significant shadows, out of which Mr Craig has long since learned to evoke stage pictures more beautiful and more suggestive than any that have been seen on the stage in our time.

The whole stage art of Mr Craig is a protest against realism, and it is to realism that we owe whatever is most conspicuously bad in the mounting of plays at the present day. Wagner did some of the harm; for he refused to realize some of the necessary limitations of stage illusion, and persisted in believing that the stage artist could compete successfully with nature in the production of landscape, light, and shadow. Yet Wagner himself protested against the heaps of unrealizing detail under which Shakespeare was buried, in his own time, on the German stage, as he is buried on the English stage in our own. No scene-painter, no scene-shifter, no limelight man, will ever delude us by his moon or meadow or moving clouds or water. His business is to aid the poet's illusion, that illusion of beauty which is the chief excuse for stage plays at all, when once we have passed beyond the 'rose-pink and dirty drab', in Meredith's sufficing phrase, of stage romance and stage reality. The distinction, the incomparable merit, of Mr Craig is that he conceives his setting as the poet conceives his drama. The verse in most Shakespearean revivals rebounds from a backcloth of metallic solidity; the scenery shuts in the players, not upon Shakespeare's dream, but upon as nearly as possible 'real' historical *bric-à-brac*. What Mr Craig does, or would do if he were allowed to do it, is to open all sorts of 'magic casements', and to thrust back all kinds of real and probable limits, and to give at last a little scope for the imagination of the playwright who is also a poet.

I do not yet know of what Mr Craig is capable, how far he can carry his happy natural gifts towards mastery. But he has done so much already that I want to see him doing more; I want to see him accepting all the difficulties of his new art frankly, and grappling with them. For the staging of Maeterlinck, especially for such a play as *La Mort de Tintagiles,* his art, just as it is, would suffice. Here are plays which exist anywhere in space, which evade reality, which do all they can to become disembodied in the very moment in which they become visible. They have atmosphere without locality, and that is what Mr Craig can give us so easily. But I would like to see him stage an opera of Wagner, *Tristan,* or the *Meistersinger* even. Wagner has perfected at Bayreuth his own conception of what scenery should be; he has done better than any one else what most other stage-craftsmen have been trying to do. He allows more than they do to convention, but even his convention aims at convincing the eye; the dragon of the *Ring* is as real a beast as Wagner could invent in his competition with nature's invention of the snake and the crocodile. But there are those who prefer Wagner's music in the concert-room to Wagner's music even at Bayreuth. Unless the whole aim and theory of Wagner was wrong, this preference is wrong. I should like, at least as an experiment, to see what Mr Craig would make of one of the operas. I am not sure that he would not reconcile those who prefer Wagner in the concert-room to this new kind of performance on the stage. He would give us the mind's attractive symbols of all these crude German pictures; he would strike away the footlights from before these vast German singers, and bring a ghostly light to creep down about their hoods and untightened drapings; he would bring, I think, the atmosphere of the music for the first time upon the stage.

Then I would like to see Mr Craig go further still; I would like to see him deal with a purely modern play, a play which takes place indoors, in the house of middle-class people. He should mount the typical modern play, Ibsen's *Ghosts*. Think of that room 'in Mrs Alving's country-house, beside one of the large fjords in Western Norway'. Do you remember the stage directions? In the first act the glimpse, through the glass windows of the conservatory, of 'a gloomy fjord landscape, veiled by steady rain'; in the second 'the mist still lies heavy over the landscape'; in the third the lamp burning on the table, the darkness outside, the 'faint glow from the conflagration'. And always 'the room as before'. What might not Mr Craig do with that room! What, precisely, I do not know; but I am sure that his method is capable of an extension which will take in that room, and, if it can take in that room, it can take in all of modern life which is of importance to the playwright.

2

Most people begin with theory, and go on, if they go on, to carry their theory into practice. Mr Gordon Craig has done a better thing, and, having begun by creating a new art of

the stage on the actual boards of the theatre, has followed
up his practical demonstration by a book of theory, in which
he explains what he has done, telling us also what he hopes
to do. *The Art of the Theatre* is a little book, hardly more than
a pamphlet, but every page is full of original thought. Until
I read it, I was not sure how much in Mr Craig's work was
intention and how much happy accident. Whether or not
we agree with every part of his theory, he has left no part un-
thought out. His theory, then, in brief, is this: he defines the
theatre as 'a place in which the entire beauty of life can be
unfolded, and not only the external beauty of the world, but
the inner beauty and meaning of life'. He would make the
theatre a temple in which a continual ceremony unfolds and
proclaims the beauty of life, and, like the churches of other
religions, it is to be, not for the few, but for the people. The
art of the theatre is to be 'neither acting nor the play, it is
not scene nor dance, but it consists of all the elements of
which these things are composed: action, which is the very
spirit of acting; words, which are the body of the play; line
and colour, which are the very heart of the scene; rhythm,
which is the very essence of dance'. The art of the theatre is
addressed in the first place to the eyes, and the first dramatist spoke through 'poetic action, which is dance, or prose
action, which is gesture'. In the modern theatre a play is no
longer 'a balance of actions, words, dance and scene, but it
is either all words or all scene'. The business of the stage
director, who is to be the artist of the theatre, is to bring back
the theatre to its true purpose. He begins by taking the
dramatist's play, and sets himself to interpret it visibly on
the boards. He reads it and gets his general impression;

he first of all chooses certain colours, which seem to him to be in
harmony with the spirit of the play, rejecting other colours as out
of tune. He then weaves into a pattern certain objects – an arch, a
fountain, a balcony, a bed – using the chosen object as the centre
of his design. Then he adds to this all the objects which are mentioned in the play, and which are necessary to be seen. To these he
adds, one by one, each character which appears in the play, and
gradually each movement of each character, and each costume. . . .

While this pattern for the eye is being devised, the designer is being guided as much by the sound of the verse or prose as by the sense or spirit.

At the first rehearsal the actors are all in their stage dresses, and have all learned their words. The picture is there; the stage director then lights his picture. He then sets it in motion, teaching each actor to 'move across our sight in a certain way, passing to a certain point, in a certain light, his head at a certain angle, his eyes, his feet, his whole body in tune with the play'. The play is then ready to begin, we may suppose? By no means. 'There will not be any play,' says the stage director to the sheep-like playgoer who has been meekly drifting with the current of dialogue, 'there will not be any play in the sense in which you use the word. When,' he is told, 'the theatre has become a masterpiece of mechanism, when it has invented a technique, it will without any effort develop a *creative art* of its own.' And that art is to be created out of three things, the three bare necessities of the stage: action, scene and voice. By action is meant 'both gestures and dancing, the prose and poetry of action'; by scene, 'all which comes before the eye, such as the lighting, costume, as well as the scenery'; by voice,

the spoken word or the word which is sung, in contradiction to the word which is read; for the word written to be spoken and the word written to be read are two entirely different things.

Up to this last surprising point, which, however, has been stealthily led up to by a very persuasive semblance of logic, how admirable is every definition and every suggestion! Everything that is said is as self-evidently true as it is commonly and consistently neglected. Who will deny that the theatre is a visible creation of life, and that life is, first of all, action; to the spectator, in the stalls or in the street, a thing first of all seen, and afterwards, to the measure of one's care or capability, heard and understood? That life should be created over again in the theatre, not in a crude material copy, but in the spirit of all art, 'by means of things that do not possess life until the artist has touched them': this also will hardly be denied. This visible creation of life is (until the words come into it) like a picture, and it is made in the spirit of the painter, who fails equally if in his picture he departs from life, or if he but imitates without interpreting it. But is it not, after all, through its power of adding the life of speech to the life of motion that the theatre attains its full perfection? Can that perfection be attained by limiting its scope to what must remain its only materials to work with: action, scene and voice?

The question is this: whether the theatre is the invention of the dramatist, and of use only in so far as it interprets his creative work; or whether the dramatist is the invention of the theatre, which has made him for its own ends, and will be able, when it has wholly achieved its mechanism, to dispense with him altogether, except perhaps as a kind of prompter. And the crux of the question is this: that to the supreme critic of literature, to Charles Lamb, a play of Shakespeare, *Lear* or *Hamlet*, seems too great for the stage, so that when acted it loses the rarest part of its magic; while to the ideal stage director, to Mr Gordon Craig, *Hamlet* should not be acted because it is not so calculated for the theatre that it depends for its ultimate achievement on gesture, scene, costume, and all that the theatre has to offer; not, that is, that it is greater or less in its art, but that it is different. If we are content to believe both, each from his own point of view, is it not Craig who will seem the more logical? for why, it will be asked, should the greatest dramatist of the world have produced his greatest work under an illusion, that it is for acting? Why should all the vital drama of the world, the only drama that is vital as literature, have been thus produced? If all this has indeed been produced under an illusion, and in the face of nature, how invaluable must such an illusion be, and how careful should we be to refrain from destroying any of its power over the mind!

An illusion is one thing, a compromise is another, and every art is made up in part of more and more ingenious compromises. The sculptor, who works in the round, and in visible competition with the forms of life, has to allow for the tricks of the eye. He tricks the eye that he may suggest, beyond the literal contour, the movement of muscle and the actual passage of blood under the skin, the momentary creasing of flesh; and he balances his hollows and bosses that he may suggest the play of air about living flesh: all his compromises are with fact, to attain life. May not the art of the dramatist be in like manner a compromise with the logic of his mechanism, a deliberate and praiseworthy twisting of ends into means? The end of technique is not in itself, but in its service to the artist; and the technique, which Mr Craig would end with, might, if it were carried out, be utilized by the dramatist to his own incalculable advantage.

Luigi Pirandello

LUIGI PIRANDELLO, 1867–1936, is the outstanding playwright of modern Italy, and deeply influenced the theatre of the rest of the world, especially through his *Six Characters in Search of an Author*, of which Bernard Shaw wrote: 'I have never come across a play *so original*.' Although he was also interested in theory, his essays seldom deal with the theory of drama as such. Even the much reprinted (and therefore not here reprinted) preface to *Six Characters* continues to tease us. However, for those who can read between the lines, some of Pirandello's pieces do provide glimpses of an Idea of drama and theatre. Two such pieces are included here. In one, dating from 1899, the young Pirandello (not yet a dramatist) gives one of the classic modern definitions of dramatic dialogue – *azione parlata*. In the other he begins to define the modern actress in a rather personal bit of polemic of which the main point is that Duse should have acted in Pirandello's plays, not D'Annunzio's. (The first has been especially translated for this volume by Fabrizio Melano. The second, not found in Pirandello's collected works in Italian, not known to his Estate in Rome, has been printed several times in English; the present text is that of *Century Magazine*, June 1924. An abridged version of the Italian original is to be found in *Eleanora Duse*, edited by Leonardo Vergani, Milan, 1958.)

Spoken Action

LUIGI PIRANDELLO*

Translated by Fabrizio Melano

I THINK this is a good time to bring the apt definition of dramatic dialogue as spoken action (though it doesn't belong to me) to the attention of my readers. Most dramatic works these days are essentially narrative, drawing upon the subject matter of novels or short stories. This can only be a mistake: first of all, because a narrative isn't, on the whole, easily reduced and adapted to stage proportions; secondly, because those proportions are further narrowed and impoverished by the excessive and (according to me) misapplied rigidity of modern technique. Shakespeare, it is true, drew the plots of some of his plays from Italian *novelle*, but what playwright has more consistently translated plot into action, without sacrificing anything to those foolish technical requirements that can only control a work's surface?

All descriptive and narrative props should be banished from the stage. Do you remember Heine's tale of Geoffroy Rudèl and Melisande? 'Every night in the castle of Blay one can hear strange noises, quivering, creaking, rustling: suddenly the figures in the tapestries begin to move. The ghostly troubadour and his lady flex their sleeping muscles, leap from the wall, and walk through the castle.' Well, a dramatic poet should perform the miracle provoked by the moonlight in Heine's old abandoned castle. Hadn't the great Greek tragedians, Aeschylus above all, performed it by breathing a powerful lyric spirit into the gigantic figures of Homer's epic tapestry? And the figures had moved, speaking. Characters should detach themselves, alive and independent, from the written pages of a play as the Lord of Blay and the Countess of Tripoli leap from their ancient tapestry.*

Now this artistic miracle can only occur if the playwright finds words that are spoken action, living words that move, immediate expressions inseparable from action, unique phrases that cannot be changed to any other and belong to a definite character in a definite situation: in short, words, expressions, phrases impossible to invent but born when the author has identified himself with his creature to the point of seeing it only as it sees itself.

In discussing dramatic dialogue, I'm not out to criticize the surface formulas of our writers – these are faulty because of a basic defect in their whole approach. Today's playwright, if he sees anything at all, sees a certain fact or situation; he has or thinks he has an original observation on some feeling or event, and believes that a play can be drawn from it. For him a play is built like a logical chain of reasoning, to which a few skilfully selected frills can be applied. Once the situation is established, he turns to the characters and looks for those most suited to illustrate it. Will three or five or ten be needed? Which stock types can we draw upon this time? How will the necessary dialogue be divided between them? What actors are available? Can the parts be tailored to their specific gifts?

* Reference is to a ballad in Heine's *Romanzero* (1851), entitled 'Geoffroy Rudèl und Melisande von Tripoli'. No Lord of Blay is mentioned in it, though the title is presumably that of the Countess's husband. The figures that Heine has leap from the tapestry are the Countess and her lover, Geoffroy Rudèl. The two stanzas quoted by Pirandello in Italian read in the original:

> *In dem Schlosse Blay allnächtlich*
> *Gibt's ein Rauschen, Knistern, Beben,*
> *Die Figuren der Tapete*
> *Fangen plötzlich an zu leben.*

> *Troubadour und Dame schütteln*
> *Die verschlafnen Schattenglieder,*
> *Treten aus der Wand und wandeln*
> *Durch die Säle auf und nieder.*

E.B.

These are the playwright's questions. But he doesn't begin to think that he should do just the opposite, that art is life, not a series of ideas. Art dies when it is based on an abstract idea or fact, when an author rationally and laboriously selects the images that will serve as symbols of some more or less philosophical conclusion. A play doesn't create people, people create a play. So first of all one must have people – free, living, active people. With them and through them the idea of the play will be born, its shape and destiny enclosed in this first seed; in every seed there already quivers a living being, the oak and all its branches already exist in an acorn.

When we speak of dramatic style, we usually mean a style that is rapid, vivacious, incisive, and passionate; but, especially in relation to the art of the theatre, we should greatly enlarge the meaning of the word style, or perhaps think of it in an altogether different manner. Why? Because the characteristic style, the personality of a dramatic author, shouldn't appear in the dialogue (the language of the characters) but in the spirit of the fable, its architecture, and the methods he has used for its development. If he really has created characters and placed men, not mannequins, on the stage, each one of them will have a specific way of expressing himself. Then the play, when read, will seem to have been written by more than one author, its dialogue made up in the heat of action by the individual characters, not by their creator.

This is what Gabriele d'Annunzio's plays lack up to now. They seem to be devised by their author rather than delivered by the individual characters: written plays, not living ones. The author (I don't know if my friends on the *Marzocco** agree with me here) evidently has not been able to forget about this style, his way of expressing himself; he has not yet managed to give each character an individual personality independent of his own.

Don't misunderstand me, though – I don't in the least agree with that small group of people we call theatre

* The name of the magazine in which this article first appeared. E.B.

professionals, who of course greeted d'Annunzio's plays with respectful indulgence, as the whims of a writer highly admired in other fields but here out of place through 'lack of experience in the tricks of the trade'. Their verdict was 'plays for reading, scarcely for acting' – not so much on account of d'Annunzio's theatrical devices, but because of his literary style.

These professionals consider the theatre a trade, not an art; for them plays do not belong to literature. The basic fabric they use to patch together their dialogue is the slovenly conversational style of French boulevard theatre; for paste glitter they sew on jokes overheard at parties or on the street, while some law-court rhetoric provides a bit of crumpled lace. In their plays too, all the characters speak in the same wretched way, without any individual style. For if d'Annunzio writes beautifully but not well, their writing is ugly, and very bad.

The situation won't change until we really understand that every action (and every idea it contains) needs a free human personality if it is to appear alive and breathing before us. It needs something that will function as its motor pathos, to use Hegel's phrase* – characters, in other words. Now the less each character is enslaved by the author's intention and style, by the demands of an imaginary plot, the less he is the passive instrument of an action, the more individual can he be, freely displaying in every action his full, specific personality. And since characters with all their complexity must, after all, be connected to a plot, it is important that they possess essential features which will always stand out, and which drive them to specific actions.

Our whole personality is always involved in each of our

* The phrase Pirandello has in mind is perhaps *bewegendes Pathos*, which is found in the section on Character in Part One, Chapter Three, of Hegel's *Aesthetik* (Philosophy of Fine Art). That section, fairly literally translated, starts out: 'Our point of departure was the general, substantive powers of action. To become actual, to find a realization, these powers require human individuality, of which they are the motor pathos . . .'

E.B.

actions. The part one can see is only the reaction to an event which is, or appears to be, momentary, but it has reference to the totality of our being; it's like one facet of a polyhedron reacting to one facet of another, without excluding all the other facets turned in other directions. The greatest difficulty an author has to overcome is fusing the subjective individuality of a character with his function in the plot or finding the word which expresses the whole of a character's being while answering the needs of an immediate stage situation.

But how many authors *can* overcome it today?

Eleanora Duse

LUIGI PIRANDELLO

I

FROM the very beginning of her long career Eleanora Duse had one controlling thought – the ambition to disappear, to merge her self, as a real person, in the character she brought to life on the stage.

Only by a hasty judgement could such an attitude be mistaken for an abdication of personality on an artist's part. As understood by Duse, it is her greatest title to glory, since this attitude implies obedience to the first duty of the actor – that supreme renunciation of self, which carries as its reward the realization not of one life only, but of as many lives as the actor succeeds in creating. And we shall see, too, that this attitude implies not, as some people conclude, an almost mechanical passiveness on the part of the actor, who must think of himself simply as an instrument for communicating an author's thought, but a spiritual creative activity of the rarest kind.

I remember that some years ago, an Italian newspaper conducted a referendum on this point among authors, actors, and dramatic critics of European distinction. The question proposed was whether or not actors have the right to judge the works which are given them for production; whether, in other words, they should or should not be regarded as more or less adequate vehicles of communication between writer and audience, which latter remains the only competent and legitimate judge. As I read the many answers to the question proposed, it seemed to me that people fail generally in appreciating the importance of one consideration which is really much more fundamental and comprehensive. It is commonly observed that, on the one hand, an author is never a good appraiser of his own work, and, on the other, that an actor is unable to recognize the artistic merits of the drama he acts; for, in a play, an actor looks only for a *good part*: if he finds it, the play is good; if he fails, it is bad.

The fact is that 'feeling', as opposed to 'thinking', plays a large part in the criticism which a writer makes of his own work. To be sure, a writer studies his creation as it is built up under his hand; but he cannot study it coldly, as an impartial critic would do, analysing it point by point. Rather he views it all at once and as a whole through the total impression which he receives of it. On its author, that is, a work of art produces an impression quite analogous to the one it arouses in reader or spectator: it is *experienced* rather than *judged*.

It is the same way with the actor, and for this reason the actor can never be considered as a mechanical or passive instrument of communication. Indeed, if an actor examined the work he is to create coolly and coldly, studying it, analysing it after the manner of a critic, and if he then tried to move on from this detached and dispassionate analysis to the interpretation of his own role, he would never succeed in giving life to an impersonation; any more than a writer could ever produce a piece of living literature if he did not start from a first feeling or inspiration, a first vision of his work as a whole, but tried to construct his book part by part, detail by detail, ultimately assembling all the separate elements in a work of deliberate composition built up as a mathematical proposition or as a theorem in logic.

The actor, in a word, *lives*. He does not *judge*. When a writer looks at a situation in life, or at an episode in history which for other people may be meaningless or commonplace, he must feel suddenly, by a spontaneous sympathy or emotion, that here is a subject which he must treat. In the same way, by a similar sympathy and emotion, the actor must recognize the part that is suitable for him. He must, that is, have an instantaneous experience within himself of the character he is to impersonate.

However, the actor is usually a professional artist living

in the theatre and on the theatre, in contact, therefore, with what is most conventional and fictitious about the drama. That is why he is very likely to see in a work of art those qualities which are most specifically theatrical; just as the illustrator in looking over a book for which he is to make the pictures will be most impressed by the parts in it which best lend themselves to illustration. I mean to say that the professional actor is inclined to overlook the deeper meaning of a play and view it as so much stage material. He will tend to subordinate the higher truth of the artistic expression before him to the fictitious reality of its stage effects.

Now, in this respect Eleanora Duse is the exact opposite of the professional actor; because, if she exaggerates in any sense, it is in her peculiar determination to see these higher meanings in a play far beyond any *experience* she can possibly have of the parts she has created or is to create – an exaggeration on her part which may be of an artistic, ethical, sentimental or 'ideal' character. The influence this tendency has had on her career is an interesting one. It does not in any way diminish, as I feel, her prodigious power as an actress on the stage; but it does do her considerable harm otherwise, since it prevents her at times from surrendering herself wholly to the *experience* of this or that character, which, were she a less complex soul, she would be able to do admirably. As it is, she is moved to limit her repertory unduly, while at the same time she is impelled, by very praiseworthy consideration, doubtless, to favour works which have an intellectual and moral rather than an artistic significance.

The point is this: Eleanora Duse is not, and never could be, a mere actress. Gradually improving and elevating her innate artistic taste, continuously developing and ripening her mind by faithful study and by a deep meditation on life which has been prompted by a variety of fortunes good and bad, Eleanora Duse has eventually become a real personality on the wider stage of our world at large. Now, a mere actress can impersonate almost any character that is proposed to her, but a personality can live only itself, and it rebels when any one attempts to impose upon it roles not in

harmony with its own clearly asserted traits. Eleanora Duse
has built up a life of her own; as I like to put it, she has
selected a 'form of being' which naturally excludes all those
other possibilities of being which once were in her – possibilities numerous indeed, because few creatures surely have
ever lived to boast vital resources as rich and varied as those
of Eleanora Duse. But venerable, noble, and worthy as any
'form' may be, and as this particular 'form' of Eleanora
Duse certainly is, it nevertheless represents an unshakable
will on her part to be just what she is, and nothing else; to
be what she is, and to exclude every other personality that
is different. This exclusiveness may be a merit, a virtue, an
attainment, in the life of a woman; but it can only be a
drawback in the professional career of an actress, since it
limits – I might say wastes – all those possibilities of being
which constitute the greatest wealth and the greatest glory
of a dramatic artist. In the case of Eleanora Duse we see
that, in proportion as her artistic, moral, and intellectual
demands have become more exacting, rigid, jealous, her
range has grown narrower and narrower. Her career on the
stage has been the sequence of one exclusion after another.

Years ago she began by disdainfully throwing aside the
repertory which had brought her her first successes, placing
her at the forefront among Italian actresses, and giving her
a world fame through her tours abroad.

2

Those who had, as I had, the fortune of seeing her as
Marguerite in *Camille*, in her youthful days indeed, but in
the full maturity of her art, can never forget the romantic
charm, the anguished tenderness, the fervent emotion which
she, and only she, was able to arouse in such great measure
in that role. At that time she seemed born, natively pre-
disposed, to become the most perfect interpreter of that
theatre which flourished in Europe, and more especially in
France, in the last thirty years of the last century, and which
was adorned with such names as Augier, Dumas *fils*, Sardou,

Porto-Riche, Donnay, and, with method and outlook somewhat changed, Henry Becque. It was a romantic, sentimental, psychological theatre – a theatre of manners, with some
tendencies toward social satire. In its various aspects, it had
echoes in Italy as well, and there also acquired distinguished
names: Ferrari, Giacosa, Rovetta, Praga, Bracco, along
with three unquestioned masterpieces to be credited to the
name of Giovanni Verga, *Cavalleria Rusticana*, *The She Wolf*,
Mine and Thine.

To this theatre Eleanora Duse brought all the richness of
her temperament, which, as we looked at it in those days,
seemed to have been made for the express purpose of
revealing not so much the anxieties of mind as the torments
and travails of the passions: an exquisitely feminine sensibility which, at one bound, as it were, and with the most
agile directness, always arrived at a wholly genuine expression of the state of the mind involved, clarifying it with
a light that shone from every line and fibre of the actress's
beautiful person – muscles vibrant, nerves tense, a facial
expression free from every conventional device, and changing only in direct correspondence with real inner trans-
formations of the soul; hands, divine hands, that seemed to
talk, and a voice such as may never again be heard on the
stage – a voice miraculous not so much for its musical
quality, as for its plasticity, its spontaneous sensitiveness to
every subtle shading of thought or sentiment. Duse's acting,
at every moment of a production, was like the surface of a
deep, still water, momentarily responsive to the subtlest
tremors of light and shadow.

And what variety! From one evening to another we used
to see her pass from the heroic passion of Marguerite
Gautier to the treachery of the *Femme de Claude*; from the
sharp, shrewd, rollicking gaiety of Goldoni's Mirandolina to
the desperation of Fedora; from the frivolous dissoluteness of
Frou Frou to the taciturn, rancorous sensuality of *The She
Wolf*, or to the exasperated humility of Santuzza; from
the spiteful, challenging obstinacy of Francillon to the light,
sarcastic capriciousness of Cyprienne in *Divorçons*.

For, at that time, Eleanora Duse was just an actress, a marvellous actress, and, to conclude from the manner in which she could give life to the separate and distinct personages of her first repertory, we have no right to doubt that she felt these women, each and one by one, alive in her, alive with her own life, with the vibration of all her own sensations, feelings and impulses.

How was it, then, that at a certain moment she suddenly seemed to feel them no longer and actually, in some cases to have a haughty disdain for them, almost a physical revulsion at having incorporated them in her own being, endowing them with theatrical life from the substance of her own soul and in the form of her own body? Certainly, to have created them with such power, she must have relived them with that experience which, as I said a moment ago, is the only legitimate judgement that an actress may pass upon one of her creations.

3

This had happened. The aesthetic criticism which Eleanora Duse had been forming on all that theatre, after her wonderful reliving of the many characters it had offered her, had so seriously disconcerted her in her professional outlook that she simply was unable to go on working with those plays. This judgement corresponded to a change, a development, that had taken place in her own personality; and Duse seemed to feel that it was somehow incompatible with her sincerity as an artist to lend this changed personality of hers to the characters of a theatre which she had come for the most part to despise. Crises of passion, tricks and artifices of female wile, needs of the flesh, petty cares and humdrum trials of daily life – in a word, the things which formed the principal content of the European theatre between 1870 and 1900, were no longer enough for Eleanora Duse. Her spirit was athirst for something else, for something less commonplace, something less matter-of-fact, something more heroic – a nobler expression of life, in short.

In Italy, meantime, people were beginning to talk of Henrik Ibsen, who was arousing great interest in most of the nations of Europe, and even in France, where importations from abroad are not readily welcome. Ibsen's theatre met both warm support and bitter hostility in the Italian public and among Italian men of letters. Luigi Capuana, the Sicilian novelist and dramatist, who had for many years been living in Rome, made a first translation (not from the Norwegian, but from the French) of *The Doll's House*. Eleanora Duse was much impressed, but her first approaches to Ibsen were timid ones. The perfect and complete understanding on her part of all the heroic spirituality contained in Ibsen's theatre – qualities which would fully have satisfied this thirst for the ideal in Eleanora Duse, at that time in the full possession of her powers – was made impossible by the distracting influence she now began to feel through contact with the spectacular and refined, but only fictitiously heroic, art of Gabriele D'Annunzio. To my way of thinking – an opinion that I have reason to believe is shared by many people in Italy – the atmosphere of D'Annunzio's theatre did harm rather than good to Eleanora Duse, and great harm, indeed. Perhaps, from the aesthetic demands of her inner life this experience was necessary to her; but it wrought a violent distortion on her art, which had once been so intimate and so profound, throwing her into false attitudes which only time, and too tardily, has been able to correct.

To make clear just what I mean, I need only put in contrast the most evident characteristics of D'Annunzio's theatre, and the most evident characteristics of the acting of Eleanora Duse as that acting used to be, and as it has again become in these later years, though now on a somewhat loftier plane.

D'Annunzio's art is wholly external. It relies on a sumptuous display of forms, on a marvellous opulence of vocabulary. It is a truly miraculous art, but it remains almost wholly superficial, since in it everything that is expressed has value not so much in itself as for the ingenuity with which it is expressed. It is an art woven entirely of sensations, but of sensations that flourish only when fed on imagery, and this imagery, if it would not cloy, must have an ever more ample development, must become ever more and more musical, ever more and more exciting to the senses. It is a sluggish art, with a very scant interior agitation, and even with a very scant external movement, since every individual state of mind, no matter how subtle, needs to be rendered explicit in all its minute shadings, so that, rather than true movement, we have a series of progressive attitudes, each one made definite and precise in its particular aesthetic value, pictorial, musical, or sculpturesque, as the case may be.

Whereas the art of Eleanora Duse is intrinsically and peculiarly opposite to all this. In her everything is internal, simple, unadorned, almost naked. Her art is a quintessential distillation of pure truth, an art that works from within outward, which shrinks from ingenious artifice, and scorns the applause of wonderment that mere brilliancy seeks. With her to feel a thing is to express it, and not to parade it; to express it in direct and immediate terms, without circumlocutions, without sonorous or sculptured or painted imagery. Imagery, in fact, was a challenge to Duse. She is natively lacking in that roundness of diction which is a prime requisite for the full elaboration of a word picture. And if she finds it by sheer effort, the effort in the end exhausts her. For her art is wholly and always an art of movement. It is a continuous, restless, momentary flow, which has neither time nor power to stop and fix itself in any given attitude, even for the pleasure of showing for a moment the beauty that a pose may have in the truth of its expression. Here is a shy and retiring art, which at a tragic moment in her career she suddenly put at the service of the least shy and the most assertive poet that ever lived. That is why I ventured to use the word 'distortion' for the effects that D'Annunzio had upon the art of Eleanora Duse.

I doubt whether I ever suffered so much inside a theatre as I suffered at the first production that Duse gave at the

'Costanzi' in Rome of D'Annunzio's *Francesca da Rimini*.
The art of the great actress seemed hampered, oppressed;
crushed even, by the gorgeous trappings of D'Annunzio's
heroine; just as the action of the tragedy itself is hampered,
oppressed, crushed by the tremendous panoply of rhetoric
that D'Annunzio's ponderous erudition thrusts upon it.
Poor Francesca! What a futile and vacuous waster of
precious words she seemed to be! To me, and I think to
everybody else, she gave a deep and almost bitter regret for
the Marguerite Gautier whom Duse, only a short time
before, had been endowing with life on our Italian stage.
And I confess that I felt the same sorrow for many other
commonplace and mediocre persons of the old theatre
which Duse had abandoned, when I listened, later on, to her
acting of two other tragedies of D'Annunzio, *La Gioconda*
and *La Città Morta*. No one will suppose that I am saying
this out of any tenderness I feel toward the old theatre. I say
it, rather, in view of an opinion I have always held about
the value that a work of dramatic art may have in itself and
of itself, and the value it may acquire or lose in the scenic
translation made of it by an actor.

As a play passes from the mind of an author through the
mind of an actor, it must inevitably undergo some modification. No matter how hard the actor tries to grasp the
intention of the writer, he will never quite succeed in seeing
a character just as the author saw it, in feeling it just as the
author felt it, in recreating it just as the author willed that
it should be. How many times does the unhappy playwright,
present at a rehearsal of his work, feel like exclaiming to the
actor, 'Oh, no! No! Not that way!' writhing in torment,
disappointment, grief, or even rage, at seeing a character of
his translated into a material reality which must perforce
be something else! But in the presence of such a protest on
the author's part, the actor will be just as much disturbed.
He sees and feels the character in his own way and he has a
right to regard the attempted imposition of the author's will
as an act of gratuitous violence cruelly inflicted on him. For
the actor is not a mere phonograph, grinding out through

a megaphone words that have been written on a sheet of paper. He must see the character in his own way and feel it in his own way. All that the author has expressed must become an organic part of the actor, and produce in the actor's being a new life sufficiently forceful to make the character a real person on the stage. An actor's interpretation must, in other words, spring palpitating and alive from the actor's own conception of his part – a conception so intimately lived by him that it is soul of his soul, body of his body. Now, since the personality the actor now assumes is not an original creation of his own, but one suggested to him by the author, how can there possibly be a perfect correspondence between the character as the author sees it, and the character as the actor sees it? There may be a more or less close approximation, a more or less exact similarity, but nothing more. The actor may repeat the lines precisely as they are written, but the very same words will express sentiments which the actor, and not the author, feels; and these sentiments will find their own peculiar manifestation in the actor's tone of voice, temper of gesture, attitude of body.

It may happen, it not infrequently does happen, that the actor improves rather than not on the drama intrusted to him. But in such cases the drama is a bad one, and all the credit belongs to the actor. He has taken from the author a piece of canvas, as it were, and given it a life which the author failed to confer upon it.

4

It was just this miracle that Duse performed in her work with the old theatre. In her repertory there may be some plays which do have a life of their own, and which will live as literature even if no actor ever again produces them. But the grandeur of Duse, in the eyes of her early audience, was the power she had of breathing the breath of life into many characters that had been barely outlined by their authors through various situations in which they were made to appear. And it was a true life that Duse thus created, holding the stage with its vivid, engrossing reality, laying hold upon every spectator witnessing the play. Duse gave a perfect form, that is, to the crude unmoulded clay her old repertory offered her. She could do this, because in the various people she came to impersonate, however commonplace and insignificant they may have been in themselves, she found a certain potentiality of humanness which she could bring to full expression; and, having done so, she rejoiced in her own creation, leaving to others the task of passing judgement on the plays as a whole.

Why could she not perform the same miracle with the works of Gabriele D'Annunzio? The answer is already implicit in what we said about the conflicting characteristics of the respective arts of D'Annunzio and of herself.

In D'Annunzio's plays Duse met a form that was artistically complete, and had to be respected in every minute particular. And this put a fatal restriction upon her own art, which is so wholly spontaneous and genuine. D'Annunzio gave her a series of beautiful, elegant, literary masks, to which she must not supply a single detail, and to which she had to fit herself much as molten metal might be poured into a mould for a statue, to harden in the attitude of that statue – attitudes, moreover, which in this case were wholly foreign to Duse's native temperament. And, in addition, behind these masks of D'Annunzio there was none of those real fundamental human elements which Duse had met even in the worst plays of her old repertory; no germ of life to bring to fruition, no formless clay to endow with perfection of form.

I should not risk asserting that the physical collapse of Eleanora Duse, and especially her growing weariness with stage life, should be attributed to the futile effort she made to adapt her own art to the art of D'Annunzio. But I am willing to state that the D'Annunzio episode was not without effect upon her career as an actress. There can be no doubt that Duse, at the peak of her development, was distracted by the D'Annunzio theatre from the one real dramatic grandeur that her time might have offered her – the theatre of Ibsen, I mean, which was surely far more harmonious with Duse's artistic temperament and with the need she has always felt of breathing a clear and rarefied atmosphere in the most lofty altitudes of the spirit.

What she was really looking for – the state of exaltation to which she had attained in her own inner life – we have been able to see from her recent return to the stage after a long retirement. She came back to us, it is true, with her old authors – Praga, D'Annunzio, Ibsen – as though to exemplify the three periods of her life. But there was a new author there – Gallarati-Scotti – significant not so much for the intrinsic merits of his *Così Sia*, as for the ethical qualities of that play and the spiritual air it breathes. The repertory exploited in this new appearance of Duse shows quite beyond the intention of the actress, as I believe, the truth of what I have said above. *La Porta Chiusa* of Praga is a mediocre work of the old theatre, but it showed us to what extent Duse was able to vitalize such amount of living material as the play contained within itself. In *La Città Morta* we have again been able to see her struggling with all the resources of her genius, but failing in the end to adapt herself to the poses required by the static exterior art of Gabriele D'Annunzio. Her *Lady of the Sea* brings back to us the sense of all that we lost in not having seen Duse approach Ibsen in full possession of her youth. A grey-haired Ellida could only awaken in us, along with a deep regret, a profound admiration for the success with which Eleanora Duse was able to give this character the incomparable freshness of a spirit that literally basks in sunshine. And if we turn to her *Ghosts*, we have the full sense of what Duse might have been at her best: a more and more lucid, a more and more direct and immediate art, which concentrates more and more intensely the essences of truth, and which has been attained by a long travail of the spirit.

Eleanora Duse is a supreme actress in whose life the real tragedy has been this, that her age did not succeed in supplying her with her author.

Bernard Shaw

BERNARD SHAW, 1856–1950, obviously the most considerable British playwright since Elizabethan times, also poured forth his views on the theatre in reviews of other men's plays and prefaces to his own. Yet, although Shaw made abundantly clear his own conception of theatre as 'a factory of thought, a prompter of conscience, an elucidator of social conduct, an armoury against despair and dullness and a temple of the Ascent of Man', and contrasted it with the feeble Idea of a Commercial Theatre which generally held the stage, he relatively seldom dealt in dramatic theory as such. The prefaces to the plays are seldom *about* the plays. They are usually about what the plays are about. From Shaw's discussions of the art of theatre and drama, one ('A Dramatic Realist to his Critics, 1894') has been chosen for inclusion here because it defines the sense in which Shaw wished to be considered a realist. It needs to be offset by passages in which he denies all interest in creating that stage illusion which in his day, as perhaps in ours, often passed for a valid realism. To save the reader trouble, one such passage can be provided forthwith. It is from *Our Theatres in the Nineties*, Volume One, under the date 13 April 1895:

For him [William Archer] there is illusion in the theatre: for me there is none. I can make imaginary assumptions readily enough; but for me the play is not the thing, but its thought, its purpose, its feeling and its execution. . . . In these criticisms by Mr Archer . . . there is little that is memorable about the execution; and that little has reference solely to its effect on the illusion . . . he still makes the congruity of the artist's performance with the illusion of the story his criterion of excellence in the acting. . . . To him acting, like scene-painting, is merely a means to an end, that end being to enable him to make believe. To me the play is only the means, the end being the expression of feeling by the arts of the actor, the poet, the musician. Anything that makes this expression more vivid, whether it be versification, or an orchestra, or a deliberately artificial delivery of the lines, is so much to the good for me, even though it may destroy all the verisimilitude of the scene.

The second Shaw selection was originally written as an appendix to *The Quintessence of Ibsenism* (1891). It has been selected because in it Shaw explains what the new drama required of the performer. Particularly interesting is the account of the new Ibsenist actress.

(Compare Pirandello on Duse p. 158 above, and Brecht on Weigel p. 105 above.) Both these Shaw pieces, written in the Nineties, were reprinted in *Shaw on Theatre*.*

* Hill and Wang, New York, 1958.

A Dramatic Realist to His Critics

BERNARD SHAW

I THINK very few people know how troublesome dramatic critics are. It is not that they are morally worse than other people; but they know nothing. Or, rather, it is a good deal worse than that: they know everything wrong. Put a thing on the stage for them as it is in real life, and instead of receiving it with the blank wonder of plain ignorance, they reject it with scorn as an imposture, on the ground that the real thing is known to the whole world to be quite different. Offer them Mr Crummles's real pump and tubs, and they will denouce both as spurious on the ground that the tubs have no handles, and the pump no bunghole.

I am, among other things, a dramatist; but I am not an original one, and so have to take all my dramatic material either from real life at first hand, or from authentic documents. The more usual course is to take it out of other dramas, in which case, on tracing it back from one drama to another, you finally come to its origin in the inventive imagination of some original dramatist. Now a fact as invented by a dramatist differs widely from the fact of the same name as it exists or occurs objectively in real life. Not only stage pumps and tubs, but (much more) stage morality and stage human nature differ from the realities of these things. Consequently to a man who derives all his knowledge of life from witnessing plays, nothing appears more unreal than objective life. A dramatic critic is generally such a man; and the more exactly I reproduce objective life for him on the stage, the more certain he is to call my play an extravaganza.

It may be asked here whether it is possible for one who every day contemplates the real world for fourteen of his waking hours, and the stage for only two, to know more of the stage world than the real world. As well might it be argued that a farmer's wife, churning for only two hours a week, and contemplating nature almost constantly, must know more about geology, forestry, and botany than about butter. A man knows what he works at, not what he idly stares at. A dramatic critic works at the stage, writes about the stage, thinks about the stage, and understands nothing of the real life he idly stares at until he has translated it into stage terms. For the rest, seeing men daily building houses, driving engines, marching to the band, making political speeches, and what not, he is stimulated by these spectacles to *imagine* what it is to be a builder, an engine-driver, a soldier, or a statesman. Of course, he imagines a stage builder, engine-driver, soldier, and so on, not a real one. Simple as this is, few dramatic critics are intelligent enough to discover it for themselves. No class is more idiotically confident of the reality of its own unreal knowledge than the literary class in general and dramatic critics in particular.

We have, then, two sorts of life to deal with: one subjective or stagey, the other objective or real. What are the comparative advantages of the two for the purposes of the dramatist? Stage life is artificially simple and well understood by the masses; but it is very stale; its feeling is conventional; it is totally unsuggestive of thought because all its conclusions are foregone; and it is constantly in conflict with the real knowledge which the separate members of the audience derive from their own daily occupations. For instance, a naval or military melodrama only goes down with civilians. Real life, on the other hand, is so ill understood, even by its clearest observers, that no sort of consistency is discoverable in it; there is no 'natural justice' corresponding to that simple and pleasant concept, 'poetic justice'; and, as a whole, it is unthinkable. But, on the other hand, it is credible, stimulating, suggestive, various, free from creeds and systems – in short, it is real.

This rough contrast will suffice to show that the two sorts of life, each presenting dramatic potentialities to the author, will, when reproduced on the stage, affect different men differently. The stage world is for the people who cannot bear to look facts in the face, because they dare not be pessimists, and yet cannot see real life otherwise than as the pessimist sees it. It might be supposed that those who conceive all the operations of our bodies as repulsive, and of our minds as sinful, would take refuge in the sects which abstain from playgoing on principle. But this is by no means what happens. If such a man has an artistic or romantic turn, he takes refuge, not in the conventicle, but in the theatre, where, in the contemplation of the idealized, or stage life, he finds some relief from his haunting conviction of omnipresent foulness and baseness. Confront him with anything like reality, and his chronic pain is aggravated instead of relieved; he raises a terrible outcry against the spectacle of cowardice, selfishness, faithlessness, sensuality – in short, everything that he went to the theatre to escape from. This is not the effect on those pessimists who dare face facts and profess their own faith. They are great admirers of the realist playwright, whom they embarrass greatly by their applause. Their cry is 'Quite right: strip off the whitewash from the sepulchre; expose human nature in all its tragi-comic baseness; tear the mask of respectability from the smug bourgeois, and show the liar, the thief, the coward, the libertine beneath.'

Now to me, as a realist playwright, the applause of the conscious, hardy pessimist is more exasperating than the abuse of the unconscious, fearful one. I am not a pessimist at all. It does not concern me that, according to certain ethical systems, all human beings fall into classes labelled liar, coward, thief, and so on. I am myself, according to these systems, a liar, a coward, a thief, and a sensualist; and it is my deliberate, cheerful, and entirely self-respecting intention to continue to the end of my life deceiving people, avoiding danger, making my bargains with publishers and managers on principles of supply and demand instead of abstract justice, and indulging all my appetites, whenever circumstances commend such actions to my judgement. If any creed or system deduces from this that I am a rascal incapable on occasion of telling the truth, facing a risk, foregoing a commercial advantage, or resisting an intemperate impulse of any sort, then so much the worse for the creed or system, since I have done all these things, and will probably do them again. The saying 'All have sinned,' is, in the sense in which it was written, certainly true of all the people I have ever known. But the sinfulness of my friends is not unmixed with saintliness: some of their actions are sinful, others saintly. And here, again, if the ethical system to which the classifications of saint and sinner belong, involves the conclusion that a line of cleavage drawn between my friends' sinful actions and their saintly ones will coincide exactly with one drawn between their mistakes and their successes (I include the highest and widest sense of the two terms), then so much the worse for the system; for the facts contradict it. Persons obsessed by systems may retort; 'No; so much the worse for your friends' – implying that I must move in a circle of rare blackguards; but I am quite prepared not only to publish a list of friends of mine whose names would put such a retort to open shame, but to take any human being, alive or dead, of whose actions a genuinely miscellaneous unselected dozen can be brought to light, to show that none of the ethical systems habitually applied by dramatic critics (not to mention other people) can verify their inferences. As a realist dramatist, therefore, it is my business to get outside these systems. For instance, in the play of mine which is most in evidence in London just now, the heroine has been classified by critics as a minx, a liar, and a *poseuse*. I have nothing to do with that: the only moral question for me is, does she do good or harm? If you admit that she does good, that she generously saves a man's life and wisely extricates herself from a false position with another man, then you may classify her as you please – brave, generous, and affectionate; or artful, dangerous, faithless – it is all one to me: you can no more prejudice me for or against her by such artificial categorizing than you could have made Molière dislike Monsieur Jourdain by a lecture on the vanity and pretentiousness of that amiable 'bourgeois gentilhomme'. The fact is, though I am willing and anxious to see the human race improved, if possible, still I find that, with reasonably sound specimens, the more intimately I know people the better I like them; and when a man concludes from this that I am a cynic, and that he, who prefers stage monsters – walking catalogues of the systematized virtues – to his own species, is a person of wholesome philanthropic tastes, why, how can I feel towards him except as an Englishwoman feels towards the Arab who, faithful to *his* system, denounces her indecency in appearing in public with her mouth uncovered?

The production of *Arms and the Man* at the Avenue Theatre, about nine weeks ago, brought the misunderstanding between my real world and the stage world of the critics to a climax, because the misunderstanding was itself, in a sense, the subject of the play. I need not describe the action of the piece in any detail: suffice it to say that the scene is laid in Bulgaria in 1885–6, at a moment when the need for repelling the onslaught of the Servians made the Bulgarians for six months a nation of heroes. But as they had only just been redeemed from centuries of miserable bondage to the Turks, and were, therefore, but beginning to work out their own redemption from barbarism – or, if you prefer it, beginning to contract the disease of civilization – they were very ignorant heroes, with boundless courage and patriotic enthusiasm, but with so little military skill that they had to place themselves under the command of Russian officers. And their attempts at Western civilization were much the same as their attempts at war – instructive, romantic, ignorant. They were a nation of plucky beginners in every department. Into their country comes, in the play, a professional officer from the high democratic civilization of Switzerland – a man completely acquainted by long, practical experience with the realities of war. The comedy arises, of course, from the collision of the knowledge of the Swiss with the illusions of the Bulgarians. In this dramatic scheme Bulgaria may be taken as symbolic of the stalls on the first night of a play. The Bulgarians are dramatic critics; the Swiss is the realist playwright invading their realm; and the comedy is the comedy of the collision of the realities represented by the realist playwright with the preconceptions of stageland. Let us follow this comedy a little into particulars.

War, as we all know, appeals very strongly to the romantic imagination. We owe the greatest realistic novel in the world, *Don Quixote*, to the awakening lesson which a romantically imaginative man received from some practical experience of real soldiering. Nobody is now foolish enough to call Cervantes a cynic because he laughed at Amadis de Gaul, or Don Quixote a worthless creature because he charged windmills and flocks of sheep. But I have been plentifully denounced as a cynic, my Swiss soldier as a coward, and my Bulgarian Don Quixote as a humbug, because I have acted on the same impulse and pursued the same method as Cervantes. Not being myself a soldier like Cervantes, I had to take my facts at second hand; but the difficulties were not very great, as such wars as the Franco-Prussian and Russo-Turkish have left a considerable number of experienced soldiers who may occasionally be met and consulted even in England; whilst the publication of such long-delayed works as Marbot's *Memoirs*, and the success with which magazine editors have drawn some of our generals, both here and in America, on the enthralling subject of military courage, has placed a mass of documentary evidence at the disposal of the realist. Even realistic fiction has become valuable in this way: for instance, it is clear that Zola, in his *Débâcle*, has gone into the evidence carefully enough to give high authority to his description of what a battle is really like.

The extent to which the method brought me into conflict with the martial imaginings of the critics is hardly to be conveyed by language. The notion that there could be any limit to a soldier's courage, or any preference on his part for life and a whole skin over a glorious death in the service of his country, was inexpressibly revolting to them. Their view was simple, manly, and straightforward, like most impracticable views. A man is either a coward or he is not. If a brave man, then he is afraid of nothing. If a coward, then he is no true soldier; and to represent him as such is to libel a noble profession.

The tone of men who know what they are talking about is remarkably different. Compare, for instance, this significant little passage from no less an authority than Lord Wolseley, who, far from being a cynic, writes about war with an almost schoolboyish enthusiasm, considering that he has seen so much of it:

> One of the most trying things for the captain or subaltern is to make their men who have found some temporary haven of refuge from the enemy's fire, leave it and spring forward in a body to advance over the open upon a position to be attacked. It is even difficult to make a line of men who have lain down, perhaps to take breath after a long advance at a running pace, rise up again. (*Fortnightly Review*, August 1888.)

This, you will observe, is your British soldier, who is quite as brave as any soldier in the world. It may be objected, however, by believers in the gameness of blue blood, that it is the British officer who wins our battles, on the playing fields of Eton and elsewhere. Let me, therefore, quote another passage from our veteran commander:

> I have seen a whole division literally crazy with terror when suddenly aroused in the dark by some senseless alarm. I have known even officers to tackle and wound their own comrades upon such occasions. Reasoning men are for the time reduced to the condition of unreasoning animals who, stricken with terror, will charge walls or houses, unconscious of what they do. [Here Lord Wolseley describes a scare which took place on a certain occasion.] In that night's panic several lost their lives; and many still bear the marks of wounds then received. (ibid., pp. 284-5.)

Now let us hear General Horace Porter, a veteran of the American War, which had the advantage of being a civil war, the most respectable sort of war, since there is generally a valuable idea of some kind at stake in it. General Porter, a cooler writer than our General, having evidently been trained in the world, and not in the army, delivers himself as follows:

The question most frequently asked of soldiers is 'How does a man feel in battle?' There is a belief, among some who have never indulged in the pastime of setting themselves up as targets to be shot at, that there is a delicious sort of exhilaration experienced in battle, which arouses a romantic enthusiasm; surfeits the mind with delightful sensations; makes one yearn for a lifetime of fighting, and feel that peace is a pusillanimous sort of thing at best. Others suppose, on the contrary, that one's knees rattle like a Spanish ballerina's castanets, and that one's mind dwells on little else than the most approved means of running away.

A happy mean between these two extremes would doubtless define the condition of the average man when he finds that, as a soldier, he is compelled to devote himself to stopping bullets as well as directing them. He stands his ground and faces the dangers into which his profession leads him, under a sense of duty and a regard for his self-respect, but often feels that the sooner the firing ceases, the better it would accord with his notion of the general fitness of things, and that if the enemy is going to fall back, the present moment would be as good a time as any at which to begin such a highly judicious and commendable movement. Braving danger, of course, has its compensations. 'The blood more stirs to rouse a lion than to start a hare.' In the excitement of a charge, or in the enthusiasm of approaching victory, there is a sense of pleasure which no one should attempt to underrate. It is the gratification which is always born of success, and, coming to one at the supreme moment of a favourable crisis in battle, rewards the soldier for many severe trials and perilous tasks. (Article in *The Century*, June 1888, p. 251.)

Probably nothing could convey a more sickening sense of abandoned pusillanimity to the dramatic critic than the ignoble spectacle of a soldier dodging a bullet. Bunn's* sublime conception of Don Caesar de Bazan, with his breast 'expanding to the ball', has fixed for ever the stage ideal of the soldier under fire. General Porter falls far beneath Bunn in this passage:

I can recall only two persons who, throughout a rattling musketry fire, always sat in their saddles without moving a muscle

* Alfred Bunn (1798–1860) was stage manager, translator of Scribe, facile versifier, and opera librettist (*The Bohemian Girl*).

or even winking an eye. One was a bugler in the regular cavalry; and the other was General Grant.

It may be urged against me here that in my play I have represented a soldier as shying like a nervous horse, not at bullets, but at such trifles as a young lady snatching a box of sweets from him and throwing it away. But my soldier explains that he has been three days under fire; and though that would, of course, make no difference to the ideal soldier, it makes a considerable difference to the real one, according to General Porter:

Courage, like everything else, wears out. Troops used to go into action during our late war, displaying a coolness and steadiness the first day that made them seem as if the screeching of shot and shell was the music on which they had been brought up. After fighting a couple of days their nerves gradually lost their tension; their buoyancy of spirits gave way; and dangers they would have laughed at the first day, often sent them panic-stricken to the rear on the third. It was always a curious sight in camp after a three days' fight to watch the effect of the sensitiveness of the nerves: men would start at the slightest sound, and dodge the flight of a bird or a pebble tossed at them. One of the chief amusements on such occasions used to be to throw stones and chips past one another's heads to see the active dodging that would follow.

A simple dramatic paraphrase of that matter-of-fact statement in the first act of *Arms and the Man* has been received as a wild topsy-turvyist invention; and when Captain Bluntschli said to the young lady, 'If I were in camp now they'd play all sorts of tricks on me,' he was supposed to be confessing himself the champion coward of the Servian army. But the truth is that he was rather showing off, in the style characteristic of the old military hand. When an officer gets over the youthful vanity of cutting a figure as a hero, and comes to understand that courage is a quality for use and not for display, and that the soldier who wins with the least risk is the best soldier, his vanity takes another turn; and, if he is a bit of a humorist, he begins to appreciate the comedy latent in the incongruity between himself and the stage soldier which civilians suppose him.

General Porter puts this characteristic of the veteran before us with perfect clearness:

At the beginning of the war officers felt that, as untested men, they ought to do many things for the sake of appearance that were wholly unnecessary. This at times led to a great deal of posing for effect and useless exposure of life. Officers used to accompany assaulting columns over causeways on horseback, and occupy the most exposed positions that could be found. They were not playing the Bravo: they were confirming their own belief in their courage, and acting under the impression that bravery ought not only to be undoubted, but conspicuous. They were simply putting their courage beyond suspicion.

At a later period of the war, *when men began to plume themselves as veterans*, they could afford to be more conservative: they had won their spurs; their reputations were established; they were beyond reproach. Officers then dismounted to lead close assaults, dodged shots to their hearts' content, did not hesitate to avail themselves of the cover of earthworks when it was wise to seek such shelter, and resorted to many acts which conserved human life and in no wise detracted from their efficiency as soldiers. There was no longer anything done for buncombe: they had settled down to practical business. (ibid., p. 249.)

In *Arms and the Man*, this very simple and intelligible picture is dramatized by the contrast between the experienced Swiss officer, with a high record for distinguished services, and the Bulgarian hero who wins the battle by an insanely courageous charge for which the Swiss thinks he ought to be court-martialled. Result: the dramatic critics pronounce the Swiss 'a poltroon'. I again appeal to General Porter for a precedent both for the Swiss's opinion of the heroic Bulgarian, and the possibility of a novice, in 'sheer ignorance of the art of war' (as the Swiss puts it), achieving just such a success as I have attributed to Sergius Saranoff:

Recruits sometimes rush into dangers from which veterans would shrink. When Thomas was holding on to his position at Chickamauga on the afternoon of the second day, and resisting charge after charge of an enemy flushed with success, General Granger came up with a division of troops, many of whom had never before been under fire. As soon as they were deployed in front of the enemy, they set up a yell, sprang over the earthworks, charged into the ranks, and created such consternation that the Confederate veterans were paralyzed by the very audacity of such conduct. Granger said, as he watched their movements, 'Just look at them: they don't know any better; they think that's the way it ought to be done. I'll bet they'll never do it again.'

According to the critics, Granger was a cynic and a worldling, incapable of appreciating true courage.

I shall perhaps here be reminded by some of my critics that the charge in *Arms and the Man* was a cavalry charge; and that I am suppressing the damning sneer at military courage implied in Captain Bluntschli's reply to Raïna Petkoff's demand to have a cavalry charge described to her:

BLUNTSCHLI: You never saw a cavalry charge, did you?

RAÏNA: No: how could I?

BLUNTSCHLI: Of course not. Well, it's a funny sight. It's like slinging a handful of peas against a window pane – first one comes, then two or three close behind them, and then all the rest in a lump.

RAÏNA [*thinking of her lover, who has just covered himself with glory in a cavalry charge*]: Yes; first one, the bravest of the brave!

BLUNTSCHLI: Hm! you should see the poor devil pulling at his horse.

RAÏNA: Why should he pull at his horse?

BLUNTSCHLI: It's running away with him, of course: do you suppose the fellow wants to get there before the others and be killed?

Imagine the feelings of the critics – countrymen of the heroes of Balaclava, and trained in warfare by repeated contemplation of the reproduction of Miss Elizabeth Thompson's pictures in the Regent Street shop windows, not to mention the recitations of Tennyson's *Charge of the Light Brigade*, which they have criticized – on hearing this speech from a mere Swiss! I ask them now to put aside these authorities for a moment and tell me whether they have ever seen a horse bolt in Piccadilly or the Row. If so, I would then ask them to consider whether it is not rather likely that in a battlefield, which is, on the whole, rather a startling place, it is not conceivable and even likely that at least one horse out of a squadron may bolt in a charge. Having gently led them to this point, I further ask them how they think they would feel if they happened to be on the back of that horse, with the danger that has so often ended in death in Rotten Row complicated with the glory of charging a regiment practically single-handed. If we are to believe their criticisms, they would be delighted at the distinction. The Swiss captain in my play takes it for granted that they would pull the horse's head off. Leaving the difference of opinion unsettled, there can be no doubt as to what their duty would be if they were soldiers. A cavalry charge attains its maximum effect only when it strikes the enemy solid. This fact ought to be particularly well known to Balaclava amateurs; for Kinglake, the popular authority on the subject, gives us specimens of the orders that were heard during the frightful advance down 'the valley of death'. The dramatic-critical formula on that occasion would undoubtedly have been, 'Charge, Chester, charge! on, Stanley, on!' Here is the reality:

The crash of dragoons overthrown by round shot, by grape and by rifle-ball, was alternated with dry technical precepts: 'Back, right flank!' 'Keep back, private This,' 'Keep back, private That!' 'Close in to your centre!' 'Do look to your dressing!' 'Right squadron, right squadron, keep back!'

There is cynicism for you! Nothing but 'keep back!' Then consider the conduct of Lord Cardigan, who rode at the head of the Light Brigade. Though he, too, said 'Keep back,' when Captain White tried to force the pace, he charged the centre gun of the battery just like a dramatic critic, and was the first man to sweep through the Russian gunners. In fact, he got clean out at the other side of the battery, happening to hit on a narrow opening by chance. The result was that he found himself presently riding down, quite alone, upon a mass of Russian cavalry. Here was a chance to cut them all down single-handed and plant the

British flag on a mountain of Muscovite corpses. By refusing it, he flinched from the first-nighter's ideal. Realizing the situation when he was twenty yards from the foe, he pulled up and converted that twenty yards into 200 as quickly as was consistent with his dignity as an officer. The stage hero finds in death the supreme consolation of being able to get up and go home when the curtain falls; but the real soldier, even when he leads Balaclava charges under conditions of appalling and prolonged danger, does not commit suicide for nothing. The fact is, Captain Bluntschli's description of the cavalry charge is taken almost verbatim from an account given privately to a friend of mine by an officer who served in the Franco-Prussian war. I am well aware that if I choose to be guided by men grossly ignorant of dramatic criticism, whose sole qualification is that they have seen cavalry charges on stricken fields, I must take the consequences. Happily, as between myself and the public, the consequences have not been unpleasant; and I recommend the experiment to my fellow dramatists with every confidence.

But great as has been the offence taken at my treating a soldier as a man with no stomach for unnecessary danger, I have given still greater by treating him as a man with a stomach for necessary food. Nature provides the defenders of our country with regular and efficient appetites. The taxpayer provides, at considerable cost to himself, rations for the soldier which are insufficient in time of peace and necessarily irregular in time of war. The result is that our young, growing soldiers sometimes go for months without once experiencing the sensation of having had enough to eat, and will often, under stress of famine, condescend to borrow florins and other trifles in silver from the young ladies who walk out with them, in order to eke out 'the living wage'. Let me quote from Cobbett's description of his soldiering days in his *Advice to Young Men*, which nobody who has read the book ever forgets:

I remember, and well I may! that, upon occasion, I, after all absolutely necessary expenses, had, on Friday, made shift to have a halfpenny in reserve, which I had destined for the purchase of a *red herring* in the morning; but, when I pulled off my clothes at night, so hungry then as to be hardly able to endure life, I found that I had *lost my halfpenny*. I buried my head under the miserable sheet and rug and cried like a child.

I am by no means convinced that the hidden tears still shed by young soldiers (who would rather die than confess to them) on similar provocation would not fill a larger cask than those shed over lost comrades or wounds to the national honour of England. In the field the matter is more serious. It is a mistake to suppose that in a battle the waiters come round regularly with soup, fish, an entrée, a snack of game, a cut from the joint, ice pudding, coffee and cigarettes, with drinks at discretion. When battles last for several days, as modern battles often do, the service of food and ammunition may get disorganized or cut off at any point; and the soldier may suffer exceedingly from hunger in consequence. To guard against this the veteran would add a picnic hamper to his equipment if it were portable enough and he could afford it, or if Fortnum and Mason would open a shop on the field. As it is, he falls back on the cheapest, most portable, and most easily purchased sort of stomach-stayer, which, as every cyclist knows, is chocolate. This chocolate, which so shocks Raïna in the play – for she, poor innocent, classes it as 'sweets' – and which seems to so many of my critics to be the climax of my audacious extravagances, is a commonplace of modern warfare. I know of a man who lived on it for two days in the Shipka Pass.

By the way, I have been laughed at in this connexion for making my officer carry an empty pistol, preferring chocolate to cartridges. But I might have gone further and represented him as going without any pistol at all. Lord Wolseley mentions two officers who seldom carried any weapons. One of them had to defend himself by shying stones when the Russians broke into his battery at Sebastopol. The other was Gordon.

The report that my military realism is a huge joke has once or twice led audiences at the Avenue Theatre to laugh at certain grim touches which form no part of the comedy of disillusionment elsewhere so constant between the young lady and the Swiss. Readers of General Marbot's *Memoirs* will remember his description of how, at the battle of Wagram, the standing corn was set on fire by the shells and many of the wounded were roasted alive. 'This often happens,' says Marbot, coolly, 'in battles fought in summer.' The Servo-Bulgarian war was fought in winter; but Marbot will be readily recognized as the source of the incident of Bluntschli's friend Stolz, who is shot in the hip in a wood-yard and burnt in the conflagration of the timber caused by the Servian shells. There is, no doubt, a certain barbarous humour in the situation – enough to explain why the Bulgarian, on hearing Raïna exclaim, 'How horrible!' adds bitterly, 'And how ridiculous!' but I can assure those who are anxious to fully appreciate the fun of the travesty of war discovered in my work by the critics, and whose rule is, 'When in doubt, laugh,' that I should not laugh at that passage myself were I looking at my own play. Marbot's picture of the fire-eaters fire-eaten is one which I recommend to our music-hall tableauists when they are in need of a change. Who that has read that Wagram chapter does not remember Marbot forcing his wretched horse to gallop through the red-hot straw embers on his way to Massena; finding that general with no aide-de-camp left to send on a probably fatal errand except his only son; being sent in the son's place as soon as he had changed his roasted horse for a fresh one; being followed into the danger by the indignant son; and, finally – Nature seldom fails with her touch of farce – discovering that the son could not handle his sabre, and having to defend him against the pursuing cavalry of the enemy, who, as Bluntschli would have prophesied, no sooner found that they had to choose between two men who stood to fight and hundreds who were running away and allowing themselves to be slaughtered like sheep, than they devoted themselves entirely to the sheep, and left Marbot to come out of the battle of Wagram with a whole skin?

I might considerably multiply my citations of documents; but the above will, I hope, suffice to show that what struck my critics as topsy-turvy extravaganza, having no more relation to real soldiering than Mr Gilbert's *Pinafore* has to real sailoring, is the plainest matter-of-fact. There is no burlesque: I have stuck to the routine of war, as described by real warriors, and avoided such farcical incidents as Sir William Gordon defending his battery by throwing stones, or General Porter's story of the two generals who, though brave and capable men, always got sick under fire, to their own great mortification. I claim that the dramatic effect produced by the shock which these realities give to the notions of romantic young ladies and fierce civilians is not burlesque, but legitimate comedy, none the less pungent because, on the first night at least, the romantic young lady was on the stage and the fierce civilians in the stalls. And since my authorities, who record many acts almost too brave to make pleasant reading, are beyond suspicion of that cynical disbelief in courage which has been freely attributed to me, I would ask whether it is not plain that the difference between my authenticated conception of real warfare and the stage conception lies in the fact that in real warfare there is real personal danger, the sense of which is constantly present to the mind of the soldier, whereas in stage warfare there is nothing but glory? Hence Captain Bluntschli, who thinks of a battlefield as a very busy and very dangerous place, is incredible to the critic who thinks of it only as a theatre in which to enjoy the luxurious excitements of patriotism, victory, and bloodshed without risk or retribution.

There are one or two general points in the play on which I may as well say a word whilst I have the opportunity. It is a common practice in England to speak of the courage of the common soldier as 'bulldog pluck'. I grant that it is an insulting practice – who would dream of comparing the spirit in which an ancient Greek went to battle with the ferocity of an animal? – though it is not so intended, as it generally comes from people who are thoughtless enough to suppose that they are paying the army a compliment. A passage in the play which drove home the true significance of the comparison greatly startled these same thoughtless ones. Can we reasonably apply such a word as valour to the quality exhibited in the field by, for instance, the armies of Frederick the Great, consisting of kidnapped men, drilled, caned and flogged to the verge of suicide, and sometimes over it? Flogging, sickeningly common in English barracks all through the most 'glorious' periods of our military history, was not abolished here by any revolt of the English soldier against it: our warriors would be flogging one another today as abjectly as ever but for the interference of humanitarians who hated the whole conception of military glory. We still hear of soldiers severely punished for posting up in the barrack stables a newspaper paragraph on the subject of an army grievance. Such absurd tyranny would, in a dockyard or a factory full of matchgirls, produce a strike; but it cows a whole regiment of soldiers. The fact is, armies as we know them are made possible, not by valour in the rank and file, but by the lack of it; not by physical courage (we test the eyes and lungs of our recruits, never their courage), but by civic impotence and moral cowardice. I am afraid of a soldier, not because he is a brave man, but because he is so utterly unmanned by discipline that he will kill me if he is told, even when he knows that the order is given because I am trying to overthrow the oppression which he fears and hates. I respect a regiment for a mutiny more than for a hundred victories; and I confess to the heartiest contempt for the warlike civilian who pays poor men a pittance to induce them to submit to be used as pawns on a battlefield in time of war, he himself, meanwhile, sitting at home talking impudent nonsense about patriotism, heroism, devotion to duty, the inspiring sound of a British cheer, and so on. 'Bulldog pluck' is much more sensible and candid. And so the idealist in my play continues to admit nightly that his bull terrier, which will fight as fiercely as a soldier, will let himself be thrashed as helplessly by the man in authority over him. One critic seems to think that it requires so much courage to say such things that he describes me as 'protecting' myself by 'ostensibly throwing the burden of my attack upon a couple of small and unimportant nationalities', since 'there would have been a certain danger in bringing my malevolent mockery too near home'. I can assure the gentleman that I meant no mockery at all. The observation is made in the play in a manner dramatically appropriate to the character of an idealist who is made a pessimist by the shattering of his illusions. His conclusion is that 'life is a farce'. My conclusion is that a soldier ought to be made a citizen and treated like any other citizen. And I am not conscious of running any risk in making that proposal, except the risk of being foolishly criticized.

I have been much lectured for my vulgarity in introducing certain references to soap and water in Bulgaria. I did so as the shortest and most effective way of bringing home to the audience the stage of civilization in which the Bulgarians were in 1885, when, having clean air and clean clothes, which made them much cleaner than any frequency of ablution can make us in the dirty air of London, they were adopting the washing habits of big western cities as pure ceremonies of culture and civilization, and not on hygienic grounds. I had not the slightest intention of suggesting that my Bulgarian major, who submits to a good wash for the sake of his social position, or his father, who never had a bath in his life, are uncleanly people, though a cockney, who by simple exposure to the atmosphere becomes more unpresentable in three hours than a Balkan mountaineer in three years, may feel bound to pretend to be shocked at them, and to shrink with disgust from even a single omission of the daily bath which, as he knows very well, the majority of English, Irish and Scotch people do not take, and which the majority of the inhabitants of the world do not even tell lies about.

Major Petkoff is quite right in his intuitive perception that soap, instead of being the radical remedy for dirt, is really one of its worst consequences. And his remark that the cultus of soap comes from the English because their climate makes them exceptionally dirty, is one of the most grimly and literally accurate passages in the play, as we who dwell in smoky towns know to our cost. However, I am sorry that my piece of realism should have been construed as an insult to the Bulgarian nation; and perhaps I should have hesitated to introduce it had I known that a passionate belief in the scrupulous cleanliness of the inhabitants of the Balkan peninsula is a vital part of Liberal views on foreign policy. But what is done is done. I close the incident by quoting from the daily papers of the 5th May last the following item of Parliamentary intelligence, which gives a basis for a rough calculation of the value of English cleanliness as measured by the pecuniary sacrifices we are willing to make for it:

ARMY BEDDING

The SECRETARY for WAR, replying to Mr Hanbury's question as to the provision made in the Army for the washing of soldiers' bedding, stated that soldiers are now allowed to have their sheets washed once a month, and their blankets once a year; and the right hon. gentleman stated that the cost of allowing clean sheets fortnightly instead of monthly would amount to something like £10,000 a year, money which might be spent more advantageously in other directions, he thought. (Hear, hear.)

I am afraid most of my critics will receive the above explanations with an indulgent sense of personal ingratitude on my part. The burden of their mostly very kind notices has been that I am a monstrously clever fellow, who has snatched a brilliant success by amusingly whimsical perversions of patent facts and piquantly cynical ridicule of human nature. I hardly have the heart to turn upon such friendly help with a cold-blooded confession that all my audacious originalities are simple liftings from stores of evidence which is ready to everybody's hand. Even that triumph of eccentric invention which nightly brings down the house, Captain Bluntschli's proposal for the hand of Raïna, is a paraphrase of an actual proposal made by an Austrian hotel proprietor for the hand of a member of my own family. To that gentleman, and to him alone, is due the merit of the irresistible joke of the four thousand table-cloths and the seventy equipages of which twenty-four will hold twelve inside. I have plundered him as I have plundered Lord Wolseley and General Porter and everyone else who had anything that was good to steal. I created nothing; I invented nothing; I imagined nothing; I perverted nothing; I simply discovered drama in real life.

I now plead strongly for a theatre to supply the want of this sort of drama. I declare that I am tired to utter disgust of imaginary life, imaginary law, imaginary ethics, science, peace, war, love, virtue, villainy, and imaginary everything else, both on the stage and off it. I demand respect, interest, affection for human nature as it is and life as we must still live it even when we have bettered it and ourselves to the utmost. If the critics really believe all their futile sermonizing about 'poor humanity' and the 'seamy side of life' and meanness, cowardice, selfishness, and all the other names they give to qualities which are as much and as obviously a necessary part of themselves as their arms and legs, why do they not shoot themselves like men instead of coming whimpering to the dramatist to pretend that they are something else? I, being a man like to themselves, know what they are perfectly well; and as I do not find that I dislike them for what they persist in calling their vanity, and sensuality, and mendacity, and dishonesty, and hypocrisy, and venality, and so forth; as, furthermore, they would not interest me in the least if they were otherwise, I shall continue to put them on the stage as they are to the best of my ability, in the hope that some day it may strike them that if they were to try a little self-respect, and stop calling themselves offensive names, they would discover that the affection of their friends, wives, and sweethearts for them is not a reasoned tribute to their virtues, but a human impulse towards their very selves. When Raïna says in the play, 'Now that you have found me out, I suppose you despise me,' she discovers that that result does not follow in the least, Captain Bluntschli not being quite dramatic critic enough to feel bound to repudiate the woman who has saved his life as 'a false and lying minx', because, at twenty-three, she has some generous illusions which lead her into a good deal of pretty nonsense.

I demand, moreover, that when I deal with facts into which the critic has never inquired, and of which he has had no personal experience, he shall not make his vain imaginations the criterion of my accuracy. I really cannot undertake, every time I write a play, to follow it up by a textbook on mortgages, or soldiering, or whatever else it may be about, for the instruction of gentlemen who will neither accept the result of my study of the subject (lest it should destroy their cherished ideals), nor undertake any study on their own account. When I have written a play the whole novelty of which lies in the fact that it is void of malice to my fellow creatures, and laboriously exact as to all essential facts, I object to be complimented on my 'brilliancy' as a fabricator of cynical extravaganzas. Nor do I consider it decent for critics to call their own ignorance 'the British public', as they almost invariably do.

It must not be supposed that the whole Press has gone wrong over *Arms and the Man* to the same extent and in the same direction. Several of the London correspondents of the provincial papers accustomed to deal with the objective world outside the theatre, came off with greater credit than the hopelessly specialized critics. Some of the latter saved themselves by a strong liking for the play, highly agreeable to me; but most of them hopelessly misunderstood me. I should have lain open to the retort that I had failed to make myself comprehensible had it not been for the masterly critical exploit achieved by Mr A. B. Walkley, whose article in *The Speaker* was a completely successful analysis of my position. Mr Walkley here saved the critics from the reproach of having failed where the actors had succeeded. Nobody who has seen Mr Yorke Stephens's impersonation of the Swiss captain will suspect him for a moment of mistaking his man, as most of the critics did, for 'a poltroon who prefers chocolate to fighting'. It was Mr Walkley who recognized that Bluntschli, 'dogged, hopelessly unromantic, incurably frank, always *terre à terre*, yet a man every inch of him, is one of the most artistic things Mr Yorke Stephens has done'.

Here we have the actor making Bluntschli appear to a fine critic, as he undoubtedly did to the gallery, a brave, sincere, unaffected soldier; and yet some of the other critics, unable to rise to the actor's level, moralized in a positively dastardly way about a 'cowardly and cynical mercenary'. Imagine English dramatic critics, who, like myself, criticize for the paper that pays them best, without regard to its politics, and whose country's regular army is exclusively a paid professional one, waxing virtuous over a 'mercenary' soldier! After that, one hardly noticed their paying tribute to the ideal woman (a sort of female George Washington) by calling Raïna a minx, and feebly remonstrating with Miss Alma Murray for charming them in such a character; whilst as to the heroic Sergius, obsessed with their own ideals, and desperately resolved to live up to them in spite of his real nature, which he is foolish enough to despise, I half expected them to stone him; and I leave Mr Bernard Gould and Mr Walkley to divide the credit, as actor and critic, the one having realized the man, and the other of having analysed him – the nicety of the second operation proving the success of the first.

Here I must break off, lest I should appear to talk too much about my own play. I should have broken off sooner but for the temptation of asserting the right of the authors to decide who is the best critic, since the critics take it upon themselves to decide who is the best writer.

Appendix to *The Quintessence of Ibsenism*

BERNARD SHAW

I HAVE a word or two to add as to the difficulties which Ibsen's philosophy places in the way of those who are called on to impersonate his characters on the stage in England. His idealist figures, at once higher and more mischievous than ordinary Philistines, puzzle by their dual aspect the conventional actor, who persists in assuming that if he is to be selfish on the stage he must be villainous; that if he is to be self-sacrificing and scrupulous he must be a hero; and that if he is to satirize himself unconsciously he must be comic. He is constantly striving to get back to familiar ground by reducing his part to one of the stage types with which he is familiar, and which he has learnt to present by rule of thumb. The more experienced he is, the more certain is he to de-Ibsenize the play into a melodrama or a farcical comedy of the common sort. Give him Helmer to play, and he begins by declaring that the part is a mass of 'inconsistencies,' and ends by suddenly grasping the idea that it is only Joseph Surface over again. Give him Gregers Werle, the devotee of Truth, and he will first play him in the vein of George Washington, and then, when he finds that the audience laughs at him instead of taking him respectfully, rush to the conclusion that Gregers is only his old friend the truthful milkman in *A Phenomenon in a Smock Frock*, and begin to play for the laughs and relish them. That is, if there are only laughs enough to make the part completely comic. Otherwise he will want to omit the passages which provoke them. To be laughed at when playing a serious part is hard upon an actor, and still more upon an actress: it is derision, than which nothing is more terrible to those whose livelihood depends on public approbation, and whose calling produces an abnormal development of self-consciousness. Now Ibsen undoubtedly does freely require from his

197

artists that they shall not only possess great skill and power on every plane of their art, but that they shall also be ready to make themselves acutely ridiculous sometimes at the very climax of their most deeply felt passages. It is not to be wondered at that they prefer to pick and choose among the lines of their parts, retaining the great professional opportunities afforded by the tragic scenes, and leaving out the touches which complete the portrait at the expense of the model's vanity. If an actress of established reputation were asked to play Hedda Gabler, her first impulse would probably be to not only turn Hedda into a Brinvilliers* or a Borgia†, or a 'Forget-me-not,'‡ but to suppress all the meaner callosities and odiousnesses which detract from Hedda's dignity as dignity is estimated on the stage. The result would be about as satisfactory to a skilled critic as that of the retouching which has made shop window photography the most worthless of the arts. The whole point of an Ibsen play lies in the exposure of the very conventions upon which are based those by which the actor is ridden. Charles Surface or Tom Jones may be very effectively played by artists who fully accept the morality professed by Joseph Surface and Blifil. Neither Fielding nor Sheridan forces upon either actor or audience the dilemma that, since Charles and Tom are lovable, there must be something hopelessly inadequate in the commercial and sexual morality which condemns them as a pair of blackguards. The ordinary actor will tell you that the authors 'do not defend their heroes' conduct', not seeing that making them lovable is the most complete defence of their conduct that could possibly be made. How far Fielding and Sheridan saw it – how far Molière or Mozart was convinced that the statue had right on his side when he threw Don Juan into the bottomless pit – how far Milton went

* In *La Marquise de Brinvilliers*, a musical pastiche with libretto by Scribe and Castil-Blaze and music by Auber, Cherubini, and others; first performed in 1831.

† Lucrezia Borgia was one of Adelaide Ristori's more lurid roles.

‡ Geneviève Ward's most popular role, in a play written for her by Merivale and Grove.

in his sympathy with Lucifer: all these are speculative points which no actor has hitherto been called upon to solve. But they are the very subjects of Ibsen's plays: those whose interest and curiosity are not excited by them find him the most puzzling and tedious of dramatists. He has not only made 'lost' women lovable; but he has recognized and avowed that this is a vital justification for them, and has accordingly explicitly argued on their side and awarded them the sympathy which poetic justice grants only to the righteous. He has made the terms 'lost' and 'ruined' in this sense ridiculous by making women apply them to men with the most ludicrous effect. Hence Ibsen cannot be played from the conventional point of view: to make that practicable the plays would have to be rewritten. In the rewriting the fascination of the parts would vanish, and with it their attraction for the performers. *A Doll's House* was adapted in this fashion, though not at the instigation of an actress; but the adaptation fortunately failed. Otherwise we might have to endure in Ibsen's case what we have already endured in that of Shakespeare, many of whose plays were supplanted for centuries by incredibly debased versions, of which Cibber's *Richard III* and Garrick's *Katharine and Petruchio* have lasted to our own time.

Taking Talma's estimate of eighteen years as the apprenticeship of a completely accomplished stage artist, there is little encouragement to offer Ibsen parts to our finished actors and actresses. They do not understand them, and would not play them in their integrity if they could be induced to attempt them. In England only two women in the full maturity of their talent have hitherto meddled with Ibsen. One of these, Miss Geneviève Ward, who 'created' the part of Lona Hessel in the English version of *Pillars of Society*, had the advantage of exceptional enterprise and intelligence, and of a more varied culture and experience of life and art than are common in her profession. The other, Mrs Theodore Wright, the first English Mrs Alving, was hardly known to the dramatic critics, though her personality and her artistic talent as an amateur reciter and actress had been familiar to the members of most of the advanced social and political bodies in London since the days of the International. It was precisely because her record lay outside the beaten track of newspaper criticism that she was qualified to surprise its writers as she did. In every other instance, the women who first ventured upon playing Ibsen heroines were young actresses whose ability had not before been fully tested and whose technical apprenticeships were far from complete. Miss Janet Achurch, though she settled the then disputed question of the feasibility of Ibsen's plays on the English stage by her impersonation of Nora in 1889, which still remains the most complete artistic achievement in the new genre, had not been long enough on the stage to secure a unanimous admission of her genius, though it was of the most irresistible and irrepressible kind. Miss Florence Farr, who may claim the palm for artistic courage and intellectual conviction in selecting for her experiment *Rosmersholm*, incomparably the most difficult and dangerous, as it is also the greatest, of Ibsen's later plays, had almost relinquished her profession from lack of interest in its routine, after spending a few years in acting farcical comedies. Miss Elizabeth Robins and Miss Marion Lea, to whose unaided enterprise we owe our early acquaintance with Hedda Gabler on the stage, were, like Miss Achurch and Miss Farr, juniors in their profession. All four were products of the modern movement for the higher education of women, literate, in touch with advanced thought, and coming by natural predilection on the stage from outside the theatrical class, in contradistinction to the senior generation of inveterately sentimental actresses, schooled in the old fashion if at all, born into their profession, quite out of the political and social movement around them – in short, intellectually naïve to the last degree. The new school says to the old, You cannot play Ibsen because you are ignoramuses. To which the old school retorts, You cannot play anything because you are amateurs. But taking amateur in its sense of unpractised executant, both schools are amateur, as far as Ibsen's plays are concerned. The old technique breaks down in the new theatre; for though in theory it is a technique of general application, making the artist so plastic that he can mould himself to any shape designed by the dramatist, in practice it is but a stock of tones and attitudes out of which, by appropriate selection and combination, a certain limited number of conventional stage figures can be made up. It is no more possible to get an Ibsen character out of it than to contrive a Greek costume out of an English wardrobe; and some of the attempts already made have been so grotesque, that at present, when one of the more specifically Ibsenian parts has to be filled, it is actually safer to entrust it to a novice than to a competent and experienced actor.

A steady improvement may be expected in the performances of Ibsen's plays as the young players whom they interest gain the experience needed to make mature artists of them. They will gain this experience not only in plays by Ibsen himself, but in the works of dramatists who will have been largely influenced by Ibsen. Playwrights who formerly only compounded plays according to the received prescriptions for producing tears or laughter are already taking their profession seriously to the full extent of their capacity, and venturing more and more to substitute the incidents and catastrophes of spiritual history for the swoons, surprises, discoveries, murders, duels, assassinations, and intrigues which are the commonplaces of the theatre at present. Others, who have no such impulse, find themselves forced to raise the quality of their work by the fact that even those who witness Ibsen's plays with undisguised weariness and aversion, find, when they return to their accustomed theatrical fare, that they have suddenly become conscious of absurdities and artificialities in it which never troubled them before. In just the same way the painters of the Naturalist school reformed their opponents much more extensively than the number of their own direct admirers indicates: for example, it is still common to hear the most contemptuous abuse and ridicule of Monet and Whistler from persons who have nevertheless had their former tolerance of the unrealities of the worst type of conventional studio picture wholly destroyed by these painters. Until quite lately, too, musicians were to be heard extolling Donizetti in the same breath with which they vehemently decried Wagner. They would make wry faces at every chord in *Tristan and Isolde*, and never suspected that their old faith was shaken until they went back to *La Favorita*, and found that it had become as obsolete as the rhymed tragedies of Lee and Otway. In the drama then, we may depend on it that though we shall not have another Ibsen, yet nobody will write for the stage after him as most playwrights wrote before him. This will involve a corresponding change in the technical stock-in-trade of the actor, whose ordinary training will then cease to be a positive disadvantage to him when he is entrusted with an Ibsen part.

No one need fear on this account that Ibsen will gradually destroy melodrama. It might as well be assumed that Shakespeare will destroy music-hall entertainments, or the prose romances of William Morris supersede the *Illustrated Police News*. All forms of art rise with the culture and capacity of the human race; but the forms rise together: the higher forms do not return and submerge the lower. The wretch who finds his happiness in setting a leash of greyhounds on a hare or in watching a terrier killing rats in a pit, may evolve into the mere blockhead who would rather go to a 'free-and-easy' and chuckle over a dull, silly, obscene song; but such a step will not raise him to the level of the frequenter of music halls of the better class, where, though the entertainment is administered in small separate doses or 'turns', yet the turns have some artistic pretension. Above him again is the patron of that elementary form of sensational drama in which there is hardly any more connexion between the incidents than the fact that the same people take part in them and call forth some very simple sort of moral judgement by being consistently villainous or virtuous throughout. As such a drama would be almost as enjoyable if the acts were played in the reverse of their appointed order, no inconvenience except that of a back seat is suffered by the playgoer who comes in for half price at nine o'clock. On a higher plane we have dramas with a rational sequence of incidents, the interest of any one of which depends on those which have preceded it; and as we go up from plane to plane we find this sequence becoming more and more organic until at last we come to a class of play in which nobody can understand the last act who has not seen the first also. Accordingly, the institution of half price at nine o'clock does not exist at theatres devoted to plays of this class. The highest type of play is completely homogeneous, often consisting of a single very complex incident; and not even the most exhaustive information as to the story enables a spectator to receive the full force of the impression aimed at in any given passage if he enters the theatre for that passage alone. The success of such plays depends upon the exercise by the audience of powers of memory, imagination, insight, reasoning, and sympathy, which only a small minority of the playgoing public at present possesses. To the rest the higher drama is as disagreeably perplexing as the game of chess is to a man who has barely enough capacity to understand skittles. Consequently, just as we have the chess club and the skittle alley prospering side by side, we shall have the theatre of Shakespeare, Molière, Goethe, and Ibsen prospering alongside that of Henry Arthur Jones and Gilbert; of Sardou, Grundy, and Pinero; of Buchanan and Ohnet, as naturally as these already prosper alongside that of Pettit and Sims, which again does no more harm to the music halls than the music halls do to the waxworks or even the ratpit, although this last is dropping into the limbo of discarded brutalities by the same progressive movement that has led the intellectual playgoer to discard Sardou and take to Ibsen. It has often been said that political parties progress serpent-wise, the tail being today where the head was formerly, yet never overtaking the head. The same figure may be applied to grades of playgoers, with the reminder that this sort of serpent grows at the head and drops off joints of his tail as he glides along. Therefore it is not only inevitable that

new theatres should be built for the new first class of
playgoers, but that the best of the existing theatres should
be gradually converted to their use, even at the cost of
ousting, in spite of much angry protest, the old patrons
who are being left behind by the movement.

The resistance of the old playgoers to the new plays will
be supported by the elder managers, the elder actors, and the
elder critics. One manager pities Ibsen for his ignorance of
effective playwriting, and declares that he can see exactly
what ought to have been done to make a real play of *Hedda
Gabler*. His case is parallel to that of Mr Henry Irving, who
saw exactly what ought to have been done to make a real
play of Goethe's *Faust*, and got Mr Wills to do it. A third
manager, repelled and disgusted by Ibsen, condemns
Hedda as totally deficient in elevating moral sentiment.
One of the plays which he prefers is Sardou's *La Tosca*!
Clearly these three representative gentlemen, all eminent
both as actors and managers, will hold by the conventional
drama until the commercial success of Ibsen forces them to
recognize that in the course of nature they are falling behind
the taste of the day. Mr Thorne, at the Vaudeville Theatre,
was the first leading manager who ventured to put a play of
Ibsen's into his evening bill; and he did not do so until Miss
Elizabeth Robins and Miss Marion Lea had given ten
experimental performances at his theatre at their own
risk. Mr Charrington and Miss Janet Achurch, who, long
before that, staked their capital and reputation on *A Doll's
House*, had to take a theatre and go into management themselves for the purpose. The production of *Rosmersholm* was
not a managerial enterprise in the ordinary sense at all: it
was an experiment made by Miss Farr, who played Rebec-
ca – an experiment, too, which was considerably hampered
by the refusal of the London managers to allow members of
their companies to take part in the performance. In short,
the senior division would have nothing to say for themselves in the matter of the one really progressive theatrical
movement of their time, but for the fact that Mr W. H.
Vernon's effort to obtain a hearing for *Pillars of Society* in

1880 was the occasion of the first appearance of the name of Ibsen on an English playbill.

But it had long been obvious that the want of a playhouse at which the aims of the management should be unconditionally artistic was not likely to be supplied either at our purely commercial theatres or at those governed by actor-managers reigning absolutely over all the other actors, a power which a young man abuses to provide opportunities for himself, and which an older man uses in an old-fashioned way. Mr William Archer, in an article in *The Fortnightly Review*, invited private munificence to endow a National Theatre; and some time later a young Dutchman, Mr J. T. Grein, an enthusiast in theatrical art, came forward with a somewhat similar scheme. Private munificence remained irresponsive – fortunately, one must think, since it was a feature of both plans that the management of the endowed theatre should be handed over to committees of managers and actors of established reputation – in other words, to the very people whose deficiencies have created the whole difficulty. Mr Grein, however, being prepared to take any practicable scheme in hand himself, soon saw the realities of the situation well enough to understand that to wait for the floating of a fashionable Utopian enterprise, with the Prince of Wales as President and a capital of at least £20,000, would be to wait for ever. He accordingly hired a cheap public hall in Tottenham Court Road, and, though his resources fell far short of those with which an ambitious young professional man ventures upon giving a dance, made a bold start by announcing a performance of *Ghosts* to inaugurate 'The Independent Theatre' on the lines of the Théâtre Libre of Paris. The result was that he received sufficient support both in money and gratuitous professional aid to enable him to give the performance at the Royalty Theatre; and throughout the following week he shared with Ibsen the distinction of being abusively discussed to an extent that must have amply convinced him that his efforts had not passed unheeded. Possibly he may have counted on being handled generously for the sake of

his previous services in obtaining some consideration for the
contemporary English drama on the continent, even to the
extent of bringing about the translation and production in
foreign theatres of some of the most popular of our recent
plays; but if he had any such hope it was not fulfilled; for he
received no quarter whatever. And at present it is clear that
unless those who appreciate the service he has rendered to
theatrical art in England support him as energetically as his
opponents attack him, it will be impossible for him to maintain the performances of the Independent Theatre at the
pitch of efficiency and frequency which will be needed if it
is to have any wide effect on the taste and seriousness of the
playgoing public. One of the most formidable and exasperating obstacles in his way is the detestable censorship exercised by the official licenser of plays, a public nuisance of
which it seems impossible to rid ourselves under existing
Parliamentary conditions. The licenser has the London
theatres at his mercy through his power to revoke their
licences; and he is empowered to exact a fee for reading each
play submitted to him, so that his income depends on his
allowing no play to be produced without going through that
ordeal. As these powers are granted to him in order that
he may forbid the performance of plays which would have
an injurious effect on public morals, the unfortunate
gentleman is bound in honour to try to do his best to keep
the stage in the right path – which he of course can set
about in no other way than by making it a reflection of his
individual views, which are necessarily dictated by his
temperament and by the political and pecuniary interests
of his class. This he does not dare to do: self-mistrust and
the fear of public opinion paralyse him whenever either
the strong hand or the open mind claims its golden opportunity; and the net result is that indecency and vulgarity
are rampant on the London stage, from which flows the
dramatic stream that irrigates the whole country; whilst
Shelley's *Cenci* tragedy and Ibsen's *Ghosts* are forbidden, and
have in fact only been performed once 'in private': that is,
before audiences of invited non-paying guests. It is now so

well understood that only plays of the commonest idealist type can be sure of a license in London, that the novel and not the drama is the form adopted as a matter of course by thoughtful masters of fiction. The merits of the case ought to be too obvious to need restating: it is plain that every argument that supports a censorship of the stage supports with tenfold force a censorship of the press, which is admittedly an abomination. What is wanted is the entire abolition of the censorship and the establishment of Free Art in the sense in which we speak of Free Trade. There is not the slightest ground for protecting theatres against the competition of music halls, or for denying to Mr Grein as a theatrical entrepreneur the freedom he would enjoy as a member of a publishing firm. In the absence of a censorship a manager can be prosecuted for an offence against public morals, just as a publisher can. At present, though managers may not touch Shelley or *Ghosts*, they find no difficulty in obtaining official sanction, practically amounting to indemnity, for indecencies from which our uncensored novels are perfectly free. The truth is that the real support of the censorship comes from those Puritans who regard Art as a department of original sin. To them the theatre is an unmixed evil, and every restriction on it a gain to the cause of righteousness. Against them stand those who regard Art in all its forms as a department of religion. The Holy War between the two sides has played a considerable part in the history of England, and is just now being prosecuted with renewed vigour by the Puritans. If their opponents do not display equal energy, it is quite possible that we shall presently have a reformed censorship ten times more odious than the existing one, the very absurdity of which causes it to be exercised with a halfheartedness that prevents the licenser from doing his worst as well as his best. The wise policy for the friends of Art just now is to use the Puritan agitation in order to bring the matter to an issue, and then to make a vigorous effort to secure that the upshot shall be the total abolition of the censorship.

As it is with the actors and managers, so it is with the

critics: the supporters of Ibsen are the younger men. In the main, however, the Press follows the managers instead of leading them. The average newspaper dramatic critic is not a Lessing, a Lamb, or a Lewes: there was a time when he was not necessarily even an accustomed playgoer, but simply a member of the reporting or literary staff told off for theatre duty without any question as to his acquaintance with dramatic literature. At present, though the special nature of his function is so far beginning to be recognized that appointments of the kind usually fall now into the hands of inveterate frequenters of the theatre, yet he is still little more than the man who supplies accounts of what takes place in the playhouses just as his colleague supplies accounts of what takes place at the police court – an important difference, however, being that the editor, who generally cares little about Art and knows less, will himself occasionally criticize, or ask one of his best writers to criticize, a remarkable police case, whereas he never dreams of theatrical art as a subject upon which there could be any editorial policy. Sir Edwin Arnold's editorial attack on Ibsen was due to the accidental circumstance that he, like Richelieu, writes verses between whiles. In fact, the 'dramatic critic' of a newspaper, in ordinary circumstances, is at his best a good descriptive reporter, and at his worst a mere theatrical newsman. As such he is a person of importance among actors and managers, and of no importance whatever elsewhere. Naturally he frequents the circles in which alone he is made much of; and by the time he has seen so many performances that he has formed some critical standards in spite of himself, he has also enrolled among his personal acquaintances every actor and manager of a few years' standing, and become engaged in all the private likes and dislikes, the quarrels and friendships, in a word, in all the partialities which personal relations involve, at which point the value of his verdicts may be imagined. Add to this that if he has the misfortune to be attached to a paper to which theatrical advertisements are an object, or of which the editor and proprietors (or their wives) do not hesitate to incur obligations to managers by asking for complimentary admissions, he may often have to choose between making himself agreeable and forfeiting his post. So that he is not always to be relied on even as a newsman where the plain truth would give offence to any individual.

Behind all the suppressive forces with which the critic has to contend comes the law of libel. Every adverse criticism of a public performer is a libel; and any agreement among the critics to boycott artists who appeal to the law is a conspiracy. Of course the boycott does take place to a certain extent; for if an artist, manager, or agent shows any disposition to retort to what is called a 'slating' by a lawyer's letter, the critic, who cannot for his own sake expose his employers to the expenses of an action or the anxiety attending the threat of one, will be tempted to shun the danger by simply never again referring to the litigiously disposed person. But although this at first sight seems to sufficiently guarantee the freedom of criticism (for most public persons would suffer more from being ignored by the papers than from being attacked in them, however abusively) its operation is really restricted on the one side to the comparatively few and powerful critics who are attached to important papers at a fixed salary, and on the other to those entrepreneurs and artists about whom the public is not imperatively curious. Most critics get paid for their notices at so much per column or per line, so that their incomes depend on the quantity they write. Under these conditions they fine themselves every time they ignore a performance. Again, a dramatist or a manager may attain such a position that his enterprises form an indispensable part of the news of the day. He can then safely intimidate a hostile critic by a threat of legal proceedings, knowing that the paper can afford neither to brave nor ignore him. The late Charles Reade, for example, was a most dangerous man to criticize adversely; but the very writers against whom he took actions found it impossible to boycott him; and what Reade did out of a natural overflow of indignant pugnacity, some of our more powerful artistic entrepreneurs occasionally threaten to do now after a deliberate calculation of the advantages of their position. If legal proceedings are actually taken, and the case is not, as usual, compromised behind the scenes, the uncertainty of the law receives its most extravagant illustration from a couple of lawyers arguing a question of fine art before a jury of men of business. Even if the critic were a capable speaker and pleader, which he is not in the least likely to be, he would be debarred from conducting his own case by the fact that his comparatively wealthy employer and not himself would be the defendant in the case. In short, the law is against straightforward criticism at the very points where it is most needed; and though it is true that an ingenious and witty writer can make any artist or performance acutely ridiculous in the eyes of ingenious and witty people without laying himself open to an action, and indeed with every appearance of good-humoured indulgence, such applications of wit and ingenuity do criticism no good; whilst in any case they offer no remedy to the plain critic writing for plain readers.

All this does not mean that the entire Press is hopelessly corrupt in its criticism of Art. But it certainly does mean that the odds against the independence of the Press critic are so heavy that no man can maintain it completely without a force of character and a personal authority which are rare in any profession, and which in most of them can command higher pecuniary terms and prospects than any which journalism can offer. The final degrees of thoroughness have no market value on the Press; for, other things being equal, a journal with a critic who is good-humoured and compliant will have no fewer readers than one with a critic who is inflexible where the interest of Art and the public are concerned. I do not exaggerate or go beyond the warrant of my own experience when I say that unless a critic is prepared not only to do much more work than the public will pay him for, but to risk his livelihood every time he strikes a serious blow at the powerful interests vested in artistic abuses of all kinds (conditions which in the long run tire out the strongest man), he must submit to compromises which detract very considerably from the trustworthiness of his criticism. Even the critic who is himself in a position to brave these risks must find a sympathetic and courageous editor-proprietor who will stand by him without reference to the commercial advantage – or disadvantage – of his incessant warfare. As all the economic conditions of our society tend to throw our journals more and more into the hands of successful moneymakers, the exceeding scarcity of this lucky combination of resolute, capable, and incorruptible critic, sympathetic editor, and disinterested and courageous proprietor, can hardly be appreciated by those who only know the world of journalism through its black and white veil.

On the whole, though excellent criticisms are written every week by men who, either as writers distinguished in other branches of literature and journalism or as civil servants, are practically independent of this or that particular appointment as dramatic critic (not to mention the few whom strong vocation and force of character have rendered incorruptible) there remains a great mass of newspaper reports of theatrical events which is only called dramatic criticism by courtesy. Among the critics properly so called opinions are divided about Ibsen in the inevitable way into Philistine, idealist, and realist (more or less). Just at present the cross-firing between them is rather confusing. Without being necessarily an Ibsenist, a critic may see at a glance that abuse of the sort quoted* is worthless; and he may for the credit of his cloth attack it on that ground. Thus we have Mr A. B. Walkley, of *The Speaker*, one of the most able and independent of our critics, provoking Mr Clement Scott beyond measure by alluding to the writers who had just been calling the admirers of Ibsen 'muck-ferreting dogs', as 'these gentry', with a good-humoured but very perceptible contempt for their literary attainments. Thereupon Mr Scott publishes a vindication of the literateness of that school, of which Mr Walkley makes unmerciful fun.

* By William Archer in 'Ghosts and Gibberings', *The Pall Mall Gazette*, 8 April 1891.

But Mr Walkley is by no means committed to Ibsenism by his appreciation of Ibsen's status as an artist, much less by his depreciation of the literary status of Ibsen's foes. On the other hand there is Mr Frederick Wedmore, a professed admirer of Balzac, conceiving such a violent antipathy to Ibsen that he almost echoes Sir Edwin Arnold, whose denunciations are at least as applicable to the author of *Vautrin* as to the author of *Ghosts*. Mr George Moore, accustomed to fight on behalf of Zola against the men who are now attacking Ibsen, takes the field promptly against his old enemies in defence, not of Ibsenism, but of Free Art. Even Mr William Archer expressly guards himself against being taken as an Ibsenist doctrinaire. In the face of all this, it is little to the point that some of the critics who have attacked Ibsen have undoubtedly done so because – to put it bluntly – they are too illiterate and incompetent in the sphere of dramatic poetry to conceive or relish anything more substantial than the theatrical fare to which they are accustomed; or that others, intimidated by the outcry raised by Sir Edwin Arnold and the section of the public typified by Pastor Manders (not to mention Mr Pecksniff), against their own conviction join the chorus of disparagement from modesty, caution, compliance – in short, from want of the courage of their profession. There is no reason to suppose that if the whole body of critics had been endowed with a liberal education and an independent income, the number of Ibsenists among them would be much greater than at present, however the tone of their adverse criticism might have been improved. Ibsen, as a pioneer in stage progress no less than in morals, is bound to have the majority of his contemporaries against him, whether as actors, managers or critics.

Finally, it is necessary to say, by way of warning, that many of the minor combatants on both sides have either not studied the plays at all, or else have been so puzzled that they have allowed themselves to be misled by the attacks of the idealists into reading extravagant immoralities between the lines, as, for instance, that Oswald in *Ghosts* is really the son of Pastor Manders, or that Lövborg is the father of Hedda Tesman's child. It has even been asserted that horrible exhibitions of death and disease occur in almost every scene of Ibsen's plays, which, for tragedies, are exceptionally free from visible physical horrors. It is not too much to say that very few of the critics have yet got so far as to be able to narrate accurately the stories of the plays they have witnessed. No wonder, then, that they have not yet made up their minds on the more difficult point of Ibsen's philosophic drift – though I do not myself see how performances of his plays can be quite adequately judged without reference to it. One consequence of this is that those who are interested, fascinated, and refreshed by Ibsen's art misrepresent his meaning benevolently quite as often as those who are perplexed and disgusted misrepresent it maliciously; and it already looks as if Ibsen might attain undisputed supremacy as a modern playwright without necessarily converting a single critic to Ibsenism. Indeed it is not possible that his meaning should be fully recognized, much less assented to, until Society as we now know it loses its self-complacency through the growth of the conviction foretold by Richard Wagner when in *The Artwork of the Future* he declared that:

Man will never be that which he can and should be until, by a conscious following of that inner natural necessity which is the only true necessity, he makes his life a mirror of nature, and frees himself from his thraldom to outer artificial counterfeits. Then will he first become a living man, who now is a mere wheel in the mechanism of this or that Religion, Nationality, or State.

Konstantin Stanislavsky

KONSTANTIN STANISLAVSKY, 1863–1938, it might be said, bestrides the narrow world of the modern theatre like a colossus. He is never out of sight. And yet few are sure what they see. Or perhaps many are sure what they see: but others are sure they don't see straight. He was a teacher, not primarily a writer. With him the style is not the man, and reading him one has quite strongly the sense of not making contact. That is why there is so marked an advantage to learning about him from a sympathetic expositor like David Magarshack (1899–1977). Stanislavsky's own works contain no such summing up as this essay.*

*Originally the Introduction to *Stanislavsky on the Art of the Stage*, London: Faber, 1950, New York: Hill & Wang Dramabook, 1960.

POSTSCRIPT, 1992
In the second half of the 20th Century, a different image of Stanislavsky has been emerging. The reader is referred to *Stanislavsky: a Biography* by Jean Benedetti (Routledge Kegan Paul, London, 1988) and two recent articles in periodicals: 'Stanislavsky's Preface to *An Actor Prepares* . . .', by Burnet M. Hobgood (Theatre Journal, May 1991) and 'The Last Decade: Stanislavsky and Stalinism', by Anatoly Smeliansky (Theater, Spring 1991.)

Stanislavsky

DAVID MAGARSHACK

I

THE theory of acting, as evolved by Stanislavsky in his famous 'system', is not based on reasoning, as many of his critics assert, so much as on experience. It is the result of a lifetime devoted to the art of the stage, of years of experiment as actor and producer, and of a feeling of dissatisfaction with what passes for 'success' both among actors and audiences. While certain general principles of acting had been laid down by a number of famous actors and playwrights, these, Stanislavsky found, had never been reduced to a system, with the result that teachers of acting have nothing on which to base their teaching, since 'inspiration' on which the theoreticians of the stage put so much stress cannot be taught, nor can it be expected to materialize itself just when the actor needs it. Neither can producers be relied on to assist the actor in capturing this elusive 'inspiration'. 'Producers,' Stanislavsky writes, 'explain very cleverly what sort of result they want to get; they are only interested in the final result. They criticize and tell the actor what he should *not* do, but they do not tell him *how* to achieve the required result. The producer,' Stanislavsky adds, 'can do a great deal, but he cannot do everything by any means. For the main thing is in the hands of the actor, who must be helped and instructed first of all.'

Stanislavsky, who was born in Moscow in 1863 (he also died there in 1938), began his career as the still all too common type of producer-autocrat. 'I treated my actors as mannequins,' he declares.

I showed them what I saw in my imagination, and they copied me. Whenever I was successful in getting the right feeling, the play came to life, but where I did not go beyond external invention, it was dead. The merit of my work at that time consisted in my endeavours to be sincere and to search for truth. I hated all false-hood on the stage, especially theatrical falsehood. I began to hate the theatre in the theatre, and I was beginning to look for genuine life in it, not ordinary life, of course, but artistic life. Perhaps at the time I was not able to distinguish between the one and the other. Besides, I understood them only externally. But even external truth helped me to create truthful and interesting mise-en-scenes, which set me on the road to truth; truth gave birth to feeling, and feeling aroused creative intuition.

What led Stanislavsky to abandon the methods of pro-ducer-autocrat and go in search of 'the elementary psycho-physical and psychological laws of acting' was his study of the methods of the great actors, and, above all, those of the famous Italian actor Tommaso Salvini (1828–1916). Those methods were so simple and yet so difficult to copy. They seemed, moreover, to possess certain qualities that were common to all great actors, and indeed, looking back on his own experience as an actor, Stanislavsky found that he too possessed the identical qualities. But the difference between him and Salvini was that while the latter seemed to be able not only to re-create them at will, but also in a way that was unique for every performance of the same play, he himself could not do it. After his first foreign tour in Ger-many with the Moscow Art Theatre in 1906, Stanislavsky went for a holiday in Finland, during which for the first time he tried to analyse his experience as an actor and producer and discover the laws of the technique of acting.

At the time Stanislavsky already enjoyed a world repu-tation. The Moscow Art Theatre, which he had founded with Nemirovich-Danchenko in 1898, was firmly established. He had behind him thirty years of theatrical activity, first among his own amateur group of actors from 1877 to 1887, then as producer of the Society of Art and Literature, founded by him, from 1888 to 1898, and lastly as one who was chiefly responsible for the stage productions of the Moscow Art Theatre. During that time, and especially since the foundation of the Moscow Art Theatre, he had created a gallery of stage characters which put him in the forefront of the greatest actors in Russia.

During those years he had learned a great deal, understood a great deal, and also discovered a great deal by accident. 'I was always looking for something new', Stanislavsky writes in *My Life in Art*, 'both in the inner work of the actor, in the work of the producer, and in the principles of stage production. I rushed about a great deal, often forgetting the important discoveries I had made and mistakenly carried away by things that were of no intrinsic value. I had collected as the result of my artistic career a sackful of material of every possible sort on the technique of the art of the stage. But everything was thrown together indiscriminately, and in such a form it is impossible to make any use of one's artistic treasures. I had to bring everything in order. I had to analyse my accumulated experience. I had, as it were, to lay the materials out on the different shelves of my mind. What was still unhewn had to be made smooth and laid, like foundation stones, at the base of my art; what had become worn, had to be repaired. For without it, any further progress was impossible.'

It was during his Finnish holiday, therefore, that Stanislavsky for the first time undertook to supply a theoretical basis for the art of the stage. Step by step he went over his past, and it became more and more obvious to him that the inner content he had put into his parts when he had first created them and the external forms which these parts had assumed in the course of time, were 'poles apart'. At first the character of every part he created seemed to depend on the exciting inner truth that he had perceived in it, but later on all that remained was its empty shell which had nothing to do with genuine art.

'During my last tour abroad', he writes,

and before it in Moscow, I kept repeating mechanically those well-drilled and firmly established 'tricks' of the part – the mechanical signs of an absence of genuine feeling. In some places I tried to be as nervous and excited as possible, and for that reason performed a series of quick movements; in others I tried to appear naive and technically reproduced childishly innocent eyes; in others still I forced myself to reproduce the gait and the typical gestures of the part – the external result of a feeling that was dead. I copied naïveté, but I was not naive; I walked with quick, short steps, but I had no feeling of an inner hurry which produced such quick steps, and so on. I exaggerated more or less skilfully, I imitated the external manifestations of feelings and actions, but at the same time I did not experience any feelings or any real need for action. As the performances went on, I acquired the mechanical habit of going through the once and for all established gymnastic exercises, which were firmly fixed as my stage habits by my muscular memory, which is so strong with actors.

In reviewing his parts, analysing his memories which contributed to their creation, and comparing them with the artificial methods he now resorted to in his acting, Stanislavsky could not help coming to the conclusion that his bad theatrical habits had crippled his soul, his body and his roles. The next thing he asked himself was how to save his parts from degeneration, from spiritual torpor, and from the despotism of acquired stage habits and external training. An actor, he thought, must have some sort of spiritual preparation before the beginning of a performance. Not only his body, but also his spirit must put on new clothes. Before beginning to act, every actor must know how to enter into that spiritual atmosphere in which alone 'the sacrament of creative art' was possible.

During his Finnish holiday Stanislavsky made a number of great discoveries, which were no less important because they were known before. His first discovery was that an actor's state of mind on the stage was not only unnatural, but also constituted one of the greatest obstacles to real acting. For in such a state of mind, an actor could only mimic and 'act a part', pretend to enter into the feelings of the character in the play, but not live and give himself up entirely to his feelings.

The theatre has invented a whole assortment of signs, expressions of human passions, theatrical poses, voice inflexions, cadences, flourishes, stage tricks, and methods of acting which become mechanical and unconscious, and are always at the service of the actor when he feels himself utterly helpless on the stage and stands there 'with an empty soul'.

The natural state of mind of the actor is, therefore, the state of mind of a man on the stage during which he has to show outwardly what he does not feel inwardly. This spiritual and physical abnormality, Stanislavsky points out, actors experience most of their lives: in the daytime between twelve and half past four at rehearsals, and at night from eight till midnight at the performance. And in an attempt to find some solution of this insoluble problem, actors not only acquire false and artificial methods of acting but also become dependent on them.

Having realized the harmfulness and anomaly of the actor's state of mind, Stanislavsky began to look for a different condition of an actor's mind and body on the stage, a condition that he calls a *creative* state of mind. Geniuses, he noticed, always seemed to possess such a creative state of mind on the stage. Less gifted people had it less often. Nevertheless, all people who are engaged in the pursuit of the art of the stage, from the genius to the man of ordinary talent, seem capable to a greater or lesser degree of achieving in some mysterious, intuitive way this creative state of mind, except that it is not given to them to achieve it as and when they like. They receive it 'as a heavenly gift from Apollo', and, Stanislavsky adds, 'we cannot, it seems, evoke it by our human methods'.

All the same, Stanislavsky could not help asking himself whether there were not some technical ways of achieving the creative state of mind. That did not mean that he wanted to produce inspiration itself in some artificial way, for that he realized was impossible. What he wanted to find out was whether there was not some way of creating the conditions favourable to the emergence of inspiration; an atmosphere in which inspiration was more likely to come to the actor. If it could not be achieved at once, could it not be done in parts, by putting it together, as it were, from different elements, even if each of these elements had to be produced by the actor within himself by a series of systematic exercises. If a genius, Stanislavsky argued, had been granted the ability to achieve the creative state of mind in the fullest possible measure, could not ordinary actors achieve it to some extent after a long and painstaking course of training?

The question Stanislavsky next set himself to answer was therefore what were the constituent elements and the nature of the creative state of mind.

He had noticed that great actors had something in common, something that only they seemed to possess, something that made them akin to each other and that reminded him of all the others. What kind of faculty was that? The question was a highly complex one, but Stanislavsky set himself to answer it by analysing this quality of greatness in the actor step by step. The first thing that struck him about this creative state of the actor was that it was invariably accompanied by a complete freedom of the body and a total relaxation of the muscles. The whole physical apparatus of the actor was, in fact, entirely at his beck and call. Thanks to this discipline, the creative work of the actor was excellently organized, and the actor could by his body freely express what his soul felt. And so excited was Stanislavsky by this discovery that he began to transform the performances in which he appeared into experimental tests.

It was then that, again by accident, Stanislavsky discovered another elementary truth. He realized that he felt so well on the stage because, in addition to the relaxation of his muscles, his public exercises riveted his attention on the sensations of his body and thereby distracted him from what was happening in the auditorium on the other side of that 'terrible black hole of the stage'. He noticed that it was at those moments that his state of mind became particularly pleasant.

Continuing his observation of himself and others, Stanislavsky realized that creative work on the stage was first of all the fullest possible concentration of the whole of the actor's spiritual and physical nature. Such a concentration, he discovered, extended not only to hearing and sight, but to all the other senses of the actor, and in addition, took possession of his body, mind, memory and imagination. The conclusion Stanislavsky arrived at was that the whole spiritual and physical nature of the actor must be centred on what was taking place in the soul of the person he was representing on the stage.

Another interesting observation Stanislavsky made relates to the attention that an audience can be expected to give to the actor's play on the stage when unaided by other actors. 'Experience has taught me', he writes,

that an actor can hold the attention of an audience by himself in a highly dramatic scene for at most *seven minutes* (that is the absolute maximum!). In a quiet scene the maximum is *one minute* (this, too, is a lot!). After that the diversity of the actor's means of expression is not sufficient to hold the attention of the audience, and he is forced to repeat himself with the result that the attention of the audience slackens until the next climax which requires new methods of presentation. But please, note that this is true only in the cases of geniuses!

The third discovery Stanislavsky made concerns the time of the arrival of the actor at the theatre. He happened one day to be at a Moscow theatre where the leading actor made a point of being late for every performance. 'A home-bred genius', Stanislavsky observes,

will always arrive five minutes late and not, like Salvini, three hours before the beginning of the performance. Why? For the simple reason that to be able to prepare something in his mind for three hours, he has to have *something* to prepare. But a home-bred genius has nothing except his talent. He arrives at the theatre with his suit of clothes in his trunk, but without any spiritual luggage. What on earth is he to do in his dressing-room from five to eight? Smoke? Tell funny stories? He could do that much better in a restaurant.

This applies not only to actors who are habitually late for a performance, but also to those who arrive just in time for its beginning. Even actors who come to the theatre in good time do so just because they are afraid to be late. They are in time to prepare their bodies, to make up their faces, Stanislavsky observes, but it never occurs to them that their souls too have to be dressed and made up. They do not care for the inner design of their parts. They hope that their parts will assume the exterior forms of a stage creation during the performance. Once this happens, they fix it in mechanical stage habits, but forgetting all about the spirit of the part, they let it wither away with time. 'An actor who disregards the wise creative feeling and is a slave of senseless stage habits,' Stanislavsky writes, 'is at the mercy of every chance, of the bad taste of the audience, of some clever stage trick, of cheap external success, of his vanity and, indeed, of anything that has nothing whatever to do with art'. No part, in fact, can be really successful unless the actor *believes* in it. The actor must believe in everything that is taking place on the stage and, above all, he must believe in himself. But he can only believe in what is true. He must, therefore, always be aware of truth and know how to find it, and to do that he must develop his artistic sensibility for truth. And Stanislavsky makes it clear that what he means by truth is the truth of the actor's feelings and sensations, the truth of the inner creative impulse which is striving to express itself.

I am not interested in the truth outside me, [he declares]. What is important to me is the truth in me, the truth of my attitude towards one scene or another on the stage, towards the different things on the stage, the scenery, my partners, who are playing the other parts in the play, and their feelings and thoughts.

The real actor, [Stanislavsky goes on], says to himself, I know that scenery, make-up, costumes, and the fact that I have to perform my work in public – is nothing but a barefaced lie. But I don't care, for things by themselves are of no importance to me . . . But – *if* everything round me on the stage were true, I should have acted this or that scene in such and such a way.

It was then that Stanislavsky realized that the work of the actor began from the moment when what he calls the 'magic', creative 'if' appeared in his soul and imagination.

While tangible reality and tangible truth, in which man could not help believing, existed, the creative work of the actor could not be said to have begun. But when the creative 'if', that is, the would-be, imaginary truth made its appearance, the actor discovered that he was able to believe in it as sincerely, if not with even greater enthusiasm, as real truth. 'Just as a little girl believes in the existence of her doll', Stanislavsky writes, 'and in the life in and around her, so the actor, the moment the creative "if" appears, is transported from the plane of real life to the plane of a different kind of life which he himself has created in his imagination. Once he believes in it, he is ready to start his creative work.'

The stage, therefore, was truth; it was what the actor sincerely believed in. In the theatre, Stanislavsky claims, even the most barefaced lie must become truth in order to be art. To make this possible, the actor must possess a highly developed imagination, a child-like naïveté and trustfulness, and an artistic sensitiveness for truth and verisimilitude both in his body and soul. For all that helped him to transform the crude stage lie into the most delicate truth of the imagination. These qualities and abilities of the actor Stanislavsky calls *the feeling for truth*. 'In it', he observes, 'is contained the play of imagination and the formation of creative belief; in it is contained the best possible defence against stage falsehood, as well as the sense of proportion, the guarantee of a child-like naïveté and the sincerity of artistic feeling.'

Stanislavsky soon discovered that the feeling for truth, like concentration and relaxation of muscles, was subject to development and could be acquired by exercises. 'This ability,' he declares, 'must be brought to so high a state of development that nothing should take place or be said or perceived on the stage without having first gone through the filter of the artistic feeling for truth.'

As soon as he made this fourth discovery, Stanislavsky put all his stage exercises for the relaxation of muscles and concentration to the test of the feeling for truth, with the result that it was only then that he succeeded in obtaining a real, natural and not forced relaxation of muscles and concentration on the stage during a performance. Moreover, in making these investigations and accidental discoveries, he found that many more truths that had been known in life had also their application on the stage. All of them, taken together, contributed to the formation of the creative state of mind as distinguished from the theatrical state of mind, which Stanislavsky regards as the real enemy of the art of the stage.

Finally, the last discovery made by Stanislavsky, 'after months of torment and doubt', was that in the art of the stage everything had to become a *habit*, which transformed everything new into something organic, into the actor's second nature. Only after having acquired this habit, could the actor make use of something new on the stage without thinking of its mechanism. This discovery, too, had a direct bearing on the creative state of mind of the actor, which could only be of any use to him when it became his normal, natural, and only means of expression. Should this not happen, the actor, Stanislavsky points out, would merely copy the external forms of any new movement without justifying it from within.

2

Stanislavsky, however, arrived at the essentials of his theory of acting only after a prolonged application of the methods of trial and error. At first he thought that the actor must start from the outer characteristics of his part in order to come to the inner feeling. Such a method, he found, was possible, though it was not by any means the best method of creative achievement in stage art.

It was the way from the conscious to the subconscious that became the pivot of his 'system'. It solved the problem of realism on the stage and supplied a reliable foot-rule for theatrical convention. Realism, Stanislavsky points out, becomes naturalism on the stage only when it is not justified by the actor from within. As soon as it is justified, it becomes either unnecessary or is not noticed at all owing to the fact that external life is filled with its internal meaning.

As for stage conventions, Stanislavsky maintains that a good stage convention is created by those conditions which are best adapted for stage representation; it is *scenic* in the best sense of the word. Only that convention can be said to be good and scenic on the stage which helps the actors and the performance to recreate *the life of the human spirit* in the play itself and in its different parts. This life must be convincing. It cannot possibly take place in conditions of barefaced lies and deceptions. A lie must become, or at any rate must seem to become, truth on the stage before it can be convincing. And truth on the stage is what the actor, the artist, and the spectator believe to be true. Therefore stage conventions, too, must bear a resemblance to truth, that is to say, be credible, and the actor himself and the spectators must believe in them. It does not matter, Stanislavsky observes, whether the production and the acting is realistic, conventional, right-wing or left-wing, impressionistic or futuristic so long as it is convincing, that is, truthful or credible, and beautiful, i.e., artistic, and lofty, and represents the genuine life of the human spirit without which there is no art. Any stage convention that does not answer those demands is, in Stanislavsky's opinion, a bad stage convention.

What Stanislavsky, therefore, set himself to do was to find the laws of the creative art of the stage that are common to all actors, great and small, and that could be perceived by their consciousness. The number of such laws, he found, was not great; neither were they of any primary importance since they did not possess the power of transforming a second-rate actor into a genius. They were nevertheless laws of nature and had, as such, to be thoroughly studied by every actor, for it was only through them that he could set in motion his subconscious creative powers, the true nature of which was apparently beyond human grasp. 'The greater the genius,' Stanislavsky writes, 'the more mysterious does its mystery grow, and the more necessary do the technical methods of creative work become for since these methods are perceived by consciousness, he can use them to explore the hidden places of his subconsciousness, which is the seat of inspiration'.

These elementary 'psycho-physical and psychological' laws form what Stanislavsky calls the 'psycho-technique' of his system, and their purpose is to teach the actor how to arouse at will his unconscious creative nature in himself for subconscious and organic creative work. 'The basis for my system', Stanislavsky writes in *My Life in Art*, 'is formed by the laws of the organic nature of the actor which I have studied thoroughly in practice. Its chief merit is that there is nothing in it I myself invented or have not checked in practice. It is the natural result of my experiences of the stage over many years.

'My "system",' he goes on,

is divided into two main parts: (1) the inner and the outer work of the actor on himself, and (2) the inner and the outer work of the actor on his part. The inner work on the actor himself is based on a psychic technique which enables him to evoke a creative state of mind during which inspiration descends on him more easily. The actor's external work on himself consists of the preparation of his bodily mechanism for the embodiment of his part and the exact presentation of its inner life. The work on the part consists of the study of the spiritual essence of a dramatic work, the germ from which it has emerged and which defines its meaning as well as the meaning of all its parts.

3

Stanislavsky's next book, *An Actor's Work On Himself*, took the form of a course of study of the art of acting. The whole aim of the course is purely practical, and in it Stanislavsky conveys what his long experience as actor, producer and teacher has taught him.

To begin with, Stanislavsky draws a clear distinction between the different types of actor to be found on the stage. There are, he maintains, broadly speaking three types of actor; the creative actor, the imitative actor, and the stage-hack, the last category including the lowest type of actor known, namely the ham-actor. So far as the creative actor is concerned his distinguishing characteristic is his ability to enter into the feelings of his part. Such an actor must be completely carried away by the play in which he is appearing, for it is only then that he can enter fully into the feelings of his part without being aware of his own feeling and without *thinking* what he is doing, everything happening by itself, that is, subconsciously. The trouble is that no actor can control his subconsciousness. What he can do, however, is to influence it indirectly, for certain parts of a man's mind can be controlled by his consciousness and will and these are capable of exerting an influence on his involuntary psychical processes.

Hence one of the main principles of the art of entering into the feelings of a part is 'the subconscious creative work of nature through the conscious psycho-technique of the actor (subconscious through conscious, involuntary through voluntary)'. The actor ought to leave the subconscious to 'magician-nature' and apply himself only to what is accessible to him, namely the conscious approach to his creative work through the conscious methods of psycho-technique, which will tell him first of all not to interfere with the subconscious when it begins to work.

The whole development of the subconscious powers of the actor therefore depends entirely on the conscious psycho-technique. It is only when the actor fully realizes that his inner and outer life is developing naturally and normally according to the laws of human nature and in the conditions that he finds on the stage, that out of the innermost recesses of his subconscious mind feelings will emerge that he himself will not always be able to understand. These feelings will take possession of him for a long or short time and lead him where something inside him will tell them.

This mysterious force which seems to be beyond human powers of comprehension, Stanislavsky calls 'nature'. The moment that the actor's true organic life on the stage is interfered with, that is, the moment the actor stops representing life truthfully on the stage, his hypersensitive subconscious mind, shy of coercion, hides itself away in its inaccessible secret places. To prevent that from happening, the actor must first of all make sure that he does his work correctly. Thus, realism and even naturalism of his inner life is indispensable to the actor for stimulating the work of his subconsciousness and the impulses of his inspiration.

However, since it is impossible always to depend on the subconscious and inspiration, the creative actor must prepare the ground for such subconscious work by seeing first of all that his conscious work is done correctly; for the conscious and correct create truth, and truth begets belief, and if nature believes in what is taking place in the actor, she will herself take a hand in whatever the actor is doing on the stage, with the result that subconsciousness and even inspiration will be given a chance of asserting themselves.

But what does correct acting mean? It means, Stanislavsky maintains, that while on the stage the actor thinks and acts correctly, logically, consistently, and in accordance with the laws of human nature, as demanded by his part and in complete agreement with it. As soon as the actor succeeds in doing that, he will identify himself with the character of his part and begin to share his feelings, that is, he will enter into the feelings of his part. The process and its definition, Stanislavsky observes, occupy a foremost position in the art of the stage. For entering into the feelings of his part helps the actor to carry out the fundamental aim of the art of the stage, namely the creation of 'the life of the human spirit' of the part and the presentation of this life on the stage in an artistic form. It is the inner nature of his part, that is to say, its inner life, brought into being with the help of the process of entering into the feelings of his part, that is the main purpose of the actor's work on the stage and should also be his chief preoccupation. Moreover, the creative actor must enter into the feelings of his part, that is experience feelings that are absolutely identical with the feelings of the character he is representing on the stage, at every performance of the play.

4

Stanislavsky's 'system' is therefore an attempt to apply certain natural laws of acting for the purpose of bringing the actor's subconscious powers of expression into play. These laws, Stanislavsky claims, are sufficiently well-defined to be studied and put into practice with the help of psychotechnique, which consists of a large number of 'elements', ten of which – 'if', given circumstances, imagination, attention, relaxation of muscles, pieces and problems, truth and belief, emotional memory, communication and extraneous aids – form the core of the famous 'system'.

Stanislavsky's genius as producer found expression at the very outset of his career in his realization of the fundamental fact that dramatic art and the art of the actor are based on purposeful and productive action. 'On the stage,' he writes, 'the actor must act both externally and internally as well as purposefully and productively, and not just "in general". A stage action, that is, must be internally justified, logical, consistent and feasible in real life. An actor must not "play" passions and characters: he must act under the influence of the passions and in character.'

How is external and internal action created on the stage? It is created, Stanislavsky replies, through one of the most powerful elements of psycho-technique expressed in the monosyllable 'if'. That is to say, the only way in which an actor can give outer and inner expression to a stage action is by asking himself, What would I do, *if* certain circumstances were true? Stanislavsky usually describes this element as the *magic if*, for, as he points out, 'it transfers the actor from the world of reality to a world in which alone his creative work can be done.'

There are all sorts of 'ifs'. There are 'ifs' which fulfil themselves at once, and 'ifs' which merely supply the stimulus for the further logical development of action. There are one-storied and many-storied 'ifs'. The secret of the powerful influence of 'if' lies in the fact that it never deals with what actually exists, but only with what might have been – 'if....' It does not affirm anything; it merely assumes. It presents a problem that has to be solved, and it is the actor who has to supply the answer to it. Moreover, it arouses in the actor an inner and outer activity, and it does it naturally and without the slightest compulsion. The word 'if', in short, is an incentive and a stimulus to the actor's creative activity. It both begins the actor's work and provides the impetus towards the further development of the constructive process of his part.

The other element out of which stage action arises is 'the given circumstances'. It supplies the fable or plot of the play, its facts, events, period, time and place of action, the conditions of life, the actor's and producer's interpretation of the play, their additions to it, the mise-en-scenes, the production, the scenery and costumes of the stage designer, the properties, the sound effects, and so on. It includes everything, in fact, the actor is asked to take into consideration in his work on the stage.

Like 'if' itself, the given circumstances are a figment of the imagination, a mere conjecture. Both 'if' and the given circumstances are of the same origin: one is an assumption ('if') and the other an addition to it ('the given circumstances'). 'If' always starts the actor's creative work, while 'the given circumstances' develop it. Their functions, however, differ somewhat: 'if' supplies the impetus to the slumbering imagination, while 'the given circumstances' provide the justification for the existence of 'if'.

So far as the nature of internal and external action is concerned, Stanislavsky points out that the art of the theatre is based on activity which finds its expression in the action on the stage. The spirit of the play is also conveyed in action. The actor's inner experience and the inner world of the play must therefore be shown in action.

An actor may attempt to present a part he does not feel inwardly as externally effective for the sake of applause. A serious actor, however, would never tolerate any interruption of a passage in which the most intimate feelings are expressed. An actor who does not mind sacrificing them to get some cheap applause merely shows that the words he utters have no meaning for him, and empty words can hardly be expected to excite serious attention. The actor wants them just as sounds to display his voice, diction and technique of speech, and his actor's temperament. As for the thought and feelings, they can only be conveyed 'in general' sorrowfully, 'in general' joyously, 'in general' tragically, and so on. Such a performance, however, is dead, formal and inartistic.

The same applies to external action. When an actor does not care what he does on the stage, when his part and his art are not devoted to what they should serve, then his actions are empty, not inwardly felt, and consequently, they have nothing of importance to convey. In such a case, all that is left for the actor to do is to act 'in general'. When an actor suffers in order to suffer, when he loves in order to love, when he is jealous and asks for forgiveness in order to be jealous and ask for forgiveness, when all this is done merely because it is in the play and not because the actor has experienced it inwardly and created the life of his part on the stage, then he will find himself in a hopeless fix, and to act 'in general' is the only solution for him.

Real art and acting 'in general' are, in fact, incompatible. The one destroys the other. Art loves order and harmony, while 'in general' is chaos and disorder.

How is the actor to save himself from his mortal enemy 'in general'? To deal with it effectively he must introduce into his purposeless 'in general' acting something that is incompatible with it and that will be sure to destroy it. 'In general' being superficial and thoughtless, the actor must introduce into his play some plan and a serious attitude towards what is happening on the stage, which will destroy superficiality and thoughtlessness. 'In general' being chaotic and absurd, the actor must introduce logic and consistency into his part, which will eliminate these bad qualities. 'In general' always starting something and never finishing it, the actor must take care that his acting is characterized by finish and completeness. As a result, there will be real, purposeful and productive human action on the stage.

To be successful in this unequal fight, the actor, Stanislavsky insists, must first of all have the courage to admit that for all sorts of reasons he loses the sense of real life when he steps on to the stage. He forgets how he acts internally and externally in real life, and he has to learn it afresh just as a child has to learn to walk, talk, look and listen. His first duty, therefore, is to learn how to act on the stage like a normal human being, simply, naturally, organically correct, and without constraint. Not as required by the conventions of the theatre, but by the laws of living, organic nature. He must, in short, learn 'how to get rid of the theatre (with a small letter) in the Theatre (with a capital T)'.

'If', 'the given circumstances', and the internal and external action that arises from them are not the only important factors in an actor's work. He requires many more special abilities, qualities, and gifts such as imagination, attention, the feeling for truth, etc. The art of controlling all these 'elements' of psycho-technique demands much practice and experience.

5

In discussing the next element of imagination, Stanislavsky first of all stresses the fact that there is no real life on the stage. Real life, he declares emphatically, is not art, a statement that ought to dispose of many of his critics who accuse him of wishing to introduce a slavish imitation of life on the stage. The nature of art, he points out, demands fiction, which is in the first place provided by the work of the author. The problem of the actor and his creative technique is, therefore, how to transform the fiction of the play into artistic stage reality. To do that the actor needs imagination.

The playwright, Stanislavsky goes on to point out, does

not give the actor everything he has to know about the play, and indeed it is hardly to be expected that an author could reveal the life of all the *dramatis personæ* in a hundred or so pages. The playwright's stage-directions are, besides, too laconic and insufficient to create the whole outward image of the characters, not to mention their manners, gaits and habits. And what about the dialogue? Is it just to be learnt by heart? There are, moreover, the producer's mise-en-scenes, and the production of the play as a whole. Could an actor possibly memorize it all and reproduce it formally on the stage? Does all this really depict the character of the person in the play and define every shade of his thoughts, feelings, impulses, and actions? According to Stanislavsky – and here one cannot help feeling that he goes perhaps a little too far and, being himself a producer of genius, is rather apt to dispose of the author in too cavalier a fashion – it is the actor himself who has to add to it all and expand it. Only if he does that will everything the author and the other artists of the theatre have given him come to life. Only then will the actor himself be able to give expression to the inner life of the person he represents on the stage and act as the author, the producer, and his own genuine feelings tell him.

In this work the actor's best friend is his imagination with its magic 'if' and 'the given circumstances'. For it not only adds to what the author, producers and others have omitted, but makes it all come to life. An actor must, therefore, possess a strong and vivid imagination, which he must use at every moment of his life and work on the stage, both when he is studying and when he is performing his part.

The actor's imagination must be active and not passive. It must also be remembered that an actor's work does not consist of the inner work of his imagination alone, but also of the outer embodiment of his creative dreams, which must always be logical and consistent. These creative dreams of the actor's imagination Stanislavsky calls the visual images of his inner eye.

The actor needs first of all an uninterrupted sequence of

'given circumstances' and, secondly, an uninterrupted series of visual images which have some connexion with the given circumstances. He needs, in short, an uninterrupted line not of plain but of illustrated given circumstances. Indeed, at every moment of his presence on the stage and at every moment of the outer and inner development of the play, the actor must be aware either of what is taking place outside him on the stage (i.e. the external given circumstances created by the producer, stage-designer, and the other artists) or of what is taking place inside him, in his own imagination, that is, those visual images which illustrate the given circumstances of the life of his part. Out of all these things there is formed, sometimes outside and sometimes inside him, an uninterrupted and endless series of inner and outer visual images, or a kind of film. While his work goes on, this film is unwinding itself endlessly, reflecting on the screen of his inner vision the illustrated given circumstances of his part, among which he lives on the stage.

These visual images create in him a corresponding mood which will influence his spirit and arouse in him a corresponding inner feeling.

An actor needs his imagination not only in order to create, but also in order to infuse new life into what he has created and what is in danger of wearing thin. Every invention of the actor's imagination must, besides, be fully justified and firmly fixed. The questions who, when, where, why and how, which the actor puts to himself to set his imagination working, should help him to create more and more definite pictures of non-existent, imaginary life. There will be times, no doubt, when they will come by themselves without the aid of his conscious mental activity and without any promptings from his reason. But it is impossible to rely on the activity of the imagination left to its own devices, and to dream 'in general' without any definite and clearly defined theme is a waste of time.

Every movement and every word on the stage must be the result of the correct life of the imagination. If an actor utters a word or does something on the stage in a mechanical way, without knowing who he is, where he comes from, why he is where he is, what he wants, where he will go to and what he will do there, he is acting without imagination, and that fraction of time he spends on the stage, whether short or long, is not truth so far as he is concerned, for he has been acting like some wound-up mechanism, like an automaton. Not a single step must be taken on the stage mechanically and without some inner justification for it, that is, without the work of the imagination. To be equal to every task, an actor's imagination, in fact, must be lively, active, responsive, and sufficiently developed.

6

To make the best use of his imagination, an actor must be able to control it. This he can only do by a well-trained attention. Hence attention is the next important 'element' of the psycho-technique of Stanislavsky's 'system'.

Like action, attention may be either internal, in which case its main function is to supply the actor with the creative material for his imagination, or external, which is no less important since it helps to concentrate the actor's mind on what is taking place on the stage and so distracts it from the terrifying black hole of the proscenium.

It is absolutely essential, Stanislavsky insists, that the actor should learn by a series of exercises how to keep his attention fixed on the stage so as to prevent it from straying into the auditorium. He must acquire a special technique that will help him to concentrate his attention so firmly on some object on the stage that the object itself should distract him from anything outside it. The actor, in short, has to learn how to look and see on the stage. For the eye of the actor who knows how to look and see attracts the attention of the spectators, concentrating it on the object they too have to look at. The empty gaze of an actor, on the other hand, merely diverts the attention of the spectators from the stage.

Attention concentrated on some object on the stage will,

in addition, evoke a natural desire to do something with it, and action will still more concentrate the actor's attention on the object. Thus attention, fusing with the object, will create the strongest possible connexion with it.

To assist the actor to concentrate his attention on the stage Stanislavsky propounds the theory of the circle of attention. He points out that in such a narrow circle, as in a circle of light, it is easy to examine the smallest details of the objects within its circumference, live with the most intimate feelings and desires, carry out the most complicated actions, solve the most difficult problems, and analyse one's feelings and thoughts. In addition, it is possible in such a circle to establish close communication with another person in it, confide to him one's most intimate thoughts, recall the past and dream of the future.

The actor's state of mind in such an imaginary circle of attention, Stanislavsky describes as 'public solitude'. It is public, he points out, because the whole audience is with the actor all the time, and it is solitude because he is separated from it by his small circle of attention. During a performance the actor can always withdraw himself to his small circle of attention and, as it were, retire into his solitude, like a snail into its shell.

With the widening of the circle of attention, the area of the actor's attention is also widened. This, however, can go on only as long as the actor can keep his attention fixed within the imaginary circle. The moment the circumference of the circle becomes blurred, the actor must narrow the circle to the limits of his visual attention. The actor has to acquire an unconscious, mechanical habit of transferring his attention from the smaller to the larger circle without breaking it. In the terrible moment of panic the actor must remember that the larger and emptier the large circle, the more compact must the middle and small circle be inside it, and the more solitary must his solitude be.

In addition to the external attention, that is, the attention directed to the objects on the stage, there is the actor's inner attention, which is also constantly diverted by the actor's memories of his private life. In the sphere of inner attention, too, there is therefore a continuous conflict in the actor's mind between the attention which is correct and useful for his part and the attention which is incorrect and harmful. Attention which is harmful draws the actor away from the problems of his part to the other side of the footlights or even beyond the walls of the theatre.

Inner attention is so important to the actor because the greater part of his life on the stage takes place on the plane of creative invention and fictitious 'given circumstances'. Hence all that resides in the actor's soul is accessible to his inner attention only. Another important quality of inner attention is that it enables the actor to transform its object from a cold, intellectual and rational one into a warm, emotional and sensuous one.

To develop his inner attention the actor must learn how to be attentive in life as well as on the stage. Stanislavsky is particularly anxious to drive home the fact that it is a great mistake to think that the actor can withdraw himself from life and take an interest only in his work on the stage. He cannot stand aside from contemporary events. Indeed, so far as the development of his inner attention is concerned, it is outside the theatre that he must learn how to look and see, hear and listen. He must train himself to discern not only what is bad in life, a thing that comes easily to any man, but also what is good and beautiful. For the good and the beautiful, Stanislavsky points out, exalt the mind and evoke a man's best feelings, leaving indelible traces on his emotional and other memories. Nature being the most beautiful thing of all, it behoves the actor to study it most.

The actor must furthermore give the same kind of attention to works of art, such as literature, music, paintings and so on, for this will help him to acquire good taste and a love of the beautiful. He must be careful, however, not to attempt to train his sense of the beautiful analytically, with a notebook in his hand, as it were, 'A true artist', Stanislavsky writes, is inspired by everything that takes place around him; life excites him and becomes the object of his study and his passion; he eagerly observes all he sees and tries to imprint it on his memory not as a statistician, but as an artist, not only in his notebook, but also in his heart. It is, in short, impossible to work in art in a detached way. We must possess a certain degree of inner warmth; we must have sensuous attention. That does not mean, however, that we must renounce our reason, for it is possible to reason warmly, and not coldly.

Since not every actor possesses the inner urge to study life in all its manifestations of good and evil, certain technical methods are necessary to arouse the actor's attention to what is happening around him in life. Stanislavsky advises such actors to use the same methods for arousing their attention as for awakening their imaginations. Let them put to themselves these questions and try to answer them honestly and sincerely: who, what, when, where, how and why is whatever they are observing taking place. Let them put into words what strikes them as beautiful or typical about a house, a room, the furniture in it or the people who own it. Let them find out the real purpose of a room or an object, why, for instance, the furniture is arranged in one way and not another, and what are the habits of their owners as indicated by the various things in a room.

Having learned how to examine everything around them and how to find their creative material in life, the actors must turn to the study of the material they require most for their creative work on the stage, namely, those emotions they receive from their personal and direct communication with people. This emotional material is so valuable because out of it the actors compose 'the life of the human spirit' of their parts, the creation of which forms the basic aim of their art. This material is so difficult to obtain because it is invisible, elusive, indefinite and only inwardly perceptible.

It is true that many invisible emotional experiences are reflected in facial expressions, in the eye, voice, speech, movements and the entire physical mechanism of man.

That may make the task of the observer easier, but it is not so easy to understand the real motives of people, because they rarely open up their hearts to strangers and show themselves as they really are. As a rule, they conceal their true feelings, with the result that their external looks deceive rather than enlighten the observer.

Stanislavsky admits that his psycho-technique has not yet discovered the methods of solving all these difficulties, and all he can do is to give just a few hints to the actor which he may find useful in certain cases. 'When the inner world of the man the actor is observing,' he writes,

is revealed in his actions, thoughts, or impulses, the actor should devote all his attention to the study of those actions. He should ask himself, 'Why did this man act thus and not thus? What was he thinking of?' and draw his own conclusions, define his attitude to the observed object, and try to understand the character of the man. When after a prolonged and penetrating process of observation and investigation he is successful in this task, he will obtain valuable creative material for his work on the stage. It often happens, however, that the inner life of the man the actor is observing is not accessible to his reason, but only to his intuition. In that case, he should try to find a way into the innermost recesses of the man's mind and look there for the material of his creative work with the help of as it were, 'the antennae of his own feelings'. This process requires very delicate powers of observation of the actor's own subconscious mind; for his ordinary attention is not sufficiently penetrating for probing into the living human soul in search of his material. In this complex process of looking for the most delicate emotional creative material, which cannot be perceived by his consciousness, the actor must rely on his common sense, experience of life, sensibility and intuition. While waiting for science to discover the practical approaches towards an understanding of a man's soul, the actor must do his best to learn how to discern the logic and consistency of its feelings and workings. This may help him to discover the best methods of finding the subconscious creative material in the external as well as the internal life of man.

7

Having dealt with the rather intangible, though not on that account less important, aspects of psycho-technique, Stanislavsky turns to its more tractable elements. The first of these is relaxation of muscles. Muscular tension, Stanislavsky observes, interferes with the actor's inner work and, particularly, with his attempts to enter into the feelings of his part. Indeed, while physical tension exists, it is a waste of time talking of correct and delicate feeling or of any normal psychical life of the part. Before beginning his work, the actor must, therefore, see that his muscles are sufficiently relaxed so as not to impede his freedom of movement. It is not, however, muscular spasms alone that interfere with the actor's work on the stage. The faintest strain anywhere can paralyze the actor's work, if not immediately discovered and dealt with.

An actor, being human, will always suffer from nervous strain during a public performance. If he relaxes it in his neck, it will appear in his diaphragm. This bodily defect of his can be fought successfully if the actor evolves in his mind a special controller or observer for that purpose. If any unnecessary strain appears anywhere, the controller must remove it at once. This process of self-analysis and removal of tension must be so developed that it becomes automatic and unconscious. It must, in fact, be transformed into a normal habit, a natural necessity not only in the quiet places of the part, but above all in the moments of the greatest nervous and physical excitement. For at such moments it is natural for the actor to intensify his muscular tension. That is why an actor must take care that his muscles are completely free from any strain whenever his part demands particularly strong emotional action from him.

The habit of relaxing the muscles must be acquired by daily systematic exercises on and off the stage. The muscle-controller must become part of the actor's own mind, his second nature.

Each pose on the stage, however, must not only be checked by the actor's muscle-controller to make sure that it is free from all strain, but must also be justified by his imagination, the given circumstances, and 'if'. When this is done, the pose ceases to be a pose and becomes action.

The actor must never forget that nature exercises greater control over the human organism than consciousness or the so highly praised actor's technique. Each pose or position of the body on the stage, Stanislavsky points out, has three phases: (1) unnecessary tension which is unavoidable in every new pose because of the actor's state of agitation at a public performance; (2) the mechanical process of the relaxation of tension with the help of the controller; and (3) the justification of the pose in the case when the actor himself does not believe in it. *Tension, relaxation, justification.*

A living pose and real action (real, that is, in the imaginary life which is justified by the given circumstances in which the actor himself believes) will force nature to take a hand in the actor's work; for it is only nature that can fully control the muscles and bring them to a state of correct tension and relaxation.

It is obvious that the more delicate the feeling, the greater must be the precision, accuracy and plasticity of its physical embodiment. This can be achieved only if the demands of the art of the stage are adapted to the demands of nature, for art lives in harmony with nature. On the other hand, nature is distorted by life and the bad habits that life engenders. The shortcomings which pass unnoticed in life become unbearable in the strong light of the stage. For in the theatre human life is shown in the narrow space of the frame of the stage, and people look at this life through binoculars; it is examined, like a miniature, through a magnifying glass. The actor, in fact, must always remember that the minutest strain in his acting will not escape the attention of the spectators.

8

The next element of psycho-technique which has a direct bearing on the methods the actor must apply to the handling of his part is that of 'pieces and problems'.

The division of a part into pieces is, according to Stanislavsky, necessary not only because this facilitates its analysis and study but also because each piece contains its own creative problem.

Both the problems and the pieces must arise out of each other logically and consistently. There are large, not so large, and small pieces and problems which, if necessary, can coalesce. Both form the basic stages of a part which the actor must take into account during a performance.

There are many varieties of stage problems of any part in a play, and not all of them are necessary or useful. The actor must, therefore, be able to differentiate between those which are useful to him and those which are not. To the former category belong: (1) problems dealing with the actor's side of the footlights, with the stage, that is, and not with the auditorium; (2) problems of the actor himself as a human being, which are analogous with the problems of his part; (3) creative and artistic problems, that is, those which contribute to the realization of the basic aim of the art of the stage, namely the creation of 'the life of the human spirit of the part' and its artistic communication; (4) real, living and active human problems, which keep the part in a state of continuous motion, as opposed to artificial, dead, theatrical ones, which have no relation to the character represented by the actor, and are merely introduced for the entertainment of the spectators; (5) problems in which the actor himself, his partner, and the spectator can believe; (6) interesting and exciting problems which are capable of stimulating the process of entering into the feelings of the part; (7) problems which are typical of the part and which are not approximately but definitely connected with the main idea of the dramatic work; and (8) problems that correspond with the inner nature of the part and are not only superficially in accord with it.

But however correct a problem may be, its chief and most important quality is the strong fascination it exerts on the actor himself. For it is very important that the problem should appeal to the actor and that he should want to solve it, since such a problem possesses a magnetic force that attracts the creative will of the actor.

These problems Stanislavsky calls *creative problems*, and each of them, he points out, must be within the capacity of the actor to solve.

As for the method of extracting these problems from the pieces into which the play has been divided, the actor, Stanislavsky advises, should invent corresponding names for each piece, for this will reveal the problem inherent in it. The problems must be defined by a verb, for a verb always implies action, and the best verb for that purpose is 'I want to'. In fact, 'I want to' acquires almost the same magic quality in Stanislavsky's system as 'if'.

9

The element of the 'pieces' into which a part is divided and the 'creative problems' of each piece expressed by 'I want to' depend for the effectiveness on the ability of the actor to represent them truthfully on the stage, which he can do only if he himself believes in them. Hence the actor's sense of truth and his belief form the next indispensable 'element' in Stanislavsky's system.

In life truth is what exists in reality and what every man knows for certain; on the stage truth is what does not exist in reality, but what could have happened 'if' the given circumstances of the play had really happened. Truth on the stage is, therefore, what the actor believes to exist in himself and in the minds and hearts of the other members of the cast. Truth and belief cannot exist without each other, and without them there can be no creative work on the stage.

But it would be a mistake to exaggerate the importance

of truth or falsehood on the stage. The actor must remember that truth is only necessary on the stage in so far as it helps to convince him and his partners and enables them to carry out correctly the creative problems inherent in their parts. As for falsehood, it too can be helpful to the actor inasmuch as it shows him the limits beyond which he cannot go.

The best way an actor can evoke a feeling of truth and belief in what he is doing on the stage is to concentrate on the simplest physical actions. What matters is not the physical actions themselves, but the feeling of truth and belief they help the actor to evoke in himself. If an actor finds it difficult to grasp at once the large truth of some big action he should divide it, like his part itself, into smaller pieces, and try to believe in the smallest of them. Quite often by the realization of one little truth and one moment of belief in the genuineness of his action, an actor will gain an insight into the whole of his part and will be able to believe in the great truth of the play.

Small physical actions, small physical truths and the moments of belief in them, Stanislavsky points out, acquire a great significance on the stage particularly in the climaxes of a tragedy. Actors ought therefore to make every possible use of the fact that small physical actions, occurring in the midst of important given circumstances, possess tremendous force. For it is in such conditions that the interaction between body and soul is created, as a result of which the external helps the internal, and the internal evokes the external. Another more practical reason why the truth of physical actions is so important during a tragic climax is that in a great tragedy an actor has to attain the highest degree of creative tension, so that to avoid overacting he must lay hold of something that is tangible and real. It is at such a moment, therefore, that what he needs most is a clear-cut, precise, exciting, and easily executed action, which will guide him along the right path naturally and mechanically, and will prevent him from being led astray. And the simpler such actions are, the quicker can he make use of them at a difficult moment of his part.

Tragic moments must consequently be approached without an undue sense of their importance and without any strain or nervousness. Nor should they be tackled all at once, as is the custom of most actors, but step by step and logically. For the actor has to *feel* each small or large truth of the physical actions and believe in it implicitly. This technique of the approach to feeling will produce a correct attitude towards tragic and dramatic climaxes in a play, and the actor will no longer be frightened by them.

Big and little physical actions are so valuable to the actor because of their clearly perceptible truth. They create the life of the actor's body, which is half the life of his part. They are also valuable because it is through them that the actor can enter into the life of his part and into its feelings easily and almost imperceptibly, and because they help to keep his attention concentrated on the stage, the play and his part.

Another important quality of physical actions is their strict logic, which introduces order, harmony and meaning into them and helps to create real and purposeful action.

In real life a man's subconsciousness generally ensures the logic and consistency of his actions, but on the stage neither the organic necessity of physical action nor its 'mechanical' logic and consistency exist, so that in place of the mechanical nature of such actions in real life, a conscious, logical and consistent stocktaking of every moment of the physical action must be introduced. As a result of frequent repetitions this process will grow into a habit.

But even logical and consistent physical actions on the stage will become artificial, that is, beget falsehood if they lack a sense of truth and if the actor does not believe in them.

'A formal approach to our complicated creative work and a narrow elementary understanding of it', Stanislavsky writes,

is the greatest danger to my method, my whole system, and its psycho-technique. To learn how to divide up large physical actions into their component parts, to establish formally their logic and their sequence, to invent corresponding exercises for them and go through them with your students without taking into account the most important thing of all, namely the necessity of infusing a sense of truth and belief into the physical actions, is not so difficult and may be made into quite a profitable business. What a temptation to the exploiters of my system! But there is nothing more harmful or more stupid so far as art is concerned than a system for the sake of a system. You cannot make it an aim in itself; you cannot transform a means into an end. That would be the greatest lie of all!

A sense of truth and belief is even more necessary in a pause of 'tragic inaction', a very complex psychological state, and the problem of infusing life into it, that is, the logic and sequence of elusive, invisible and unstable inner feelings, is one of great importance. The actor has to ask himself what he would have done in real life if he had fallen into a state of tragic inaction. In life a man is active inwardly in his imagination before he takes any decision; he sees with his inner eye what is going to happen and how it is going to happen, and he carries out the indicated action in his mind. An actor, in addition, feels his thoughts physically, and can hardly restrain his inner calls to action, which crave to give an outward form to inner life. For this reason, an actor will find that his mental ideas about action will help him to evoke his inner activity. For an actor's whole work takes place not in actual but in imaginary and non-existent life, a life which might have existed. This life the actors have a right to regard as real, and their physical actions on the stage as genuine physical acts. So far as the actor is concerned, the method of perception of the logic and sequence of feelings through the logic and sequence of physical actions is, therefore, entirely justified.

What the actor has to do in such cases, Stanislavsky advises, is to leave the complex psychological problem alone, since he could not possibly analyse it himself, and transfer his attention to an entirely different sphere, namely the logic of actions, where the problem can be solved in a purely practical and not scientific way with the help of his human nature, his experience of life, his instinct, sensibility, logic and the subconsciousness itself.

The logical sequence of the physical actions and feelings will lead the actor to truth, and truth will evoke belief, and together they will create what Stanislavsky calls 'I am', which means 'I exist, I live, I feel, and I think in the same way as the character I am representing on the stage does.' In other words, 'I am' evokes emotion and feeling and enables the actor to enter into the feelings of his part. 'I am' is, according to Stanislavsky, the condensed and almost absolute truth on the stage. 'I am' is the result of the desire for truth, and where there is truth, belief, and 'I am', there is inevitably also true human (not theatrical) experience. One of the consequences of this is that the spectator too is drawn into the action as an involuntary participant; he is drawn into the very midst of the life that is taking place on the stage, which he accepts as truth.

Truth on the stage, however, must be not only realistic, but also artistic. The actor, though, must remember that it is impossible to create artistic truth all at once, but that it is created in the course of the whole process of the gestation and growth of his part. In concentrating on the main inner features of his part, investing them with a correspondingly beautiful stage form and expression, and getting rid of anything that is superfluous, the actor, guided by his subconscious, his artistic flair, his talent, sensibility and taste, makes his part poetic, beautiful and harmonious, comprehensible and simple, and ennobling and purifying to all those who watch him. All these qualities help the stage creation to be not only right and truthful, but also artistic.

The actor must, therefore, avoid everything that is not in his powers to express and is contrary to his nature, logic and common sense. For all that leads to distortion, violence, overacting and falsehood. The more frequently these appear on the stage, the worse for the actor's sense of truth, which becomes demoralized and perverted by untruth. The actor must fear the habits of deceit and falsehood on the stage. He must not let those evil seeds take root in him, for otherwise they will spread like weeds and smother the tender shoots of truth.

The basic principle of Stanislavsky's 'system' being, as stated earlier, the subconscious through the conscious, it is not surprising that he should include among the elements of psycho-technique one whose main function it is to arouse inspiration. This element is emotional memory, that is, the memory that resides in the actor's feelings and is brought to the surface of his consciousness by his five senses, though mostly by sight and hearing.

Stanislavsky illustrates the meaning of emotional memory by asking the actor to imagine a large number of houses, a large number of rooms in each house, a large number of cupboards in each room, drawers in each cupboard, large and small boxes in each drawer, and among the boxes one that is very small and is filled with beads. It is easy to find the house, the room, the cupboard, the drawer, and the boxes, and even the smallest box of all, but it will take a very sharp eye to find a tiny bead that fell out of the little box and, flashing for a moment, has gone for good. If it is found, it is by sheer accident. The same thing is true of the store-house of an actor's memory. It too has its cupboards, drawers, and large and small boxes. Some of them are more and others less accessible. But, Stanislavsky asks, how is the actor to find one of the 'beads' of his emotional memory, which flashed across his mind once and then vanished for ever? When they occasionally appear the actor ought to be grateful to Apollo for having sent him those visual images, but he need not expect to be able to recover a feeling that has gone for good. He must be content with the things of today and not wait for something he had the day before to come to him again. He must never attempt to hunt after the old bead that is irretrievably lost, but every time do his best to achieve a new and fresher inspiration, even if it is weaker than that of the day before. The important thing is that it should be natural and come by itself out of the innermost recesses of his mind. Every new flash of inspiration is beautiful in its own way just because it is inspiration.

Feelings the actor has never before experienced on the stage are desirable because they are spontaneous, strong and vivid, though they only appear in brief flashes and are introduced into the part in separate episodes. The surprise hidden in these feelings contains an irresistibly stimulating force. But the trouble is that the actor cannot control these feelings, but is controlled by them. The whole thing, therefore, must be left to nature in the hope that when these flashes of inspiration do occur, they will do so when the actor wants them and will not be contrary to the play or the part. Unexpected and unconscious 'inspiration' is, of course, very welcome, but that does not in any way minimize the importance of the conscious and repetitive memories that are also a result of the actor's emotional memory, because it is through them that he can to a certain extent influence inspiration. Such conscious memories should be particularly dear to an actor because they are woven out of the carefully chosen material of his emotional memory.

An actor, according to Stanislavsky, cannot help playing himself all his life, but he has to do it in different combinations and permutations of problems and given circumstances which he himself conceives for his part and melts in the furnace of his own emotional memories, which are the best materials for his inner creative work. Hence the actor must always make use of them and never rely on what he may get from others.

Stanislavsky points out that the germs of all the human vices and virtues are to be found in the actor himself, who must use his art and technique for the discovery in a natural way of all those germs of human passions and then develop them for any of his parts. The 'soul' of the character represented on the stage is in this way composed of the living human elements of the actor's own 'soul', of his own emotional memories, etc. What the actor must do first of all is to find the methods of extracting this emotional material from his own soul and, secondly, the methods of creating out of them endless combinations in the human souls of his parts.

Since the stage sets and the mood they evoke in the actor stimulate his feelings, he must learn how to look, see and absorb everything that surrounds him on the stage so as to submit himself to the mood created by the stage illusion. But unfortunately not all good scenery stimulates an actor's emotional memory because producers and stage designers do not always realize that the sets, lighting, sound and other stage effects are much more important to the actor than to the audience, for it helps him to concentrate his entire attention on the stage, and distracts it from anything outside it. If the mood created on the stage by these effects is in harmony with the spirit of the play, an atmosphere will be created which will be favourable to the actor's work, rouse his emotional memory, and help him to enter into the feelings of his part. That is why an actor must learn how to look and see on the stage, and how to respond to his surroundings. He must, in short, know how to use all the stimuli of the stage.

Occasionally, however, the actor may find it necessary to reverse the process and, instead of going from stimulus to feeling, go from feeling to stimulus, especially if he wants to fix an inner experience that came to him by chance.

The actor must never think about the feeling itself, but try to find out what has caused it. It is the conditions that have produced the experience that matter. For these conditions are the soil which, after having been watered and manured, produce the feeling. When this happens, nature herself will as a rule produce a new feeling analogous to the feeling experienced by the actor before.

As for the character and quality of emotional memory, there is all the difference in the world, Stanislavsky points out, between an experience an actor has lived through himself and one which he has only heard of or read about. The actor has to transform the second type of emotional memory from sympathy into feeling. This will sometimes happen automatically. The actor enters into the position of the character he is representing on the stage so completely that he feels himself to be in his place, in which case sympathy will automatically be transformed into feeling. But if this does not happen, the actor has to call to his aid the magic 'if', the given circumstances, and all the other stimuli which will strike a responsive chord in his emotional memory.

The actor, that is, must be able to call to his aid all the different inner and outer stimuli that arouse the right feeling in him. He must know how to find the stimuli for each feeling and he must be able to determine which stimulus produces which feeling.

The actor, however, can never rely on observation alone to replenish the storehouses of his emotional memory. It is not enough to widen the circle of attention by including in it different spheres of life; he must also understand the meaning of the facts he observes and be able to digest inwardly the received impressions of his emotional memory. For his acting to become creative and to represent 'the life of the human spirit', the actor must not only study this life, but take an active part in all its mainfestations, wherever and whenever possible. Without it his art will dry up and become artificial.

If an actor, therefore, is to fulfil what is expected of a real artist, he must lead 'a full, interesting, beautiful, varied, exciting and exalted life'. He must possess 'an infinitely wide horizon,' for he will be called upon to present 'the life of the human spirit' of all the peoples of the world, present, past and future.

'The ideal of our creative work at all times has been and will be what is eternal in art', Stanislavsky writes,

what never grows old and dies, and what is always young and dear to people. The actor takes from real or imaginary life all it can give to man. But he transforms all the impressions, passions and joys of life into the material for his creative work. Out of what is transitory and personal he creates a whole world of poetic images and ideas which will live for ever.

II

Stanislavsky's theory of acting is quite properly mainly concerned with elucidating the problems which bear directly on the ways in which an actor can enter into the feelings of his part. But since drama is an art in which several persons are engaged in re-creating 'the life of the human spirit' on the stage, it is no less important that the actor should be able to communicate the feelings of the character he is representing. He must, besides, be able to understand what is passing in the minds of the other characters in the play when they say something. Thought transmission, therefore, plays an essential role in the actor's technique, all the more so as the audience too must be able to gain an understanding of what is passing in the minds of the characters in the play both when they say something and when they are silent. Hence communication forms an important element of the actor's psycho-technique.

Indeed, as Stanislavsky points out, if a correct and an uninterrupted process of communication is necessary in life, then it is ten times more necessary on the stage. Such a process of stage communication, however, is only possible if the actor succeeds in banishing all his own personal thoughts and feelings during the performance. Since in most cases the private life of the actor does not cease when he comes on the stage, the line of the life of his part and his communication of it is interrupted by interpolations from the actor's private life which have nothing to do with the character he is representing. This is the first difficulty an actor must learn to overcome, for the nature of the theatre and its art are based on uninterrupted communication between the different members of the cast among themselves and each individual member with himself. Indeed, the spectators can understand and take part indirectly in the action only when the process of communication between the actors on the stage occurs. If, therefore, actors want to hold the attention of the audience they must take care that they communicate their thoughts, feelings and actions to their partners without interruption.

In soliloquies the process of self-communication can only be justified, Stanislavsky maintains, if it has a definite object of concentration. Similar difficulties exist in establishing mutual communication between the actor and his partner, and Stanislavsky advises the actor who experiences such difficulties to choose some particular point on his partner through which to communicate with him.

An actor, besides, must not only learn to convey his thoughts and feelings to his partner, but must make sure that they have reached his partner's mind and heart. To achieve this a short pause is necessary, for during this pause the actor can communicate with his eyes what his words cannot express. In his turn, the actor must know how to absorb the words and thoughts of his partner each time differently.

As for establishing communication with imaginary and non-existing objects (such as the ghost of Hamlet's father), it is a mistake, Stanislavsky thinks, for the actor to imagine its presence on the stage. Experienced actors know that what matters is not 'the ghost' but their own inner attitude towards it, and that is why they put in the place of the imaginary object (the ghost), their magic 'if' and try to find an honest answer to the question how they would have acted if there had been a ghost in the empty space before them.

So far as the audience is concerned, the actor must never try to communicate with it directly, but always indirectly. The peculiar difficulty of stage communication is that it takes place simultaneously between the actor, his partner, and the audience. However, there is this difference that between the actor and his partner on the stage the communication is always direct and conscious, while between the actor and the audience it is always indirect and unconscious. The remarkable thing is that in either case the communication is reciprocal.

'Many people are of the opinion', Stanislavsky writes,

that the external movements of hands, feet and trunk, which are visible to the eye, are an expression of activity, while the inner actions of spiritual communication, which are invisible to the eye, are inactive. This is a mistake, and all the more annoying since in our art, which creates the life of the human spirit of the part, every expression of inner action is highly important and valuable.

Inner communication, therefore, is one of the most important active actions on the stage, which is indispensable to the process of the creation and transmission of 'the life of the human spirit' of the part.

As usual, Stanislavsky invents an utterly unscientific term for the definition of this inner and invisible communication. He calls it *ray-emission* and *ray-absorption*, or *irradiation* and *absorption*. In a calm state of mind, he explains, a person's ray-emissions and ray-absorptions are almost imperceptible, but in moments of emotional stress, ecstasy, or heightened feelings, the ray-emissions and ray-absorptions grow more definite and perceptible both to those who are emitting them and those who are absorbing them. 'It is as though the inner feelings and desires,' he writes, 'emitted rays which, issuing through the eyes and body, poured in a stream over other people.'

If the actor makes full use of the long series of logically and consistently interwoven experiences and feelings, the connexion between them will grow stronger till, finally, they assume the form of reciprocal communication which Stanislavsky defines as *grip*, and which will invariably make the processes of ray-emission and ray-absorption stronger. On the stage there must be a grip in everything – in the eyes, hearing and all the rest of the five senses. 'If an actor listens,' Stanislavsky writes, 'he must both listen and hear. If he smells, he must inhale. If he looks, he must look and see, and not just glance at an object without hanging on to it as it were, with his teeth, which', Stanislavsky is careful to observe, 'does not mean at all that he should strain himself unnecessarily'. On the stage and particularly in tragedy, such a grip is absolutely necessary. To represent passions which impinge violently upon life, the actor must possess both an inward and an outward grip, either of which will result in ray-emission. As for the method of mastering this process, Stanislavsky again points out that if the actor finds it impossible to go from the inner to the outer, he has to go from the outer to the inner.

There are all sorts of ways in which actors can bring out some hidden nuance of a feeling to attract attention to their particular state of mind at some moment in the performance. What matters about these aids which actors use when communicating with each other on the stage is their vividness, subtlety, refinement and taste. There are two things an actor has to consider when inventing these aids, namely the way in which to choose them and the way in which to carry them out. The most effective of these aids to communication are subconscious. They appear in moments of genuine inspiration, and their main strength lies in their surprise, daring and boldness. Conscious aids suggested by the producer or fellow-actors must never be accepted by the actor as given. He must always adapt them and make them his own.

There is no direct way of evoking subconscious aids and the best thing is to leave everything to nature. As for the half-conscious aids, that is, aids which are only to a certain extent subconscious, something may be achieved there with the help of psycho-technique, but not very much, since the technique of originating aids is not very prolific. The actor must remember, however, always to introduce a new nuance into the aids he has already used and justify the change, and then his acting will gain a new freshness.

12

Having mustered all the main elements through which the actor can re-create 'the life of the human spirit' of his part, the question that still remains unanswered is what it is that puts them all into motion. In other words, if an actor is given the script of a play in which he is to act one of the characters, what is it that rouses the elements into activity so as to assure a good performance of his part? First his reason enables him to understand the text of the play.

Secondly, his will infuses the necessary courage in him to proceed with his work. Thirdly, his feeling enables him to transform mere sympathy for his character into experience. Reason, will and feeling are, therefore, what Stanislavsky calls the motive forces of the actor's inner life.

Reason (intellect), Stanislavsky points out, has two main functions, namely, the moment of its first impact which leads to the emergence of the idea, and the one originating from it, leading to the emergence of judgment. Reason, will and feeling always act together, simultaneously, and in close dependence on one another (reason-will-feeling, feeling-will-reason or will-feeling-reason). Will and feeling are automatically included in the actor's creative work once he begins to use his reason, or, to put it another way, an idea about something naturally evokes judgment about it. The interdependence and close connexion between one creative force and the rest is very important, and it would be a mistake not to make use of them for the actor's practical purposes. The technique of this mental process consists in rousing to action every member of the triumvirate, as well as all the elements of the actor's creative mechanism, naturally and organically, by the interaction of all its members. Sometimes the motive forces of inner life start working at one and the same time, in which case the actor must submit himself entirely to the ensuing natural creative tendencies of these forces. But when reason, will and feeling remain unresponsive to the actor's creative appeal he has to make use of the stimuli or baits, which not only each of the elements, but also each motive force, possesses. The actor must be careful, however, not to arouse them all at once. He should start with one, preferably reason, which is more accommodating than the other two. In such a case, the actor gets a corresponding idea from the formal thought of the text and begins to see what the words mean. The idea, in turn, evokes the corresponding judgment, and the thought, no longer formal and dry but animated by ideas, naturally arouses will and feeling.

It is quite possible that if the actor approaches the play

or his part by taking feeling, and not intellect, for his starting point, all the other motive forces of inner life will be brought into action at once; but if not, he will have again to use some bait, which in this case will be reason. Will, on the other hand, can be indirectly roused by a problem.

The correctness of the statement that the motive forces of inner life are reason, will and feeling is confirmed, Stanislavsky maintains, by nature herself in the existence of actors in whose characters emotion, reason or will prevails. The actors in whom feeling predominates over reason will, in playing Romeo or Othello, emphasize the emotional side of these parts. Actors in whose creative work will predominates over reason and feeling will, in playing Macbeth or Brand, emphasize their ambition or religious proclivities. While actors in whose creative nature reason predominates over will and feeling will, when playing Hamlet, involuntarily give an intellectual tinge to their part.

The predominance of one or another of the motive forces of inner life must, however, never be strong enough to suppress the others. There must, Stanislavsky insists, be a harmonious correlation between all the motive forces.

The direction taken by the motive forces of inner life, Stanislavsky maintains, must form one unbroken line. It is very rarely that the actor's reason, will and feeling grasp the chief meaning of a new play, are inspired by it creatively, and produce the inner state of mind which is necessary for his work. More often the text of the play is assimilated only to a certain extent by reason, only partially encompassed by feeling, and only arouses indefinite, scrappy impulses of will. During the first period of his acquaintance with the playwright's work, therefore, the actor only gets a vague idea of it, and his judgement of it cannot but be superficial. His will and feeling also react rather hesitatingly to his first impressions, and he only gets a 'general' perception of the life of his part.

This is only what can be expected, since in the majority of cases a great deal of work is required before the actor can grasp the inner meaning of a play. It may also happen sometimes that the actor finds it impossible to make head or tail of the text of a play at the first reading, his will and feeling remain passive, and he can form no idea or judgment of the work. This is often the case with symbolic or impressionistic plays. He has, therefore, to rely on someone else's opinions and judgement, and try to understand the text of the play with their help. After a great deal of hard work he will at last get a vague idea of what it all means, but he will still have no independent opinions about it, for these emerge only gradually. When they do, the actor will in the end succeed one way or another in getting all the motive forces of his inner life to take a hand in his work.

At first, while the aim is still obscure, the invisible currents of direction of the motive forces are in an embryonic stage. Only single moments of the life of the part, perceived by the actor when he made his first acquaintance with the play, have aroused the motive forces of inner life strongly enough to move in a certain direction. Thoughts and desires appear in spurts. They emerge, come to a halt, reappear and again vanish. If these lines, issuing from the motive forces of inner life, were to be represented graphically, one would get a large number of short jerky lines going in all directions. But the more familiar the actor gets with his part and the deeper his understanding of its chief aim, the straighter do these lines of direction become. It is then that the first stage of the actor's creative work arises.

The art of the stage, like any other art, must have an unbroken line, and the moment the different lines of direction of the motive forces straighten out, that is, become one unbroken line, the creative work of the actor can be said to start. The actor, though, must have many such unbroken lines, that is to say, lines of the inventions of his imagination, attention, objects, logic and consistency, pieces and problems, inclinations and actions, uninterrupted moments of truth and belief, emotional memories, communication, extraneous aids and other elements that are necessary in his work.

The man who is the actor and the man who is the part

have to live with all these lines on the stage almost without interruption. These lines impart life and movement to the character the actor is representing. The moment they come to a stop, the life of the part comes to an end and paralysis or death sets in. But such an alternation of death and revival is abnormal, for the part demands continuous life and an almost unbroken line.

In each part and play, moreover, the larger lines are composed of a large number of small lines, and on the stage they can encompass different intervals of time, days, weeks, months, years and so on. The author who creates the line of life of the play, however, does not indicate the whole line, but only parts of it, leaving intervals between each part. He does not describe many things that happen off stage, and the actor has often to use his imagination to fill in the gaps in the play left by the author. For without it, it is impossible to present on the stage the entire 'life of the human spirit' of the actor in his part, but only separate bits of it. To enter into the feelings of his character, however, the actor must have a relatively unbroken line of the life of his part and the play.

It is important to realize that the life of a part is one unbroken sequence of objects and circles of attention on the plane of imagined reality, on the plane of memories of the past, or on the plane of dreams of the future. The fact that the line is unbroken is of great importance to the actor, and he must train himself to keep it unbroken, and always fixed on the stage, never for a moment letting it stray into the auditorium. If the attention of the actor is constantly moving from one object to another, then this constant change of the objects of his attention creates the unbroken line. Should the actor concentrate his attention only on one object, keeping it fixed on it during the whole of the act or during the whole of the play, there would be no line of movement, and even if one had been formed, it would have been the line of a madman, an *idée fixe*.

What direction do the lines of the motive forces of the actor's inner life take? They move in the direction of those inner creative powers in the actor which they influence, that is, in the direction of his inner and physical nature, and in the direction of his inner elements. Reason, will and feeling raise the alarm, and with the strength, temperament and persuasion peculiar to them mobilize all the actor's inner creative powers. 'The endless inventions of the imagination, the objects of attention, the elements of communication, problems, desires and actions, truth and belief and the emotional memories', Stanislavsky writes, 'form long lines, and the motive forces of inner life pass along them in review, arousing the elements to action and as a result of it becoming themselves even more powerfully infected with creative enthusiasm. Moreover, they absorb from the elements particles of their natural qualities, and grow more active in consequence.'

This merging of all the elements of the actor-part in their general movement towards artistic truth creates the important inner condition which Stanislavsky calls the inner creative state of mind of the actor on the stage, which is both worse and better than the normal state of mind: worse because it contains a bit of the theatre and the stage with its self-exhibiting impulses, and better because it contains the feeling of public solitude which is unknown in normal life.

All the actor's artistic abilities and natural qualities as well as some of the methods of psycho-technique, which Stanislavsky has called 'elements', are, in fact, elements of the inner creative state of the actor on the stage. When an actor comes out on the stage and faces a large audience, he is apt to lose his self-control from stage-fright, or from a sense of responsibility or from a realization of the difficulties of his part. At such a moment the elements of his creative state tend to disintegrate and live apart from each other: attention for the sake of attention, objects for the sake of objects, the feeling of truth for the sake of truth, extraneous aids for the sake of extraneous aids, and so on. This is abnormal; for the elements which create his inner state of mind should, as in life, be inseparable. In fact, owing to the abnormal conditions of stage work, the actor's creative state of mind is intrinsically unstable, and he tends to act just for the sake of 'acting', and to communicate with the spectators rather than with his partners. What the actor must do, therefore, is to see that his creative state of mind on the stage approaches the natural state of mind that he normally experiences in real life. He must do his best to induce such a normal state of mind artificially with the help of inner technique.

All actors make up and dress for their parts before the beginning of a performance, but what most of them forget is that it is no less important to make up and dress their souls for the creation of 'the life of the human spirit' of their parts. How are they to do it? First of all, they must arrive at the theatre in good time, that is at least two hours before the beginning of the performance in the case of a leading part. They must then 'tune their inner strings', check the different elements and 'baits' which help to bring their creative mechanism into action. They ought to start with the relaxation of their muscles, for without that no creative work is possible on the stage. 'And then?' Stanislavsky writes, 'Why, take any object. It is a picture. What does it represent? What is its size? Its colours? Take some remote object. The small circle – not farther than your feet or just up to your chest. Think of a physical problem. Justify it and bring it to life, first with one, then with another, invention of your imagination. Bring your action to the point of truth and belief. Think of the magic "if", the given circumstances, etc. After having brought all the elements into play, choose any element you like to start your work with, and the rest will come as a result of the natural inclination for team-work of the motive forces of inner life and the elements. And the same applies to the actor's creative state of mind.'

These preliminary exercises before the performances are merely a 'check-up' of the actor's expressive apparatus, 'the tuning of his inner creative instrument'. If the actor's part has reached the stage where he can start his work, this preliminary process of self-adjustment will be easy and comparatively quick. If not, it will be more difficult, but not less necessary. At the rehearsals too and during his work at home, the actor must try to achieve the right creative state of mind, which usually suffers most from instability at the very beginning, when he has not yet come to grips with his part, and at the end when his part shows signs of wear and tear. The correct inner creative state of mind is always in a state of disequilibrium and demands constant adjustment, which in the course of time becomes automatic. An actor must always possess sufficient self-control to enable him to carry on with his acting and at the same time correct any inner element that has gone awry.

'An actor', Stanislavsky quotes Salvini again, 'lives, weeps and laughs on the stage, and while weeping or laughing, he observes his laughter and tears. And it is in this dualism, in this equilibrium between life and acting, that art finds its true expression.'

The inner state of mind of the actor depends on the nature of each problem and action. Hence the quality, strength, stability, firmness, depth, duration, sincerity and composition of the inner creative state are infinitely various. If in addition one takes into consideration the fact that in each of these aspects of the creative state a certain element, or one of the motive forces of inner life, or some natural idiosyncrasy of the actor usually predominates, then their diversity seems truly limitless. Occasionally the creative state will be reached accidentally and it will itself look for the theme of inner action. More often, however, it will be some interesting problem, or part, or play that will impel the actor to engage in his creative work and arouse in him the right creative state of mind.

13

If all the elements of the actor's creative state form one unbroken line, then what is the direction in which this line is moving? Or, in other words, what is the whole purpose of the performance? Its purpose, surely, is to provide a scenic embodiment of the playwright's ruling idea. Hence the unbroken lines formed by the elements of the creative states of all the actors taking part in the performance must all be moving in the direction of the play's ruling idea.

It is, therefore, the duty of the actor to grasp the meaning of the ruling idea for the sake of which the author wrote his play. In addition he must make sure that the ruling idea appeals to him – both intellectually and emotionally. For the playwright's intentions will never be fully expressed by the actor if the ruling idea of the play does not strike a chord in the heart of the actor himself. It will be found, as a rule, that the same ruling idea will strike a different chord in the heart of each actor playing the same part; for if each performer does not reveal his individuality in his part, his creation is dead. The actor, in short, must know how to make every ruling idea his own, that is, 'find in it an inner meaning which is akin to his soul'.

The process of finding the ruling idea will be facilitated if the actor defines it by a phrase, for this will impart a meaning and a direction to his work on the play. If the ruling idea enters firmly into the actor's imagination, thoughts, feelings and all the elements of his creative state; if it reminds him constantly of the inner life of his part and of the aim of his work; and if it helps him to keep his sensory attention in the sphere of the life of his part, then the process of entering into the feelings of his character will take its normal course. If, on the other hand, there should be a conflict between the inner aim of the play and the actor's own aims, his part will be a failure, and the whole play may suffer disastrous distortion.

This active inner movement of the motive forces of the inner life of the actor-part through the play forms what Stanislavsky calls the 'through-action' of the actor-part. But for the through-action all the pieces and problems, the given circumstances, communication, extraneous aids, moments of truth and belief, etc., would have remained quiescent, separated from each other, and without hope of coming to life. But the line of through-action welds them together, threading all the elements like beads on one string and directing them towards the ruling idea. If an actor acts his part without taking through-action into account, he is not acting on the stage in the given circumstances and with the magic 'if', nor is he drawing nature herself with her subconsciousness into his work, nor is he creating 'the life of the human spirit' of his part. Indeed, everything in Stanislavsky's 'system' exists for the sake of through-action and the ruling idea. The graph of through-action represents a straight line made up of the different lines of the actor's part, some short and some long, but all moving in one direction, thus:

These short lines of the life of the part are inter-connected and form one long line of through-action, which passes through the whole of the play. But if the actor lacks a ruling idea, each of the lines of the life of his part will be moving in different directions thus:

Under such conditions the through-action is destroyed, the whole play is torn into bits and pieces, moving in different directions, and each part of it has to exist by itself. But however beautiful each of these parts may be when considered separately, it is by itself quite useless so far as the play as a whole is concerned.

The task of defining the ruling idea of a play and so making sure that the through-action follows the course the author had intended for it becomes even more tricky than it is if the producer wishes to introduce some tendentious interpretation into it. Stanislavsky is very outspoken about the dangers of tendentiousness in general. 'Tendentiousness and art', he writes in *My Life in Art*, 'are incompatible: the one excludes the other. As soon as one approaches the art of the stage with tendentious, utilitarian, or any other non-artistic idea, it withers away. It is impossible to accept a sermon or a propaganda piece as true art.' If, therefore, a tendentious idea having nothing to do with the play's ruling idea is introduced into a play, some parts of the play will be torn out of the straight line of the through-action and diverted from the ruling idea, thus:

$$\longrightarrow \searrow \longrightarrow \searrow_{\substack{\longrightarrow \searrow \\ tendency}} \downarrow \longrightarrow ruling\ idea$$

If, on the other hand, the tendentious idea corresponds to the ruling idea, then the creative process will take its normal course, thus:

$$\longrightarrow\!\!-\!\!\longrightarrow\!\!-\!\!\rightarrow\!\!\rightarrow\!\!\rightarrow\!\!-\!\!\rightarrow\!\!\rightarrow\!\!\rightarrow \qquad ruling\ idea \\ tendency$$

This is particularly true if the producer of a classical play tries to graft 'new' ideas on it in order to 'bring it up-to-date'. In such a case the 'new' ideas will ruin the old masterpiece if they are forcibly imposed on the old play for the sake of topical interest; if, however, the modern tendencies, as sometimes happens, agree with the ruling idea of the old play, they will cease to exist independently and merge with the ruling idea.

14

What makes every performance of a play, no matter how many times it may be repeated, always fresh, sincere, truthful, and above all, quite surprisingly different? It is not the actor's technique, nor the producer's ingenuity, nor even the playwright's genius. It is only, Stanislavsky suggests, the actor's subconscious and intuitive creative ability which can infuse a different sort of life into every performance of the same play. The actor who repeats himself is lost; for there is nothing more unendurable than a well-drilled performance in which everything has been thought out beforehand. It is the actor who can invest his 'now' with ever new and ever fascinating properties who is the creative actor *par excellence*.

What, however, must the actor do to evoke the subconscious powers of creative art? First of all, he must get rid of all muscular and inner strains. But even if he achieves a complete relaxation of outer and inner tension, it is only very seldom that he will obtain a complete illusion of reality on the stage. He will mostly find in the imagined life of his part truth alternating with verisimilitude and belief with probability. It is all the more necessary, therefore, that he should make friends with his subconscious mind, so active in real life but so rarely met with on the stage. Without the subconscious work of his inner organic nature, his performance is false as well as rational, lifeless as well as conventional, uninspired as well as formal. The actor must consequently give his creative subconsciousness a free pass to the stage. He must eliminate everything that interferes with it, and strengthen everything that helps to evoke it. It is the basic task of psycho-technique, therefore, so to mould the actor's mind as to awaken in him the subconscious processes of organic nature.

But how is the actor to approach consciously something that is unamenable to consciousness? This serious objection to his 'system' Stanislavsky meets by pointing out that fortunately there is no sharp division between conscious and subconscious experience. Besides, consciousness quite often indicates the direction in which subconsciousness is moving when carrying out its creative work. This fact is very widely used by psycho-technique, that is, by the methods of Stanislavsky's system whose aim it is to stimulate the actor's subconscious creative powers through his conscious inner technique.

The process has already been discussed. The actor must see that the activities of all the elements of his inner creative state as well as the motive forces of his inner life (reason, will, feeling) and through-action become indistinguishable from normal human activities, for it is only then that he will experience the inner life of his organic nature in his part and will find in himself the real truth of the life of the person he is representing on the stage. Since it is impossible not to believe in truth, the 'I am' of the part will be created by itself.

In fact, every time truth and belief are born in the actor involuntarily, organic nature with her subconsciousness will take a hand in his work. It is thus that through the conscious psycho-technique of the actor, carried to its fullest extent, the ground is prepared by nature herself for the creative subconscious process. The important thing is that the actor must carry out the methods of psycho-technique to their fullest extent, for only then can he hope for assistance from his subconsciousness. And he must further realize that it is a mistake to think that every moment of creative work on the stage must needs be something great, complicated and exalted. The opposite is true: the most insignificant action and the most unimportant technical device can become of vital importance if they are carried out to their fullest extent, for it is there that truth, belief, and 'I am' arise. When that happens, the actor's inner and physical mechanism is working normally on the stage, just as in life, in spite of the abnormal conditions of work in front of an audience. What comes about normally in life, is brought about on the stage by psycho-technique.

The actor must therefore never forget that the most insignificant physical and inner action, if driven to the absolute limit of 'I am', is capable of drawing his inner organic nature with its subconsciousness into his work.

As for the psycho-technical methods of bringing it about, Stanislavsky points out that in chemistry when two solutions produce too weak a reaction, a minute quantity of a third acts as a catalytic agent which at once brings the reaction to the required strength. The actor, too, must introduce such a catalytic agent into his work in the form of some impromptu action or some small detail of truth, as soon as he has been successful in achieving the correct inner creative

state, and as soon as he feels that with the aid of psycho-
technique everything in him is only waiting for a push for
nature to start her work. Such catalytic agents must be
sought everywhere – in the performances, the visual images,
feelings, desires, in the small details of the inventions of the
imagination, in an object with which the actor is in communication, in the hardly perceptible details of the stage
setting, or mise-en-scene. There are hundreds of ways in
which the actor can discover some tiny grain of human
truth which will evoke belief and create the condition of 'I
am'. As a result of these few moments of unexpected and
complete fusion between the life of the character in the play
and the life of the actor on the stage, the actor will feel the
presence of bits of himself in his part and bits of his part in
himself, after which truth, belief in it, and 'I am' will deliver
him into the hands of organic nature and her subconsciousness.

Another method of inducing subconsciousness to take
over more and more of the actor's conscious work, is for him
to concentrate on his big problems, which will automatically
leave the small problems to his subconsciousness. The big
problems of his part are, therefore, his best psycho-technical
methods for exerting an indirect influence on his subconscious nature. The same thing happens to the big problems
the moment the actor's mind is beginning to be preoccupied with the ruling idea of the play. They too are then
to a large extent carried out subconsciously. Since, moreover, through-action consists of a long line of big problems,
each of which contains an enormous number of small
problems which are carried out subconsciously, the total
number of moments of subconscious creative work concealed
in the through-action, pervading the whole play from beginning to end, will also be enormous. Through-action is
consequently the most powerful method for influencing
subconsciousness the actor can possibly find.

Through-action, however, does not arise by itself. Its
creative impetus is directly dependent on the interest which
the ruling idea can arouse. Hence, through-action and the

ruling idea, which also contain many properties capable of giving rise to subconscious creative moments, are the most powerful 'baits' for stimulating the subconscious creative work or organic nature. It must therefore be the chief aim of every actor to be fully aware of all their manifold implications, for then he can safely leave the rest to be carried out subconsciously by 'the supreme magician – nature'.

Since conscious psycho-technique helps to create the methods and the favourable conditions for the creative work of nature, the actor ought always to think of the things which stimulate the action of the motive forces of his inner life and which help him to achieve his inner creative state. He must also always keep in mind the ruling idea and through-action, and indeed everything that is accessible to his consciousness, with whose help he must learn to prepare the ground for the subconscious work of his artistic nature. What he ought never to do is to try to achieve inspiration in a direct way, just for the sake of inspiration. Stanislavsky's 'system' does not manufacture inspiration; it merely prepares the ground for its manifestation in a natural way. That does not mean, however, that Stanislavsky is against the actor's making use of 'happy accidents', that is to say, accidents which, though unforeseen by the producer or actor, give a touch of truth to a certain scene. On the contrary, Stanislavsky strongly advises the actor to use such accidents as a 'tuning fork' which will give him the right note of life among the conventional lies of the stage and make everybody feel and believe in 'I am'. It may, accidentally, also help the actor to find a subconscious approach to his part. Coincidences and accidents on the stage, however, must be used wisely: the actor must never overlook them, but he must not rely on them either.

The fundamental principle of Stanislavsky's theory of acting is, as we see, that the actor's work is not a technical conjuring trick or a game of 'let's pretend'; it is, on the contrary, in every way a natural process, a natural creative act, resembling, Stanislavsky suggests, the birth of a human being, in this particular case, the man-part.

The analysis of this process, Stanislavsky observes, convinces him that organic nature always acts according to certain well-established laws whenever it is creating something new in the world, whether it is something biological or something created by the imagination of man. In short, the creation of a living human being on the stage (or a part) is a natural act of the organic creative nature of the actor.

Emotional Memory[*]

ERIC BENTLEY

IN an essay entitled 'Emotional Memory' (Tulane Drama Review, Summer 1962) the American stage director Robert Lewis traces the phrase 'emotional memory' back as far as 1925 and adds:

> During the Group Theatre days in the Thirties, we called it 'Affective Memory' (a term borrowed from an earlier French psychologist). But, by whatever name, it is accomplished roughly as follows.

The name is actually given in David Magarshack's *Stanislavsky: a Life* in these words:

> Stanislavsky was struck by the fact that in his most successful part of Dr Stockmann he had unconsciously endowed it with a number of external traits which he had observed in life and kept buried in his memory till the moment came for them to be combined in the delineation of a character with whom he felt a strong affinity. He at once realized the importance of these hidden memories, which he embodied in his system first under the name of 'affective memories' (he had presumably been reading Th. Ribot's *Problèmes de psychologie affective*) and later under the name of 'emotional memories'.

If Mr Magarshack means to suggest that Stanislavsky necessarily took the phrase Affective Memory from one particular book of Ribot's, that would be a mistake, but one which the English-speaking reader might have difficulty in tracking down, for this is how the only published translation of the key passage reads. It is to be found on pages 156–67 of *An Actor Prepares* (Theatre Arts Books, 16th printing, 1958):

*Copyright © 1962 by Tulane Drama Review. Published by permission of Eric Bentley. The original title was: 'Who was Ribot? or: Did Stanislavsky Know Any Psychology?'

... 'As for *emotion memory*: there was no sign of it today.' When he was asked to explain that term he said: 'I can best illustrate it as did Ribot, who was the first person to define this type of memories, by telling you a story...'

However, some of us who may not be up to reading all of Stanislavsky in Russian have read quite a lot of him in the admirably complete German translations. I will translate literally this same passage from the German edition (*Das Geheimnis des Schauspielerischen Erfolges*: Scientia, Zurich, n.d.):

...As for the memory of feelings, there was no sign of it today.' 'The memory of feelings?' I tried to make this clear to myself. 'Yes, or, as we wish to call it, the 'emotional memory'. Earlier – following Ribot – we called it the 'affective memory'. This term is now rejected without having been replaced. But we have *some* word for it and so, provisionally, we're agreeing to call it the memory of feelings: Emotional Memory.' The pupils asked him to explain more clearly what was understood by this word. 'You will best understand it from the example which Ribot gave....

In short, there is no mystery at all as to where the term comes from. Mystery is created only when a translator decides to leave out so much that is of interest or when a teacher decides to relegate a distinguished scientist to the status of an unnamed 'earlier French psychologist'. Even Mr Magarshack, himself a scrupulous translator of Stanislavsky, is not, evidently, so close a student of psychology or he would know that it need not have been the *Problèmes* that Stanislavsky was reading, as Ribot mentions Affective Memory in other places, some of them better known. Nor must the American reader study French to become acquainted with Ribot, several of whose books were published in English.

All this, however, does not mean that we can trace Stanislavsky's teaching on emotional memory back to the scientific psychologists. Even on the terminology Stanislavsky seems misinformed. It is not true that Ribot spoke exclusively of Affective Memory, and that only later writers spoke of Emotional Memory; nor is it true that, for Ribot, Affective Memory was an earlier term, Emotional Memory a later one. We find him using the former expression in the late work (1910) which Mr Magarshack cites, whereas the phrase Emotional Memory is found more than once in such an earlier work as *The Psychology of the Emotions*. I cite the latter title in English because it was published in that language (1897) in quite a popular series, 'The Contemporary Science Series', as edited by Havelock Ellis. The fact is that both terms were common currency among psychologists of the time.

So much for terminology. The ideas are quite another matter. Whether there was really such a thing as Affective or Emotional Memory was NOT agreed upon by the psychologists. Ribot himself, though inclined to accept the notion, records the doubts of his colleagues, and surrounds his own assent with such stern provisos as: 'The emotional memory is nil in the majority of people'. Even this debate was not quite in Stanislavsky's field for it concerned whether people spontaneously do have emotional (as against intellectual) memories, not whether emotional memories can be induced by exercises. Ribot's answer is that *some* people have them. And he cites a contemporary man of letters as saying that women have them and are therefore monogamous, while men don't have them and are polygamous. Hence, when Mr Robert Lewis speaks of Emotional Memory as something that is 'accomplished' he is not talking about what Ribot was talking about. And when he implies that, though the *name* may vary, the *process* is the same which both the psychologists and the theatre people have been referring to, he is exactly inverting the truth. For what has happened is that theatre people have been invoking scientific terminology *for the sake of its authoritative sound* on the assumption that anything with a scientific name must have a scientific basis. Once we see through this fallacy, we realize that 'exercises' given to actors may not actually do the work they are supposed to do. But this is not to say that they have no value. By way of analogy, take prayer. There may not be a God sitting Up There listening to it, but that is not to say the person praying feels no better for it. Some of the older actors did pray before going out on stage: and prayer was probably a better preparation than dressing-room chatter, let alone alcohol or drugs. Likewise exercises in Emotional Memory. They are the prayers of the age of science. As such it is doubtful if they could be improved by the study of science itself. I do not recommend Ribot to actors. Rather, perhaps, Ignatius Loyola's *Spiritual Exercises*, a book which embodies the science of the age of prayer. Ribot, for that matter, does refer to St Ignatius's great work, and years ago Mr Francis Fergusson introduced the topic into the discussion of the Stanislavsky system. When the news reaches the Moscow Art Theatre, Russia will perhaps get reconverted to Christianity.

Richard Wagner

RICHARD WAGNER, 1813–83, was thought by many to have discovered The Music of the Future, and not a few, like Appia, thought he had at the same stroke discovered The Theatre of the Future too. And he not only wrote his own libretti. He theorized on an equally grand scale. His prose works seemed to Bernard Shaw, and many of his generation, very impressive even in English translation. Today it is hard to see how this could ever have been so. Yet Wagner's importance, even the importance of some of his ideas, is undeniable. The 'prose works' cannot just be passed by. One solution is to condense them, as was done by two American scholars (*Wagner on Music and Drama*, edited by Albert Goldman and Evert Sprinchorn)*. Even so there are few outstanding pages, nor is there any competent summary of Wagner's scheme of things. The best such summary, and it is more readable than Wagner himself, still seems to be the essay reprinted here. It appeared first in *The Quarterly Review*, July 1905, and then was reprinted in Symons's book *Studies in the Seven Arts* (Dutton, New York, 1907).

* New York, E. P. Dutton, 1964.

POSTSCRIPT, 1992
The eight-volume edition of Wagner's Prose Works remains out of print on both sides of the Atlantic but in 1973 Peter Owen, London, issued a 187-page selection: *Richard Wagner, Stories and Essays*, selected, edited and introduced by Charles Osborne. Valuable, too, is *Selected Letters of Richard Wagner*, translated and edited by Stewart Spencer and Barry Millington, J. M. Dent & Sons Ltd, London and Melbourne, 1987.

P.P.S., 2007
The eight-volume edition of *Wagner's Prose Works* is now in print with the University of Nebraska Press.

The Ideas of Richard Wagner

ARTHUR SYMONS

I

ONE of the good actions of Baudelaire, whose equity of conscience in matters of art was flawless, may be seen in a pamphlet published in 1861, with the title 'Richard Wagner et Tannhäuser à Paris'. In this pamphlet Baudelaire has said the first and the last word on many of the problems of Wagner's work; and perhaps most decisively on that problem of artist and critic which has so often disturbed the judgement of reasoners in the abstract. Can the same man, people have said, of Wagner as of others, be a creator and also a thinker, an instinctive artist and a maker of theories? This is Baudelaire's answer, and it is sufficient: 'It would be a wholly new event in the history of the arts if a critic were to turn himself into a poet, a reversal of every pyschic law, a monstrosity; on the other hand, all great poets become naturally, inevitably, critics. I pity the poets who are guided solely by instinct; they seem to me incomplete. In the spiritual life of the former there must come a crisis when they would think out their art, discover the obscure laws in consequence of which they have produced, and draw from this study a series of precepts whose divine purpose is infallibility in poetic production. It would be prodigious for a critic to become a poet, and it is impossible for a poet not to contain a critic.'

The chief distinction and main value of Wagner's theoretical writing lies in this fact, that it is wholly the personal expression of an artist engaged in creative work, finding out theories by the way, as he comes upon obstacles or aids in the nature of things. It may be contended that only this kind of criticism, the criticism of a creative artist, is of any real value; and Wagner's is for the most part more than criticism, or the judging of existent work; it is a building up of scaffolding for the erection of work to come. In 'A Communication to my Friends' (1851), which is an auto-biography of ideas, he has taken great pains to trace the unconscious, inevitable evolution of his work and of his ideas. He not only tells us, he proves to us, step by step, that none of his innovations was 'prompted by reflection, but solely by practical experience, and the nature of his artistic aim'. In this philosophical autobiography we see the growth of a great artist, more clearly perhaps than we see it in any similar document; certainly in more precise detail. Wagner's progress as an artist was vital, for it was the pro-gress of life.

He looked upon genius as an immense receptivity, a receptivity so immense that it filled and overflowed the being, thus forcing upon it the need to create. And he dis-tinguished between the two kinds of artists, feminine and masculine; the feminine who absorbs only art, and the masculine who absorbs life itself, and from life derives the new material which he will turn into a new and living art. He shows us, in his own work, the gradual way in which imitation passed into production, the unconscious moulding of the stuff of his art from within, as one need after another arose; the way in which every innovation in form came from a single cause: the necessity 'to convey to others as vividly and intelligibly as possible what his own mind's eye had seen.' He learns sometimes from a failure, his failure to achieve a plan wrongly attempted; sometimes from a dis-appointment, the disappointment of seeing work after work fail, and then that more hopeless one of being applauded for something other than he wanted to do, with 'the good-humoured sympathy shown to a lunatic by his friends'. Sometimes it is from a woman he learns, from an artist-woman like Schröder-Devrient, of whom he says: 'The remotest contact with this extraordinary woman electrified me; for many a long year, down even to the present day, I saw, I heard, I felt her near me, whenever the impulse to artistic production seized me.' He learns from the Revolution of 1848, from the whistles of the Jockey Club at the first night of 'Tannhäuser' in Paris, from a desperate realization of what opera is, of what the theatre is, of what the public is. Nothing ever happens to him in vain; nothing that touches him goes by without his seizing it; he seizes nothing from which he does not wring out its secret, its secret for him. Thus alike his work and all his practical energies grow out of the very soil and substance of his life; thus they are vital, and promise continuance of vitality, as few other works and deeds of art in our time can be said to do.

Nor must it be forgotten that we owe, if not the whole, at all events the main part, of Wagner's theoretical writing to the impossibility of putting his work before the public under the conditions which he judged indispensable to its proper realization. Writing in 1857 on Liszt's Symphonic Poems, he declares proudly, 'I will hold by my experience that whoever waits for recognition by his foes, before he can make up his mind about himself, must have indeed his share of patience, but little ground for self-reliance.' And in the admirable 'Communication to my Friends', he tells those friends why he addresses them and not the general, indifferent public; and why 'my friends must see the whole of me in order to decide whether they can be wholly my friends.' He confesses how 'tragical' it is that, under modern conditions, the artist must address himself to the understanding rather than to the feeling; and this alike in his work and in his attempt to explain that work to the world which refuses to let him achieve it. So early as 1857 he decides, solemnly, publicly, that he will write no more theory; twenty-five years before the time he announces his plans, absolutely completed, and declares, 'Only with my work shall you see me again!'

To read the pages which come after (by far the larger half of the prose works) is to follow step by step what seems a life's tragedy; only that it is to end, one knows, as a divine comedy. A few ideas, a few needs, growing more and more precise, adjusted more and more definitely within their own limits, we find repeated and reiterated, without haste and without rest, through book, article, letter, speech. All this gathered energy presses forward in one direction, and from all points, with an attack as of the Japanese on Port Arthur, unweariable, self-forgetful, scientific. It is only in the last few years of his life that we get theory for theory's sake, in by no means the most valuable part of his work: discussions of religion (partly against Nietzsche), of civilization (partly on behalf of Gobineau), dreams that had always been his, prophesyings, doctrine; a kind of 'Latter-day Pamphlets', or that dogma into which the last words of a great artist so often harden.

2

Wagner's fundamental ideas, with the precise and detailed statement and explanation of his conception of art, and of that work of art which it was his unceasing endeavour to create, or rather to organize, are contained in two of the earliest of his prose writings, 'The Art-work of the Future' (1849) and 'Opera and Drama' (1851). Everything else in his theoretical writing is a confirmation, or a correction, or (very rarely) a contradiction, of what is to be found in these two books; and their thorough understanding is so essential to any realization of why Wagner did what he did, that I shall attempt to give as complete a summary as possible of the main ideas contained in them, as much as possible in his own words.

Here and elsewhere all my quotations will be taken from the monumental translation of Wagner's prose works by Mr William Ashton Ellis, a heroic undertaking, achieved nobly. The translation of Wagner (and especially of these two books) is a task of extraordinary difficulty, and can never quite seem to have been wholly concluded. Wagner's prose, his earlier prose particularly, is clouded by the smoke of German metaphysics and contorted by the ruthless con-scientiousness of the German temperament. He will leave nothing unsaid, even if there is no possible way of saying clearly what he wants to say. And he does somehow say things that have never been said before, or never from so near the roots. Often he says them picturesquely, always truthfully, energetically, and, above all, logically; rarely with much ease or charm. He is terribly in earnest, and words are things to be used for their precise and honest uses. He takes them captive, thrusts them together from the ends of the earth, and lets the chains clank between them. It is therefore not to be expected that even Mr Ellis, with his knowledge, skill and patience, should have been able to make Wagner always what is called readable: and in his admirable fidelity to the sense and words of the original, there are times (especially in those difficult early volumes) when what we read may indeed be strictly related to the German text, but can hardly be said to be strictly English. With a courtesy for which one has little precedent, he has permitted me on occasion to modify a word here and there in my quotations. The permission was unconditional: my use of it has been infrequent, but, I think, requires explanation.

In 'The Art-work of the Future' Wagner defines art as 'an immediate vital act', the expression of man, as man is the expression of nature. 'The first and truest fount of Art reveals itself in the impulse that urges from Life into the work of art; for it is the impulse to bring the unconscious, instinctive principle of Life to understanding, and acknowledgment as Necessity.' 'Art is an inbred craving of the natural, genuine, and uncorrupted man,' not an artificial product, and not a product of mind only, which produces science, but of that deeper impulse which is unconscious. From this unconscious impulse, this need, come all great creations, all great inventions; conscious intellect does but exploit and splinter those direct impulses which come straight from the people. The people alone can feel 'a common and collective want'; without this want there can be no need; without need no necessary action; where there is no necessary action, caprice enters, and caprice is the mother of all unnaturalness. Out of caprice, or an imagined need, come luxury, fashion and the whole art-traffic of our shameless age. 'Only from Life, from which alone can even the need for her grow up, can Art obtain her matter and her form; but where Life is modelled upon fashion, Art can never fashion anything from Life.'

In his consideration of art Wagner sets down two broad divisions: art as derived directly from man, and art as shaped by man from the stuff of nature. In the first division he sets dance (or motion), tone and poetry, in which man is himself the subject and agent of his own artistic treatment; in the second, architecture, sculpture and painting, in which man 'extends the longing for artistic portrayal to the objects of surrounding, allied, ministering Nature.'

The ground of all human art is bodily motion. Into bodily motion comes rhythm, which is 'the mind of dance and the skeleton of tone'. Tone is 'the heart of man, through which dance and poetry are brought to mutual understanding'. This organic being is 'clothed upon with the flesh of the world'. Thus, in the purely human arts, we rise from bodily motion to poetry, to which man adds himself as singer and actor; and we have at once the lyric art-work out of which comes the perfected form of lyric drama. This, as he conceives it, is to arise when 'the pride of all three arts in their own self-sufficiency shall break to pieces and pass over into love for one another.' Attempts, it is true, have been made to combine them, conspicuously in opera; but the failure of opera comes from 'a compact of three egoisms', without mutual giving as well as taking.

The limits of dance are evident; mere motion can go no further than pantomime and ballet. What then are the limits of tone? Harmony is the unbounded sea; rhythm and melody, in which dance and poetry regain their own true essence, are the limiting shores to this unbounded sea. Yet, within the confines of these shores, the sea is for ever tossing, for ever falling back upon itself. Christianity first set bounds to it with words, 'the toneless, fluid, scattering word of the Christian creed.' When the limits of this narrow world were broken, and the sea again let loose, an arbitrary measure was set upon it from without, counterpoint, 'the mathematics of feeling', the claim of tone to be an end in itself, unrelated to nature, a matter of the intellect instead of a voice of the heart. Life, however, was never extinct, for there arose the folk-tune, with its twin-born folk-song; which, however, was seized upon by the makers of music and turned into the 'aria': 'not the beating heart of the nightingale, but only its warbling throat.' Then, out of that unending source, bodily motion, expressed in the rhythm of the dance, came the final achievement of instrumental music, the symphony, which is made on the basis of the harmonized dance. Beethoven carries instrumental music to the verge of speech, and there pauses; then, in the Ninth Symphony, in which he calls in the word, 'redeems music out of her own peculiar element into the realm of universal art'. Beyond what Beethoven has there done with music, 'no further step is possible, for upon it the perfect art-work of the future alone can follow, the universal drama to which he has forged for us the key.'

But poetry, has that also its limits? Literary poetry still exists, even the literary drama, written, as Goethe wrote it, from outside, as by one playing on a lifeless instrument; even 'the unheard-of, drama written for dumb reading!' But poetry was once a living thing, a thing spoken and sung; it arose from the midst of the people, and was kept alive by them, alike as epic, lyric and drama. 'Tragedy flourished for just so long as it was inspired by the spirit of the people,' and, at its greatest moment, among the Greeks, 'the poetic purpose rose singly to life upon the shoulders of the arts of dance and tone, as the head of the full-fledged human being.' Where we see tragedy supreme in Shakespeare and music supreme in Beethoven we see two great halves of one universal whole. It remains for the art of the future to combine these two halves in one; and, in the process of joining, all the other arts, those arts not derived directly from man but shaped by man from the stuff of nature, will find their place, as they help towards the one result.

The sections which follow, dealing with architecture, sculpture and painting, form a special pleading to which it is hardly necessary to give much attention. Each art may indeed legitimately enough be utilized in the production and performance of such an art-work as Wagner indicates, and as he actually produced and performed; architecture building the theatre, sculpture teaching man his own bodily beauty, and the beauty and significance of his grouping and movement on the stage, and painting creating a landscape which shall seem to set this human figure in the midst of nature itself. In going further than this, in asserting that sculpture is to give place to the human body, and painting to limit itself to the imitation of nature as a background of stage-scenery for the actor, we see the German.* We see also the propagandist, who has a doctrine to prove; perhaps the enthusiast, who has convinced himself of what he desires to believe. In his conclusion of the whole matter he goes one step further, and identifies the poet and the performer; then finds in the performer 'the fellowship of all the artists', and, in that fellowship, the community of the people, who, having felt the want, have found out the way. 'The perfectly artistic performer is therefore the unit man extended to the essence of the human species by the utmost evolution of his own particular nature. The place in which this wondrous process comes to pass is the theatric stage; the collective art-work which it brings to the light of day, the Drama.'

In a letter to Berlioz, written in 1860, Wagner reminds his critic, who has chosen to fasten upon him the title, 'Music of the Future' (the hostile invention of a Professor Bischof of Cologne), that the essay was written at a time when 'a violent crisis in his life' (the Revolution of 1848, and his exile from Germany) had for a time withdrawn him

* A more temperate, indeed a wholly just view of the relations of the plastic arts, is to be found in the 'Letter to Liszt on the proposed Goethe Institute,' written in 1851 ('Prose Works,' iii. 19–20), where Wagner points out the necessity of the due and helpful subordination of painting and sculpture to architecture in any complete and living organism of plastic art.

from the practice of his art. 'I asked myself,' he says, 'what position Art should occupy towards the public, so as to inspire it with a reverence that should never be profaned; and, not to be merely building castles in the air, I took my stand on the position which art once occupied towards the public life of the Greeks.' In the thirty thousand Greeks assembled to listen to a tragedy of Æschylus he found the one ideal public; and, in the whole situation, a suggestion towards an art which should be no pedantic revival of that, but a similar union of the arts, in the proportions demanded by their present condition and by the present condition of the world. For, as no one has realized more clearly, there is no absolute art-work; but each age must have its own art-work, as that of the preceding age ceases to be living and becomes monumental. 'The Shakespeare who can alone be of value to us is the ever new creative poet who, now and in all ages, is to that age what Shakespeare was to his own age.'

'Opera and Drama,' which closely followed 'The Art-work of the Future,' was written at Zürich in four months; it fills 376 large pages in Mr Ellis's translation. In a letter to Uhlig, written 20 January 1851, Wagner says, 'The first part is the shortest and easiest, perhaps also the most entertaining; the second goes deeper, and the third goes right to the bottom.' In the dedication to the second edition, written in 1868, he says, 'My desire to get to the bottom of the matter and to shirk no detail that, in my opinion, might make the difficult subject of æsthetic analysis intelligible to simple feeling betrayed me into a stubbornness of style which to the reader who looks merely for entertainment, and is not directly interested in the subject itself, is extremely likely to seem a bewildering diffuseness.' And the translator confesses that no other of Wagner's prose works has given him half so much difficulty as the third and portions of the second part of 'Opera and Drama'; for in them, as he says, 'we are presented with a theory absolutely in the making.'

'Opera and Drama' is an attempt to state, in minute particulars, what 'The Art-work of the Future' stated in general terms. It is based upon a demonstration of the fundamental error in the construction of opera: 'that a means of expression (music) has been made the end, while the end of expression (drama) has been made a means.' How fatal have been the results of this fundamental error can be realized only when it is seen how many of the greater musicians have thus spent their best energies in exploring a labyrinth which does but lead back, through many vain wanderings, to the starting-point.

The musical basis of opera was the *aria*, i.e. 'the folk-song as rendered by the art-singer before the world of rank and quality, but with its word-poem left out and replaced by the product of the art-poet to that end composed.' The performer was rightly the basis of the performance, but a basis set awry; for the performer was chosen only for his dexterity in song, not for his skill as an actor. Dance and dance-tune, 'borrowed just as waywardly from the folk-dance and its tune as was the operatic *aria* from the folk-song, joined forces with the singer in all the sterile immisci-bility of unnatural things'. Between these alien elements a shifting plank-bridge was thrown across, recitative, which is no more than the intoning of the Church, fixed by ritual into 'an arid resemblance to, without the reality of, speech', and varied a little by musical caprice for the convenience of opera.

This unsound structure was untouched by the theory and practice of Gluck, whose 'revolution' was no more than a revolt on the part of the composer against the domination of the singer. The singer was made to render more faithfully the music which the composer set before him; but the poet 'still looked up to the composer with the deepest awe', and no nearer approach was made to drama. In Spontini we see the logical filling out of the fixed forms of opera to their fullest extent. Along these lines nothing further can be done; it is for the poet to step into the place usurped by the musician. The poet did nothing, but still continued to work to order, not once daring to pursue a real dramatic aim. He contented himself with stereotyped phrases, the make-believe of rhetoric, straitened to the measure of the musician's fixed forms, knowing that to make his characters speak 'in brief and definite terms, surcharged with meaning,' would have caused his instant dismissal. Thus music, which in the nature of things can only be expression, is seen endeavouring to fill the place of that which is to be expressed, to be itself its own object. 'Such a music is no longer any music, but a fantastic hybrid emanation from poetry and music, which, in truth, can only materialize itself as caricature.'

Mozart's importance in the history of opera is this, that, taking the forms as he found them, he filled them with living music, setting whatever words were given him, and giving those words 'the utmost musical expression of which their last particle of sense was capable.' Had Mozart met a poet who could have given him the foundation for his musical interpretation, he would have solved the problem for himself, unconsciously, by mere sincerity to his genius for musical expression.

After Mozart, in whom form was nothing and the musical spirit everything, came imitators who fancied they were imitating Mozart when they copied his form. It was Rossini who showed how hollow that form really was, and he did so by reducing *aria*, the essence of opera, to its own real essence, melody. In the folk-song words and tune had always grown together; in the opera there had been always some pretence of characterization. Rossini abandoned everything but just 'naked, ear-delighting, absolute, melodic melody,' a delicious meaningless sound. 'What reflection and æsthetic speculation had built up, Rossini's opera melodies pulled down and blew into nothing, like a baseless dream.' Rossini gave every one what he wanted. He gave the singer what he wanted, display; and the player what he wanted, again display; and the poet a long rest, and leave to rhyme as he chose. Above all he gave the public what it wanted: not the people, but that public which need only be named to be realized, the modern opera public. 'With Rossini the real life-history of the opera comes to an end.

It was at an end when the unconscious seedling of its being had evolved to naked and conscious bloom.'

The one genuine, yet futile attempt to produce living opera was the attempt of Weber, who saw in opera only melody, and who went to the true source, to the folk-song, for his melody. But he saw only the flower of the woods, and plucked it, taking it where it could but fade and die, because it had lost the sustenance of its root. On his heels came Auber, and then Rossini himself, who pilfered national melodies and stuck them together like a dressmaker giving variety to an old dress. The chorus came forward, and played at being the people; and there was 'a motley, con-glomerate surrounding, without a centre to surround'. Music tried to be outlandish, to express nothing, but in a more uncommon way. Opera became French, and, partly through a misunderstanding of Beethoven, neo-romantic.

Until Beethoven had done what he did, no one could have been quite certain 'that the expression of an altogether definite, a clearly intelligible individual content, was in truth impossible in this language that had only fitted itself for conveying the general character of an emotion': the language, that is, of absolute music. Beethoven attempts 'to reach the artistically necessary within an inartistically impossible'; he chooses, in music, a form which 'often seems the mere capricious venting of a whim, and which, loosed from any purely musical cohesion, is only bound together by the bond of a poetic purpose impossible to render into music with full poetic plainness.' Thus, much of his later work seems to be so many sketches for a picture which he could never make visible in all its outlines.

What in Beethoven was a 'struggle for the discovery of a new basis of musical language' has been seized upon by later composers only in its external contrasts, excesses, in-articulate voices of joy and despair, and made the basis of a wholly artificial construction, in which 'a programme reciting the heads of some subject taken from nature or human life was put into the hearer's hands; and it was left to his imaginative talent to interpret, in keeping with the hint once given, all the musical freaks that one's unchecked licence might now let loose in motley chaos.' Berlioz seized upon what was most chaotic in the sketchwork of Beethoven, and, using it as a misunderstood magic symbol, called unnatural visions about him.

What he had to say to people was so wonderful, so unwonted, so entirely unnatural, that he could never have said it out in homely, simple words; he needed a huge array of the most complicated machines in order to proclaim, by the help of many-wheeled and delicately-adjusted mechanism, what a simple human organism could not possibly have uttered, just because it was so entirely unhuman. ... Each height and depth of this mechanism's capacity has Berlioz explored, with the result of developing a positively astounding knowledge; and, if we mean to recognize the inventors of our present industrial machinery as the benefactors of modern State-humanity, then we must worship Berlioz as the veritable saviour of our world of absolute music; for he has made it possible to musicians to produce the most wonderful effect from the emptiest and most inartistic content of their music-making, by an unheard-of marshalling of mere mechanical means.

In Berlioz, Wagner admits, 'there dwelt a genuine artistic stress,' but Berlioz was but a 'tragic sacrifice'. His orchestra was annexed by the opera-composer; and its 'splintered and atomic melodies' were now lifted from the orchestra into the voice itself. The result was Meyerbeer, who, when Wagner wrote, could be alluded to, without need of naming, as the most famous opera-composer of modern times.

Weber, in 'Euryanthe', had endeavoured in vain to make a coherent dramatic structure out of two contradictory elements, 'absolute, self-sufficing melody and unflinchingly true dramatic expression'. Meyerbeer attempted the same thing from the standpoint of effect, and with the aid of the Rossini melody. Thus, while

Weber wanted a drama that could pass with all its members, with every scenic *nuance*, into his noble soulful melody, Meyerbeer, on the contrary, wanted a monstrous piebald, historico-romantic, diabolico-religious, fanatico-libidinous, sacro-frivolous, mysteriocriminal, autolyco-sentimental, dramatic hotch-potch, therein to find material for a curious chimeric music – a want which, owing to the indomitable buckram of his musical temperament, could never be quite suitably supplied.

In his summing-up of the whole discussion on opera and the nature of music, Wagner tells us that the secret of the barrenness of modern music lies in this, that music is a woman who gives birth but does not beget. 'Just as the living folk-melody is inseparable from the living folk-poem, at pain of organic death, so can music's organism never bear the true, the living melody, except it first be fecundated by the poet's thought. Music is the bearing woman, the poet the begetter; and music had therefore reached the pinnacle of madness when she wanted not only to bear, but to beget.' He now turns, therefore, to the poet.

The second part of 'Opera and Drama' is concerned with 'The Play, and the Nature of Dramatic Poetry'. Wagner first clears the way for his theory by pointing out that when Lessing, in his 'Laocoon', mapped out the boundaries of the arts, he was concerned, in poetry, only with that art as a thing to be read, even when he touches on drama; and that, figuring it as addressed wholly to the imagination, not to the sight and hearing, he was rightly anxious only to preserve its purity; that is, to make it as easy as possible for the imagination to grasp it. But, just as the piano is an abstract and toneless reduction backward through the organ, the stringed instrument, and the wind instrument, from the 'oldest, truest, most beautiful organ of music', the human voice, so, if we trace back the literary drama, or indeed any form of poetry, we shall find its origin in the tone of human speech, which is one and the same with the singing tone.

Modern drama has a twofold origin: through Shakespeare from the romance, and through Racine from misunderstood Greek tragedy. At the time of the Renaissance poetry was found in the narrative poem, which had culminated in the fantastic romance of Ariosto. To this fantastic romance Shakespeare gave inner meaning and outward show; he took the inconsequential and unlimited stage of the mummers and mystery-players, narrowed his action to the limits of the spectator's attention, but, through the conditions of that stage, left the representation of the scene to the mind's eye, and thus left open a door to all that was vague and unlimited in romance and history. In France and Italy the drama, played, not before the people, but in princes' palaces, was copied externally from ancient drama. A fixed scene was taken as its first requirement, and thus an endeavour was made to construct from without inwards, 'from mechanism to life': talk on the scene, action behind the scene. Drama passed over into opera, which was thus 'the premature bloom on an unripe fruit, grown from an unnatural, artificial soil'.

It was in Germany, in whose soil the drama has never taken root, that a mongrel thing, which is still rampant on the European stage, came into being. When Shakespeare was brought over to Germany, where the opera was already in possession of the stage, an attempt was made to actualize his scenes, upon which it was discovered that dramatized history or romance was only possible so long as the scene need only be suggested. In the attempt to actualize Shakespeare's mental pictures, all the resources of mechanism were employed in vain; and the plays themselves were cut and altered in order to bring them within the range of a possible realistic representation. It was seen that the drama of Shakespeare could only be realized under its primitive conditions, with the scene left wholly to the imagination. Embodied, it became, so far as embodiment was possible, 'an unsurveyable mass of realisms and actualisms'.

It therefore remained evident that the nature of romance can never wholly correspond with the nature of drama; that, as an art in which drama was at once its inner essence and its embodied representation, the drama of Shakespeare remained, as a form, imperfect. The result of this consciousness was that the poet either wrote literary dramas for reading, or attempted an artificial reconstruction of the antique. Such was the drama of Goethe and Schiller. Goethe, after repeated attempts, produces his only organic work in 'Faust', which is dramatic only in form, and in 'Wilhelm Meister', which returns frankly to romance. Schiller 'hovers between heaven and earth' in an attempt to turn history into romance and romance into classical drama. Both, and all that resulted from both, prove 'that our literary drama is every whit as far removed from the genuine drama as the pianoforte from the symphonic song of human voices; that in the modern drama we can arrive at the production of poetry only by the most elaborate devices of literary mechanism, just as on the pianoforte we only arrive at the production of music through the most complicated devices of technical mechanism – in either case, a soulless poetry, a toneless music.'

The stuff of the modern drama, then, being romance, what is the difference between this romance and the myth which was the stuff of ancient Greek drama? Myth Wagner defines as 'the poem of a life-view in common', the instinctive creation of the imagination of primitive man working upon his astonished and uncomprehending view of natural phenomena. 'This incomparable thing about the *mythos* is that it is true for all time, and its content, how close soever its compression, is inexhaustible throughout the ages.' The poet's business was merely to expound the myth by expressing it in action, an action which should be condensed and unified from it, as it, in its turn, had been a condensation and unification of the primitive view of nature.

The romance of the Middle Ages is derived from the mingling of two mythic cycles, the Christian legend and the Germanic saga. Christian legend can only present pictures, or, transfigured by music, render moments of ecstasy, which must remain 'blends of colour without drawing'. The essence of drama is living action, in its progress towards a clearly defined end; whereas Christianity being a passage through life to the transfiguration of death, 'must perforce begin with the storm of life, to weaken down its movement to the final swoon of dying out'. The Germanic saga begins with a myth older than Christianity, then, when Christianity has seized upon it, becomes 'a swarm of actions whose true idea appears to us unfathomable and capricious, because their motives, resting on a view of life quite alien to the Christian's, had been lost to the poet'. Foreign stuffs are patched upon it; and it becomes wholly unreal and outlandish, a medley of adventures, from whose imaginary pictures, however, men turned to track them in reality, by voyages of discovery, and by the scientific discoveries of the intellect. Nature, meanwhile, unchanged, awaits a new interpretation.

The first step in this interpretation is to seize and represent actual things as they are, individually. History comes forward with a more bewildering mass of material than fancy had ever found for itself; and from this tangle of conditions and surroundings the essence of the man is to be unravelled. This can be done by the romance writer, not by the dramatist. The drama, which is organic, presupposes all those surroundings which it is the business of the romance writer to develop before us. The romance writer works from without inwards, the dramatist from within outwards. And now, going one step further, and turning to actual life as it exists before our eyes, the poet can no longer 'extemporize artistic fancies'; he can only render the whole horror of what lies naked before him; 'he needs only to feel pity, and at once his passion becomes a vital force.' Actual things draw him out of the contemplation of actual things; the poem turns to journalism, the stuff of poetry becomes politics.

It was Napoleon who said to Goethe that, in the modern world, politics play the part of fate in the ancient world.

The Greek Fate is the inner nature-necessity, from which the Greek – because he did not understand it – sought refuge in the arbitrary political state. Our Fate is the arbitrary political state, which to us shows itself as an outer necessity for the maintenance of society; and from this we seek refuge in the nature-necessity, because we have learnt to understand the latter, and have recognized it as the conditionment of our being and all its shapings.

In the myth of Oedipus is seen a prophetic picture of the 'whole history of mankind, from the beginnings of society to the inevitable downfall of the state'. The modern state is a necessity of an artificial and inorganic kind; it is not, as society (arising from the family, and working through love rather than through law) should rightly be, 'the free self-determining of the individuality'. Within these artificial bounds of the state only thought is free; and the poet who would render the conflict of the individual and of the state must content himself with appealing to the understanding; he cannot appeal to the understanding through the feeling. Dramatic art is 'the emotionalizing of the intellect', for, in drama, the appeal is made directly to the senses and can completely realize its aim.

In drama, therefore, an action can only be explained when it is completely justified by the feeling; and it is thus the dramatic poet's task not to invent actions but to make an action so intelligible through its emotional necessity that we may altogether dispense with the intellect's assistance in its justification. The poet, therefore, has to make his main scope the choice of the action, which he must so choose that, alike in its character and in its compass, it makes possible to him its entire justification by the feeling, for in this justification alone resides the reaching of his aim.

This action he cannot find in the present, where the fundamental relations are no longer to be seen in their simple and natural growth; nor in the past, as recorded by history, where an action can only become intelligible to us through a detailed explanation of its surroundings. It must be found in a new creation of myth, and this myth must arise from a condensation into one action of the image of all man's energy, together with his recognition of his own mood in nature, nature apprehended, not in parts by the under-standing, but as a whole by the feeling. This strengthening of a moment of action can only be achieved 'by lifting it above the ordinary human measure through the poetic figment of wonder'.

Poetic wonder is the highest and most necessary product of the artist's power of beholding and displaying. ... It is the fullest understanding of Nature that first enables the poet to set her phenomena before us in wondrous shaping: for only in such shaping do they become intelligible to us as the conditionments of human actions intensified.

The motives which tend towards this supreme moment of action are to be condensed and absorbed into one; and from this one motive 'all that savours of the particular and accidental must be taken away, and it must be given its full truth as a necessary, purely human utterance of feeling.'

Only in tone-speech can this fully realized utterance of feeling be made. Modern speech, alike in prose and in the modern form of verse, in which 'Stabreim', or the root alliteration by which words were once fused with melody, has given place to end-rhyme ('fluttering at the loose ends of the ribands of melody'), is no longer able to speak to the feeling, but only to the understanding, and this through a convention by which we 'dominate our feelings that we may demonstrate to the understanding an aim of the understanding.' Speech, therefore, has shrunk to 'absolute intellectual speech', as music has shrunk to 'absolute tone-speech'. The poet can thus only adequately realize his 'strengthened moments of action' by a speech proportionately raised above its habitual methods of expression. Tone-speech is this 'new, redeeming and realizing tongue'; tone-speech not separately made, an emotional expression ungoverned by this aim (as we see it in modern opera), but tone-speech which is the fullest expression of this aim, and thus 'the expression of the most deeply roused human feelings, according to their highest power of self-expression.'

Wagner now passes, in the third part, to a consideration of 'The Arts of Poetry and Tone in the Drama of the Future'. He begins by pointing out in minute detail, through the physiology of speech (the actual making of speech by breath), that it is only from a heightening of ordinary speech, and not from the recognized prosody of verse, that we can hope to find the means of ultimate expression; and that, our language having lost all direct means of emotional appeal, we must go back to its very roots before we can fit it to combine with that tone-speech which does possess such an appeal. He shows that the metre of Greek choric verse can only properly be understood by taking into account its musical accompaniment, by which a long-held note could be justified to the ear. That these lyrics were written to fixed tunes, tunes probably fixed by dance movements, is evident from the great elaboration of a rhythm which could never have arisen directly out of the substance of poems so largely grave and philosophic. The oldest lyric arises out of tone and melody, in which human emotion at first uttered itself in the mere breathing of the vowels, then through the individualization of the vowels by consonants. In a word-root we have not only the appeal to thought of that root's meaning, but also the sensuous appeal of the open sound which is its 'sensuous body' and primal substance. Tone, with its appeal to feeling, begins by passing into the word, with its appeal to the understanding; the final return is that of the word, through harmony, to that tone-speech in which the understanding is reached through the feeling, and both are satisfied.

Primitive melodies rarely modulate from one key into another; and, if we wish to address the feeling intelligibly through tone alone, we must return to this simplicity of key. This Beethoven did in the melody to which he set Schiller's verse in the Ninth Symphony; but if we compare this, in its original form, with the broad melodic structure of the musical setting of the line, 'Seid umschlungen, Millionen!' we shall see the whole difference between a melody which is made separately and, so to speak, laid upon the verse, and a melody which grows directly out of the verse itself. It is the poetic aim which causes and justifies modulation, for by it the change and gradation of emotion can be rendered intelligible to the feeling. Harmony is 'the bearing element which takes up the poetic aim solely as a begetting seed, to shape it into finished semblance by the prescripts of its own, its womanly organism'. Modern music has taken harmony as sufficient in itself, and by so doing has but 'worked bewilderingly and benumbingly upon the feeling'. The tone-poet must, instead, add to a melody, conditioned by its speaking verse, the harmony implicitly contained therein. Now 'harmony is in itself a thing of thought; to the senses it becomes first actually discernible as polyphony, or, to define it still more closely, as polyphonic symphony.' This, for the purposes of the drama, cannot be supplied by vocal symphony, because each voice, in a perfectly proportioned action, can but be the expression of an individual character, present on the stage for his own ends, and not as a mere vocal support for others. 'Only in the full tide of lyric outpour, when all the characters and their surroundings have been strictly led up to a joint expression of feeling, is there offered to the tone-poet a polyphonic mass of voices to which he may make over the declaration of his harmony.' Only by the orchestra can it find expression, for the orchestra is 'the realized thought' of harmony.

The timbre of the human voice can never absolutely blend with that of any instrument; it is the duty of the orchestra to subordinate itself to, and support, the vocal melody, never actually mingling with it. The orchestra possesses a distinct faculty of speech, 'the faculty of uttering the unspeakable', or rather that which, to our intellect, is the unspeakable. This faculty it possesses in common with gesture, which expresses something that cannot be expressed in words. The orchestra expresses to the ear what gesture expresses to the eye, and both combined carry on or lead up to what the verse-melody expresses in words. It is able to transform thought ('the bond between an absent and a present emotion') into an actually present emotion. 'Music cannot think, but she can materialize thoughts. A musical motive can produce a definite impression on the feeling, inciting it to a function akin to thought, only when the emotion uttered in that motive has been definitely conditioned by a definite object and proclaimed by a definite individual before our very eyes.' The orchestra, then, can express foreboding or remembrance, and it can do this with perfect clearness and direct appeal to the emotions by the recurrence of a musical motive which we have already associated with a definite emotion, or whose significance is interpreted to us by a definite gesture. What has been called tone-painting in instrumental music is an attempt to do this by the suggestion of tones, or with the aid of a written programme; in either case by a 'chilling' appeal to mere fancy in place of feeling. 'The life-giving focus of dramatic expression is the verse-melody of the performer; towards it the absolute orchestral melody leads on, as a foreboding; from it is led the instrumental-motive's "thought", as a remembrance.' In order to arrive at perfect unity of form and content there must be something more than a mere juxtaposition of poetic and musical expression, or the musician will have roused a feeling in vain, and the poet will have failed to fix this feeling incompletely roused. Unity can be secured only when the expression fully renders the content, and renders it unceasingly; and this can be done only when the poet's aim and the musician's expression are so blended that neither can be distinguished from the other, 'the chief motives of the dramatic action, having become distinguishable melodic moments which fully materialize their content, being moulded into a continuous' texture, binding the whole art-work together, and, in the final result, the orchestra so completely 'guiding our whole attention away from itself as a means of expression, and directing it to the object expressed,' that, in a sense, it shall not 'be heard at all'. Thus, at its height of realized achievement, 'art conceals art.'

3

This, then, was the task to which Wagner addressed himself; this was his ideal, and this remains his achievement. We have seen how wholly the theory was an outcome of the work itself; and Wagner assures us that he brought on 'a fit of brain cramp' by his endeavour to 'treat as a theorem a thing which had become quite clear and certain to him in his artistic intention and production'. The theory came out of the preliminary labour at what afterwards became the 'Ring des Nibelungen.' It was in the midst of that long labour that, as we know, he stopped to write 'Tristan'; we know now, since the publication of the letters to Mathilde Wesendonck, why he stopped, and why he 'clean forgot every theory' in the calm fever of that creation, 'to such an extent that during the working out I myself was aware of how far I had outstripped my system'.

What Coleridge said of Wordsworth may be applied even more fitly to Wagner: 'He had, like all great artists, to create the taste by which he was to be realized, to teach the art by which he was to be seen and judged.' Thus we see him first of all explaining himself to himself before he explains himself to the world; and, in this final explanation, giving no place to the thinker's vanity in thought or the artist's in self-consciousness, but making an appeal for help, a kind of persistent expostulation. Wagner wanted people to understand him in order that they might carry out his ideas, that particular part of his ideas which he was powerless to carry out without their aid. He was creating the 'art-work of the future', the work itself which he had once dreamed was to be the spontaneous and miraculous outcome of his ideal 'community'; he still wanted to make that community come to him; he believed in it until belief was quite worn out; and we see him, in essay after essay, expecting less and less, as revolution has brought it no nearer to him, and 'German policy' has brought it no nearer. At last he sees only two possibilities: one, a private association of art-loving men and women, and he doubts if enough lovers of art are to be found; the other, a German prince, who would devote his opera-budget to the creation of a national art. 'Will this prince be found?' he asks, not expecting an answer; and he adds: 'Patience and long-suffering have worn me out. I no longer hope to live out the production of my "Bühnenfestspiel".' This is in 1863. The prince was at hand: 'for it was indeed a king who called to me in chaos: "Hither! Complete thy work! I will it!"'

What was begun in 1864 by King Ludwig of Bavaria had to wait many years for its completion; and that completion was to come about by the additional help of a private association of art-lovers, of whose existence Wagner had doubted. Nothing ever came from any 'community'; and Wagner, like all other believers in 'the people', had to realize in the end that art, in our days, can be helped only by a few powerful individuals: a king, a popular favourite like Liszt, an enthusiastic woman like the Countess von Schleinitz. In the modern world money is power; and with money even Bayreuth may be forced upon the world. It must be forced upon it; it will not be chosen; afterwards, the thing once done, the public will follow; for the public, like the work itself, has to be created. Having failed to produce his art-work with the help of the public, Wagner proceeded to produce a public with the help of the art-work. He built Bayreuth for the production of his own works in his own way, and arranged, down to the minutest details, the manner of their representation.

Few of Wagner's theories were not the growth of many times and many ideas. The idea, or first glimpse, of Bayreuth itself may perhaps be found, as Mr Ashton Ellis finds it, in a flourish of mere rhetoric in one of Berlioz's articles in the 'Gazette Musicale', which Wagner caught up in one of his own articles of that year (1841):

So Berlioz lately dreamed of what he would do were he one of those unfortunate beings who pay five hundred francs for the singing of a romance not worth five sous; he would take the finest orchestra in the world to the ruins of Troy to play to him the 'Sinfonia Eroica'.

It has always been Wagner's desire that all the seats in his theatre should be equalized, and, if possible, that they should be free. It was not possible; and the uniform price of seats had to be a high one; but in the 'stipendiary fund', formed at Wagner's express wish, not long before his death (by which free seats and travelling expenses are still given to a certain number of poor musicians), we find some approximation towards his original desire. The advisability of the form of the amphitheatre, with its consequent equalizing of seats and prices, had been discerned by Wagner at least as early as 1851, when in 'A Communication to my Friends', he describes the modern opera-house, with its threefold and mutually contradictory appeal to the gallery, the pit, and the boxes, 'the vulgar, the Philistine, and the exquisite, thrown into one common pot'.

But it was a need even more fundamental which finally brought about the exact shape of the Bayreuth theatre: the need, whose importance gradually grew upon him, of having the orchestra out of sight, and sunk below the level of the stage. The first consciousness of this need is seen in one of those *feuilletons*, written in 1840 or 1841, which Wagner afterwards brought together under the title, 'A German Musician in Paris'. Here he comments, in passing, on the distraction and unloveliness of 'seeing music as well as hearing it', and on the amazing people who like to sit as near the orchestra as possible in order to watch the movements of the fiddles and to wait on the next beat of the kettle-drum. In 1849, in 'The Art-work of the Future', he symbolizes the orchestra as 'the loam of endless universal feeling', from which renewed strength is to be drawn, as Antaeus drew a renewal of strength from contact with the earth. As such, and 'by its essence diametrically opposed to the scenic landscape which surrounds the actor', it is, 'as to locality, most rightly placed in the deepened foreground outside the scenic frame,' to which it forms 'the perfect complement', the undercurrent.

In the preface to the poem of 'The Ring' (1863), in which the Bayreuth idea is definitely proposed, Wagner dwells in more detail on the advantages of an invisible orchestra. In 1873, in the 'report' on Bayreuth, he points out how the desire to render the mechanical means of the music invisible had led step by step to the transformation of the whole auditorium. As the first necessity was that the orchestra should be sunk so deep that no one in the audience could look down into it, it was evident that the seats would have to be arranged tier above tier, in gradually ascending rows, 'their ultimate height to be governed solely by the possibility of a distinct view of the scenic picture'. In order to frame in the empty space between the stage and the first row of seats ('the mystic gulf', as Wagner called it, because it had to divide the real from the ideal world), a second wider proscenium was set up, which threw back the stage picture into a further depth (as Whistler would have easel pictures thrown back into the depths of the frame, 'the frame being the window through which the painter looks at his model'). A difficulty, caused by the side-walls of the auditorium, suggested a further development of this scheme; and proscenium after proscenium was added through the whole interior, in the form of broadening rows of columns, which framed it into a single vista, widening gradually outwards from the stage. Thus, for the first time in the modern world, a literal 'theatron', or looking-room, had been constructed, solely for the purpose of looking, and of looking in one direction only.

Wagner's attitude towards the public was never intentionally an autocratic one. His whole conception of art was unselfish, never in any narrow sense 'art for art's sake', but art concealing art for the joy of the world. Certainly no one in modern times has longed so ardently, or laboured so hard, that the whole world might see itself transfigured in art and might rejoice in that transfiguration. Is not his whole aim that of universal art? and can art be universal except through universality of delight? His dissatisfaction with the performances of his own works in the ordinary theatres arose from the impossibility of directly addressing the actual feeling of the public through those conditions. When one of his operas has at last had a clamorous success, he is dissatisfied, because he is conscious that its meaning has not been rightly apprehended. He does not want to be admired, as strange things are admired; but to be understood, and, being understood, to be loved, and thus to become a living bond between art and the world. In a footnote to 'Opera and Drama' he says emphatically:

By this term, the public, I can never think of those units who employ their abstract art-intelligence to make themselves familiar with things which are never realized upon the stage. By the public I mean that assemblage of spectators without any specifically cultivated art-understanding, to whom the represented drama should come for their complete, their entirely toilless, emotional understanding; spectators, therefore, whose interest should never be led to the mere art media employed, but solely to the artistic object realized thereby, to the drama as a represented action, intelligible to every one. Since the public, then, is to enjoy without the slightest effort of an art-intelligence, its claims are grievously slighted when the performance does not realize the dramatic aim.

Bayreuth is the endeavour to satisfy the legitimate, un-recognized, often disputed rights, not of the artist, as an outside solitary individual, but of the public, of which the artist is himself to become a sympathetic and more conscious member. Do we not here return, very significantly, to what seemed like words in the air in that conclusion of 'The Art-work of the Future', where the creative artist identifies himself with the performer, and the performer becomes, or typifies, 'the unit man expanded to the essence of the human species'?

4

In the realizing of this achievement, as we have seen from 'The Art-work of the Future' and 'Opera and Drama', Wagner demanded, in the combination of the arts, two main factors: poetry, carried to its utmost limits in drama; and music carried to its utmost limits as the interpreter and deepener of dramatic action. In one of the admirable letters to Mathilde Wesendonck, Wagner delights quite frankly in the thought that no one could so fitly supplement Schopenhauer's theory of music, because, 'there never was another man who was a poet and a musician at once.' It is this double faculty which permitted him to achieve the whole of his aim, and it is through his possession of this double faculty that his ideas about music and about drama are almost equally significant and fundamental. We shall be more likely to realize their full meaning if we take them not, as he generally insisted on taking them, together, but, as far as we can, separately; and we will begin, as he began, with the foundation of his scheme, with drama.

Drama, 'the one, indivisible, supreme creation of the mind of man', was, as we know, celebrated by the Greeks as a religious festival. Now, as in ancient Greece, the theatre is the chronicle and epitome of the age; but with what a difference! With us, in the most serious European countries, religion is forbidden to be dealt with on the stage; 'our evil conscience has so lowered the theatre in public estimation that it is the duty of the police to prevent the stage from meddling in the slightest degree with religion.' What has killed art in the modern world is commercialism. 'The rulership of public taste in art', says Wagner in 'Opera and Drama', 'has passed over to the person . . . who orders the art-work for his money, and insists on ever novel variations of his one beloved theme, but at no price a new theme itself; and this ruler and order-giver is the Philistine.' 'I simply take in view,' he says in 1878, in his article on 'The Public and Popularity', 'our public art-conditions of the day when I assert that it is impossible for anything to be truly good if it is to be reckoned in advance for presentation to the public, and if this intended presentation rules the author in his sketch and composition of an art-work'. Thus the playwright has to endure 'the sufferings of all the other artists turned into one', because what he creates can only become a work of art by 'entering into open life', that is, by being seen on the open stage. 'If the theatre is at all to answer to its high and natural mission it must be completely freed from the necessity of industrial speculation.' For the playwright, therefore, a public is a necessary part of his stock-in-trade. The Greeks had it, supremely; Shakespeare, Molière, had it; but, though Wagner himself has violently conquered it for music, for drama it still remains unconquered.

Wagner points out the significant fact that from Aeschylus to Molière, through Lope de Vega and Shakespeare, the great dramatic poet has always been himself an actor, or has written for a given company of actors. He points out how in

Paris, where alone the stage has a measure of natural life, every genre has its theatre, and every play is written for a definite theatre. Here, then, is the very foundation of the dramatic art, which is only realized by the complete inter-dependence of poet and actor, the poet 'forgetting himself' as he creates his poetry in terms of living men and women, and the actor divesting himself of self in carrying out the intentions of the poet. Wagner defines the Shakespearian drama as 'a fixed mimetic improvization of the highest poetic value', and he shows how, in order to rise to drama, poetry must stoop to the stage; it must cease to be an absolute thing, pure poetry, and must accept aid from life itself, from the actor who realizes it according to its inten-tion. The form of a Shakespeare play would be as unintelli-gible to us as that of a Greek play without our knowledge of the stage necessities which shaped both the one and the other. Neither, though both contain poetry which is supreme as poetry, took its form from poetry; neither is intelligible as poetic form. The actor's art is like 'the life-dew in which the poetic aim was to be steeped, to enable it, as in a magic transformation, to appear as the mirror of life'.

In the Greek play the chorus appeared in the orchestra, that is, in the midst of the audience, while the personages, masked and heightened, were seen in a ghostly illusion of grandeur on the stage. Shakespeare's stage is planted with-in the orchestra; his actors, who acted in the midst of the audience, had to be absolutely natural if they were not to be wholly ridiculous. We expect, since his time, no less of nature from the actor, a power of illusion which must be absolute.

Man interprets or is the ape of nature; the actor is the ape of, and interprets man. He is 'Nature's intermediate link through which that absolutely realistic mother of all being incites the ideal within us'. And now Wagner takes his further step from drama into music, which he justifies, in one place, by representing the mirrored image of life, which is the play, 'dipped in the magic spring of music, which frees it from all the realism of matter', and, in another place, by the affirmation: 'What to Shakespeare was practically impossible, namely, to be the actor of all his parts, the tone-composer achieves with complete certainty, for out of each executant musician he speaks to us directly.' Into these speculations we must not now follow him. One point, however, which he raises in a later footnote to 'The Art-work of the Future' has a significance, apart from his special intention, in its choice of music as a test or touchstone of drama. He imagines the playwright resenting the intrusion of music, and he asks him in return of what value can be 'those thoughts and situations to which the lightest and most restrained accompaniment of music should seem importunate and burdensome'? Could there be a more essential test of drama, or a test more easily applied by a moment's thought? Think of any given play, and imagine a musical accompaniment of the closest or loosest kind. I can hear a music as of Mozart coming up like an atmosphere about Congreve's 'Way of the World', as easily as I can hear Beethoven's 'Coriolan'* overture leading in Shake-speare's 'Coriolanus'. Tolstoy's 'Power of Darkness' is itself already a kind of awful tragic music; but would all of Ibsen go quite well to a musical setting? Conceive of music and Dumas *fils* together, and remember that, rightly or wrongly Maeterlinck's 'Pelléas et Mélisande' has only succeeded on the stage since it has been completed by the musical interpretation of Debussy.

The root of all evil in modern art, and especially in the art of drama, Wagner finds to be the fact that 'modern art is a mere product of culture, and not sprung from life itself'. The drama written as literature, at a distance from the theatre, and with only a vague consciousness of the actor, can be no other than a lifeless thing, not answering to any need. The only modern German dramatic work in which there is any vitality, Goethe's 'Faust', springs from the puppet-stage of the people; but German actors are incap-able of giving it, for the verse must be spoken with absolute

---

* But the *Coriolan* Beethoven wrote his overture to was not by Shake-speare. E.B.

naturalness, and the actor has lost the secret of speaking verse naturally. Thus the actor must be trained; must be taught above all to speak. 'Only actors can teach each other to speak; and they would find their best help in sternly refusing to play bad pieces, that is, pieces which hinder them from entering that ecstasy which alone can ennoble their art.' Wagner is never tired of proclaiming his debt to Wilhelmine Schröder-Devrient, who first inspired in him, he tells us, the desire to write music worthy of her singing. Was her voice so wonderful? 'No,' answers Wagner; 'she had no "voice" at all; but she knew how to use her breath so beautifully, and to let a true womanly soul stream forth in such wonderful sounds, that we never thought of either voice or singing. . . . All my knowledge of mimetic art,' he goes on to say, 'I owe to this great woman; and through that teaching I can point to truthfulness as the foundation of that art.'

Wagner's best service to drama, in his theories as in his practice, is the insistence with which he has demonstrated the necessary basis of the play in the theatre. 'The thorough "stage-piece",' he says, 'in the modernest of senses, would assuredly have to form the basis, and the only sound one, of all future dramatic efforts.' And not merely does he see that the play must be based upon the theatre, but that the particular play must be conditioned by the particular theatre. No one has seen more clearly the necessity of 'tempering the artistic ends to be realized' to the actual 'means of execution' which are at the artist's disposal. 'Even the scantiest means are equal to realizing an artistic aim, provided it rules itself for expression through these means.' Thus there is not one among his many plans of theatre reform which has not some actual building in view, whether the Vienna Opera-house there visibly before him, or that 'Bühnenfestspielhaus' which he saw no less clearly in his mind before the first stone of the foundation had been set in the earth at Bayreuth. And whenever he speaks of the theatre it is as of a kind of religious service and with a kind of religious awe, which, in one of his essays, bursts out into a flame of warning exultation. 'If we enter a theatre,' he says gravely, 'with any power of insight, we look straight into a dæmonic abyss of possibilities, the lowest as well as the highest. . . . Here in the theatre the whole man, with his lowest and his highest passions, is placed in terrifying nakedness before himself, and by himself is driven to quivering joy, to surging sorrow, to hell and heaven. . . . In awe and shuddering have the greatest poets of all nations and of all times approached this terrible abyss,' from whose brink those heavenly wizards are thrust back by the modern world, that they may give place to 'the Furies of vulgarity, the sottish gnomes of dishonouring delights'.

5

It has sometimes been said that there is a contradiction between Wagner's conception of music at various periods of his life; and so in appearance there is, but only in appearance. The reading of Schopenhauer, at Zürich and Venice, during the composition of 'Tristan und Isolde', did indeed supply him with a complete theory, or what may be called a transcendental philosophy, of music, which he later on transferred to his book on Beethoven, developing it after his own fashion. It is true also that, in the more important of his previous writings, as in 'Opera and Drama', nothing had been said of any such transcendental view of music, music being treated indeed almost wholly in regard to its dependence upon words and action. But it must be remembered that Wagner was concerned only with a particular form of music, with dramatic music, and that he was arguing with a purpose, and to convince people, already attentive enough to music in itself, of certain new possibilities in its union with drama.

In Wagner's theoretical writing everything is a matter of focus; that once established, nothing is seen except in relation to it. He is literally unable to see things in unrelated detail. This is why he is so impatient with 'absolute' music in its modern developments, and with 'absolute' literature, in more than Verlaine's sense, when he cries, 'Et tout le reste est Littèrature!' That is why he is unable to consider a

single question, the question of the Jews,* of a Goethe
institute, of musical criticism, without focusing it where the
rays of thought will best converge upon it. Every idea comes
to Wagner from circumstances. A king becomes his friend,
and he sets himself to find out the inner and primal meaning
of kingship. Long before, he had guessed at the idea which
he is only now able to develop out of the material actually
under his hand; and it is thus no less with all his studies of
race, religion, politics.

So, wholly concentrated upon one aspect of music, he may
well have seemed to do somewhat less than justice to music
itself; and the Beethoven book may seem like the sudden,
odd, theoretical awakening of a musician to the whole
greatness of his own art. It is therefore instructive to turn
to one of those newspaper articles which Wagner wrote
when he was in Paris in 1840 and 1841; and there we shall
find, and in reference to Beethoven, a singularly clear
anticipation of almost everything that he was afterwards to
say on the inner meaning of music. Why, he asks, should
people 'take the useless trouble to confound the musical
with the poetic tongue', seeing that 'where the speech of
man stops short, there music's reign begins'? Tone-painting,
he admits, may be used in jest, but, in purely instrumental
music, in no other sense, without ceasing to be humorous
and becoming absurd. Where, he asks, in the 'Eroica
Symphony', is 'the Bridge of Lodi, where the battle of
Arcole, where the victory under the Pyramids, where the
18th Brumaire'? These things would have been found set
down in a 'biographic symphony' of his time, as indeed we
find them in biographic or autobiographic tone-poems of
Richard Strauss in our time. But Beethoven saw Bonaparte,
not as a general but as a musician; 'and in *his* domain he
saw the sphere where he could bring to pass the self-same
thing as Bonaparte in the plains of Italy.' A mood in music,
he admits, may be produced by no matter what external
cause, for the musician is, after all, a man, and at the mercy

* See the essay 'Judaism in Music' in *Stories and Essays*.

of his temperament in its instinctive choice among the sounds in which he hears the footsteps of events. But these moods, once profoundly set in motion, 'when they force him to production, have already turned to music in him, so that, at the moment of creative inspiration, it is no longer the outer event that governs the composer, but the musical sensation which it has begotten in him'. And, further, what music can express in her universal voice is not merely the joy, passion, or despair of the individual, but joy itself, or passion or despair, raised to infinity, and purified by the very 'semblance of the world'.*

Do we not already see music, as Schopenhauer saw it, as 'an idea of the world'? and the musician 'speaking the highest wisdom in a language his reason does not understand'? It is in the wonderful book on Beethoven, written in 1870, that Wagner goes deepest into music as music, led by Schopenhauer, but going beyond him. He shows us Beethoven, surrounded by silence, like 'a world walking among men'; and he shows us how the action of music is to shut us off from the outer world, where we can dream, as it were, awake, redeemed from the strivings of the individual will, and at one with nature, with our inmost selves. Music, he shows us, blots out civilization as the daylight blots out lamplight.

To this voice of nature in sound it seemed to Wagner that Beethoven had given as complete an interpretation as the human individual could give. What, then, he asks, remains for instrumental music to do? If one refuses the help of what Beethoven finally came to accept, words, and if one refuses to make a servile copy of Beethoven, there remains only that riddle without an answer, the tone-poem, and that riddle whose answer has already been given, programme music. We have already seen, from 'Opera and Drama',

* Note also that in 1857, in his letter on Liszt's 'Symphonic Poems', Wagner says: 'Hear my creed: music can never and in no possible alliance cease to be the highest, the redeeming art. It is of her nature that what all the other arts but hint at, through her and in her becomes the most indubitable of certainties, the most direct and definite of truths.'

what Wagner thought of the form of programme music, as Berlioz employed it. In a later article on Liszt, he points out in more precise detail how Berlioz, by his method, only succeeded in losing the musical idea without finding a poetic one, music being capable of giving only 'the quintessence of an emotional content', and Berlioz trying to force music to suggest, without words or action, definite scenes in a play. In Liszt, however, he found a more genuinely musical conception, an attempt, whether wholly successful or not, to translate the fundamental intention of a poem or of a poet into terms of music; and this seemed to him to be realized in the Dante Symphony, where 'the soul of Dante's poem is shown in purest radiance'. The danger of this new form he sees to be that of attempting to do the work of drama without the visible or audible accompaniments of drama, and, in particular, to use, for mere effect, and effect never really explicit, modulations which in his own music he had used for definite and obvious reasons. He counsels the composer never to quit a key so long as what he has to say can be said in it; and he shows by his own practice how carefully he has observed his rule.

Nothing is more interesting in Wagner's comments on himself than the account, in 'A Communication to my Friends', of his early struggle after originality in melody; his failure to achieve originality by seeking it; and how the quality he sought came to him when he had given up every thought but that of expressing his meaning, the meaning of the words or the situation which he wanted to express. 'I no longer,' he says, 'tried intentionally for customary melody, or, in a sense, for melody at all, but absolutely let it take its rise from the emotional utterance of the words themselves.' We may compare one of the wisest of Coleridge's jottings: 'Item, that dramatic poetry must be poetry hid in thought and passion, not thought and passion disguised in the dress of poetry.' Wagner and Coleridge, two great masters of technique, teach us equally that the greatest art can be produced only by the abandonment of art itself to that primal energy which works after its own laws, not conscious of anything but of the need of exquisitely truthful speech.

There is a certain part of Wagner's writing about music which is fiercely polemical, not only such broad attacks as the famous 'Judaism in Music', but in regard to individual composers. Except when he jeers at 'S. Johannes' Brahms, with what seems a literally personal irritation, there is hardly an instance in which the personal element is not scrupulously subordinated to a conception of right and wrong in music. The musicians whom he attacks are always and only those who were charlatans, like Meyerbeer ('the starling who follows the plough-share down the field, and merrily picks up the earth-worm just uncovered in the furrow'), or triflers, like 'sickly' Gounod, or those who turned back on their earlier selves, like the 'turgid' later Schumann, or were superficial and did harm to art by their superficiality, like Mendelssohn: 'I fancied I was peering into a veritable abyss of superficiality, an utter void.'

He is scrupulously just to a musician like Rossini, who, being merely heedless and selfish, let his genius drift with the tide;* he sees the sincerity and right direction of an incomplete talent like Spontini's; picks out of the great rubbish-heap of lighter French operas one work in which there is something, if not good, vital, Auber's 'Masaniello'; and, in spite of personal differences and personal affections, can be scrupulously accurate in his analysis of the contradictory genius of Berlioz and in his characterization of the misunderstood genius of Liszt. But he was incapable of seeing an abuse without trying to set it right, or a sham without trying to stamp it out. In writing a letter of advice to the editor of a new musical journal, he bids him above all wage war against that null and void music, which is made as a separate manufacture, music which follows the rules and has no other reason for existence. He hates it as

---

* One of Wagner's subtlest and most fundamental pages of criticism is contained in a 'Reminiscence of Rossini', written in 1868, in which he shows that Rossini as truly represents his own trivial age as Palestrina, Bach, Mozart, represented each his own age 'of more hopeful effort'.

he hates that 'whole clinking, twinkling, glittering, glistening show, Grand Opera!' As you must knock down one structure if you would build another in its place, no detail is too minute for Wagner to define and denounce in the art-traffic of the modern world, and he has not only said finally, and said fruitfully, everything that is to be said in criticism of opera and opera-houses, and the performing and staging of opera, but he has done a special and often overlooked service to music in general by his insistence on the proper rendering of orchestral music. It is to Wagner that we owe almost a revolution in the art of conducting.

In his scheme for a music-school for Munich (1865), Wagner laments that in Germany 'we have classical works, but as yet no classical rendering for them', and he shows how, through the lack of a national Conservatoire, there is no musical tradition in Germany, such a tradition, for instance, for the performance of Mozart as the Paris Conservatoire has preserved for the performance of Gluck. In regard to Beethoven, the condition of things is still worse, for 'it is an established fact that Beethoven himself could never obtain an entirely adequate performance of his difficult instrumental works'. Here, again, he points out how the Paris Conservatoire spent three years in studying the Ninth Symphony, and how needful such study was, seeing that, in so many cases, 'the master's thought is only to be brought to really cognizable utterance through a most intelligent, refined, and dexterous combination and modification of its orchestral expression'. In the very important essay of 1870, 'On Conducting', and in separate studies in the rendering of the Ninth Symphony, he explains in detail what these 'quite new demands on rendering' are which 'arrive with Beethoven's uncommonly expressive use of rhythm', with his minute orchestral shading, and also with those practical errors in scoring which he overlooked because he could not hear them. He shows how not only Beethoven, but Weber (and in Dresden, where Weber had conducted) had come to be given in wholly wrong *tempo*; how Gluck and Mozart had been misinterpreted by being taken twice too fast or twice too slow. Then in still greater detail, he explains (writing from exile, where he was unable to come into personal contact with musicians) how his own overtures are to be given, and the reason of every shade of expression. Few parts of his writing on music are more valuable than these technical instructions; and it must be remembered that from Wagner arose the whole modern German school of conductors, from Bülow to Weingartner, and that the greatest of them, Richter, was the most intimately under his influence. Thus Wagner not only reformed the actual conditions of music, not only created a new and wonderful music of his own, but brought about a scarcely less significant reform in the interpretation of music, which, existing on paper, could be heard nowhere according to the intentions of the composer.

6

More than any artist of our time, Wagner may be compared with the many-sided artists of the Renaissance; but he must be compared only to be contrasted. In them an infinity of talents led to no concentration of all in one; each talent, even in Leonardo, pulls a different way, and painting, science, literature, engineering, the many interpretations and mouldings of nature, are nowhere brought together into any unity, or built up into any single structure. In Wagner, the musician, the poet, the playwright, the thinker, the administrator, all worked to a single end, built up a single structure; there was no waste of a faculty, nor was any one faculty sacrificed to another. In this he is unique as a man of genius, and in this his creation had its justification in nature. Whether or no the 'art-work of the future' is to be on the lines which Wagner laid down; whether Beethoven may not satisfy the musical sense more completely on one side, and Shakespeare the dramatic sense on the other; whether, in any case, more has been demonstrated than that in Germany, the soil of music and the only soil in which drama has never taken root, music is required to give dramatic poetry life: all this matters little. A man with a genius for many arts has brought those arts, in his own work, more intimately into union than they have ever before been brought; and he has delighted the world with this combination of arts as few men of special genius have ever delighted the world with their work in any of these arts. To find a parallel for this achievement we must look back to the Greeks, to the age of Æschylus and Sophocles; and we shall not even here find a parallel; for, if the dramatic poetry was on a vastly higher plane than in the music-drama of Wagner, it is certain that the music was on a vastly lower one. Of the future it is idle to speak; but, at the beginning of the twentieth century, may we not admit that the typical art of the nineteenth century, the art for which it is most likely to be remembered, has been the art, musical and dramatic, of Richard Wagner?

W. B. Yeats

w. b. yeats, 1865–1939, was so great a poet that his contributions to the theatre tend to get overlooked. Yet he should rank as one of the few theatre *managers* of our century whose management has had the slightest cultural value. His views on the drama can scarcely be done justice to in an anthology, but his philosophy of the theatre probably can, and it was with that in mind that the following excerpt was made.

I took the title (says Yeats) from a book by Romain Rolland on some French theatrical experiments. 'A People's Theatre' is not quite the same thing as 'A Popular Theatre'. The essay was published in *The Irish Statesman* in the autumn of 1919.

An excerpt from the Rolland book is to be found below, p. 455 ff. Between Yeats and Rolland the reader becomes acquainted with the question of theatre and democracy as a whole. Appended here is a short essay from *Plays, Acting and Music** by a member of Yeats's entourage, Arthur Symons. It is little known, but packs in much of the thinking current in Yeatsian circles of half a century ago. It seemed more sensible to choose this than to reprint what has already appeared of Yeats in such collections as Toby Cole's *Playwrights on Playwriting* and Henry Popkin's revision of the Barrett H. Clark *European Theories of the Drama*.

* London: Duckworth, 1928.

A People's Theatre

W. B. YEATS

A LETTER TO LADY GREGORY

1

MY DEAR LADY GREGORY – Of recent years you have
done all that is anxious and laborious in the supervision of
the Abbey Theatre and left me free to follow my own
thoughts. It is therefore right that I address to you this
letter, wherein I shall explain, half for your ears, half for
other ears, certain thoughts that have made me believe that
the Abbey Theatre can never do all we had hoped. We set
out to make a 'People's Theatre', and in that we have
succeeded. But I did not know until very lately that there
are certain things, dear to both our hearts, which no
'People's Theatre' can accomplish.

2

All exploitation of the life of the wealthy, for the eye and the
ear of the poor and half poor, in plays, in popular novels, in
musical comedy, in fashion papers, at the cinema, in *Daily
Mirror* photographs, is a travesty of the life of the rich; and
if it were not would all but justify some red terror; and it
impoverishes and vulgarizes the imagination, seeming to
hold up for envy and to commend a life where all is display
and hurry, passion without emotion, emotion without intellect, and where there is nothing stern and solitary. The
plays and novels are the least mischievous, for they still
have the old-fashioned romanticism – their threepenny bit,
if worn, is silver yet – but they are without intensity and
intellect and cannot convey the charm of either as it may
exist in those they would represent. All this exploitation is a
rankness that has grown up recently among us and has come

out of an historical necessity that has made the furniture and the clothes and the brains, of all but the leisured and the lettered, copies and travesties.

Shakespeare set upon the stage Kings and Queens, great historical or legendary persons about whom all was reality, except the circumstance of their lives which remain vague and summary because – his mind and the mind of his audience being interested in emotion and intellect at their moment of union and at their greatest intensity – he could only write his best when he wrote of those who controlled the mechanism of life. Had they been controlled by it, intellect and emotion entangled by intricacy and detail could never have mounted to that union which, as Swedenborg said of the marriage of the angels, is a conflagration of the whole being. But since great crowds, changed by popular education with its eye always on some objective task, have begun to find reality in mechanism alone,* our popular commercial art has substituted for Lear and Cordelia the real millionaire and the real peeress, and seeks to make them charming by insisting perpetually that they have all that wealth can buy, or rather all that average men and women would buy if they had wealth. Shakespeare's groundlings watched the stage in terrified sympathy, while the British working man looks perhaps at the photographs of these lords and ladies, whom he admires beyond measure, with the pleasant feeling that they will all be robbed and murdered before he dies.

3

Then, too, that turning into ridicule of peasant and citizen and all lesser men could but increase our delight when the great personified spiritual power, but seems unnatural when the great are but the rich. During an illness lately I read two popular novels which I had borrowed from the servants.

* I have read somewhere statistics that showed how popular education has coincided with the lessening of Shakespeare's audience. In every chief town before it began Shakespeare was constantly played.

They were good stories and half consoled me for the sleep
I could not get, but I was a long time before I saw clearly
why everybody with less than a thousand a year was a
theme of comedy and everybody with less than five hundred
a theme of farce. Even Rosencrantz and Guildenstern,
courtiers and doubtless great men in their world, could be
but foils for Hamlet because Shakespeare had nothing to
do with objective truth, but we who have nothing to do with
anything else, in so far as we are of our epoch, must not
allow a greater style to corrupt us.

An artisan or a small shopkeeper feels, I think, when he
sees upon our Abbey stage men of his own trade, that they
are represented as he himself would represent them if he
had the gift of expression. I do not mean that he sees his own
life expounded there without exaggeration, for exaggeration
is selection and the more passionate the art the more marked
is the selection, but he does not feel that he has strayed into
some other man's seat. If it is comedy he will laugh at
ridiculous people, people in whose character there is some
contortion, but their station of life will not seem ridiculous.
The best stories I have listened to outside the Theatre have
been told me by farmers or sailors when I was a boy, one or
two by fellow-travellers in railway carriages, and most had
some quality of romance, romance of a class and its particular capacity for adventure; and our Theatre is a people's
theatre in a sense which no mere educational theatre can be,
because its plays are to some extent a part of that popular
imagination. It is very seldom that a man or woman bred up
among the propertied or professional classes knows any class
but his own, and that a class which is much the same all
over the world, and already written of by so many dramatists that it is nearly impossible to see its dramatic situations
with our own eyes, and those dramatic situations are perhaps
exhausted – as Nietzsche thought the whole universe would
be some day – and nothing left but to repeat the same
combinations over again.

When the Abbey Manager sends us a play for our opinion
and it is my turn to read it, if the handwriting of the MSS.

329

or of the author's accompanying letter suggests a leisured life I start prejudiced. There will be no fresh observation of character, I think, no sense of dialogue, all will be literary second-hand, at best what Rossetti called 'The soulless self-reflections of man's skill'. On the other hand, until the Abbey plays began themselves to be copied, a hand-writing learned in a national school always made me expect dialogue, written out by some man who had admired good dialogue before he had seen it upon paper. The construction would probably be bad, for there the student of plays has the better luck, but plays made impossible by rambling and redundance have often contained some character or some dialogue that has stayed in my memory for years. At first there was often vulgarity, and there still is in those comic love scenes which we invariably reject, and there is often propaganda with all its distortion, but these weigh light when set against life seen as if newly created. At first, in face of your mockery, I used to recommend some reading of Ibsen or Galsworthy, but no one has benefited by that reading or by anything but the Abbey audience and our own rejection of all gross propaganda and gross imitation of the comic column in the newspapers. Our dramatists, and I am not speaking of your work or Synge's but of those to whom you and Synge and I gave an opportunity, have been excellent just in so far as they have become all eye and ear, their minds not smoking lamps, as at times they would have wished, but clear mirrors.

Our players, too, have been vivid and exciting because they have copied a life personally known to them, and of recent years, since our Manager has had to select from the ordinary stage-struck young men and women who have seen many players and perhaps no life but that of the professional class, it has been much harder, though players have matured more rapidly, to get the old, exciting, vivid playing. I have never recovered the good opinion of one recent Manager because I urged him to choose instead some young man or woman from some little shop who had never given his or her thoughts to the theatre. Put all the names into a hat, I think I said, and pick the first that comes. One of our early players was exceedingly fine in the old woman in *Riders to the Sea*. 'She has never been to Aran, she knows nothing but Dublin, surely in that part she is not objective, surely she creates from imagination,' I thought; but when I asked her she said, 'I copied from my old grandmother.' Certainly it is this objectivity, this making of all from sympathy, from observation, never from passion, from lonely dreaming, that has made our players, at their best, great comedians, for comedy is passionless.

We have been the first to create a true 'People's Theatre', and we have succeeded because it is not an exploitation of local colour, or of a limited form of drama possessing a temporary novelty, but the first doing of something for which the world is ripe, something that will be done all over the world and done more and more perfectly: the making articulate of all the dumb classes each with its own knowledge of the world, its own dignity, but all objective with the objectivity of the office and the workshop, of the newspaper and the street, of mechanism and of politics.

4

Yet we did not set out to create this sort of theatre, and its success has been to me a discouragement and a defeat. Dante in that passage in the *Convito* which is, I think, the first passage of poignant autobiography in literary history, for there is nothing in St Augustine not formal and abstract beside it, in describing his poverty and his exile counts as his chief misfortune that he has had to show himself to all Italy and so publish his human frailties that men who honoured him unknown honour him no more. Lacking means he had lacked seclusion, and he explains that men such as he should have but few and intimate friends. His study was unity of being, the subordination of all parts to the whole as in a perfectly proportioned human body – his own definition of beauty – and not, as with those I have described, the unity of things in the world; and like all subjectives he shrank, because of what he was, because of what others were, from contact with many men. Had he written plays he would have written from his own thought and passion, observing little and using little, if at all, the conversation of his time – and whether he wrote in verse or in prose his style would have been distant, musical, metaphorical, moulded by antiquity. We stand on the margin between wilderness and wilderness, that which we observe through our senses and that which we can experience only, and our art is always the description of one or the other. If our art is mainly from experience we have need of learned speech, of agreed symbols, because all those things whose names renew experience have accompanied that experience already many times. A personage in one of Turgenev's novels is reminded by the odour of, I think, heliotrope, of some sweetheart that had worn it, and poetry is any flower that brings a memory of emotion, while an unmemoried flower is prose, and a flower pressed and named and numbered science; but our poetical heliotrope need bring to mind no sweetheart of ours, for it suffices that it crowned the bride of Paris, or Peleus' bride. Neither poetry nor any subjective art can exist but for those who do in some measure share its traditional knowledge, a knowledge learned in leisure and contemplation. Even Burns, except in those popular verses which are as lacking in tradition, as modern, as topical, as Longfellow, was, as Henley said, not the founder but the last of a dynasty.

Once such men could draw the crowd because the circumstance of life changed slowly and there was little to disturb contemplation and so men repeated old verses and old stories, and learned and simple had come to share in common much allusion and symbol. Where the simple were ignorant they were ready to learn and so became receptive, or perhaps even to pretend knowledge like the clowns in the medieval poem that describes the arrival of Chaucer's Pilgrims at Canterbury, who that they may seem gentlemen pretend to know the legends in the stained-glass windows. Shakespeare, more objective than Dante – for, alas, the world must move – was still predominantly subjective, and he wrote during the latest crisis of history that made possible a Theatre of his kind. There were still among the common people many traditional songs and stories, while court and university, which were much more important to him, had an interest Chaucer never shared in great dramatic persons, in those men and women of Plutarch, who made their death a ritual of passion; for what is passion but the straining of man's being against some obstacle that obstructs its unity?

You and I and Synge, not understanding the clock, set out to bring again the Theatre of Shakespeare or rather perhaps of Sophocles. I had told you how at Young Ireland Societies and the like, young men when I was twenty had read papers to one another about Irish legend and history, and you yourself soon discovered the Gaelic League, then but a new weak thing, and taught yourself Irish. At Spiddal or near it an innkeeper had sung us Gaelic songs, all new village work that though not literature had *naïveté* and sincerity. The writers, caring nothing for cleverness, had tried to express emotion, tragic or humorous, and great masterpieces, *The Grief of a Girl's Heart,* for instance, had been written in the same speech and manner and were still sung. We know that the songs of the Thames boatmen, to name but these, in the age of Queen Elizabeth had the same relation to great masterpieces. These Gaelic songs were as unlike as those to the songs of the Music Hall with their clever ear-catching rhythm, the work of some mind as objective as that of an inventor or of a newspaper reporter. We thought we could bring the old folk-life to Dublin, patriotic feeling to aid us, and with the folk-life all the life of the heart, understanding heart, according to Dante's definition, as the most interior being; but the modern world is more powerful than any Propaganda or even than any special circumstance, and our success has been that we have made a theatre of the head, and persuaded Dublin playgoers to think about their own trade or profession or class and their life within it, so long as the stage curtain is up, in relation to Ireland as a whole. For certain hours of an evening they have objective modern eyes.

5

The objective nature and the subjective are mixed in different proportions as are the shadowed and the bright parts in the lunar phases. In Dante there was little shadow, in Shakespeare a larger portion, while you and Synge, it may be, resemble the moon when it has just passed its third quarter, for you have constant humour – and humour is of the shadowed part – much observation and a speech founded upon that of real life. You and he will always hold our audience, but both have used so constantly a measure of lunar light, have so elaborated style and emotion, an individual way of seeing, that neither will ever, till a classic and taught in school, find a perfect welcome.

The outcry against *The Playboy* was an outcry against its style, against its way of seeing; and when the audience called Synge 'decadent' – a favourite reproach from the objective everywhere – it was but troubled by the stench of its own burnt cakes. How could they that dreaded solitude love that which solitude had made? And never have I heard any, that laugh the loudest at your comedies, praise that musical and delicate style that makes them always a fit accompaniment for verse and sets them at times among the world's great comedies. Indeed, the louder they laugh the readier are they to rate them with the hundred ephemeral farces they have laughed at and forgotten. Synge they have at least hated. When you and Synge find such an uneasy footing, what shall I do there who have never observed anything, or listened with an attentive ear, but value all I have seen or heard because of the emotions they call up or because of something they remind me of that exists, as I believe, beyond the world? Oh, yes, I am listened to – am I not a founder of the theatre? – and here and there scattered solitaries delight in what I have made and return to hear it again; but some young Corkman, all eyes and ears, whose first rambling play we have just pulled together or half together, can do more than that. He will be played by players who have spoken dialogue

like his every night for years, and sentences that it had been
a bore to read will so delight the whole house that to keep my
hands from clapping I shall have to remind myself that I
gave my voice for the play's production and must not applaud
my own judgement.

6

I want to create for myself an unpopular theatre and an
audience like a secret society where admission is by favour
and never to many. Perhaps I shall never create it, for you
and I and Synge have had to dig the stone for our statue and
I am aghast at the sight of a new quarry, and besides I want
so much – an audience of fifty, a room worthy of it (some
great dining-room or drawing-room), half-a-dozen young
men and women who can dance and speak verse or play
drum and flute and zither, and all the while, instead of a
profession, I but offer them 'an accomplishment'. However, there are my *Four Plays for Dancers* as a beginning, some
masks by Mr Dulac, music by Mr Dulac and by Mr Rummell. In most towns one can find fifty people for whom one
need not build all on observation and sympathy, because they
read poetry for their pleasure and understand the traditional language of passion. I desire a mysterious art, always re-
minding and half-reminding those who understand it of
dearly loved things, doing its work by suggestion, not by
direct statement, a complexity of rhythm, colour, gesture,
not space-pervading like the intellect but a memory and a
prophecy: a mode of drama Shelley and Keats could have
used without ceasing to be themselves, and for which even
Blake in the mood of *The Book of Thel* might not have been
too obscure. Instead of advertisements in the press I need a
hostess, and even the most accomplished hostess must choose
with more than usual care, for I have noticed that city-living
cultivated people, those whose names would first occur to
her, set great value on painting, which is a form of property,
and on music, which is a part of the organization of life, while
the lovers of literature, those who read a book many times,

either are young men with little means or live far away from big towns.

What alarms me most is how a new art needing so elaborate a technique can make its first experiments before those who, as Molière said of the courtiers of his day, have seen so much. How shall our singers and dancers be welcomed by those who have heard Chaliapin in all his parts and who know all the dances of the Russians? Yet where can I find Mr Dulac and Mr Rummell or any to match them, but in London* or in Paris, and who but the leisured will welcome an elaborate art or pay for its first experiments? In one thing the luck might be upon our side. A man who loves verse and the visible arts has, in a work such as I imagine, the advantage of the professional player. The professional player becomes the amateur, the other has been preparing all his life, and certainly I shall not soon forget the rehearsal of *The Hawk's Well,* when Mr Ezra Pound, who had never acted on any stage, in the absence of our chief player rehearsed for half an hour. Even the forms of subjective acting that were natural to the professional stage have ceased. Where all now is sympathy and observation no Irving can carry himself with intellectual pride, nor any Salvini in half-animal nobility, both wrapped in solitude.

I know that you consider Ireland alone our business, and in that we do not differ, except that I care very little where a play of mine is first played so that it find some natural audience and good players. My rooks may sleep abroad in the fields for a while, but when the winter comes they will remember the way home to the rookery trees. Indeed, I have Ireland especially in mind, for I want to make, or to help some man some day to make, a feeling of exclusiveness, a bond among chosen spirits, a mystery almost for leisured and lettered people. Ireland has suffered more than England from democracy, for since the Wild Geese fled, who might have grown to be leaders in manners and in taste, she has

* I live in Dublin now, and indolence and hatred of travel will probably compel me to make my experiment there after all. – W.B.Y., 1923.

had but political leaders. As a drawing is defined by its outline and taste by its rejections, I too must reject and draw an outline about the thing I seek; and say that I seek, not a theatre but the theatre's anti-self, an art that can appease all within us that becomes uneasy as the curtain falls and the house breaks into applause.

7

Meanwhile the Popular Theatre should grow always more objective; more and more a reflection of the general mind; more and more a discovery of the simple emotions that make all men kin, clearing itself the while of sentimentality, the wreckage of an obsolete popular culture, seeking always not to feel and to imagine but to understand and to see. Let those who are all personality, who can only feel and imagine, leave it, before their presence become a corruption and turn it from its honesty. The rhetoric of d'Annunzio, the melodrama and spectacle of the later Maeterlinck, are the insincerities of subjectives, who being very able men have learned to hold an audience that is not their natural audience. To be intelligible they are compelled to harden, to externalize and deform. The popular play left to itself may not lack vicissitude and development, for it may pass, though more slowly than the novel which need not carry with it so great a crowd, from the physical objectivity of Fielding and Defoe to the spiritual objectivity of Tolstoy and Dostoievsky, for beyond the whole we reach by unbiased intellect there is another whole reached by resignation and the denial of self.

8

The two great energies of the world that in Shakespeare's day penetrated each other have fallen apart as speech and music fell apart at the Renaissance, and that has brought each to greater freedom, and we have to prepare a stage for the whole wealth of modern lyricism, for an art that is close to pure music, for those energies that would free the arts from imitation, that would ally acting to decoration and to the dance. We are not yet conscious, for as yet we have no philosophy while the opposite energy is conscious. All visible history, the discoveries of science, the discussions of politics, are with it; but as I read the world, the sudden changes, or rather the sudden revelation of future changes, are not from visible history but from its anti-self. Blake says somewhere in a Prophetic Book that things must complete themselves before they pass away, and every new logical development of the objective energy intensifies in an exact correspondence a counter energy, or rather adds to an always deepening unanalysable longing. That counter longing, having no visible past, can only become a conscious energy suddenly, in those moments of revelation which are as a flash of lightning. Are we approaching a supreme moment of self-consciousness, the two halves of the soul separate and face to face? A certain friend of mine has written upon this subject a couple of intricate poems called 'The Phases of the Moon' and 'The Double Vision' respectively, which are my continual study, and I must refer the reader to these poems for the necessary mathematical calculations. Were it not for that other gyre turning inward in exact measure with the outward whirl of its fellow, we would fall in a generation or so under some tyranny that would cease at last to be a tyranny, so perfect our acquiescence.

> Constrained, arraigned, baffled, bent and unbent
> By these wire-jointed jaws and limbs of wood,
> Themselves obedient,
> Knowing not evil and good;
>
> Obedient to some hidden magical breath.
> They do not even feel, so abstract are they,
> So dead beyond our death,
> Triumph that we obey.*

*These lines are from 'The Double Vision' which, like 'The Phases of the Moon', is by Yeats. E.B.

A Theory of the Stage

ARTHUR SYMONS

LIFE and beauty are the body and soul of great drama. Mix
the two as you will, so long as both are there, resolved into a
single substance. But let there be, in the making, two ingredients, and while one is poetry, and comes bringing
beauty, the other is a violent thing which has been scornfully
called melodrama, and is the emphasis of action. The greatest plays are melodrama by their skeleton, and poetry by the
flesh which clothes that skeleton.

The foundation of drama is that part of the action which
can be represented in dumb show. Only the essential parts
of action can be represented without words, and you would
set the puppets vainly to work on any material but that which
is common to humanity. The permanence of a drama might
be tested by the continuance and universality of its appeal
when played silently in gestures. I have seen the test applied.
Companies of marionette players still go about the villages
of Kent, and among their stock pieces is *Arden of Feversham*,
the play which Shakespeare is not too great to have written,
at some moment when his right hand knew not what his left
hand was doing. Well, that great little play can hold the
eyes of every child and villager, as the puppets enact it; and
its power has not gone out of it after three centuries. Dumb
show apes the primal forces of nature, and is inarticulate, as
they are; until relief gives words. When words come, there is
no reason why they should not be in verse, for only in verse
can we render what is deepest in humanity of the utmost
beauty. Nothing but beauty should exist on the stage. Visible
beauty comes with the ballet, an abstract thing; gesture adds
pantomime, with which drama begins; and then words
bring in the speech by which life tries to tell its secret. Because poetry, speaking its natural language of verse, can let
out more of that secret than prose, the great drama of the

past has been mainly drama in verse. The modern desire to escape from form, and to get at a raw thing which shall seem like what we know of the outside of nature, has led our latest dramatists to use prose in preference to verse, which indeed is more within their limits. It is Ibsen who has seemed to do most to justify the use of prose, for he carries his psychology far with it. Yet it remains prose, a meaner method, a limiting restraint, and his drama a thing less fundamental than the drama of the poets. Only one modern writer has brought something which is almost the equivalent of poetry out of prose speech: Tolstoy, in *The Power of Darkness*. The play is horrible and uncouth, but it is illuminated by a greater inner light. There is not a beautiful word in it, but it is filled with beauty. And that is because Tolstoy has the vision which may be equally that of the poet and of the prophet.

It is often said that the age of poetry is over, and that the great forms of the future must be in prose. That is the 'exquisite reason' of those whom the gods have not made poetical. It is like saying that there will be no more music, or that love is out of date. Forms change, but not essence; and Whitman points the way, not to prose, but to a poetry which shall take in wider regions of the mind.

Yet, though it is by its poetry that, as Lamb pointed out, a play of Shakespeare differs from a play of Banks or Lillo, the poetry is not more essential to its making than the living substance, the melodrama. Poets who have written plays for reading have wasted their best opportunities. Why wear chains for dancing? The limitations necessary to the drama before it can be fitted to the stage are but hindrances and disabilities to the writer of a book. Where can we find more spilt wealth than in the plays of Swinburne, where all the magnificent speech builds up no structure, but wavers in orchestral floods, without beginning or ending? It has been said that Shakespeare will sacrifice his drama to his poetry, and even *Hamlet* has been quoted against him. But let *Hamlet* be rightly acted, and whatever has seemed mere lingering meditation will be recognized as a part of that thought which makes or waits on action. If poetry in Shakespeare may sometimes seem to delay action, it does but deepen it. The poetry is the life blood, or runs through it. Only bad actors and managers think that by stripping the flesh from the skeleton they can show us a more living body. The outlines of *Hamlet* are crude, irresistible melodrama, still irresistible to the gallery; and the greatness of the play, though it comes to us by means of the poetry, comes to us legitimately, as a growth out of melodrama.

The failure, the comparative failure, of every contemporary dramatist, however far he may go in one direction or another, comes from his neglect of one or another of these two primary and essential requirements. There is, at this time, a more serious dramatic movement in Germany than in any other country; with mechanicians, like Sudermann, as accomplished as the best of ours, and dramatists who are also poets, like Hauptmann. I do not know them well enough to bring them into my argument, but I can see that in Germany, whatever the actual result, the endeavour is in the right direction. Elsewhere, how often do we find even so much as this, in more than a single writer here and there? Consider Ibsen, who is the subtlest master of the stage since Sophocles. At his best he has a firm hold on structural melodrama, he is a marvellous analyst of life, he is the most ingenious of all the playwrights; but ask him for beauty and he will give you a phrase, 'vine-leaves in the hair' or its equivalent; one of the clichés of the minor poet. In the end beauty revenged itself upon him by bringing him to a no-man's-land where there were clouds and phantasms that he could no longer direct.

Maeterlinck began by a marvellous instinct, with plays 'for marionettes', and, having discovered a forgotten secret, grew tired of limiting himself within its narrow circle, and came outside his magic. *Monna Vanna* is an attempt to be broadly human on the part of a man whose gift is of another kind: a visionary of the moods. His later speech, like his later dramatic material, is diluted; he becomes, in the conventional sense, eloquent, which poetry never is. But he has brought back mystery to the stage, which has been banished, or retained in exile, among phantasmagoric Faust-lights. The dramatist of the future will have more to learn from Maeterlinck than from any other playwright of our time. He has seen his puppets against the permanent darkness, which we had cloaked with light; he has given them supreme silences.

In d'Annunzio we have an art partly shaped by Maeterlinck, in which all is atmosphere, and a home for sensations which never become vital passions. The roses in the sarcophagus are part of the action in *Francesca*, and in *The Dead City* the whole action arises out of the glorious mischief hidden like a deadly fume in the grave of Agamemnon. Speech and drama are there, clothing but not revealing one another; the speech always a lovely veil, never a human outline.

We have in England one man, and one only, who has some public claim to be named with these artists, though his aim is the negation of art. Mr Shaw is a mind without a body, a whimsical intelligence without a soul. He is one of those tragic buffoons who play with eternal things, not only for the amusement of the crowd, but because an uneasy devil capers in their own brains. He is a merry preacher, a petulant critic, a great talker. It is partly because he is an Irishman that he has transplanted the art of talking to the soil of the stage: Sheridan, Wilde, Shaw, our only modern comedians, all Irishmen, all talkers. It is by his astonishing skill of saying everything that comes into his head, with a spirit really intoxicating, that Mr Shaw has succeeded in holding the stage with undramatic plays, in which there is neither life nor beauty. Life gives up its wisdom only to reverence, and beauty is jealous of neglected altars. But those who amuse the world, no matter by what means, have their place in the world at any given moment. Mr Shaw is a clock striking the hour.

With Mr Shaw we come to the play which is prose, and nothing but prose. The form is familiar among us, though it is cultivated with a more instinctive skill, as is natural, in

France. There was a time, not so long ago, when Dumas *fils* was to France what Ibsen afterwards became to Europe. What remains of him now is hardly more than his first 'fond adventure' the supremely playable *Dame aux Camélias*. The other plays are already out of date, since Ibsen; the philosophy of '*Tue-la!*' was the special pleading of the moment, and a drama in which special pleading, and not the fundamental 'criticism of life', is the dramatic motive can never outlast its technique, which has also died with the coming of Ibsen. Better technique, perhaps, than that of *La Femme de Claude*, but with less rather than more weight of thought behind it, is to be found in many accomplished playwrights, who are doing all sorts of interesting temporary things, excellently made to entertain the attentive French public with a solid kind of entertainment. Here, in England, we have no such folk to command; our cleverest playwrights, apart from Mr Shaw, are what we might call practitioners. There is Mr Pinero, Mr Jones, Mr Grundy; what names are better known, or less to be associated with literature? There is Anthony Hope, who can write, and Mr Barrie who has something both human and humorous. There are many more names, if I could remember them; but where is the serious playwright? Who is there that can be compared with our poets or our novelists, not only with a Swinburne or a Meredith, but, in a younger generation, with a Bridges or a Conrad? The Court Theatre has given us one or two good realistic plays, the best being Mr Granville-Barker's, besides giving Mr Shaw his chance in England, after he had had and taken it in America. But is there, anywhere but in Ireland, an attempt to write imaginative literature in the form of drama? The Irish Literary Theatre has already, in Mr Yeats and Mr Synge, two notable writers, each wholly individual, one a poet in verse, the other a poet in prose. Neither has yet reached the public, in any effectual way, or perhaps the limits of his own powers as a dramatist. Yet who else is there for us to hope in, if we are to have once more an art of the stage, based on the great principles, and a theatre in which that art can be acted?

The whole universe lies open to the poet who is also a dramatist, affording him an incomparable choice of subject. Ibsen, the greatest of the playwrights of modern life, narrowed his stage, for ingenious plausible reasons of his own, to the four walls of a house, and, at his best, constrained his people to talk of nothing above their daily occupations. He got the illusion of everyday life, but at a cruel expense. These people, until they began to turn crazy, had no vision beyond their eyesight, and their thoughts never went deep enough to need a better form for expression than they could find in their newspapers. They discussed immortal problems as they would have discussed the entries in their ledger. Think for a moment how the peasants speak in that play of Tolstoy's which I have called the only modern play in prose which contains poetry. They speak as Russians speak, with a certain childishness, in which they are more primitive than our more civilized peasants. But the speech comes from deeper than they are aware, it stumbles into a revelation of the soul. A drunken man in Tolstoy has more wisdom in his cups than all Ibsen's strange ladies who fumble at their lips for sea-magic.

And as Tolstoy found in this sordid chaos material for tragedy which is as noble as the Greeks' (a like horror at the root of both, a like radiance at both summits), so the poet will find stories, as modern as this if he chooses, from which he can take the same ingredients for his art. The ingredients are unchanging since *Prometheus*; no human agony has ever grown old or lost its pity and terror. The great plays of the past were made out of great stories, and the great stories are repeated in our days and can be heard wherever an old man tells us a little of what has come to him in living. Verse lends itself to the lifting and adequate treatment of the primary emotions, because it can render them more as they are in the soul, not being tied down to probable words, as prose talk is. The probable words of prose talk can only render a part of what goes on among the obscure imageries of the inner life; for who, in a moment of crisis, responds to circumstances or destiny with an adequate answer? Poetry, which is spoken thought, or the speech of something deeper than thought, may let loose some part of that answer which would justify the soul, if it did not lie dumb upon its lips.

Émile Zola

ÉMILE ZOLA, 1840–1902, did a four-month stint as a drama critic in 1873, then wrote weekly reviews for *Le Bien public* (1876–8), *Le Voltaire* (1878–80) and *Le Figaro* (1880–81). His pieces are collected in two volumes published in 1881: *Le Naturalisme au Théâtre* and *Nos auteurs dramatiques*. Although Zola's preface to *Thérèse Raquin* has been widely printed in English, as has the chapter on theatre from *The Experimental Novel*, nothing from his two volumes on theatre – his principal contribution, after all – seems to have been done into English until now. The passages here were chosen with a view to showing that Zola did not merely deliver orations in favour of Naturalism as a general proposition but had a clear vision of a new kind of theatre and could describe it, department by department. When we see what the idea was we realize that it is no passing fashion of the eighteen eighties that is at stake. Many of these words are very close to the thinking of Brecht in 1950. Zola was not a great playwright, but like another minor playwright who was a major writer, Diderot, he knew how to speak for an epoch and also how to see into the future. From Zola's own writings, one would pass to such things as Bernard Shaw's preface to *Three Plays of Brieux* and Strindberg's preface to *Miss Julie*. These two are widely available. Chosen for inclusion here is the manifesto on German Naturalism, 'To Begin' by Otto Brahm (1856–1912), which prefaced the first issue of *Freie Buehne für modernes Leben*, 1889, but which did not appear in English until the essay came out from which it is taken for use here, 'The Freie Bühne and Its Influence' by Lee Baxandall.*

* *Modern Drama* (Lawrence, Kansas), February 1963.

From Naturalism in the Theatre*

ÉMILE ZOLA

Translated by Albert Bermel

NATURALISM

I

EACH winter at the beginning of the theatre season I fall
prey to the same thoughts. A hope springs up in me, and I
tell myself that before the first warmth of summer empties
the playhouses, a dramatist of genius will be discovered.
Our theatre desperately needs a new man who will scour the
debased boards and bring about a rebirth in an art degraded
by its practitioners to the simple-minded requirements of the
crowd. Yes, it would take a powerful personality, an innovator's mind, to overthrow the accepted conventions and
finally install the real human drama in place of the ridiculous
untruths that are on display today. I picture this creator
scorning the tricks of the clever hack, smashing the imposed
patterns, remaking the stage until it is continuous with the
auditorium, giving a shiver of life to the painted trees, letting
in through the backcloth the great, free air of reality.

Unfortunately, this dream I have every October has not
yet been fulfilled, and is not likely to be for some time. I
wait in vain, I go from failure to failure. Is this, then, merely
the naive wish of a poet? Are we trapped in today's dramatic
art, which is so confining, like a cave that lacks air and light?
Certainly, if dramatic art by its nature forbids this escape
into less restricted forms, it would indeed be vain to delude
ourselves and to expect a renaissance at any moment. But
despite the stubborn assertions of certain critics who do not
like to have their standards threatened, it is obvious that
dramatic art, like all the arts, has before it an unlimited
domain, without barriers of any kind to left or right.

* English translation copyright © 1968 by Albert Bermel.

351

Inability, human incapacity, is the only boundary to an art.

To understand the need for a revolution in the theatre, we must establish clearly where we stand today. During our entire classical period tragedy ruled as an absolute monarch. It was rigid and intolerant, never granting its subjects a touch of freedom, bending the greatest minds to its inexorable laws. If a playwright tried to break away from them he was condemned as witless, incoherent and bizarre; he was almost considered a dangerous man. Yet even within the narrow formula genius did build its monument of marble and bronze. The formula was born during the Greek and Latin revival; the artists who took it over found in it a pattern that would serve for great works. Only later, when the imitators – that line of increasingly weaker and punier disciples – came along, did the faults in the formula show up: outlandish situations, improbabilities, dishonest uniformity, and uninterrupted, unbearable declaiming. Tragedy maintained such a sway that two hundred years had to pass before it went out of date. It tried slowly to become more flexible, but without success, for the authoritarian principles in which it was grounded formally forbade any concession to new ideas, under pain of death. Just when it was trying to broaden its scope, it was overturned, after a long and glorious reign.

In the eighteenth century romantic drama was already stirring inside tragedy. On occasion the three unities were violated, more importance was given to scenery and extras, violent climaxes were now staged, where formerly they had been described in speeches so that the majestic tranquillity of psychological analysis might not be disturbed by physical action. In addition, the passion of the *grande époque* was replaced by commonplace acting; a grey rain of mediocrity and staleness soaked the stage. One can visualize tragedy, by the beginning of this century, as a long, pale, emaciated figure without a drop of blood under its white skin, trailing its tattered robes across a gloomy stage on which the footlights had gone dark of their own accord. A rebirth of dramatic art out of a new formula was inevitable. It was then that romantic drama noisily planted its standard in front of the prompter's box. The hour had come; a slow ferment had been at work; the insurrection advanced on to terrain already softened-up for the victory. And never has the word insurrection seemed more apt, for romantic drama bodily seized the monarch tragedy and, out of hatred for its impotence, sought to destroy every memory of its reign. Tragedy did not react; it sat still on its throne, guarding its cold majesty, persisting with its speeches and descriptions. Whereas romantic drama made action its rule, excesses of action that leapt to the four corners of the stage, hitting out to right and left, no longer reasoning or analysing, giving the public a full view of the blood-drenched horror of its climaxes. Tragedy had chosen antiquity for its setting, the eternal Greeks and Romans, immobilizing the action in a room or in front of the columns of a temple; romantic drama chose the Middle Ages, paraded knights and ladies, manufactured strange sets with castles pinnacled over sheer gorges, armories crowded with weapons, dungeons dripping with moisture, ancient forests pocked with moonlight. The war was joined on all fronts; romantic drama ruthlessly made itself the armed adversary of tragedy and assaulted it with every method that defied the old formula.

This raging hostility, which characterized the romantic drama at its high tide, needs to be stressed, for it offers a precious insight. The poets who led the movement undoubtedly talked about putting real passion on stage and laying claim to a vast new realm that would encompass the whole of human life with its contradictions and inconsistencies; it is worth remembering, for example, that romantic drama fought above all for a mixture of laughter and tears in the same play, arguing that joy and pain walk side by side on earth. Yet truth, reality, in fact counted for little – even displeased the innovators. They had only one passion, to overthrow the tragic formula that inhibited them, to crush it once and for all under a stampede of every kind of audacity. They did not want their heroes of the Middle Ages to be more real than the heroes of tragic antiquity; they wanted

them to appear as passionate and splendid as their predecessors had appeared cold and correct. A mere skirmish
over dress and modes of speech, nothing more: one set of
puppets at odds with another. Togas were torn up in favour
of doublets; a lady, instead of addressing her lover as 'My
lord', called him 'My lion'. After the transition fiction still
prevailed; only the setting was different.

I do not want to be unfair to the romantic movement. Its
effect has been outstanding and unquestionable; it has made
us what we are: free artists. It was, I repeat, a necessary
revolution, a violent struggle that arose just in time to
sweep away a tragic convention that had become childish.
Still, it would be ridiculous to arrest the evolution of dramatic art at romanticism. These days, especially, it is astounding to read certain prefaces in which the 1830 movement is
announced as the triumphal entry into human truth. Our
forty-year distance is enough to let us see clearly that the
alleged truth of the romanticists is a persistent and monstrous
exaggeration of reality, a fantasy that has declined into
excesses. Tragedy, to be sure, is another type of falseness, but
it is not *more* false. Between the characters who pace about in
togas, endlessly discussing their passions with confidants,
and the characters in doublets who perform great feats and
flit about like insects drunk with the sun, there is nothing to
choose; both are equally and totally unacceptable. Such
people have never existed. Romantic heroes are only tragic
heroes bitten by the mardi .gras bug, hiding behind false
noses, and dancing the dramatic cancan after drinking. For
the old sluggish rhetoric the 1830 movement substituted an
excited, full-blooded rhetoric, and that is all.

Without believing that art progresses, we can still say that
it is continuously in motion, among all civilizations, and that
this motion reflects different phases of the human mind.
Genius is made manifest in every formula, even in the most
primitive and innocent ones, though the formulas become
transmuted according to the intellectual breadth of each
civilization; that is incontestable. If Aeschylus was great,
Shakespeare and Molière showed themselves to be equally

great, each within his differing civilization and formula. By this I mean that I set apart the creative genius who knows how to make the most of the formula of his time. There is no progress in human creation but there is a logical succession to the formulas, to methods of thought and expression. Thus, art takes the same strides as humanity, is its very language, goes where it goes, moves with it towards light and truth; but for that, we could never judge whether a creator's efforts were more or less great, depending on whether he comes at the beginning or end of a literature.

In these terms, it is certain that when we left tragedy behind, the romantic drama was a first step in the direction of the naturalistic drama, towards which we are now advancing. The romantic drama cleared the ground, proclaimed the freedom of art. Its love of action, its mixture of laughter and tears, its research into accuracy of costume and setting show the movement's impulse towards real life. Is this not how things happen during every revolution against a secular regime? One begins by breaking windows, chanting and shouting, wrecking relics of the last regime with hammer blows. There is a first exuberance, an intoxication with the new horizons faintly glimpsed, excesses of all kinds that go beyond the original aims and degenerate into the despotism of the old, hated system, those very abuses the revolution has just fought against. In the heat of the battle tomorrow's truths evaporate. And not until all is calm and the fever has abated is there any regret for the broken windows, any understanding of how the effort has gone awry, how the new laws have been prematurely thrown together so that they are hardly any improvement over the laws that were destroyed. Well, the whole history of romantic drama is there. It may have been the formula necessary for its time, it may have had truthful intuitions, it may have been the form that will always be celebrated because a great poet used it to compose his masterpieces. At the present time it is, nonetheless, a ridiculous, outdated formula, with a rhetoric that offends us. We now wonder why it was necessary to push in windows, wave swords, bellow without a break, to go a scale too shrill in sentiment and language. All that leaves us cold, it bores and annoys us. Our condemnation of the romantic formula is summed up in one severe remark: To destroy one rhetoric it was not necessary to invent another.

Today, then, tragedy and romantic drama are equally old and worn out. And that is hardly to the credit of the latter, it should be said, for in less than half a century it has fallen into the same state of decay as tragedy, which took two centuries to die. There it lies, flattened in its turn, overwhelmed by the same passion it showed in its own battle. Nothing is left. We can only guess at what is to come. Logically all that can grow up on that free ground conquered in 1830 is the formula of naturalism.

2

It seems impossible that the movement of inquiry and analysis, which is precisely the movement of the nineteenth century, can have revolutionized all the sciences and arts and left dramatic art to one side, as if isolated. The natural sciences date from the end of the last century; chemistry and physics are less than a hundred years old; history and criticism have been renovated, virtually re-created since the Revolution; an entire world has arisen; it has sent us back to the study of documents, to experience, made us realize that to start afresh we must first take things back to the beginning, become familiar with man and nature, verify what is. Thenceforward, the great naturalistic school, which has spread secretly, irrevocably, often making its way in darkness but always advancing, can finally come out triumphantly into the light of day. To trace the history of this movement, with the misunderstandings that might have impeded it and the multiple causes that have thrust it forward or slowed it down, would be to trace the history of the century itself. An irresistible current carries our society towards the study of reality. In the novel Balzac has been the bold and mighty innovator who has replaced the observation of the scholar with the imagination of the poet.

But in the theatre the evolution seems slower. No eminent writer has yet formulated the new idea with any clarity.

I certainly do not say that some excellent works have not been produced, with characters in them who are ingeniously examined and bold truths taken right on to the stage. Let me, for instance, cite certain plays by M. Dumas *fils*, whose talent I scarcely admire, and M. Émile Augier, the most humane and powerful of all. Still, they are midgets beside Balzac; they lack the genius to lay down the formula. It must be said that one can never tell quite when a movement is getting under way; generally its source is remote and lost in the earlier movement from which it emerged. In a manner of speaking, the naturalistic current has always existed. It brings with it nothing absolutely novel. But it has finally flowed into a period favourable to it; it is succeeding and expanding because the human mind has attained the necessary maturity. I do not, therefore, deny the past; I affirm the present. The strength of naturalism is precisely that it has deep roots in our national literature which contains plenty of wisdom. It comes from the very entrails of humanity; it is that much the stronger because it has taken longer to grow and is found in a greater number of our masterpieces.

Certain things have come to pass and I point them out. Can we believe that *L'Ami Fritz* would have been applauded at the Comédie-Française twenty years ago? Definitely not! This play, in which people eat all the time and the lover talks in such homely language, would have disgusted both the classicists and the romantics. To explain its success we must concede that as the years have gone by a secret fermentation has been at work. Lifelike paintings, which used to repel the public, today attract them. The majority has been won over and the stage is open to every experiment. This is the only conclusion to draw.

So that is where we stand. To explain my point better – I am not afraid of repeating myself – I will sum up what I have said. Looking closely at the history of our dramatic literature, one can detect several clearly separated periods.

First, there was the infancy of the art, farces and the mystery plays of the Middle Ages, the reciting of simple dialogues which developed as part of a naïve convention, with primitive staging and sets. Gradually, the plays became more complex but in a crude fashion. When Corneille appeared he was acclaimed most of all for his status as an innovator, for refining the dramatic formula of the time, and for hallowing it by means of his genius. It would be very interesting to study the pertinent documents and discover how our classical formula came to be created. It corresponded to the social spirit of the period. Nothing is solid that is not built on necessity. Tragedy reigned for two centuries because it satisfied the exact requirements of those centuries. Geniuses of differing temperaments had buttressed it with their masterpieces. And it continued to impose itself long afterwards, even when second-rate talents were producing inferior work. It acquired a momentum. It persisted also as the literary expression of that society, and nothing would have overthrown it if the society had not itself disappeared. After the Revolution, after that profound disturbance that was meant to transform everything and give birth to a new world, tragedy struggled to stay alive for a few more years. Then the formula cracked and romanticism broke through. A new formula asserted itself. We must look back at the first half of the century to understand the meaning of this cry for liberty. The young society was in the tremor of its infancy. The excited, bewildered, violently unleashed people were still racked by a dangerous fever; and in the first flush of their new liberty they yearned for prodigious adventures and superhuman love affairs. They gaped at the stars; some committed suicide, a very curious reaction to the social enfranchisement which had just been declared at the cost of so much blood. Turning specifically to dramatic literature, I maintain that romanticism in the theatre was an uncomplicated revolt, the invasion by a victorious group who took over the stage violently with drums beating and flags flying. In these early moments the combatants dreamed of making their imprint with a new form; to one rhetoric they opposed another: the

Middle Ages to Antiquity, the exalting of passion to the exalting of duty. And that was all, for only the scenic conventions were altered. The characters remained marionettes in new clothing. Only the exterior aspect and the language were modified. But for the period that was enough. Romanticism had taken possession of the theatre in the name of literary freedom and it carried out its revolutionary task with incomparable bravura. But who does not see today that its role could extend no farther than that? Does romanticism have anything whatever to say about our present society? Does it meet one of our requirements? Obviously not. It is as outmoded as a jargon we no longer follow. It confidently expected to replace classical literature which had lasted for two centuries because it was based on social conditions. But romanticism was based on nothing but the fantasy of a few poets or, if you will, on the passing malady of minds overwhelmed by historical events; it was bound to disappear with the malady. It provided the occasion for a magnificent flowering of lyricism; that will be its eternal glory. Today, however, with the evolution accomplished, it is plain that romanticism was no more than the necessary link between classicism and naturalism. The struggle is over; now we must found a secure state. Naturalism flows out of classical art, just as our present society has arisen from the wreckage of the old society. Naturalism alone corresponds to our social needs; it alone has deep roots in the spirit of our times; and it alone can provide a living, durable formula for our art, because this formula will express the nature of our contemporary intelligence. There may be fashions and passing fantasies that exist outside naturalism but they will not survive for long. I say again, naturalism is the expression of our century and it will not die until a new upheaval transforms our democratic world.

Only one thing is needed now: men of genius who can fix the naturalistic formula. Balzac has done it for the novel and the novel is established. When will our Corneilles, Molières and Racines appear to establish our new theatre? We must hope and wait.

3

The period when romantic drama ruled now seems distant. In Paris five or six of its playhouses prospered. The demolition of the old theatres along the Boulevard du Temple was a catastrophe of the first order. The theatres became separated from one another, the public changed, different fashions arose. But the discredit into which the drama has fallen proceeds mostly from the exhaustion of the genre – ridiculous, boring plays have gradually taken over from the potent works of 1830.

To this enfeeblement we must add the absolute lack of new actors who understand and can interpret these kinds of plays, for every dramatic formula that vanishes carries away its interpreters with it. Today the drama, hunted from stage to stage, has only two houses that really belong to it, the Ambigu and the Théâtre-Historique. Even at the Saint-Martin the drama is lucky to win a brief showing for itself, between one great spectacle and the next.

An occasional success may renew its courage. But its decline is inevitable; romantic drama is sliding into oblivion, and if it seems sometimes to check its descent, it does so only to roll even lower afterwards. Naturally, there are loud complaints. The tail-end romanticists are desperately unhappy. They swear that except in the drama – meaning their kind of drama – there is no salvation for dramatic literature. I believe, on the contrary, that we must find a new formula that will transform the drama, just as the writers in the first half of the century transformed tragedy. That is the essence of the matter. Today the battle is between romantic drama and naturalistic drama. By romantic drama I mean every play that mocks truthfulness in its incidents and characterization, that struts about in its puppet-box, stuffed to the belly with noises that flounder, for some idealistic reason or other, in pastiches of Shakespeare and Hugo. Every period has its formula; ours is certainly not that of 1830. We are an age of method, of experimental science; our primary need is for precise analysis. We hardly understand the liberty we have won if we use it only to imprison ourselves in a new tradition. The way is open: we can now return to man and nature.

Finally, there have been great efforts to revive the historical drama. Nothing could be better. A critic cannot roundly condemn the choice of historical subjects, even if his own preferences are entirely for subjects that are modern. It is simply that I am full of distrust. The manager one gives this sort of play to frightens me in advance. It is a question of how history is treated, what unusual characters are presented bearing the names of kings, great captains or great artists, and what awful sauce they are served up in to make the history palatable. As soon as the authors of these concoctions move into the past they think everything is permitted: improbabilities, cardboard dolls, monumental idiocies, the hysterical scribblings that falsely represent local colour. And what strange dialogue – François I talking like a haberdasher straight out of the Rue Saint-Denis, Richelieu using the words of a criminal from the Boulevard du Crime, Charlotte Corday with the weeping sentimentalities of a factory girl.

What astounds me is that our playwrights do not seem to suspect for a moment that the historical genre is unavoidably the least rewarding, the one that calls most strongly for research, integrity, a consummate gift of intuition, a talent for reconstruction. I am all for historical drama when it is in the hands of poets of genius or men of exceptional knowledge who are capable of making the public see an epoch come alive with its special quality, its manners, its civilization. In that case we have a work of prophecy or of profoundly interesting criticism.

But unfortunately I know what it is these partisans of historical drama want to revive: the swaggering and sword-play, the big spectacle with big words, the play of lies that shows off in front of the crowd, the gross exhibition that saddens honest minds. Hence my distrust. I think that all this antiquated business is better left in our museum of dramatic history under a pious layer of dust.

There are, undeniably, great obstacles to original experiments: we run up against the hypocrisies of criticism and the long education in idiocies that has been foisted on the public. This public, which titters at every childishness in melodramas, nevertheless lets itself be carried away by outbursts of fine sentiment. But the public is changing. Shakespeare's public and Molière's are no longer ours. We must reckon with shifts in outlook, with the need for reality which is everywhere getting more insistent. The last few romantics vainly repeat that the public wants this and the public wants that; the day is coming when the public will want the truth.

4

The old formulas, classical and romantic, were based on the rearrangement and systematic amputation of the truth. They determined on principle that the truth is not good enough; they tried to draw out of it an essence, a 'poetry', on the pretext that nature must be expurgated and magnified. Up to the present the different literary schools disputed only over the question of the best way to disguise the truth so that it might not look too brazen to the public. The classicists adopted the toga; the romantics fought a revolution to impose the coat of mail and the doublet. Essentially the change of dress made little difference; the counterfeiting of nature went on. But today the naturalistic thinkers are telling us that the truth does not need clothing; it can walk naked. That, I repeat, is the quarrel.

Writers with any sense understand perfectly that tragedy and romantic drama are dead. The majority, though, are badly troubled when they turn their minds to the as-yet-unclear formula of tomorrow. Does the truth seriously ask them to give up the grandeur, the poetry, the traditional epic effects that their ambition tells them to put into their plays? Does naturalism demand that they shrink their horizons and risk not one flight into fantasy?

I will try to reply. But first we must determine the methods used by the idealists to lift their works into poetry. They begin by placing their chosen subject in a distant time. That provides them with costumes and makes the framework of the story vague enough to give them full scope for lying. Next, they generalize instead of particularizing; their characters are no longer living people but sentiments, arguments, passions that have been induced by reasoning. This false framework calls for heroes of marble or cardboard. A man of flesh and bone with his own originality would jar in such a legendary setting. Moreover, when we see the characters in romantic drama or tragedy walking about they are stiffened into an attitude, one representing duty, another patriotism, a third superstition, a fourth maternal love; thus, all the abstract ideas file by. Never the thorough analysis of an organism, never a character whose muscles and brain function as in nature.

These, then, are the mannerisms that writers with epic inclinations do not want to give up. For them poetry resides in the past and in abstraction, in the idealizing of facts and characters. As soon as one confronts them with daily life, with the people who fill our streets, they blink, they stammer, they are afraid; they no longer see clearly; they find everything ugly and not good enough for art. According to them, a subject must enter the lies of legend, men must harden and turn to stone like statues before the artist can accept them and make them fit the disguises he has prepared.

Now, it is at this point that the naturalistic movement comes along and says squarely that poetry is everywhere, in everything, even more in the present and the real than in the past and the abstract. Each event at each moment has its poetic, superb aspect. We brush up against heroes who are great and powerful in different respects from the puppets of the epic-makers. Not one playwright in this century has brought to life figures as lofty as Baron Hulot,

Old Grandet, César Birotteau, and all the other characters of Balzac, who are so individual and so alive. Beside these real, giant creations Greek and Roman heroes quake; the heroes of the Middle Ages fall flat on their faces like lead soldiers.

With the superior works being produced in these times by the naturalistic school – works of high endeavour, pulsing with life – it is ridiculous and false to park our poetry in some antiquated temple and bury it in cobwebs. Poetry flows at its full force through everything that exists; the truer to life, the greater it becomes. And I mean to give the word poetry its widest definition, not to pin it down exclusively to the cadence of two rhymes, nor to bury it in a narrow coterie of dreamers, but to restore its real human significance which concerns the expansion and encouragement of every kind of truth.

Take our present environment, then, and try to make men live in it: you will write great works. It will undoubtedly call for some effort; it means sifting out of the confusion of life the simple formula of naturalism. Therein lies the difficulty: to do great things with the subjects and characters that our eyes, accustomed to the spectacle of the daily round, have come to see as small. I am aware that it is more convenient to present a marionette to the public and name it Charlemagne and puff it up with such tirades that the public believes it is watching a colossus; it is more convenient than taking a bourgeois of our time, a grotesque, unsightly man, and drawing sublime poetry out of him, making him, for example, Père Goriot, the father who gives his guts for his daughters, a figure so gigantic with truth and love that no other literature can offer his equal.

Nothing is as easy as persuading the managers with known formulas; and heroes in the classical or romantic taste cost so little labour that they are manufactured by the dozen, and have become standardized articles that clutter up our literature. But it takes hard work to create a real hero, intelligently analysed, alive and performing. That is probably why naturalism terrifies those authors who are used to fishing up great men from the troubled waters of history. They would have to burrow too deeply into humanity, learn about life, go straight for the greatness of reality and make it function with all their power. And let nobody gainsay this true poetry of humanity; it has been sifted out in the novel and can be in the theatre; only the method of adaptation remains to be found.

I am troubled by a comparison; it has been haunting me and I will now free myself of it. For two long months a play called *Les Danicheff* has been running at the Odéon. It takes place in Russia. It has been very successful here, but is apparently so dishonest, so packed with gross improbabilities, that the author, a Russian, has not even dared to show it in his country. What can you think of this work which is applauded in Paris and would be booed in St Petersburg? Well, imagine for a moment that the Romans could come back to life and see a performance of *Rome vaincue*. Can you hear their roars of laughter? Do you think the play would complete one performance? It would strike them as a parody; it would sink under the weight of mockery. And is there one historical play that could be performed before the society it claims to portray? A strange theatre, this, which is plausible only among foreigners, is based on the disappearance of the generations it deals with, and is made up of so much misinformation that it is good only for the ignorant!

The future is with naturalism. The formula will be found; it will be proved that there is more poetry in the little apartment of a bourgeois than in all the empty, worm-eaten palaces of history; in the end we will see that everything meets in the real: lovely fantasies that are free of capriciousness and whimsy, and idylls, and comedies, and dramas. Once the soil has been turned over, the task that seems alarming and unfeasible today will become easy.

I am not qualified to pronounce on the form that to-morrow's drama will take; that must be left to the voice of some genius to come. But I will allow myself to indicate the path I consider our theatre will follow.

First, the romantic drama must be abandoned. It would be disastrous for us to take over its outrageous acting, its rhetoric, its inherent thesis of action at the expense of character analysis. The finest models of the genre are, as has been said, mere operas with big effects. I believe, then, that we must go back to tragedy – not, heaven forbid, to borrow more of its rhetoric, its system of confidants, its declaiming, its endless speeches, but to return to its simplicity of action and its unique psychological and physiological study of the characters. Thus understood, the tragic framework is excellent; one deed unwinds in all its reality, and moves the characters to passions and feelings, the exact analysis of which constitutes the sole interest of the play – and in a contemporary environment, with the people who surround us.

My constant concern, my anxious vigil, has made me wonder which of us will have the strength to raise himself to the pitch of genius. If the naturalistic drama must come into being, only a genius can give birth to it. Corneille and Racine made tragedy. Victor Hugo made romantic drama. Where is the as-yet-unknown author who must make the naturalistic drama? In recent years experiments have not been wanting. But either because the public was not ready or because none of the beginners had the necessary staying-power, not one of these attempts has had decisive results.

In battles of this kind, small victories mean nothing; we need triumphs that overwhelm the adversary and win the public to the cause. Audiences would give way before the onslaught of a really strong man. This man would come with the expected word, the solution to the problem, the formula for a real life on stage, combining it with the illusions necessary in the theatre. He would have what the newcomers have as yet lacked: the cleverness or the might to impose himself and to remain so close to truth that his cleverness could not lead him into lies.

And what an immense place this innovator would occupy in our dramatic literature! He would be at the peak. He would build his monument in the middle of the desert of mediocrity that we are crossing, among the jerry-built houses strewn about our most illustrious stages. He would put everything in question and remake everything, scour the boards, create a world whose elements he would lift from life, from outside our traditions. Surely there is no more ambitious dream that a writer of our time could fulfil. The domain of the novel is crowded; the domain of the theatre is free. At this time in France an imperishable glory awaits the man of genius who takes up the work of Molière and finds in the reality of living comedy the full, true drama of modern society.

PHYSIOLOGICAL MAN*

... In effect, the great naturalistic evolution, which comes down directly from the fifteenth century to ours has everything to do with the gradual substitution of physiological man for metaphysical man. In tragedy metaphysical man, man according to dogma and logic, reigned absolutely. The body did not count; the soul was regarded as the only interesting piece of human machinery; drama took place in the air, in pure mind. Consequently, what use was the tangible world? Why worry about the place where the action was located? Why be surprised at a baroque costume or false declaiming? Why notice that Queen Dido was a boy whose budding beard forced him to wear a mask? None of that mattered; these trifles were not worth stooping to; the play was heard out as if it were a school essay or a law case; it was on a higher plane than man, in the world of ideas, so far away from real man that any intrusion of reality would have spoiled the show.

Such is the point of departure – in Mystery plays, the religious point; the philosophical point in tragedy. And from that beginning natural man, stifling under the rhetoric and dogma, struggled secretly, tried to break free, made lengthy, futile efforts, and in the end asserted himself, limb

---

* What precedes is a complete chapter. Two brief excerpts follow from the chapter on Costume.

by limb. The whole history of our theatre is in this conquest by the physiological man, who emerged more clearly in each period from behind the dummy of religious and philosophical idealism. Corneille, Molière, Racine, Voltaire, Beaumarchais and, in our day, Victor Hugo, Émile Augier, Alexandre Dumas *fils*, even Sardou, have had only one task, even when they were not completely aware of it: to increase the reality of our corpus of drama, to progress towards truth, to sift out more and more of the natural man and impose him on the public. And inevitably, the evolution will not end with them. It continues; it will continue forever. Mankind is very young. . . .

COSTUME, STAGE DESIGN, SPEECH

Modern clothes make a poor spectacle. If we depart from bourgeois tragedy, shut in between its four walls, and wish to use the breadth of larger stages for crowd scenes we are embarrassed and constrained by the monotony and the uniformly funereal look of the extras. In this case, I think, we should take advantage of the variety of garb offered by the different classes and occupations. To elaborate: I can imagine an author setting one act in the main marketplace of les Halles in Paris. The setting would be superb, with its bustling life and bold possibilities. In this immense setting we could have a very picturesque ensemble by displaying the porters wearing their large hats, the saleswomen with their white aprons and vividly-coloured scarves, the customers dressed in silk or wool or cotton prints, from the ladies accompanied by their maids to the female beggars on the prowl for anything they can pick up off the street. For inspiration it would be enough to go to les Halles and look about. Nothing is gaudier or more interesting. All of Paris would enjoy seeing this set if it were realized with the necessary accuracy and amplitude.

And how many other settings for popular drama there are for the taking! Inside a factory, the interior of a mine, the gingerbread market, a railway station, flower stalls, a racetrack, and so on. All the activities of modern life can take place in them. It will be said that such sets have already been tried. Unquestionably we have seen factories and railway stations in fantasy plays; but these were fantasy stations and factories. I mean, these sets were thrown together to create an illusion that was at best incomplete. What we need is detailed reproduction: costumes supplied by tradespeople, not sumptuous but adequate for the purposes of truth and for the interest of the scenes. Since everybody mourns the death of the drama our playwrights certainly ought to make a try at this type of popular, contemporary drama. At one stroke they could satisfy the public hunger for spectacle and the need for exact studies which grows more pressing every day. Let us hope, though, that the playwrights will show us real people and not those whining members of the working class who play such strange roles in boulevard melodrama.

As M. Adolphe Jullien has said – and I will never be tired of repeating it – everything is interdependent in the theatre. Lifelike costumes look wrong if the sets, the diction, the plays themselves are not lifelike. They must all march in step along the naturalistic road. When costume becomes more accurate, so do sets; actors free themselves from bombastic declaiming; plays study reality more closely and their characters are more true to life. I could make the same observations about sets I have just made about costume. With them too, we may seem to have reached the highest possible degree of truth, but we still have long strides to take. Most of all we would need to intensify the illusion in reconstructing the environments, less for their picturesque quality than for dramatic utility. The environment must determine the character. When a set is planned so as to give the lively impression of a description by Balzac; when, as the curtain rises, one catches the first glimpse of the characters, their personalities and behaviour, if only to see the actual locale in which they move, the importance of exact reproduction in the decor will be appreciated. Obviously, that is the way we are going. Environment, the study of which has transformed science and literature, will have to take a large role in the theatre. And here I may mention again the question of metaphysical man, the abstraction who had to be satisfied with his three walls in tragedy – whereas the physiological man in our modern works is asking more and more compellingly to be determined by his setting, by the environment that produced him. We see then that the road to progress is still long, for sets as well as costume. We are coming upon the truth but we can hardly stammer it out.

Another very serious matter is diction. True, we have got away from the chanting, the plainsong, of the seventeenth century. But we now have a 'theatre voice', a false recitation that is very obtrusive and very annoying. Everything that is wrong with it comes from the fixed traditional code set up by the majority of critics. They found the theatre in a certain state and, instead of looking to the future, and judging the progress we are making and the progress we shall make by the progress we have already made, they stubbornly defend the relics of the old conventions, swearing that these relics must be preserved. Ask them why, make them see how far we have travelled; they will give you no logical reason. They will reply with assertions based on a set of conditions that are disappearing.

In diction the errors come from what the critics call 'theatre language'. Their theory is that on stage you must not speak as you do in everyday life. To support this viewpoint they pick examples from traditional practices, from what was happening yesterday – and is happening still – without taking account of the naturalistic movement, the phases of which have been established for us by M. Jullien's book.* Let us realize that there is no such thing as 'theatre language'. There has been a rhetoric which grew more and more feeble and is now dying out. Those are the facts. If you compare the declaiming of actors under Louis XIV with that of Lekain, and if you compare Lekain's with that

* Adolphe Jullien 1845–1932, writer on music and the theatre. The book Zola cites is *Histoire du costume au théâtre*, 1880. E.B.

of our own artists today, you will clearly distinguish the phases, from tragic chanting down to our search for the natural, precise tone, the cry of truth. It follows that 'theatre language', that language of booming sonority, is vanishing. We are moving towards simplicity, the exact word spoken without emphasis, quite naturally. How many examples I could give if I had unlimited space! Consider the powerful effect that Geoffroy has on the public; all his talent comes from his natural personality. He holds the public because he speaks on stage as he does at home. When a sentence sounds outlandish he cannot pronounce it; the author has to find another one. That is the fundamental criticism of so-called 'theatre language'. Again, follow the diction of a talented actor and at the same time watch the public; the cheers go up, the house is in raptures when a truthful accent gives the words the exact value they must have. All the great successes of the stage are triumphs over convention.

Alas, yes, there is a 'theatre language'. It is the clichés, the resounding platitudes, the hollow words that roll about like empty barrels, all that intolerable rhetoric of our vaudevilles and dramas, which is beginning to make us smile. It would be very interesting to study the style of such talented authors as MM. Augier, Dumas and Sardou. I could find much to criticize, especially in the last two with their conventional language, a language of their own that they put into the mouths of all their characters, men, women, children, old folk, both sexes and all ages. This irritates me, for each character has his own language, and to create living people you must give them to the public not merely in accurate dress and in the environments that have made them what they are, but with their individual ways of thinking and expressing themselves. I repeat that that is the obvious aim of our theatre. There is no theatre language regulated by such a code as 'cadenced sentences' or sonority. There is simply a kind of dialogue that is growing more precise and is following – or rather, leading – sets and costumes towards naturalistic progress. When plays are more truthful, the actors' diction will gain enormously in simplicity and naturalness.

To conclude, I will repeat that the battle of the conventions is far from being finished, and that it will no doubt last forever. Today we are beginning to see clearly where we are going, but our steps are still impeded by the melting slush of rhetoric and metaphysics.

To Begin

OTTO BRAHM*

Translated by Lee Baxandall

WE are launching a Free Stage for Modern Life.

Art shall be the object of our strivings – the new art, which fixes its attention on reality and contemporary existence.

There was once an art which fled before the day, which sought poetry solely in the twilight of the past, and, by timid flight from reality, strived for those deep ideal distances where blooms eternally youthful that which never was. The art of today, like a clinging organism, embraces all that lives, both nature and society; therefore the closest and the keenest interactions of modern art and modern life are brought into harmony, and whosoever wishes to understand the former must strive also to comprehend the latter in its thousand fluctuating contours, its interwoven and embattled life impulses.

The banner slogan of the new art, written up in golden letters by the leading spirits, is the single word Truth; and Truth it is, Truth on every path of life, which we too strive for and demand. Not the objective truth which eludes those who stand in battle; but the individual Truth which is freely created out of the most personal conviction and which is freely expressed – the Truth of the independent spirit who has nothing to euphemize and nothing to conceal. And who has therefore but a single foe, his arch enemy and mortal antagonist: lies, of every shape and manner.

No other programme do we enter upon in these pages. We disavow every formula, and do not presume to chain life and art, which are in eternal motion, to the rigid constraint of rule. We direct our efforts toward what is Becoming; and the gaze is more attentively directed toward what will come than upon that Eternal Yesterday which loses itself in trying to base itself once and for all upon conventions and precepts about the infinite possibilities of mankind. We bow in humility before everything great which former epochs have handed down to us. But not from them do we obtain our models and norms for existence; for not he who makes the views of a vanished world into his own, but only he who freely feels the demands of the present hour within himself will be suffused by the vital intellectual forces of the age. Only he will be a modern man.

Whosoever bows his ear to the ground in warlike times will hear the sound of what is coming but not yet seen; and thus, with all our senses alert, in the midst of an age full of the stress of creation and the thirst of Becoming, we too want to catch the cadence of what is coming, the onstorming New in all its effervescent lawlessness. No turnstile of theory and no sacredly held examples from the past will restrain the infinity of development which is the essence of the human race.

Wherever the New is greeted with happy cry, a feud must be declared against the Old and it must be conducted with all weapons of the spirit. We do not speak of the Old which lives still, for the great leaders of mankind are not our enemy; but our war cry is pitted against the dead Old, the rigid rule and the outlived criticism which with learned logic oppose themselves to the Becoming. We speak of causes, not of persons – but whenever the clash of views calls out the young against the old, and we cannot deal with the cause without dealing with the person, we want to fight for the demands of our generation with free minds and without obeisance to established authority. And since these pages are given over to the life which is becoming and which marches forward to unknown goals, we will strive as best we can to group around us the youth, the fresh and unexhausted talents. We avoid only the washouts without talent who threaten with noisy excesses to distort a good cause; for we are as well armed against the miserable camp followers of the new art, the pillagers of its successes, as we are against the blindly zealous antagonists.

Wherever modern art has applied its most lively energies,

it has put down roots in the soil of Naturalism. Hearkening to an internal urgency of the age, it has based itself upon the acknowledgement of natural forces and with ruthless striving for honesty it shows us the world as it is. We are friends of Naturalism and we want to go a good stretch of the way with it – but we should not be surprised if, in the course of the journey, at some point which we cannot today ascertain, the road should suddenly turn and astonishing new vistas in art and life should emerge. For human culture is bound by no formula, not even the most recent; and in this conviction, with faith in the Eternally Becoming, we have launched a Free Stage for Modern Life. . . .

PART TWO

Towards a Historical Over-view

Georg Brandes

GEORG BRANDES, 1842–1927, a Dane, was one of the most widely read and influential of nineteenth-century scholars. The excerpt from his writings that follows began as the Inaugural Lecture in a series that later became the six-volume set of *Main Currents in Nineteenth-Century Literature*. The lecture was delivered at the University of Copenhagen on 3 November 1871. Henrik Ibsen read it when the first volume of lectures appeared in the following year. In his letter to Brandes dated 4 April 1872, he wrote:

... I must turn to what has lately been constantly in my thoughts and has even disturbed my sleep. I have read your Lectures.

No more dangerous book could fall into the hands of a pregnant writer. It is one of those works which place a yawning gap between yesterday and today.... Your book reminds of the goldfields of California, when they were first discovered, which either made men millionaires or ruined them. Can our Northern lands take it? I don't know, but it doesn't matter – what cannot stand the ideas of the times must succumb.

What will be the outcome of this mortal combat between two epochs I do not know, but anything rather than the existing state of affairs, say I. I do not promise myself that any permanent improvement will result from victory; hitherto, all development has been no more than a stumbling from one error to another. But the struggle is good, wholesome, invigorating; to me your revolt is a great, shattering, and emancipating outbreak of genius.

The Inaugural Lecture is the only item in the present book not addressed specifically to the subject of drama or theatre. It was thought well worth including, nonetheless, partly because of its influence on Ibsen, and partly because it provides a lucid account of the context of all serious drama in Ibsen's time: the drama does not lead its life in a context of other drama. Also, the Lecture has unaccountably been omitted from the English-language edition of Brandes' *Main Currents*. It was specially translated for publication here.

Inaugural Lecture, 1871*

GEORG BRANDES

Translated by Evert Sprinchorn

BEFORE I embark upon this series of lectures, I feel it is necessary to ask your indulgence. This is the first time that I speak from this platform, and I bring with me all the faults and failings of inexperience. I lack as much in the way of ability as I do in the way of knowledge. What I thereby do or say to offend you will, I believe, be corrected as I gain experience. But with regard to my basic views, my principles and my beliefs, I do not ask any indulgence whatsoever. What I may say or do to offend you in this respect will not be changed. I consider it a duty and a privilege to follow the principles to which I have committed myself: a belief in the right of free inquiry and in the eventual triumph of free thought. After these introductory remarks, expressed here once and for all, I ask you now to consider what I have to say.†

The central subject of this study is the reaction against the literature of the eighteenth century during the first decades of the nineteenth, and the triumph of this reaction. This historic event is European in scope and can only be understood through a study of comparative literature. I am going to attempt such a study as I endeavour to follow simultaneously the main movements in the literatures of Germany, France and England, these being the most important of the period. The study of comparative literature has the double virtue of bringing foreign literatures closer to us, thus making them our own, and of separating us from our own so that we are able to see it as a whole. The eye does not see what lies too close or too far away. The scientific study of

* English translation copyright © 1968 by Evert Sprinchorn.

† This translation of Brandes' lecture is based on the second edition, revised, of *Hovedstrømninger i det nittende Aarhundreds Literatur* (Copenhagen, 1877); but this first paragraph is taken from the first edition.

literature provides us with a telescope, one end magnifying, the other end reducing the size of what we see. The point is to use it to correct the illusions of normal vision. Until now the different nations have, as far as literature is concerned, stood far apart from each other and only in the smallest measure taken any interest in the products of each other's cultures. To illustrate conditions as they exist, or at least did exist, let me remind you of the fable about the fox and the stork. The fox invited the stork to dinner, but he served all the delicious bits on a flat plate so that the stork with his long beak got virtually nothing. You know how the stork avenged himself. He served drink and food in a high and narrow vase into which his long beak could reach, but not the fox's pointed nose. In much the same way the different countries have played fox and stork to each other. A major task in the study of aesthetics is and has been to serve the stork's menu on the fox's china, and vice versa.

A national literature is complete and well-rounded only if it presents the whole history of the thoughts and feelings of its people. The great literatures, such as those of England and France, contain a sufficient number of documents for determining how the English and French people felt and thought in each period of their histories. Other literatures, as, for example, the German, which had its real beginning in the middle of the previous century, are less interesting because they are less complete. This is even more true of a literature so new as our own. It is not possible to study the inner life of the Danish people completely because there are too many large gaps in their literature. Long periods in our history are hidden from us because there were no poetic or psychological manifestos or monuments of any significance. Whatever may have been felt and thought at that time is lost to us. Furthermore, it has been the fate of our little, out-of-the-way country not to have given birth to any important European movement. Nor have we given any support to the great changes that have taken place; we have simply gone through them, that is, if we have been affected by them at all. We got the Reformation from

Germany, the Revolution from France. Our literature is like a little chapel in a big church: it has an altar, but the main altar is somewhere else. Not only are there periods in which we do not know how our people thought and felt, but there are periods in which our thoughts and feelings were more dull and feeble than those of other nations. Consequently, some important European movements reached us while others did not. We rallied behind one slogan of the day but not the next. Indeed, it sometimes happened that, without having participated at all in the main action, whose broad waves were flat and spent before they reached our sandy beaches, we found ourselves participating in the reaction.

I believe that that is what has occurred in this century, and I was so struck by this that I decided to undertake the investigations that make up my lectures.

Everyone knows of the vast revolutionary movement that broke out over the world towards the end of the eighteenth century and of the changes accompanying it in politics and religion. But consider: the essence of it never touched us. To take one example: one of the slogans of this revolutionary literature was freedom of thought. But free thought, which appeared elsewhere in such daring forms and produced such enormous results, reached us in the sadly faded form of theological rationalism. Hegel puts it neatly: 'As long as the sun stood in the firmament, and as long as the planets revolved around it, no one noticed that man was standing on the principle of pure thought – one might say, standing on his head – and was trying to reshape and rebuild the universe according to his own point of view. All the earlier revolutions had had limited aims; this was the first that wished to re-create mankind.' One cannot deny that we Danes respected decorum. We did not stand on our heads. But by the time this powerful movement, brought about by the self-confidence of the humanitarians, which amounted to a fanatic faith in the principle of pure thought, had, like any great river that overflows its banks, given rise to defensive measures and a reaction, we Danes joined in the reaction. In all our literature during the first part of this century, in the poetry of Oehlenschläger, in the sermons of Grundtvig, the speeches of Mynster, and the stories of Ingemann, there is a strong element of reaction against the eighteenth century. The reaction itself was justified and natural. But what I am saying is unjustified and unnatural is that this reaction still continues with us long after it has been stopped and defeated elsewhere.

You must not suppose that I identify reaction with retrogression. Far from it. On the contrary, a true, supplementary, and corrective reaction constitutes progress. But the current of such a reaction is fast and strong and does not stagnate. After having fought for some time against the excesses of the preceding period and after having retrieved what had been repressed, the next period takes up the worthwhile features of the preceding one, reconciles itself with the latter, and continues the movement. But this has not happened. When a plant has been bent to one side, one corrects it by bending it the other way. The reaction against the eighteenth century still moves on, slowly, sluggishly, spasmodically, and it does not seem to want to come to an end. And the consequence is that our literature has sunk into a lethargy which is beginning to amaze even us. That is why I have wanted to describe how the reaction – yes, this very same reaction – has been brought to an end in other countries.

What I shall describe is a historical movement, partaking of the form and character of a play. The accomplishments of the six different groups of literature I intend to describe may be regarded as the six acts of a mighty drama. The first group, the French emigrant writers, inspired by Rousseau, begin the reaction; but with them the reactionary currents are still everywhere mingled with the revolutionary. With the second group, the semi-Catholic romantic school of Germany, the reaction is on the rise, making headway, and holding itself more aloof from the contemporary struggle for progress and liberty. The third group, comprising such authors as Joseph de Maistre, Lamennais in his orthodox period, and Lamartine and Victor Hugo after the restoration of the monarchy when they were still the mainstays of the legitimists and the clerical party, represents the militant and triumphant reaction. Byron and his English contemporaries form the fourth group. It is this man Byron who produces the reversal in the great drama. The Greek War of Independence breaks out; a fresh breeze blows across the face of Europe; Byron falls like a hero in the cause of Greece; and his death makes an extraordinary impression on all the writers of the continent. Shortly before the July revolution the great writers of France turn about to form the fifth group, the French romantic school, and the new liberal movement is represented by such names as Lamennais, Hugo, Lamartine, Musset, George Sand and many others. And when the movement passes from France to Germany, the liberal ideas score a victory there too. The writers forming the sixth and last group which I shall describe are inspired by the Greek War of Independence and the July Revolution and, like the French writers, see in Byron's great shade the leader of the liberal movement. The writers of Young Germany, among whom the most important, like Heine and Börne, are of Jewish extraction, prepare, together with their contemporary French writers, the upheaval of 1848.

I believe that this great drama in six acts has something to teach us. We are now as usual forty years behind the rest of Europe. The current of revolution in the chief literatures has long ago swallowed its tributaries, burst the dikes thrown up against it, and been led off into thousands of channels. We are still trying to hold it back and divert it to the swamp of reaction. But we have only succeeded in holding back our literature.

It should not be difficult for us to agree that Danish literature has at no time in this century been in such a decline as at present. Literary production has virtually ceased, and there are no human or social problems able to awaken any interest or provoke any discussion except in the newspapers and in other fugitive writings. We have never possessed a strongly original creative spirit, and now that we are so thoroughly indifferent to foreign ideas, our spiritual deafness has brought with it, as in the case of deaf-mutes, complete dumbness.

What keeps a literature alive in our days is that it submits problems to debate. Thus, for example, George Sand debates the problem of the relations between the sexes. Byron and Feuerbach religion, John Stuart Mill and Proudhon property, Turgenev, Spielhagen and Émile Augier social conditions. A literature that does not submit problems to debate loses all meaning. The people who produce such a literature may long believe that the redemption of the world will ensue, but they will eventually see their expectations disappointed. Such people have as little to do with development and progress as the fly that thought it was driving the wagon forward because it occasionally gave the four horses some harmless stings.

In such a society many virtues may have been preserved – courage in war, for instance – but these virtues cannot support literature when intellectual courage has vanished. Any reactionary current that stagnates exercises a tyrannical power, and when a society has so changed that it conceals the face of tyranny behind the mask of freedom, when every liberal opinion or statement carelessly expressed in public exposes one to banishment by one's acquaintances, the respectable part of the press, and the larger number of government officials, then naturally only the most extraordinary qualities will suffice to produce the kind of ability and character on which the progress of society depends. If such a society produces any kind of serious literature, one should not be very surprised if its essential aim is to cast scorn on the present and put it to shame. This literature will repeatedly call the people of its time miserable wretches, and one may even find that the works which are most highly praised and most widely sold (Ibsen's *Brand*, for example) are those in which the reader may discover first with horror and then with delight what a worm he is, how pitiful he is, and how cowardly! One may also notice that Will becomes the watchword of such a people, and that everywhere plays about Will and philosophies of Will are being peddled. One demands what one does not possess. One calls for what one misses most bitterly. And one peddles what is most called for. But in spite of all this it would be wrong to come to the pessimistic conclusion that there is less courage, determination, enthusiasm, and Will in such a people than in the average. There is just as much courage and desire for freedom as usual, but now more is needed. For when the current of reaction holds back the new forces in literature, and when, mind you, the society producing it has not, like the English, daily heard itself accused, derided, and even damned for its conventionality and hypocrisy, but has on the contrary been persuaded of its liberalness and has had incense burned every day under its collective nose, then exceptional qualities and conditions are demanded of those who are to bring new blood to the literature of their country. A soldier needs no unusual courage to shoot at the enemy from behind the ramparts, but if he has been led out where there is no cover, it is no wonder that his courage deserts him.

Our literature has worked less for the cause of progress than the more important national literatures because of a combination of circumstances. Even the circumstances that favoured the development of Danish letters in the past stand in our way in this instance. Let me single out the trait of childlikeness in the Danish folk. To this quality we owe the almost unique naïveté of our poetry. Naïveté is, in the highest sense a poetic quality, encountered again and again in nearly all of our poets from Oehlenschläger through Ingemann and Andersen to Hostrup. But naïveté is scarcely a revolutionary quality. Let me point out next the highly abstract idealism of our literature. It deals not with life but with dreams. Like idealism and fear of reality in all literatures, this trait is due to the fact that our poetry developed as a kind of solace for the very real troubles of a politically sick and corrupt period, as a kind of spiritual victory to compensate for the material defeat.

But it has preserved a tragic deficiency as a memory of its victory.

The Dane who goes abroad is sometimes asked, 'How can one learn to know the culture of your country? Has your modern literature produced any clear and distinct types?' The Dane is embarrassed to answer. Most of us know the nature of the types and ideals bequeathed by the eighteenth to the nineteenth century. Let me name a couple of the chief representative types of one country, Germany. There is Nathan the Wise, the ideal of the Enlightenment, symbol of tolerance, or a noble humanity, and a thoroughgoing rationalism. It can hardly be said that we have held on to this ideal or furthered it as was done in Germany, first by Schleiermacher and later by many others. Mynster was our Schleiermacher, but what a vast distance separates his orthodoxy from Schleiermacher's liberalism. Step by step we have departed from the ideals of rationalism and left them far behind us. Clausen* was once their spokesman, but he is no longer. Heiberg† was followed by Martensen, and Martensen's *Speculative Dogmatics* gave way to his *Christian Dogmatics*. There was still a breath of rationalism in the poetry of Oehlenschläger, but the generation of Oehlenschläger and Ørsted‡ gave birth to the generation of Kierkegaard and Paludan-Müller.

German literature of the eighteenth century passed on to us many other representative types. Among these are: Werther, the ideal of the Storm and Stress, representing the struggle of nature and the passions against the restraints of conventionally ordered society; Faust, the most important of them, embodying and comprehending the new spirit of the times, that, dissatisfied with the gains won by the Enlightenment, presages a higher truth, a higher level of

* H. N. Clausen, a Danish theologian who espoused the higher criticism.

† P. A. Heiberg, novelist and social critic who was banished from Denmark in 1799 for his republican views.

‡ H. C. Ørsted was a scientist (discoverer of electromagnetism), and friend of Oehlenschläger.

happiness, and an immensely higher power; Wilhelm Meister, representing humanitarianism, who goes through the school of life from apprenticeship to mastership, who begins by looking for the ideal in a flight away from life and ends by finding it in reality, and for whom the ideal and the real melt into one. There is the Prometheus of Goethe, who expounds the philosophy of Spinoza in intense and moving verse while he creates man in his own image. And there is finally Marquis Posa, the incarnation of the Revolution, the apostle and prophet of freedom, the true representative of the generation that wanted to make mankind happier and progress possible by revolting against all the traditions that had been handed down from on high.

Our Danish literature begins with these types behind it. Does it develop them and carry them further? One cannot say that it does. How can one tell? Only by looking at what has happened since then. Let me tell you what has happened although none of the accounts print it this way. One fine day as Werther went about in despair, madly in love with Lotte, it occurred to him that the bond between her and Albert meant very little indeed, and he took her away from Albert. One fine day Marquis Posa, wearying of preaching freedom at the court of Philip II to the deaf ears of the tyrant, pulled out his sword and ran him through. And Prometheus rose from his mountain and cleaned out Mount Olympus. And Faust, kneeling before the Earth Spirit, rose up and took possession of the earth and subjugated it with steam, electricity and systematic research.

Let us turn our attention now to the figure in which our poetic literature first embodies itself. This is Aladdin* and Aladdin stands for the right of poetry and of poetic naïveté to exist and to triumph. This is poetry about poetry, poetry listening to its own voice, poetry looking at its own reflection and marvelling at its beauty, and very much in danger of becoming a spineless and sensual Narcissus. There is another aspect to Aladdin. He is a genius; and with the sublime audacity of the supremely talented, Oehlenschläger

* In the play by Oehlenschläger, printed 1805.

has dethroned the Faust-figure, transformed Faust into a Noureddin* and let him end as a Wagner. I refrain from expressing my virtually unlimited admiration for this poem in order to pursue my thought. Aladdin is a genius; but what kind of a genius is he? What kind of genius does he remind one of? Geniuses like Oehlenschläger himself perhaps, or like his contemporary Lamartine, but certainly not geniuses like Shakespeare, like Leonardo, like Michelangelo, Beethoven, Goethe, and Schiller, Hugo, and Byron, and least of all like Napoleon, who was perhaps the most immediate inspiration for Aladdin. For a genius is not a man who idles his time away with genius but a man who creates with genius; and his inborn gifts are only so much material for him, not the work itself.

After Aladdin came Oehlenschläger's Nordic heroes, Hakon, Palnatoke, Axel, Hagbarth, ideal figures of great strength and love, who without being portrayed with such imaginative power that they assume an existence of their own in antiquity are still too far removed from the present age to have any meaning for it. With all their beauty they are too abstract and ideal to mirror completely the age in which they were created; and their practical effect is severely limited by their proclaiming themselves to be the heroes of the past. There is in them none of the spirit of modern times. Individual psychology is suppressed, and everything about them that might seem clearly and unambigously modern is deliberately purged away. It is instructive to compare these heroes with those in the contemporary drama of Victor Hugo. The latter are perhaps inferior as poetic creations, but one feels more keenly the breath of a new era when one of Hugo's low-born heroes or heroines strides across the stage. That is why all of Hugo's tragedies were prohibited by the government, something which has never happened to a Dane, a peculiarity which one can attribute, according to one's sympathies, either to the purely poetic quality of our literature or to its complete lack of contact with reality. Even more abstract – I should

* The enchanter who steals the magic lamp from Aladdin.

say bloodless – are the characters in the literary works which derive from Oehlenschläger's dramas and deal with the Middle Ages as Oehlenschläger had dealt with antiquity. I am referring to the novels of Ingemann. The experience and knowledge of life on which these novels are built is infinitesimal. They have other values, but they have little or no relation to reality, although they belong to a group of books that have made the greatest impression on the public. They belong to an irritating and now nearly abandoned genre imported from Scotland, the historical novel, which, having been created by a full-blooded Tory, derived from a spirit whose ideals remained in the past, just as ours have.

Because of this spirit, far too many of the great events of this century were wasted on us. The Greek War of Independence, which elsewhere signalled a revolt so violent that old schools were destroyed and new ones born, occasioned in Denmark a few charming poems but left no deeper mark than that famous line in *King Solomon and George the Hatter*,* 'What does the Baron think of the affairs in Greece?' An event like the July Revolution of 1830 leaves in the works of so outspoken and liberal a soul as Poul Møller no other trace than that certainly beautiful and characteristic poem, 'The Artist among the Rebels', a poem which in its loyalty, its aesthetic indifference to the events of this world, and its contempt for all social agitation mirrors the whole epoch here in Denmark. For Poul Møller the revolutionists were indeed exemplified by 'two liberal-minded boys and a lame editor'. When Byron's poetry finally reached us, after having reigned supreme for a quarter of a century and having spread throughout the world after his proud death, only the trimmings appealed to us. We were on our guard against his heroes and his ideas. One of our noblest and finest poets, Frederik Paludan-Müller, the son of a bishop, appropriated the verse forms, the rhythms, the changes of tone, the baroque leaps between pathos and irony that are characteristic of Byron's epics, but only in order to invest them all with the traditional ways of thinking and feeling.

* A popular farce by J. L. Heiberg, performed 1825.

He poured the old wine in new bottles, and gradually made his poetry into a sounding board for an ascetic morality and the most rigid orthodoxy.

One of the reasons for this state of affairs is certainly to be found in the nature of the social class that has been responsible in this century not only for our literature but also for a large part of our scholarship. While the literature of England and France is composed to a great extent by independent persons, often occupying high positions and having broad horizons, and while German literature in spite of its academic qualities possesses spiritual independence, nature's dearest blessing when Germany was in political bondage, our recent literature has been written almost exclusively by civil servants and by men with an illiberal professional education. While the French and English nobility, the great landowners and the important statesmen, contributed significantly to their cultures, and while their professional writers often lived like nomads and gypsies far from an orderly bourgeois existence, our nobility, the old as well as the new, has played no part in recent literature, and the contributions of our prosperous classes and our few bohemians have not been significant. Our literature like our culture in general has its roots in the university at Copenhagen and in the rectories in the country. An altogether disproportionate number of the men who set the taste of the times have been clergymen or the sons of clergymen or students of theology. The influence of the theologians has been so pervasive that if one conceived an imaginary land and passed an imaginary law according to which only graduates of seminaries could have a voice in literature or be permitted to pass foreign ideas on to their countrymen, I doubt that such a literature, created exclusively by students of divinity, would differ very much from ours.

It seems that we are destined to express ourselves only in the forms of abstract ideals and abstract caricatures. After all the positive heroes I have mentioned come a series of negative ones. Heiberg gathers together all the character traits sketched in his farces and *vaudevilles* to portray in *A*

Soul after Death the typical Philistine of Copenhagen; and Paludan-Müller creates his *Adam Homo*, properly speaking the only genuinely typical and, for a foreigner, the only instructive Danish novel. It represents the quintessence of the spinelessness and the wretchedness of the European reaction. Adam Homo may be the average man but he is the average man during the reign of Christian VIII. Also at this time the imported ideas in philosophy lose ground here, the newly started Hegelian schools suspend their activities, Heiberg gives way to Kierkegaard, and the passion for thought to the passion for faith. The philosophical movement ceases temporarily without having produced a single work, even a short work, while the ethical, religious movement that now begins does find a parallel and a continuation in literature. A group of charming but childish novels of peasant life, the pastorals of our century, are caught in the religious current. Higher and higher mounts the enthusiasm for asceticism and positive religion. One writer outdoes the other in piling up ideals, from the top of which pile reality appears only as a distant black dot.

Where does this current finally emerge? In such figures as Paludan-Müller's Kalanus,* who ecstatically commits himself to the stake, and Ibsen's Brand, whose moral principles if realized would cause half of mankind to starve to death for the sake of an ideal.

This is where we have ended. Nowhere in all of Europe can one find more exalted ideals and only in a few places a duller intellectual life. For one would be extremely naïve to believe that these heroes have their counterparts in our actual life. So strong has the current been that even a spirit as revolutionary as Ibsen's has been seized by it. Does *Brand* stand for revolution or reaction? I cannot tell, there is so much of both in it.

The two main principles of the previous century were

---

* The Indian ascetic in *Kalanus* (printed 1854) greets Alexander the Great as an incarnation of Brahma. Later, appalled by Alexander's voluptuous life, he repudiates him and, despite Alexander's pleadings, kills himself.

freedom of research in science and the unimpeded development of humanity in literature. Whatever does not hold with this current flows down into decadence and takes the way to Byzantium. For all other movements are Byzantine: in science, Byzantine scholasticism, and in poetry, bodies and souls that do not resemble bodies and souls, but are abstract and all alike.

If one were to put into the hands of a man from outer space who had read only our Danish classics a few contemporary foreign plays, such as Alexandre Dumas' *Le Fils naturel*, Émile Augier's *Le Fils de Giboyer* and *Les Effrontés*, he would be confronted with innumerable social conditions and social problems he had no idea existed, because, although they exist in our society, they do not exist in our literature. Our moral zealousness has its complement in our moral prudery. What have we made of those first advances gained at the beginning of the century when we like everyone else for the first time glimpsed a world of poetry beyond the three unities, another god beyond the Holy Trinity, the happiness of true love beyond conventional marriage, a truth beyond dogmas, an equality beyond differences of class and profession, and a freedom far beyond the restraints of propriety, social conventions and morals?

Oehlenschläger emancipated our poetry from the ethics of utilitarianism. Heiberg freed criticism from the subjective school, gained for logic a position as honourable as that of creative literature, and won new territory for philosophy. Then came the first demands for political freedom. But the standard-bearers in literature asked, 'Why on earth do you want political freedom when the true freedom is the inner freedom of the will? It is always permissible to gain this and, once gained, the other freedom is absolutely without significance.' Bulky metaphysical dissertations on the freedom of the will, determinism, and madness had been written before; now there appeared political dissertations on freedom and constitutional rights which demonstrated that a nation could have a constitution without having a constitutional form of government, and genuine freedom without stipulated freedoms. But these arguments did not appease the public, and we won our political freedom.

Now if once again the slogan for further progress were, 'Freedom, the freedom of the spirit', I think a chorus of voices would cry out in unison, 'We mean freedom of thought and the freedom of mankind.' These voices would not be silenced by being asked, 'Why on earth call for freedom when you already have all you could wish for?' – political freedom being understood. The people would not be satisfied with that. For it is not so much our laws that need changing as it is our whole conception of society. The younger generation must plough it up and replant it before a new literature can bloom and flourish. Their chief task will be to channel into our country those currents that have their origin in the revolution and in the belief in progress, and to halt the reaction at all points where its historic mission has been fulfilled.

Arnold Hauser

ARNOLD HAUSER (1892–1978) is known chiefly for his monumental *Social History of Art*, 1952, in which 'The Origins of Domestic Drama' constitutes one chapter. That he appears in an anthology of dramatic theory might at first seem bizarre, but it is precisely by his range that Hauser is remarkable. The same cannot be said for the historians of theatre and drama, few of whom seem ever to have noticed anything in this universe except theatre and drama. If the topic 'Origins of Domestic Drama' seems rather special and narrow, in Professor Hauser's hands it proves to be quite otherwise – the key, or at least *a* key, to modern drama as a whole.

The Origins of Domestic Drama

ARNOLD HAUSER

Translated in collaboration with the author by Stanley Godman

THE middle-class novel of manners and family life represented a complete innovation compared with the various
forms of heroic, pastoral and picaresque novel, which had
dominated the whole field of light fiction until the middle
of the eighteenth century, but it was by no means so
deliberately and methodically opposed to the older literature as the middle-class drama, which arose in conscious
antithesis to classical tragedy and became the mouthpiece of
the revolutionary bourgeoisie. The mere existence of an
elevated drama, the protagonists of which were all members
of the middle class, was in itself an expression of the claim of
this class to be taken just as seriously as the nobility from
which the heroes of tragedy had sprung. The middle-class
drama implied from the very outset the relativizing and be-
littling of the heroic and aristocratic virtues and was in itself
an advertisement for bourgeois morality and the middle-class
claim to equality of rights. Its whole history was determined
by its origins in bourgeois class-consciousness. To be sure, it
was by no means the first and only form of the drama to have
its source in a social conflict, but it was the first example of a
drama which made this conflict its very theme and which
placed itself openly in the service of a class struggle. The
theatre had always propagated the ideology of the classes by
which it had been financed, but class differences had never
before formed more than the latent, never the manifest and
explicit content of its productions. Such speeches as, shall
we say, the following had never been heard before: 'Ye
Athenian aristocrats, the injunctions of your kinship morality
are inconsistent with the principles of our democratic state:
your heroes are not only fratricides and matricides, they are
also guilty of high treason.' Or: 'Ye English barons, your
reckless manners threaten the peace of our industrious cities;

your crown-pretenders and rebels are no more than imposing criminals.' Or: 'You Paris shopkeepers, money-lenders
and lawyers, know that if we, the French nobility, go under,
a whole world will go under which is too good to compromise with you.' But now such things were stated quite
frankly: 'We, the respectable middle class, will not and
cannot live in a world dominated by you parasites, and
even if we ourselves must perish, our children will win the
day and live.'

Because of its polemical and programmatical character,
the new drama was burdened from the very outset with
problems unknown to the older forms of the drama. For,
although these also were 'tendentious', they did not result
in plays with a thesis to propound. It is one of the peculiari-
ties of dramatic form that its dialectical nature makes it a
ready vehicle for polemics, but the dramatist himself is prevented from taking sides in public by its 'objectivity'. The
admissibility of propaganda has been disputed in this form
of art more than in any other. The problem first arose,
however, after the enlightenment had turned the stage into
a lay-pulpit and a platform and had in practice completely
renounced the Kantian 'disinterestedness' of art. Only an
age which believed as firmly as this one in the educable and
improvable nature of man could commit itself to purely tendentious art; every other age would have doubted the effectiveness of such clumsy moral teaching. The real difference,
however, between the bourgeois and the pre-bourgeois
drama did not consist exactly in the fact that the political
and social purpose which was formerly latent was now
given direct expression, but in the fact that the dramatic
conflict no longer took place between single individuals but
between the hero and institutions, that the hero was now
fighting against anonymous forces and had to formulate his
point of view as an abstract idea, as a denunciation of the
prevailing social order. The long speeches and indictments
now usually begin with a plural 'Ye' instead of the singular
'You'. 'What are your laws, of which you make your boast,'
declaims Lillo, 'but the fool's wisdom, and the coward's

valour, the instrument and screen of all your villainies? By them you punish in others what you act yourselves, or would have acted, had you been in their circumstances. The judge who condemns the poor man for being a thief, had been a thief himself, had he been poor.'* Speeches like that had never been heard before in any serious play. But Mercier goes even further: 'I am poor, because there are too many rich' – says one of his characters. That is already almost the voice of Gerhart Hauptmann. But, in spite of this new tone, the middle-class drama of the eighteenth century no more implies the criteria of a people's theatre than does the proletarian drama of the nineteenth; both are the result of a development in which all connexion with the common people has long been lost, and both are based on theatrical conventions which have their source in classicism.

In France the popular theatre, which had masterpieces like *Maître Pathelin* to its credit, was completely forced out of literature by the court theatre; the biblical-historical play and the farce were supplanted by high tragedy and the stylized, intellectualized comedy. We do not precisely know what had survived of the old medieval tradition on the popular stage in the provinces in the age of classical drama, but in the literary theatre of the capital and the court hardly any more of it had been preserved than was contained in the plays of Molière. The drama developed into the literary genre in which the ideals of court society in the service of absolute monarchy found the most direct and imposing expression. It became the representative genre, if only for the reason that it was suitable for presentation with an impressive social framework and theatrical performances offered a special opportunity for displaying the grandeur and splendour of the monarchy. Its motifs became the symbol of a feudalistic-heroic life, based on the idea of authority, service and loyalty, and its heroes the idealization of a social class which, thanks to its exemption from the trivial cares of everyday life, was able to see in this service and loyalty the

* George Lillo: *The London Merchant or the History of George Barnwell*, 1731, iv 2.

highest ethical ideals. All those who were not in a position to devote themselves to the worship of these ideals were regarded as a species of humanity beyond the pale of dramatic dignity. The tendency to absolutism, and the attempt to make court culture more exclusive and more like the French model, led in England, too, to the displacement of the popular theatre that, at the turn of the sixteenth century, had been still completely fused with the literature of the upper classes. Since the reign of Charles I, dramatists had limited themselves more and more to producing for the theatre of the court and the higher ranks of society, so that the popular tradition of the Elizabethan age had soon been lost. When the Puritans proceeded to close down the theatres, the English drama was already on the decline.*

The peripeteia had always been regarded as one of the essentials of tragedy and until the eighteenth century every dramatic critic had felt that the sudden turn of destiny makes the deeper impression, the higher the position from which the hero falls. In an age like that of absolutism this feeling must have been particularly strong, and in the poetic theory of the baroque, tragedy is simply defined as the genre whose heroes are princes, generals and suchlike notabilities. However pedantic this definition may appear to us today, it does lay hold of a basic characteristic of tragedy and even points perhaps to the ultimate source of the tragic experience. It was, therefore, really a decisive turning point when the eighteenth century made ordinary middle-class citizens the protagonists of serious and significant dramatic action and showed them as the victims of tragic fates and the representatives of high moral ideas. In earlier times this kind of thing would never have occurred to anyone, even though the assertion that middle-class persons had always been portrayed on the older stage merely as comic figures is by no means in accordance with the facts. Mercier is slandering Molière when he reproaches him for having tried to

* L. Stephen, *Engl. Lit. and Soc. in the 18th Cent.*, 1960, p. 66.

'ridicule and humiliate' the middle class.* Molière generally characterizes the bourgeois as honest, frank, intelligent and even witty. He usually combines such descriptions, moreover, with a sarcastic thrust at the upper classes.† In the older drama, however, a person from the middle class had never been made to bear a lofty and soul-stirring destiny and to accomplish a noble and exemplary deed. The representatives of the bourgeois drama now emancipate themselves so completely from this limitation and from the prejudice of considering the promotion of the bourgeois to the protagonist of a tragedy as the trivialization of the genre, that they can no longer understand a dramaturgical sense in raising the hero above the social level of the average man. They judge the whole problem from the humanitarian angle, and think that the high rank of the hero only lessens the spectator's interest in his fate, since it is possible to take a genuinely sympathetic interest only in persons of the same social standing as oneself.‡ This democratic point of view is already hinted at in the dedication of Lillo's *London Merchant*, and the middle-class dramatists abide by it on the whole. They have to compensate for the loss of the high social position held by the hero in classical tragedy by deepening and enriching his character, and this leads to the psychological overloading of the drama and creates a further series of problems unknown to earlier playwrights.

Since the human ideals followed by the pioneers of the new middle-class literature were incompatible with the traditional conception of tragedy and the tragic hero, they emphasized the fact that the age of classical tragedy was past and described its masters, Corneille and Racine, as mere word-spinners.§ Diderot demanded the abolition of the tirades, which he considered both insincere and unnatural, and in his fight against the affected style of the *tragédie*

* Mercier: *Du Théâtre ou Nouvel essai sur l'art dramatique*, 1773. Quoted by F. Gaiffe, p. 91.

† Clara Stockmeyer: *Soziale Probleme im Drama des Sturmes und Dranges*, 1922, p. 68.

‡ Beaumarchais: *Essai sur le genre dramatique sérieux*, 1767.

§ Rousseau: *La Nouvelle Héloïse*, II, Lettre 17.

classique, Lessing also attacked its mendacious class character.
It was now discovered for the first time that artistic truth is
valuable as a weapon in the social struggle, that the faithful
reproduction of facts leads automatically to the dissolution
of social prejudices and the abolition of injustice, and that
those who fight for justice need not fear the truth in any of
its forms, that there is, in a word, a certain correspondence
between the idea of artistic truth and that of social justice.
There now arose that alliance, so familiar in the nineteenth
century, between radicalism and naturalism, that solidarity
which the progressive elements felt existed between themselves and the naturalists even when the latter, as in the case
of Balzac, thought differently from them in political matters.

Diderot already formulated the most important principles
of naturalistic dramatic theory. He requires not merely the
natural, psychologically accurate motivation of spiritual
processes but also exactness in the description of the milieu
and fidelity to nature in the scenery; he also desires, as he
imagines, still in accordance with the spirit of naturalism,
that the action should lead not to big scenic climaxes but to a
series of optically impressive tableaux, and here he seems to
have in mind 'tableaux vivants' in the style of Greuze. He
obviously feels the sensual attractiveness of the visual more
strongly than the intellectual effects of dramatic dialectics.
Even in the linguistic and acoustic field he favours purely
sensual effects. He would prefer to restrict the action to
pantomime, gestures and dumb-show and the speaking to
interjections and exclamations. But, above all, he wants to
replace the stiff, stilted Alexandrine by the unrhetorical,
unemotional language of every day. He attempts everywhere to tone down the loudness of classical tragedy and to
curb its sensational stage effects, guided as he is by the
bourgeois fondness for the intimate, the direct and the
homely. The middle-class view of art, which sees in the
representation of the immanent, self-sufficient present the
real aim, strives to give the stage the character of a self-contained microcosm. This approach also explains the idea of
the fictitious 'fourth wall', which is first hinted at by Diderot.

The presence of spectators on the stage had been felt to be a disturbing influence in earlier times, it is true, but Diderot goes so far as to desire that plays should be performed as if no audience were present at all. This marks the beginning of the reign of total illusion in the theatre – the displacement of the play-element and the concealment of the fictitious nature of the representation.

Classical tragedy sees man isolated and describes him as an independent, autonomous intellectual entity, in merely external contact with the material world and never influenced by it in his innermost self. The bourgeois drama, on the other hand, thinks of him as a part and function of his environment and depicts him as a being who, instead of controlling concrete reality, as in classical tragedy, is himself controlled and absorbed by it. The milieu ceases to be simply the background and external framework and now takes an active part in the shaping of human destiny. The frontiers between the inner and the outer world, between spirit and matter, become fluid and gradually disappear, so that in the end all actions, decisions and feelings contain an element of the extraneous, the external and the material, something that does not originate in the subject and which makes man seem the product of a mindless and soulless reality. Only a society that had lost its faith in both the necessity and the divine ordinance of social distinctions and in their connexion with personal virtue and merit, that experiences the daily growing power of money and sees men becoming merely what external conditions make them, but which, nevertheless, affirms the dynamism of human society, since it either owes its own ascendancy to it or promises itself that it will lead to its ascendancy, only that kind of society could reduce the drama to the categories of real space and time and develop the characters out of their material environment. How strongly this materialism and naturalism was conditioned by social factors is shown most strikingly by Diderot's doctrine of the characters in the drama – namely, the theory that the social standing of the characters possesses a higher degree of reality and relevance than their personal, spiritual habitus and that the question whether a man is a judge, an official or a merchant by profession is more important than the sum total of his individual qualities. The origin of the whole doctrine is to be found in the assumption that the spectator is able to escape from the influence of a play much less easily, when he sees his own class portrayed on the stage, which he must acknowledge to be his class if he is logical, than when he merely sees his own personal character portrayed, which he is free to disown if he wants to.* The psychology of the naturalistic drama, in which the characters are interpreted as social phenomena, has its origin in this urge which the spectator feels to identify himself with his social compeers. Now, however much objective truth there may be in such an interpretation of the characters in a play, it leads, when raised to the status of an exclusive principle, to a falsification of the facts. The assumption that men and women are merely social beings results in just as arbitrary a picture of experience as the view according to which every person is a unique and incomparable individual. Both conceptions lead to a stylization and romanticizing of reality. On the other hand, however, there is no doubt that the conception of man held in any particular epoch is socially conditioned and that the choice as to whether man is portrayed in the main as an autonomous personality or as the representative of a class depends in every age on the social approach and political aims of those who happen to be the upholders of culture. When a public wishes to see social origins and class characteristics emphasized in the human portraiture, that is always a sign that that society has become class-conscious, no matter whether the public in question is aristocratic or middle-class. In this context the question whether the aristocrat is only an aristocrat and the bourgeois only a bourgeois is absolutely unimportant.

The sociological and materialistic conception of man, which makes him appear to be the mere function of his environment, implies a new form of drama, completely different from classical tragedy. It means not only the

*Diderot: 'Entretiens sur le Fils naturel'. *Oeuvres*, 1875-7, VII, p. 150.

degradation of the hero, it makes the very possibility of the drama in the old sense of the term questionable, since it deprives man of all autonomy and, therefore, to some extent of responsibility for his actions. For, if his soul is nothing but the battle-ground for contending anonymous forces, for what can he himself still be called to account? The moral evaluation of actions must apparently lose all significance or at least become highly problematical, and the ethics of the drama become dissolved into mere psychology and casuistry. For, in a drama in which the law of nature and nothing but the law of nature predominates, there can be no question of anything beyond an analysis of the motives and a tracking down of the psychological road at the end of which the hero attains his deed. The whole problem of tragic guilt is in question. The founders of the bourgeois drama renounced tragedy, in order to introduce into the drama the man whose guilt is the opposite of tragic, being conditioned by everyday reality; their successors deny the very existence of guilt, in order to save tragedy from destruction. The romantics eliminate the problem of guilt even from their interpretation of earlier tragedy and, instead of accusing the hero of wrong, make him a kind of superman whose greatness is revealed in the acceptance of his fate. The hero of romantic tragedy is still victorious in defeat and overcomes his inimical destiny by making it the pregnant and inevitable solution of the problem with which his life confronts him. Thus Kleist's Prince of Homburg overcomes his fear of death, and thereby abolishes the apparent meaninglessness and inadequacy of his fate, as soon as the decisive power over his life is put into his own hands. He condemns himself to death, since he recognizes therein the only way to resolve the situation in which he finds himself. The acceptance of the inevitability of fate, the readiness, indeed the joyfulness, with which he sacrifices himself, is his victory in defeat, the victory of freedom of necessity. The fact that in the end he does not have to die, after all, is in accordance with the sublimation and spiritualization which tragedy undergoes. The acknowledgement of guilt, or of what remains over of guilt, that is, the successful struggle to escape from the throes of delusion into the clear light of reason, is already equivalent to expiation and the restoration of the balance. The romantic movement reduces tragic guilt to the wilfulness of the hero, to his mere personal will and individual existence, in revolt against the primal unity of all being. According to Hebbel's interpretation of this idea, it is absolutely indifferent whether the hero falls as a result of a good or evil action. The romantic conception of tragedy, culminating in the apotheosis of the hero, is infinitely remote from the melodramas of Lillo and Diderot, but it would have been inconceivable without the revision to which the first bourgeois dramatists submitted the problem of guilt.

Hebbel was fully aware of the danger by which the form of the drama was threatened by the middle-class ideology, but, in contrast to the neo-classicists, he in no way failed to recognize the new dramatic possibilities inherent in middle-class life. The formal disadvantages of the psychological transformation of the drama were obvious. The tragic deed was an uncanny, inexplicable, irrational phenomenon in Greek drama, in Shakespeare and still, to some extent, in French classical drama; its shattering effect was due, above all, to its incommensurability. The new psychological motivation gave it a human measure and, as the representatives of the domestic drama intended, it was made easier for the audience to sympathize with the characters on the stage. The opponents of the domestic drama forget, however, when they deplore the loss of the terrors, the incalculability and inevitability of tragedy, that the irrational effect of tragedy was not lost as a consequence of the invention of psychological motivation and that the irrational content of tragedy had already lost its influence, when the need for that kind of motivation was first felt. The greatest danger with which the drama, as a form, was threatened by psychological and rational motivation was the loss of its simplicity, of its overwhelmingly direct, brutally realistic character, without which 'good theatre' in the old sense was impossible. The dramatic treatment became more and more intimate, more and more intellectualized and withdrawn from mass effects. Not merely the action and stage procedure but also the characters themselves lost their former sharpness of definition; they became richer but less clear, more true to life but less easy to grasp, less immediate to the audience and more difficult to be reduced to a directly evident formula. But it was precisely in this element of difficulty that the main attraction of the new drama resided, though it thereby became increasingly remote from the popular theatre.

The ill-defined characters were involved in obscure conflicts, situations in which neither the opposing figures nor the problems with which they were concerned were fully brought to light. This indefiniteness was conditioned, above all, by the comprehensive and conciliatory bourgeois morality which attempted to discover explanatory and extenuating circumstances and stood for the view that 'to understand everything is to forgive everything'. In the older drama a uniform standard of moral values had prevailed, accepted even by the villains and scoundrels;* but now that an ethical relativism had emerged from the social revolution, the dramatist often wavered between two ideologies and left the real problem unsolved, just as Goethe, for example, left the conflict between Tasso and Antonio undecided. The fact that motives and pretexts were now open to discussion weakened the element of inevitability in the dramatic conflict, but this was compensated for by the liveliness of the dramatic dialectic, so that it is by no means possible to maintain that the ethical relativism of the domestic drama merely had a destructive influence on dramatic form. The new bourgeois morality was all in all dramatically no less fertile than the feudal-aristocratic morality of the old tragedy. The latter knew of no other duties than those owed to the feudal lord and to honour, and it offered the impressive spectacle of conflicts in which powerful and violent personalities raged against themselves and each other. The domestic drama, on the other hand, discovers the duties

* George Lukács: 'Zur Soziologie des Dramas'. *Archiv f. Sozialwiss. u. Sozialpolit.*, 1914, vol. 38, pp. 330 f.

which are owed to society,* and describes the fight for freedom and justice waged by men who are materially more
narrowly tied, but are, nevertheless, spiritually free and
brave – a fight which is perhaps less theatrical but in itself no
less dramatic than the bloody conflicts of heroic tragedy.
The outcome of the struggle is not, however, inevitable to the
same degree as hitherto, when the simple morality of feudal
loyalty and knightly heroism allowed of no escape, no compromise, no 'having it both ways'. Nothing describes the
new moral outlook better than Lessing's words in *Nathan der
Weise*: 'Kein Mensch muss muessen' – words which do not,
of course, imply that man has no duties at all, but that he is
inwardly free, that is to say, free to choose his means, and that
he is accountable for his actions to none but himself. In the
older drama inward, in the new drama outward ties are
stressed; but oppressive as the latter are in themselves, they
allow absolutely free play to the dramatically relevant
action. 'The old tragedy rests on an unavoidable moral
duty' – Goethe says in his essay *Shakespeare and No End*: '...
All duty is despotic ... the will, on the other hand, is free
... It is the god of the age ... Moral duty makes tragedy
great and strong, the will makes it weak and slight.' Goethe
here takes a conservative standpoint and evaluates the drama
according to the pattern of the old, quasi-religious immola-
tion, instead of according to the principles of the conflict of
will and conscience into which the drama has developed. He
reproaches the modern drama for granting too much freedom to the hero; later critics usually fall into the opposite
error and think that the determinism of the naturalistic
drama makes any question of freedom, and therefore of
dramatic conflict, impossible. They do not understand that
it is dramaturgically completely irrelevant where the will
originates, by what motives it is guided, what is 'intellectual'
and what 'material' in it, provided that a dramatic conflict
takes place one way or another.†

These critics put quite a different interpretation on the

* A. Eloesser: *Das buergerliche Drama*, 1898, p. 13. Paul Ernst: *Ein Credo*,
1912, I, p. 102.   † Cf. G. Lukács, loc. cit., p. 343.

principle which they oppose to the hero's will from that of Goethe; it is a matter of two entirely different kinds of necessity. Goethe is thinking of the antinomies of the older drama, the conflict of duty and passion, loyalty and love, moderation and presumption, and deplores that the power of the objective principles of order has diminished in the modern drama, in comparison with that of the subjectivity. Later, necessity is usually taken as meaning the laws of empirical reality, especially those of the physical and social environment, the inescapability of which was discovered by the eighteenth century. In reality, therefore, three different things are in question here: a wish, a duty and a compulsion. In the modern drama individual inclinations are confronted by two different objective orders of reality: an ethical-normative and a physical-factual order. Philosophical idealism described the conformity to law of experience as accidental, in contrast to the universal validity of ethical norms, and in accordance with this idealism, modern classicistic theory regards the predominance of the material conditions of life in the drama as depraving. But it is no more than a prejudice of romantic idealism to assert that the hero's dependence on his material environment thwarts all dramatic conflict, all tragic effects and makes the very possibility of true drama problematical. It is true, however, that, as a consequence of the conciliatory morality and nontragic outlook of the middle class, the modern world offers tragedy less material than former ages. The modern bourgeois public likes to see plays with a 'happy ending' more than great, harrowing tragedies, and feels, as Hebbel remarks in his preface to *Maria Magdalene,* no real difference between tragedy and sadness. It simply does not understand that the sad is not tragic and the tragic not sad.

The eighteenth century loved the theatre and was an extraordinarily fertile period in the history of the drama, but it was not a tragic age, not an epoch which saw the problems of human existence in the form of uncompromising alternatives. The great ages of tragedy are those in which subversive social displacements take place, and a ruling class suddenly loses its power and influence. Tragic conflicts usually revolve around the values which form the moral basis of the power of this class and the ruinous end of the hero symbolizes and transfigures the ruinous end which threatens the class as a whole. Both Greek tragedy and the English, Spanish and French drama of the sixteenth and seventeenth centuries were produced in such periods of crisis and symbolize the tragic fate of their aristocracies. The drama heroizes and idealizes their downfall in accordance with the outlook of a public that still consists for the most part of members of the declining class itself. Even in the case of the Shakespearian drama, the public of which is not dominated by this class, and where the poet does not stand on the side of the social stratum threatened with destruction, tragedy draws its inspiration, its conception of heroism and its idea of necessity from the sight afforded by the fate of the former ruling class. In contrast to these ages, the periods in which the fashion is set by a social class which believes in its ultimate triumph are not favourable for tragic drama. Their optimism, their faith in the capacity of reason and right to achieve victory, prevents the tragic outcome of dramatic entanglements, or seeks to make a tragic accident out of tragic necessity and a tragic error out of tragic guilt. The difference between the tragedies of Shakespeare and Corneille, on the one hand, and those of Lessing and Schiller, on the other, is that in the one case the destruction of the hero represents a higher and in the other case a mere historical necessity. There is no conceivable order of society in which a Hamlet or Antony would not inevitably come to ruin, whereas the heroes of Lessing and Schiller, Sara Sampson and Emilia Galotti, Ferdinand and Luise, Carlos and Posa, could be happy and contented in any other society and any other time except their own, that is to say, except that of their creator. But an epoch which sees human unhappiness as historically conditioned, and does not consider it an inevitable and inescapable fate, can certainly produce tragedies, even important ones; it will, however, in no way utter its final and deepest word in this form. It may, therefore, be right that 'every age produces its own necessity and thus its own tragedy',[*] yet the representative genre of the age of the enlightenment was not tragedy but the novel. In the ages of tragedy the representatives of the old institutions combat the world-view and aspirations of a new generation; in times in which the non-tragic drama prevails, a younger generation combats the old institutions. Naturally, the single individual can be wrecked by old institutions just as much as he can be destroyed by the representatives of a new world. A class, however, that believes in its ultimate victory, will regard its sacrifices as the price of victory, whereas the other class, that feels the approach of its own inevitable ruin, sees in the tragic destiny of its heroes a sign of the coming end of the world and a twilight of the gods. The destructive blows of blind fate offer no satisfaction to the optimistic middle class which believes in the victory of its cause; only the dying classes of tragic ages find comfort in the thought that in this world all great and noble things are doomed to destruction and wish to place this destruction in a transfiguring light. Perhaps the romantic philosophy of tragedy, with its apotheosis of the self-sacrificing hero, is already a sign of the decadence of the bourgeoisie. The middle class will, at any rate, not produce a tragic drama in which fate is resignedly accepted until it feels threatened with the loss of its very life; then, for the first time, it will see, as happens in Ibsen's play, fate knocking at the door in the menacing shape of triumphant youth.

The most important difference between the tragic experience of the nineteenth century and that of earlier ages was that, in contrast to the old aristocracies, the modern middle class felt itself threatened not merely from outside. It was a class made up of such multifarious and contrary elements that it seemed menaced by the danger of dissolution from the very outset. It embraced not only elements siding with reactionary groups and others who felt a sense of solidarity with the lower ranks of society, but, above all, the socially rootless intelligentsia that flirted now with the upper now with the lower classes, and, accordingly, stood partly for the

[*] A. Eloesser, op. cit., p. 215.

ideas of the anti-revolutionary and anti-rationalist romantics, partly agitated for a state of permanent revolution. In
both cases it aroused in the mind of the middle class doubts
about its right to exist at all and about the lasting quality of
its own social order. It bred a 'super-bourgeois' attitude to
life – a consciousness that the middle class had betrayed its
original ideals and that it now had to conquer itself and
struggle to attain a universally valid humanism. On the
whole, these 'super-bourgeois' tendencies had an anti-
bourgeois origin. The development through which Goethe,
Schiller and many other writers passed, especially in Germany, from their revolutionary beginnings to their later,
conservative and often anti-revolutionary attitude, was in
accordance with the reactionary movement in the middle
class itself and with its betrayal of the enlightenment. The
writers were merely the spokesmen of their public. But it
often happened that they sublimated the reactionary convictions of their readers and, with their less robust conscience
and their greater readiness to sham, simulated higher, super-
bourgeois ideals, when they had really sunk back to a pre-
and anti-bourgeois level. This psychology of repression and
sublimation created such a complicated structure that it is
often difficult to differentiate the various tendencies. It has
been possible to establish that in Schiller's *Kabale und Liebe*,
for example, three different generations and, therefore, three
ideologies intersect each other: the pre-bourgeois of the
court circles, the bourgeois of Luise's family and the 'super-
bourgeois' of Ferdinand.* But the super-bourgeois world
here differs from the bourgeois merely by reason of its
greater breadth and lack of bias. The relation between the
three attitudes is really much more complicated in a work
like *Don Carlos*, in which the super-bourgeois philosophy of
Posa enables him to understand Philip and even to sympathize to a certain degree with the 'unhappy' king. In a word,
it becomes increasingly difficult to ascertain whether the

* Fritz Brueggemann: 'Der Kampf um die buergerliche Welt- und
Lebensanschauung i.d. deutschen Lit. d. 18. Jahrh.' *Deutsche Viertels-
jahrsschr. f. Literaturwiss. u. Geistesgesch.*, III 1, 1925.

dramatist's 'super-bourgeois' ideology corresponds to a progressive or a reactionary disposition, and whether it is a question of the middle class achieving victory over itself or simply one of desertion. However that may be, the attacks on the middle class become a basic characteristic of the bourgeois drama, and the rebel against the bourgeois morality and way of life, the scoffer at bourgeois conventions and philistine narrow-mindedness, becomes one of its stock figures. It would shed an extraordinarily revealing light on the gradual alienation of modern literature from the middle classes, to examine the metamorphoses this figure underwent from the 'Storm and Stress' right up to Ibsen and Shaw. For he does not represent simply the stereotyped insurgent against the prevailing social order, who is one of the basic types of the drama of all times, nor is he merely a variant of rebellion against the particular ruler of the moment, which is one of the fundamental dramatic situations, but he represents a concrete and consistent attack on the bourgeoisie, on the basis of its spiritual existence and on its claim to stand for a universally valid moral norm. To sum up, what we are here confronted with is a literary form which from being one of the most effective weapons of the middle class developed into the most dangerous instrument of its self-estrangement and demoralization.

George Lukács

The Hungarian critic GEORGE (Georg, Gyorgy) LUKÁCS (1885–1971), regarded by Thomas Mann as the most important literary critic of our time, has been chiefly interested in the novel, and might be said to have neglected poetry and the drama, about which there is little in his better-known publications, such as *Studies in European Realism*, *The Historical Novel* and *Realism in Our Time*. Yet a couple of hundred pages on modern drama formed one of Lukács's first significant contributions. Written in Hungarian, and finished in 1909, it was then re-done in German and appeared in two parts in the periodical *Archiv für Sozialwissenschaft und Sozial-politik* in 1914 under the title 'Die Soziologie des Modernen Dramas'. What follows is taken from this study; it did not appear in English until 1965, when *The Tulane Drama Review* published it.

The Sociology of Modern Drama*

GEORGE LUKÁCS

Translated by Lee Baxandall

MODERN drama is the drama of the bourgeoisie; modern drama is bourgeois drama. By the end of our discussion, we believe, a real and specific content will have filled out this abstract formulation. . . .

The drama has now taken on new social dimensions.† This development became necessary, and necessary at this particular time, because of the specific social situation of the bourgeoisie. For bourgeois drama is the first to grow out of conscious class confrontation; the first with the set intention of expressing the patterns of thought and emotion, as well as the relations with other classes, of a class struggling for power and freedom. . . . Although in Elizabethan drama the representatives of several classes appear, the true human beings, the dramatic characters, are derived on the whole from a single class. Infrequently, we find a figure that represents the petty nobility, as in *Arden of Feversham*. The lower classes merely take part in comic episodes, or they are on

* Copyright, © 1965, by Lee Baxandall.

† Discussed in detail in a portion of the essay here omitted, which dealt chiefly with development of the stage as an institution. Lukács argues that truly bourgeois plays were first written by the Germans Lenz, Grabbe, Goethe, Schiller, and others who were the first dramatists to develop historicist ideas. Emphasis upon reasoned argument, together with environmental determinism, is seen to distinguish bourgeois playwrights from their predecessors, who had enjoyed spontaneous communication with their audiences by virtue of shared religious sensibility. According to Lukács, this unity was shattered by a new rationalism, introduced to society by the bourgeoisie's organization of economy and social relations along the most productive lines. The playwright found himself isolated from the broad public; he produced intellectualist compositions for minority audiences, while the public, cut off alike from the rationalist stage and from religious drama, sought theatre offering amusement for its own sake. The Little Theatre movement which emerged after 1885 sought to provide bourgeois drama with a stage, but with poor results.

hand simply so their inferiority will highlight the refinements of the heroes. For this reason, class is not decisive in
structuring the character and action of these plays. . . .

A new determinant is joined to the new drama: value
judgement. In the new drama not merely passions are in conflict, but ideologies, *Weltanschauungen*, as well. Because men
collide who come from differing situations, value judgements
must necessarily function as importantly, at least, as purely
individual characteristics. . . . The moral outlooks of Hamlet
and Claudius, and even of Richard and Richmond, are at
bottom identical. Each man is resolute, and feels contempt-
ible if he acts contrary to this moral view. Claudius knows
the murder of his brother to be a sin; he is even incapable of
seeking motives that might justify his action, and it is inconceivable that he would attempt a relativist justification
(as Hebbel's Herodes will, following the murder of Aristo-
bolus). Also the 'sceptical' and 'philosophical' Hamlet never
for a moment doubts that he is impelled as though by
categorical imperative to seek blood revenge. So long as he
remains incapable of acting as he knows he must, he feels
sinful and blameworthy. Hegel is therefore correct when he
says the deeds of Shakespeare's heroes are not 'morally
justified'. For the ethical value judgement of that epoch
rested upon such solid metaphysical foundations, showed
such little tolerance for any kind of relativity, and gained
universality from such mystic, non-analyzable emotions,
that no person violating it – for whatever reasons and
motive – could justify his act even subjectively. His deed
could be explained by his soul's condition, but no amount of
reasoning could provide absolution. . . .

The conflict of generations as a theme is but the most
striking and extreme instance of a phenomenon new to
drama, but born of general emotion. For the stage has
turned into the point of intersection for pairs of worlds
distinct in time; the realm of drama is one where 'past'
and 'future', 'no longer' and 'not yet', come together in a
single moment. What we usually call 'the present' in
drama is the occasion of self-appraisal; from the past is born

the future, which struggles free of the old and of all that stands in opposition. The end of each tragedy sees the collapse of an entire world. The new drama brings what in fact is new, and what follows the collapse differs qualitatively from the old; whereas in Shakespeare the difference was merely quantitative. Looked at from an ethical perspective: the bad is replaced by the good, or by something better than the old, and at any rate decidedly different in kind. In *Götz von Berlichingen* Goethe depicts the collapse of a world; a tragedy is possible in this case only because Götz was born at that particular time. A century or perhaps even a generation earlier, and he would have become a hero of legend, perhaps rather like a tragi-comic Don Quixote; and a scant generation later as well, this might have been the result. . . .

What we are discussing here is the increased complexity which determines dramatic character. We find it can be viewed from different sides, in numerous perspectives; characters in the new drama are more complicated than in the old, threads that are more intricate run together and knot with one another and with the external world, to express the interrelationship. In turn the concept of the external world grows more relative than ever. We have said of the drama that, in general, destiny is what confronts man from without. In Greek and even in Shakespearean drama we can still easily distinguish between man and his environment, or, speaking from the viewpoint of drama, between the hero and his destiny. But now these lines of division have blurred. So much of the vital centre streams out of the peripheries, and so much streams from there into the vital centre of man, that the concepts which distinguish man from his environment, flesh from spirit, free will from circumstance, hero from destiny, character from situation, are nearly deprived of meaning in the face of the complexity of constant interactions. Destiny is what comes to the hero from without. If we are to continue composing dramas, we must hold to this definition regardless of whether it is true in life; otherwise we would find it impossible to maintain the contending parties in equilibrium (supposing a two-dimension composition), nor would there be foreground or background. . . . Most simply, what must be located is the equilibrium between man and the external world; the relation of a man to his action, to the extent that his action is really still his.

The more that circumstances define man, the more difficult this problem seems, and the more the very atmosphere appears to absorb all into itself. Man, distinct contours, no longer exist; only air, only the atmosphere. All that modern life has introduced by way of enriching the perceptions and emotions seems to vanish into the atmosphere, and the composition is what suffers. . . .

To what extent is modern man the enactor of his actions? In his actions man elaborates his entire being, he arrives at himself in them: how much are they really his? How much is the vital centre of man really deep within him? This relation will be the prime determinant of style in every drama. All stylization, all structure bases itself on where the one and the other diverge and coincide, how the one determines the other. . . . All reflection on the drama comes to this: how does man achieve a tragic action? Is it indeed he who achieves it? By what means? The question truly at the bottom of the theory of tragic guilt is this: did the tragic personage really do his tragic deed, and if he did not, can it be tragic? And the real meaning of 'constructing the guilt' exists in building bridges between the deed and the doer, in finding a point from which one will see that all proceeds from within despite every opposition, a perspective which rescues the autonomy of tragic man. . . .

We have to ask whether there can still be a drama. The threat to it is indisputably great, and in naturalism, for instance, we see that it virtually ceases to be dramatic. And yet only the origin of the mutually-opposing forces has been altered; the forces themselves must not be allowed in turn to grow so out of balance that a drama is not possible. In other words, we are faced in the final analysis with a problem of expression, and need not necessarily concern ourselves with the problem of the drama's existence. It matters little whether the will which is set against destiny originates entirely from within; it matters as little whether it is free or constrained, or determined by circumstances of whatever sort. These matters count for little, because a drama remains possible so long as the dynamic force of the will is strong enough to nourish a struggle of life and death dimensions, where the entire being is rendered meaningful.

Hebbel was the first to recognize that the difference between action and suffering is not quite so profound as the words suggest; that every suffering is really an action directed within, and every action which is directed against destiny assumes the form of suffering. Man grows dramatic by virtue of the intensity of his will, by the outpouring of his essence in his deeds, by becoming wholly identical with them. So long as this capacity retains sufficient force to symbolize the entirety of man and his destiny, the displacement earlier noted results merely in a new form of the same relation. The heroes of the new drama – in comparison to the old – are more passive than active; they are acted upon more than they act for themselves; they defend rather than attack; their heroism is mostly a heroism of anguish, of despair, not one of bold aggressiveness. Since so much of the inner man has fallen prey to destiny, the last battle is to be enacted within. We can best summarize by saying that the more the vital motivating centre is displaced outward (*i.e.*, the greater the determining force of external factors), the more the centre of tragic conflict is drawn inward; it becomes internalized, more exclusively a conflict in the spirit. For up to a certain limit, the inner powers of resistance upon which the spirit can depend become greater and more intense in direct proportion to the greatness and intensity of the outwardly opposing forces. And since the hero now is confronted not only with many more external factors than formerly, but also by actions which have become not his own and turn against him, the struggle in which he engages will be heightened into anguish. He must engage in the struggle: something drives him into it which he cannot resist; it is not his to decide whether he even wishes to resist.

This is the dramatic conflict: man as merely the intersection point of great forces, and his deeds not even his own. Instead something independent of him mixes in, a hostile system which he senses as forever indifferent to him, thus shattering his will. And the why of his acts is likewise never wholly his own, and what he senses as his inner motivating energy also partakes of an aspect of the great complex which directs him toward his fall. The dialectical force comes to reside more exclusively in the idea, in the abstract. Men are but pawns, their will is but their possible moves, and it is what remains forever alien to them (the *abstractum*) which moves them. Man's significance consists only of this, that the game cannot be played without him, that men are the only possible hieroglyphs with which the mysterious inscription may be composed. . . .

The new drama is nevertheless the drama of individualism, and that with a force, an intensity and an exclusiveness no other drama ever had. Indeed, one can well conceive an historical perspective on the drama which would see in this the most profound distinction between the old and new drama; such an outlook would place the beginnings of new drama at the point where individualism commences to become dramatic. . . . We said previously that new drama is bourgeois and historicist; we add now that it is a drama of individualism. And in fact these three formulas express a single point of demarcation; they merely view the parting of ways from distinct vantage-points. The first perspective is the question of sociological basis, the foundation on which the other two are based and from which they grow. It states simply that the social and economic forms which the bourgeoisie opposed to remaining vestiges of the feudal order became, from the eighteenth century onward, the prevailing forms. Also, that life proceeds within this framework, and in the tempo and rhythm it dictates, and thus the problems this fact provokes are precisely the problems of life; in a word, that culture today is bourgeois culture. . . . Both historicism and individualism have their roots in the soil of this one culture, and though it may seem from several points of view that they would be sharply conflicting, mutually exclusive opposites, we must nevertheless ask how much this opposition really amounts to an antagonism. . . .

In the course of German Romanticism the historicist sense grew to consciousness together with and parallel to Romantic Individualism, and the two were never felt to exclude one another. We must regard as no accident the way both of these sensibilities rose to consciousness coincidentally and closely associated with the first great event of bourgeois culture, and perhaps its most decisive, the French Revolution, and all that happened around and because of it. . . .

If we examine even the superficial externals of modern life, we are struck by the degree to which it has grown uniform, though it theoretically has engendered a most extreme individualism. Our clothing has grown uniform, as has the communications system; the various forms of employment, from the employee's viewpoint, have grown ever more similar (bureaucracy, mechanized industrial labour); education and the experiences of childhood are more and more alike (the effect and increasing influence of big-city life); and so on. Parallel to this is the ongoing *rationalizing* of our life. Perhaps the essence of the modern division of labour, as seen by the individual, is that ways are sought to make work independent of the worker's capacities, which, always irrational, are but qualitatively determinable; to this end, work is organized according to production outlooks which are objective, super-personal and independent of the employee's character. This is the characteristic tendency of the economics of capitalism. Production is rendered more objective, and freed from the personality of the productive agent. An objective abstraction, capital, becomes the true productive agent in capitalist economy, and it scarcely has an organic relation with the personality of its accidental owner; indeed, personality may often become superfluous, as in corporations.

Also, scientific methodologies gradually cease to be bound up with personality. In medieval science a single individual personally would command an entire sphere of knowledge (*e.g.*, chemistry, astrology), and masters passed on their knowledge or 'secret' to the pupils. The same situation was true in the medieval trades and commerce. But the modern specialized methodologies become continually more objective and impersonal. The relation between work and its performers grows more loose; less and less does the work engage the employee's personality, and conversely, the work is related ever less to the worker's personal qualities. Thus work assumes an oddly objective existence, detached from the particularities of individual men, and they must seek means of self-expression outside their work. The relations between men grow more impersonal as well. Possibly the chief characteristic of the feudal order was the way men's dependencies and relations were brought into unity; by contrast, the bourgeois order rationalizes them. The same tendency to depersonalize, with the substitution of quantitative for qualitative categories, is manifested in the overall state organization (electoral system, bureaucracy, military organization, etc.). Together with all this, man too develops a view of life and the world which is inclined toward wholly objective standards, free of any dependency upon human factors.

The style of the new individualism, especially the aspect of importance to us, is defined by this displacement in the relations of liberty and constraint. The transformation can be briefly formulated: previously, life itself was individualistic, now men, or rather their convictions and their outlooks on life, are. Earlier ideology emphasized constraint, because man felt his place within a binding order to be natural and consistent with the world system; and yet, all occasions of concrete living offered him the opportunity to inject his personality into the order of things by means of his deeds. Hence a spontaneous and continuous individualism of this sort was feasible, whereas today it has grown conscious and problematic as a result of the transformation we have sketched. Previously it was – in Schiller's sense – naïve, and today sentimental. The formulation is this, applied to drama: the old drama, by which we mean here primarily that of the Renaissance, was drama of great individuals, today's is that of individualism. In other words, the realization of personality, its *per se* expression in life, could in no wise become a theme of earlier drama, since personality was not yet problematic. It is, in the drama of today, the chief and most central problem. Though it is true that in most tragedies the action consisted of the clash at some point of someone's maximum attainment with what lay outside him, and the existing order of things refused to let a figure rise to the peak of his possibilities without destroying him, yet this was never associated, consciously at least, with the blunt concept of maximized attainment. The arrangement of the situation was never such that the tragedy had necessarily to result, as it were, from the bare fact of willing, the mere realization of personality. In summary: where the tragedy was previously brought on by the particular *direction* taken by the will, the mere *act* of willing suffices to induce it in the new tragedy. Once again Hebbel offers the most precise definition. He stated that it did not matter for the purposes of drama whether the hero's fall was caused by good or bad actions.

The realization and maintenance of personality has become on the one hand a conscious problem of living; the longing to make the personality prevail grows increasingly pressing and urgent. On the other hand, external circumstances, which rule out this possibility from the first, gain ever greater weight. It is in this way that survival as an individual, the integrity of individuality, becomes the vital centre of drama. Indeed the bare fact of Being begins to turn tragic. In view of the augmented force of external circumstance, the least disturbance or incapacity to adjust is enough to induce dissonances which cannot be resolved. Just so, the aesthetic of Romanticism regarded tragedy – with a metaphysical rationale and explanation, to be sure – as a consequence of mere being, and the necessary inevitable consequence and natural correlate of individuation. Thus, the contention of these mutually opposed forces is emphasized with increasing sharpness. The sense of being constrained grows, as does its dramatic expression; likewise the longing grows for a man to shatter the bonds which bind men, even though the price he pays is his downfall.

Both these tendencies already had become conscious by the time of *Sturm und Drang* drama, but – in theory at least – they were considered as complementary elements serving to differentiate the genres of art. Lenz saw here the distinction between comedy and tragedy. For him, comedy portrayed society, the men rooted in it, and relationships against which they were incapable of successful struggle; whereas tragedy presented great personalities, who challenged relationships and struggled though it might mean ruin. As early as Goethe's tragedy *Götz* and the first dramas of Schiller, however, relationships are nearly as emphasized as in Lenz's comedies; moreover, what prevents Lenz's comedies from qualifying as real tragedies is not to be found in his idea of what distinguishes the genres (here he was influenced by Diderot and Mercier).

Thus we can say that the drama of individualism (and historicism) is as well the drama of milieu. For only this much-heightened sense of the significance of milieu enables it to function as a dramatic element; only this could render individualism truly problematic, and so engender the drama of individualism. This drama signals the collapse of eighteenth century doctrinaire individualism. What then was treated as a formal contention between ideologies and life, now becomes a portion of content, an integral part of the historicist drama. Modern life liberates man from many old constraints and it causes him to feel each bond between men (since these are no longer organic) as a bondage. But in turn, man comes to be enclasped by an entire chain of abstract bondages, which are yet more complicated. He feels, whether or not he is conscious of it, that every bond whatsoever is bad and so every bond between men must be resisted as an imposition upon human dignity. In every case, however, the bondage will prove stronger than the resistance. In this perspective Schiller's first play is one typical commencement of the new drama, just as Goethe's play was in another perspective.

Artistically this all implies, in the first place, a paradox in the dramatic representation of character. For in the new drama, compared to the old, character becomes much more important and at the same time much less important. Our perspective alone determines whether we count its formal significance as everything or as nothing. Even as the philosophies of Stirner and Marx are basically drawn from the same source, Fichte, so every modern drama embodies this duality of origin, this dialectic out of the life that gives it birth. (We perhaps see this conflict most clearly in the historical dramas of Grabbe.) Character becomes everything, since the conflict is entirely for the sake of character's vital centre; for it alone and for nothing peripheral, because the force disposed of by this vital centre alone determines the dialectic, that is, the dramatic, quality of drama. Conversely, character becomes nothing, since the conflict is merely *around* and *about* the vital centre, solely for the *principle* of individuality. Since the great question becomes one of to what degree the individual will finds community possible, the direction of the will, its strength, and other specifics which might render it individual in fact, must remain unconsidered. Thus – and the essence of the stylistic problem is here – character is led back to more rational causes than ever before, and becomes at the same time ever more hopelessly irrational. The old drama was founded in a universal sensibility, unifying and meta-rational, which circumscribed as well as permeated its composition and psychology. The old drama's religious origins thus afforded man what was virtually an unconscious and naïve mode of expression. Indeed, to the extent that this drama grew conscious of its tendency, efforts were made to eliminate it. (Euripides is perhaps the best example here.) By contrast, the foundations of the new drama are rational: from its origins it lacks the quality of mystical religious emotion. Only when this emotion once again appears in life does a real drama again appear; to be sure, it re-emerges at first as an exclusively artistic demand, but later it seeks to serve as the unifying foundation of life and art. And yet this meta-rational, indissoluble sensibility could never again escape the mark of consciousness, of being *a posteriori*; never could it be once more the unifying, enveloping atmosphere of all things. Both character and destiny had acquired a paradoxical duality, had become at once mystically irrational and geometrically constructed. The expression of the meta-rational becomes in this way more mysterious in psychology than it was earlier, but also, in its technique, more rational and conceptual. The drama comes to be built upon mathematics, a complicated web of abstractions, and in this perspective character achieves significance merely as an intersection; it becomes, as Hofmannsthal once remarked, equivalent to a contrapuntal necessity. And yet, no such systemization can contain the real sum of what humanity makes out of a human being (and drama without human beings is inconceivable). Therefore the dramatic and the characteristic aspects of modern man do not coincide. That which is truly human in the human being must remain to a degree outside the drama. Seen in the perspective of a single life, the personality turns inward, becomes spiritualized, whereas the outward data in turn become abstract and uniform, until a true connexion between the two is impossible. The data, actions manifested in the external world, fail to account for the whole man, who in turn is not able to arrive at an action revelatory of his entire self. (Here lies the most profound stylistic contradiction of the intimate drama: as drama increasingly becomes an affair of the spirit, it increasingly misses the vital centre of personality.) This – in context with that indissoluble irrationality whereby man is represented – explains the heavy burden of theory encumbering much of the new drama. Since the vital centre of character and the intersecting point of man and his destiny do not necessarily coincide, supplemental theory is brought in to contrive a dramatic linkage of the two. One could indeed say that the maintenance of personality is threatened by the totality of external data. The data perhaps cannot drain the personality dry – but personality can, by a process of internalization, seek to flee the individual data, avoiding them, keeping out of contact with them.

In sum, life as the subject of poetry has grown more epic, or to be precise, more novelistic than ever (we refer, of course, to the psychological rather than the primitive form of the novel). The transposition of life into the drama is achieved only by the symptomatic rendering of the life data. For the significance of life's external particulars has declined, if we regard them with the task in mind of rendering man dramatic. Thus, the threat to personality becomes almost of necessity the subject of theoretical discussion. Only if the problem is presented abstractly, dialectically, can we succeed in turning the particular event, which is the basic stuff of drama, into an event touching upon, and expressive of, dramatic man's inner essence. The personage must be consciously aware that in the given case directly involving him, the perpetuation of his personality is at stake. The new drama is on this account the drama of individualism: a drama of demands upon personality made conscious. For this reason men's convictions, their ideologies, are of the highest artistic importance, for they alone can lend a symptomatic significance to the naked data. Only they can bring the vital centres of drama and of character into adjustment. However, this adjustment will always remain problematic; it will never be more than a 'solution', an almost miraculous coherence of mutually antagonistic forces, for the ideology threatens in turn to reduce character to a 'contrapuntal necessity'.

Thus heroism in the new drama is quite different from what it was in the old; and the French *tragédie classique* relates most intimately to the old in this regard. Heroism is now more passive, requires less of outward splendour, success, and victory (here again we refer to Hebbel's theory of suffering and action); but on the other hand it is more conscious, judicious and, in expression, more pathetic and rhetorical than was the old. Perhaps we will be somewhat

dubious about this last assertion, in view of the sparse simplicity of language in many modern dramas; even so, the
essence of the question here concerns not so much rhetoric
or its absence in direct expression, but rather the underlying
tone in the pathetic scenes, and how much or relatively little
this approaches expression. When Hebbel's Clara, Ibsen's
Hedda, or even Hauptmann's Henschel dies (to name but
the least obtrusively pathetic dénouements) the death partakes of the very same tone as did the emotions of heroes in
Corneille and Racine. In the face of death, the heroes of
Greek and Shakespearian drama were composed; their
pathos consists of bravely looking death in the eye, of
proudly bearing what is not to be averted. The heroes of the
new drama always partake of the ecstatic; they seem to have
become conscious of a sense that death can vouchsafe them
the transcendence, greatness, and illumination which life
withheld (*e.g.*, the *Antigone* of Sophocles compared with that
of Alfieri), and together with this a sense that death will
fulfil and perfect their personalities. This sense arose only
among the spectators in the old drama. That is why Schopenhauer valued the modern tragedy more highly than the
ancient; he called the tone resignation, and regarded it as the
essence of tragedy. With this the outer event becomes wholly
inward – that is, at the moment when the two vital centres
coincide most exactly – and form has in a sense become content. We might well say that the ancients regarded tragedy
naïvely. The tragedy is *a posteriori* to the viewpoint of the
acting personages and the stylistic means. Thus it is not so
important that the problem be thought through to its end.
By contrast, in the new tragedies the tragedy is asserted as
primary; the various particular phenomena of man, life,
and the events of drama are all regarded as tragic; here the
tragedy is *a priori* to life.

A dramatic problem exists in this antimony of an individualism which relates to the external world within a reduced
scope of expressive significations. It is not the only problem.
As we have seen, one of the important new forms of our life
results from the slackening and loosening of constraints in

the realm of the particular and the immediate, while the abstract constraints correspondingly grow and assume augmented force. The individual's sense of autonomy in his relations with others is ever-increasing, he tolerates less and less any purely personal bond between men, which by its nature will demand more of personality than do those bonds which are purely abstract. Simmel provides an interesting case of this transformation in sensibility. At the beginning of the modern epoch, he states, should an impoverished Spanish nobleman enter the personal service of a rich man (*i.e.*, work as a servant or lackey), he would not lose his title of nobility, whereas he would should he turn to a trade. In contrast, a young American woman today is not ashamed to work in a factory, but she does feel shame if she takes up housework in another's employ. Thus the relations among men have grown much more complex. For if the realization of personality is not to become a hollow ideology, somebody must achieve it. But since this someone will feel his personal autonomy to be sacred, he will tolerate intrusion upon it no more than will those who aspire to be his master. In this way new conflicts result from the new patterning of sensibility, and this at precisely the juncture where, in the old order of society, the relation of higher to lower rank (master to servant, husband to wife, parents to children, etc.) found stability, the point where a tradition which dated back countless centuries had the energy to confirm and perpetuate tendencies through which the lives of men mingled in the most intimate manner. And so again, and in yet another perspective, the new drama emerges as the drama of individualism. For one of individualism's greatest antimonies becomes its foremost theme: the fact that realization of personality will be achieved only at the price of suppressing the personalities of others (which, in turn, require for their realization the ruin of the personalities of others).

As a formal relationship, this adds a new development to human relations in drama. Behind a belief that man's full personality is realized in his relationships with others, lies an emotion, a sensibility that suffuses all of life. When the emotion vanishes or diminishes, characters whose spirit functions chiefly on the basis of that emotion (the servant, confidante, etc.) will vanish from the drama. As the emotion ceases to be universal they become no more than hollow, illusion-disrupting technical properties. This is an evident fact of the French and Spanish drama, and we might better mention that Kent's whole personality is fulfilled in the relationship to Lear, as is Horatio's in his relationship to Hamlet. By contrast, in Goethe's first play, and in Schiller's, we find the theme of a servant at the crucial moment turning against his master (Weislingen – Franz; Franz Moor – Herman), thus ceasing to exist merely in relationship to the master. Here the means elude the one who proposes to use them, they take on new life, become an end. As in many other realms we see here, too, how purely decorative relationships are shattered by the new life; relations become more complex, and where once only gestures made contact, psychological bonds and complex reciprocal effects that are barely expressible are now produced.

The stylistic problem is defined under these conditions, that is, by displacements in the relations among men as caused by the new life (the dramatic material) and by the new ways men have of regarding and evaluating their relationships (the dramatic *principium stilisationis*). Limitations set by these possibilities become the limits of the new drama's expressive potential; and both types of limitation produce the questions which can set the stylistic problem. Perhaps we may briefly formulate these questions: what kind of man does this life produce, and how can he be depicted dramatically? What is his destiny, what typical events will reveal it, how can these events be given adequate dramatic expression?

How does man in the new life relate to the men in the world about him? We must phrase the question thus, if we wish to arrive at a man suitable for drama. Man in isolation is not suited to the drama; no literary art can result from an isolation of human existence which would correspond to the art of portraiture. Literature shows man only in the succession of his feelings and thoughts, which means it cannot entirely exclude the causes of the feelings and thoughts; at most it will somewhat conceal a portion of these causes, that is, the external world, which is their immediate origin. Every other literary form can if it wishes, however, present causes as though sprung straight from the soul of man, as though impressions were drawn but from the soul. They can, in other words, depict arbitrarily the relation of man to his external world, showing it as something other than a web of complex interactions. The dramatic form forbids such an approach, and it moreover focuses relations to the external world in relations to other men. Thus investigation of a man suited for drama coincides with an investigation of the problem of man's relation to other men. (Elsewhere we have discussed, and will discuss again, this relation in its totality, *i.e.*, so-called destiny, the unity that symbolizes this totality.) How do men make contact with one another? Or better, what is their maximum potential for approaching one another, and what is the maximum distance they can place between themselves? Better yet, to what extent is man isolated in modern drama, to what degree is he alone?

Doubtless the old drama offers numerous examples of incomprehension between men. They can be of social origin, resulting because men of low origins and temperament must always see an eternal riddle in all refinement. However, this kind of incomprehension is not an aspect of the problem, for it depends merely upon social distinctions. Other instances are of a moral origin, inasmuch as a refined spirit (Claudius says of Hamlet), 'being remiss, most generous, and free from all contriving', just cannot imagine that other men are otherwise. This is the blindness of noble soul, confronted by a calculating evil which sees quite through it. Incomprehension such as this always has a rational basis, either in the qualities of particular men, or in the consequences of certain specific circumstances. It is part of the dramatic groundplan, built in from the first as a 'given'. As some men will understand one another, others will not, and the one relationship is as absolute and constant as the other. Yet the continued viability of the confidante should be a sign that the potential of absolute understanding among men was never in doubt. Confidantes are almost eliminated in the modern drama, and where they remain, they are felt to function as a disruptive technical device. Now gone out of life is that universal emotion for which alone they could function as symbol, which lifted them above their merely technical function so they might appear as the stylization of a palpable something in reality, rather than a mere convention. The emotion for which they stood could only have been one of the absolute possibility of understanding. If we consider the most complex of these relationships, the one closest to our own emotion, we will see that the functioning of Horatio vis-à-vis Hamlet only confirms that no discord of spirits did or could exist between them; all Hamlet's actions and all his motives are rightly regarded and valued by Horatio, in their original sense. What one says to the other is understood and felt as the other understood and felt. Hamlet – remarkable as this may sound – is thus not alone. When he dies he does so with sure knowledge that a man lives in whom his own spirit is mirrored, pure, without the distortion of incomprehension. The new drama has no confidantes, and this is a symptom that life has robbed man of his faith that he can understand another man; *'nous mourrons tous inconnus'*, Balzac says somewhere. . . . I do not allude here to Faust's *Alleinsein*, nor to that of Tasso, nor to the loneliness of Grillparzer's Kaiser Rudolf nor to that of Hebbel's Herodes, next to whom an understanding friend never stood nor ever could stand. Rather I will direct attention to the first great friendship of the new drama, that between Carlos and Posa (and, to a lesser degree to be sure, that between Clavigo and Carlos); and to that of Kandaules and Gyges, Gregers Werle and Ekdal, Borkmann and Foldal, etc. This is no result of spiritual greatness, either, for neither Hebbel's Clara, nor Hauptmann's Henschel, nor Rose Bernd ever finds a person so near to them as Horatio is to Hamlet. Men become simply incapable of expressing the truly essential in them and what truly directs their actions; even should they in rare moments find words to fit the inexpressible, these words will at any rate go unheard past the spirits of others, or reach them with meaning transformed.

A new element is correspondingly introduced into the dialogue – or rather, a new style problem confronts dialogue. . . . What is said becomes ever more peripheral to what is not expressible. The melody in dialogue is ever more submerged in the accompaniment, the openly spoken in the allusion, in silence, in effects achieved by pauses, change of tempo, etc. For the process which proceeds exclusively within, which will not even seek for words, which *can* not, is better expressed by word groupings than by their sense, and better by their associative power than by their real meaning, by their painterly or musical rather than compressive energy. The more lonely men in drama become (and the development is ever more in this direction, or at least toward awareness of it), the more the dialogue will become fragmented, allusive, impressionistic in form rather than specific and forthright. As a form, monologue is not capable of fulfilling this task. . . . A monologue is in fact the compression of a situation, or else a commentary in programmatic form upon what will come later. In a monologue the loneliness of a specific situation is compressed and expressed together with all that must remain unsaid because of the situation; and certain matters at most remain concealed: shame, for instance. But because the monologue always comes either at the start or the end of a dialogue, it cannot express the ever-shifting nuances of understanding and incomprehension which evade formulation and which we speak of here. The new dramatic man is not isolated because he must conceal certain matters for specific reasons, but because he strongly feels he wants, and is aware of wanting, to come together – and knows he is incapable of it. . . .

The only ideology which men will not feel to be an ideology is one which prevails absolutely and tolerates no opposition or doubt; only such a one ceases to be abstract and intellectual and is entirely transformed into feeling, so that it is received emotionally just as though no problem of value-judgement were ever involved (*e.g.*, the medieval ideology of Revenge as still found in Shakespeare, or the dictates of Honour among the Spanish). Until the ideologies motivating men became relativized, a man was right or he was wrong. If right, he recognized no relative justification of his opponents whatsoever; nothing might justify them since they were wrong. Were one to suppose that demonic passions drove them to transgress norms which otherwise were absolutely binding, then the nature of the motivating forces was itself enough to forbid sympathy for the others' state of mind, especially with opponents. The final implication of a struggle between persons was such that one could scarcely see in the opponent anyone less than a mortal enemy, and this is precisely because the struggle was irrational. How different are conflicts where the individual is taken for the mere proxy of something external to him, something objective, conflicts where the pairing of particular opponents is virtually accidental, the result of intersected necessities. This is why the man of Shakespeare's time, ripping and tearing his opponent in the wild grip of unbridled passions, could hardly be thought to conceive a sense of community with those whom he destroyed and who destroyed him. . . .

In the main, this explains why intrigue has become superfluous and even disruptive. When every action can be 'understood', man's wickedness (though its forms remain unchanged) can no longer be regarded as the ultimate cause of events (as, *e.g.*, Shakespeare's Iago still was). The Count in Lessing's *Emilia Galotti* represents the first stage of this development; and, after the wild excesses of his initial dramas, Schiller comes to this point almost against his will, in the opinion of Philipp. Again it is Hebbel who grasps the situation in its theoretical purity, when he declares that a dramatist's worth is in inverse ratio to the number of scoundrels he requires. . . . In this way the tragic experience is elevated entirely into the realm of absolute necessity. Everything which is merely personal, merely empirical, disappears from it, even from its form as a phenomenon.

Nothing remains but the bare tragic content, a perspective upon life in the form of inevitably tragic conflicts. ... In this way the dramatic conflicts grow not merely more profound, but at either side of certain limits they vanish entirely. All becomes a matter of viewpoint. The subjective extreme descends from the minds of acting personages, as it were, and into the very foundations of the play. Whether or not a matter is tragic becomes strictly a matter of viewpoint. The tragi-comedy appears, a genre of art whose essence is that an event played out before us is, at one and the same time, inseparably comic and tragic. The genre has little positive significance and it is simply impracticable in performance, since the simultaneous duality of vision cannot become spontaneous experience, and the tragic aspect in a comic situation, or the comic in a tragic situation, will only be felt subsequently and then for the most part intellectually. Thus, though this sort of effort may deepen comedy from the perspective of a *Weltanschauung*, it nevertheless disrupts the purity of style and keeps tragedy to the level of the banal and trivial, if indeed it is not distorted into grotesquery. ...

The conflicts become ever more decisively and exclusively inward, they become so much an affair of man's spirit that they can scarcely be communicated to others; and no data, no actions may be conceived which might express the conflicts, leaving nothing in reserve. Thus does action become not merely superfluous (for the release of tragic emotions does not inherently require it), but it may be felt as positively disruptive. Often enough action is no more than an accidental instigation of the real event, which occurs somewhere beyond its reach and independent of it. 'Our life has become too inward,' Hebbel laments, 'and, barring a miracle, it will never again become external.' Goethe too was aware of the immense advantages which Shakespeare had over him; for in his time the decisive conflicts might still occur in a form which worked strongly upon the senses. ...

The new life lacks a mythology; what this means is that the thematic material of tragedies must be distanced from life artificially. For the aesthetic significance of mythology is twofold. In the first place it projects, in the concrete symbols of concrete fables, man's vital emotions concerning the most profound problems of his life. These fables are not so rigid that they cannot incorporate displacements of the general sensibility, should these occur. Should it happen, however, the retained elements will always outweigh the added elements; the perceptible event will amount to more than the new way of valuing it. The second aspect, and possibly the more important, is that the tragic situation so expressed is held at a constant natural distance from the public – a constant distance, since the event is projected into vast dark distances of time. A natural distance, since subject and content, and indeed form, have been moulded in the public's midst as something their own life partakes of, something passed along from their ancestors and without which life itself could scarcely be imagined. Whatever can be made into myth is by its nature poetic. This means, in the always paradoxical fashion of every poetic work, that it is both distant and near to life, and bears in itself, without conscious stylization, the real and irreal, the naïve and all-signifying, the spontaneous and symbolic, adornment and simple pathos. At its origins, or in the process of turning the past into myth (as for instance, Shakespeare with the War of the Roses), everything that is accidental or superfluous or derives from the individual will, or depends for its effect upon the wilfulness of individual taste – everything which, despite its 'interestingness', renders the profound trivial – is torn from the subjects of poetry. . . .

The bourgeois drama is by nature problematic, as theory and practice both agree, and countless circumstantial and formal signs indicate. Apart from the general stylistic problems of any new drama, drama becomes problematic at its base as soon as its subject is a bourgeois destiny enacted among bourgeois personages. The thematic material of bourgeois drama is trivial, because it is all too near to us; the natural pathos of its living men is nondramatic and its most subtle values are lost when heightened into drama; the fable is wilfully invented and so cannot retain the natural and poetic resonance of an ancient tradition. In consequence, most modern dramas are historical, whether they are set in a definite epoch or the timeless past, and, in view of the foregoing, their historicity gains new meaning. History is meant as a substitute for mythology, creating artificial distances, producing monumentality, clearing away trivia and injecting a new pathos. However, the distance to be gained by projecting back in history is more conscious than formerly, and it is for this reason less spirited and forced to appeal more to the facts, forced, because more timid, to cling more strongly to empirical data. The essence of historical distancing is that it substitutes what happened long ago for what happens today. But always, one event takes the place of another; never does a symbol replace a reality. (Naturally I am not concerned here with trivial 'historical truth'. A modern fantasy drama is historical; it is less free of the facts than are Shakespeare's historical dramas.) . . .

Tragedy itself has become problematic. There are, that is, no longer any absolute, overriding, external, easily discerned criteria by which one judges whether a given man and a given destiny are tragic. The tragic becomes strictly a matter of viewpoint, and – important as a problem of expression – strictly an inward, spiritual problem. Something becomes tragic only by the suggestive force of expression, and only spiritual intensities can lend the pathos of tragedy to it. . . . This is why the heroism of the new drama has grown more stylized, more rhetorical, than in the old: the heroism of the hero must be asserted consciously. On the one hand, this serves to hold his tragic experience at the distance of tragedy, as compared to the corresponding events of his life which will refuse to assume a tragic figuration. On the other hand, this affords the possibility of lending a certain force of pathos, of nay-saying significance, to this destiny within the drama, which otherwise lacks the means to render itself objectively conspicuous. What is essential in the hero, what involves him in tragedy, is in this fashion overtly stylized on the plan of a conscious heroism. Dramatic character depiction becomes artificed, hard, places distance between itself and life, whenever it endeavours to rise to tragedy. And the more it aspires to the true tragic peaks of life, or attains them, the more will it be gripped by an obstinate and cold majesty, which will in turn exclude more and more of life's richness and subtleties. . . .

The stylization, however, can no longer be simply the pathos of abstract and conscious heroism. It can be only the stylization of a single quality, exaggerated to a degree beyond any found in life, so that this single quality will be seen to rule the entire man and his destiny as well. To use the language of life, a pathology will be needed. For what does such extremism signify, if not a kind of illness, a pathological overgrowth of a certain specific into the whole life of a man? . . .

Pathology is a technical necessity and as such is related to the problems we have sketched – as even Schiller could sense, when he wrote of Goethe's *Iphigenie*: 'On the whole, Orestes is the most self-aware among them; without the Furies he would not be Orestes, and yet, since the cause of his condition is not perceptible to the eye, but remains wholly in his spirit, his condition becomes an overly long and unrelieved torment without an object.'

When a mythology is absent – which explains why this case is perhaps more striking than others – the basis on which everything must be justified is character. When the motivations are wholly based upon character, however, the wholly inward origin of this destiny will drive the character relentlessly to the limits of pathology. The non-pathological Orestes of Aeschylus was driven from without by what drives Goethe's from within; what once was destiny, becomes character for the modern poets. When we find a pathological trait in one or another personage of the ancient poets (Heracles, Ajax, Lear, Ophelia, etc.), then it is the destiny of that personage to so become and his tragedy is that this is what becomes of him; but his tragedy does not originate in his being so. Even where the tragedy is built upon a pathological situation, as in *Phaedra*, it is still projected entirely from without: the gods have inflicted it. Perhaps this seems only a technical problem; it may appear to matter little whether Orestes is pursued by the Furies or his own heated imagination, whether it is the witches' enticing words which bring Macbeth's stormy hunger for power to ripeness, or whether Holophernes seeks his own ruin. In practice, however, we will see that what comes from without, what is sent upon man by the gods, is universal; it is destiny. In the same way, to the same degree, it might happen to anyone, and in the final analysis it becomes a destiny without reference to the composition of the particular character – or at any rate, not solely with reference to it. But when all has become an inner event and can follow only from the character – if, indeed, all is not so infinitely far from the nature of the concerned that they become incapable of dramatic action (as Oswald, Rank) – its intensity must be heightened into an illness if it is to be seen and heard. In pathology and in it alone lies the possibility of rendering undramatic men dramatic. Nothing else is capable of lending them that concentration of action, that intensity of the senses, which will make the act and the situation symbolic and raise the figures above the ordinary, above the everyday. Says Kerr, 'in disease we find the permitted poetry of naturalism. . . . The figure is lent infinitely more dimensions and yet can be justified in reality.' . . .

We must therefore ask whether today pathology is to be avoided, if the content and form of life are to be expressed in dramatic form. It is a tendency destructive of the true dramatic essence, since it relegates causation to the Universal and becomes lost in a maze of psychological subtleties and imponderables. But can we see another possibility that remains open to the drama? . . .

As we see, it is a question transcending the realm of purely artistic or technical problems. To solve this technical task becomes a problem of life itself: it becomes a search for the vital centre of life. For the ancients and their drama, this question offered no problem; the vital centre was their point of departure and everything else grouped itself around it. . . . Now the vital centre is invented by the poet himself;

no longer is it to be discovered, except as an inspiration or vision, as a profound philosophy or the intuition of genius; and even then, on an individual basis, as a particular, thus wholly accidental, insight. . . .

This is the crux of the paradox: the material of drama consists of the interrelatedness of ethical systems, and the dramatic structure which arises from this relationship is aesthetic-formal. From a different viewpoint, what is involved is an equilibrium of forces, of aesthetic interrelations, and this equilibrium can be achieved only in the medium of ethics. More simply, so long as tragedy did not become ethically problematic, either inwardly or outwardly, the pure aesthetics of structure functioned quite naturally: from a given beginning only a single given result can follow, since the ethical structure is a given precondition known to the poet and public alike. But when ethics cease to be a given, the ethical knotting within the drama – thus, its aesthetics – has to be created; whereupon ethics, as the cornerstone of the artistic composition, move necessarily into the vital centre of motivation. In this way the great and spontaneous unity of ethics and aesthetics, within the tragic experience, commences to be the problem.

Romain Rolland

ROMAIN ROLLAND, 1866–1944, is another major man of letters who wrote minor plays. It is not, of course, as a playwright that he finds a place here, but as a spokesman for a democratic theatre. His viewpoint offsets those of Yeats (p. 327 above) and Tocqueville (p. 479 below), spokesmen for aristocracy. There are two excerpts here, both from his book *The People's Theatre*, translated by Barrett H. Clark.* In the first, a general ideal is set forth. In the second, the background of this ideal in French history is described. Appended is a short essay by Erwin Piscator (1893–1966), 'The Theatre Can Belong to Our Century'. Rolland was one of Piscator's models, and since Rolland, as quoted here, deals mainly with the past, it is of interest to hear what his admirer has to say of the present and future. Piscator's book-length statement, *Das Politische Theater*, came out in 1929 and has been translated by H. Rorison as *The Political Theatre*, Eyre Methuen, 1980. (It came out in Berlin in 1929, and is in print today as a paperback published by Rowohlt in Hamburg.) 'The Theatre Can Belong to Our Century' first appeared in *Producing the Play* by John Gassner.†

* Published by Allen and Unwin, London, 1919 and Holt, New York, 1918, and long out of print. The French original came out in book form in 1903, and had run serially in the *Revue d'art dramatique*, 1900–1903.

† Dryden Press, New York, 1941.

From *The People's Theatre*

ROMAIN ROLLAND

Translated by Barrett H. Clark

THREE REQUISITES

SUPPOSING that the capital is secured and the public ready. What conditions are necessary to a real People's Theatre?

I shall not try to lay down absolute rules of procedure: we must remember that no laws are eternally applicable, the only good laws being made for an epoch that passes and a country that changes. Popular art is essentially changeable. Not only do the people feel in a manner far different from the 'cultured' class, there exist different groups among the people themselves: the people of today and the people of tomorrow; those of a certain part of a certain city, and those of a part of another city. We cannot presume to do more than establish an average, more or less applicable to the people of Paris at the present time.

The first requisite of the People's Theatre is that it must be a recreation. It must first of all give pleasure, a sort of physical and moral rest to the working-man weary from his day's work. It will be the task of the architects of the future People's Theatre to see that cheap seats are not instruments of inquisitorial torture. It will be the task of the dramatists to see that their works produce joy, and not sadness and boredom. The greatest vanity or else downright stupidity are the only excuses for offering the people the latest products of a decadent art, which produces evil effects sometimes even on the minds of the torpid. As for the sufferings and doubts of the 'cultured', let them keep these to themselves: the people have more than enough already. There is no use adding to their burden. The man of our times who best understood the people – Tolstoy – has not always himself escaped this artistic vice, and he has bravely humbled

455

himself for his pride. His vocation as an apostle, that imperious need of his to impose his faith on others, and the exigencies of his artistic realism, were greater in *The Power of Darkness* than this fundamental goodness. Such plays, it seems to me, discourage rather than help the people. If we offered them no other fare, they would be right in turning their backs on us and seeking to drown their troubles at the cabaret. It would be pitiless of us to try to divert their sad existences with the spectacle of similar existences. If certain of the 'cultured few' take pleasure 'sucking melancholy as a weasel sucks an egg', we at least cannot demand the same intellectual stoicism from the people. The people are fond of violent acts, provided they do not, as in life, crush the hero. No matter how discouraged or resigned the people are in their lives, they are extravagantly optimistic where their dream-heroes are concerned, and they suffer when a play turns out sadly. But does this mean that they want tearful melodramas with uniformly happy endings? Surely not. The crude concoction of lies that forms the basis of most melodrama merely stupefies them, acting as a soporific, and contributes, like alcohol, to general inertia. The factor of amusement which we have desiderated in this art should not be allowed to take the place of moral energy. On the contrary!

The theatre ought to be a source of energy: this is the second requisite. The obligation to avoid what is depressing and discouraging is altogether negative; an antidote is necessary, something to support and exalt the soul. In giving the people recreation, the theatre is obliged to render them better able to set to work on the morrow. The happiness of simple and healthy men is never complete without some sort of action. Let the theatre be an arena of action. Let the people make of their dramatist a congenial travelling-companion, alert, jovial, heroic if need be, on whose arm they may lean, on whose good humour they may count to make them forget the fatigue of the journey. It is the duty of this companion to take the people straight to their destination – without of course neglecting to teach them to observe along the road.

This, it seems to me, is the third requisite of our People's Theatre:

The theatre ought to be a guiding light to the intelligence. It should flood with light the terrible brain of man, which is filled with shadows and monsters, and is exceeding narrow and cramped. We have just spoken of the need of guarding against giving every product of the artist to the people; I do not wish, however, to imply that they must be spared all incentive to thought. The working-man does not as a rule think while his body is working. It is good to exercise his brain and, no matter how little he may understand, it will afford him pleasure, just as violent exercise is always gratifying to any normal man after prolonged inaction. He must be taught, then, to see *things* clearly as well as himself, and to judge.

Joy, energy and *intelligence*: these are the three fundamental requisites of our People's Theatre. So far as a moral purpose is concerned – lessons, that is, in virtue, social solidarity, and the like – we need not bother much about that. The mere existence of a permanent theatre, where great emotions are shared and shared often, will create at least for the time being a bond of brotherhood. In place of virtue, give them more intelligence, more happiness, and more energy: virtue and moral lessons will take care of themselves. People are not so much downright bad as ignorant: their badness is only the result of ignorance. Our great problem is to bring more light, purer air, and better order into the chaos of the soul. It is enough if we set the people to thinking and doing; let us not think and do for them. Let us above all avoid preaching morality; only too often have the truest friends of the people made art repellent to them by this means. The People's Theatre must avoid these two excesses: moral pedagogy, which seeks to extract lifeless lessons from living works (a stupid thing to do, for the keenly alert will immediately scent the bait and avoid it), and mere impersonal dilettantism, whose only purpose is to amuse the people at any cost – a dishonourable thing, with which the people are not always pleased, for they can judge those who amuse them; and often there is a mixture of disdain in their laughter. No moral purpose, then, and no mere empty amusement, in and for itself. Morality is no more than the hygiene of the heart and the brain.* Let us found a theatre full to the brim with health and joy. '*Joy, the abounding strength of nature . . . joy, which turns the wheels of the world's clocks; joy, which revolves the spheres in space; joy, which brings forth the flower from the seed, and suns from the firmament!*'

SEVERAL PRECURSORS

THE first men who appear to have conceived the idea of a new dramatic art for the new society, a People's Theatre for the sovereign people, are among the precursors of the Revolution, the philosophers of the eighteenth century, whose epoch-making suggestions sowed in every corner of the earth the seeds for a new life: above all, Jean-Jacques Rousseau and Diderot – Rousseau, who was always preoccupied with the nation's education, and Diderot, so anxious to enrich life, exalt its powers, and unite men in a Dionysiac and fraternal joy.

Rousseau, in his admirable *Lettre sur les spectacles*,† that profoundly sincere work in which some have pretended to discover a paradox in order to escape the application of its stern moral – Rousseau, after having analyzed the theatre and the life of his day with the pitilessly clear vision of a Tolstoy, does not however conclude by condemning the stage in general, for he perceives the possibility of a regeneration of dramatic art, provided it is given a national and popular character, as with the Greeks. He says:

I see for these ills but one remedy, and that is that we write our own plays for our own theatre, and that we have dramatists in preference to actors. For it is not good to witness imitations of everything under the sun, but only of what is fitting for free men. The Greek plays, based upon the past misfortunes of the nation or

* 'The ineffable joy we feel when we are perfectly healthy in mind and spirit.' (Schiller to Goethe, 7 January 1795).
† *Lettre à d'Alembert*, 1758.

the present faults of the people, might well offer useful lessons to the audience. . . . But the plays of the Greeks had none of the nastiness observable in the plays of our own time. Their theatres were not built for purposes of personal aggrandizement; theirs were not obscure prisons; the actors were not under the necessity of levying contributions on the audience, nor to count the number of spectators out of the corner of their eye, in order to be sure of their supper. Their grave and superb spectacles, given under the open heavens before the whole nation, presented nothing but combats, victories, prizes – things capable of inspiring emulation and sentiments of honour and glory in the breasts of all the people. These great plays were a constant source of instruction.

But Rousseau had another, a far more original and democratic idea for a people's theatre: People's festivals. I shall touch upon this point a little later on.

At about the same time Diderot, the most enlightened and broad-minded of the geniuses of the eighteenth century, and perhaps the most fertile, who was less concerned with the educational value of the stage than with the aesthetic, said in his *Paradoxe sur le comédien*: 'We have yet to discover true tragedy.' And he added, in his *Deuxième entretien sur le Fils naturel*:

Strictly speaking, there are no popular spectacles. The theatres of antiquity held as many as eighty thousand spectators at one time. . . . Think of the power in that great assemblage, when you consider the influence of one man on another and the immediate transmission of emotion in such crowds. Forty or fifty thousand people, gathered together, will not be restrained by motives of decency. . . . He who cannot feel within him an emotion arising from the fact that he is one of a great assemblage, must be vicious: his character has something solitary that I dislike. And if the size of this tremendous audience increases the emotion of the spectator, what will it not do for the author and the actor? How vastly different is our petty theatre, wherein we amuse our audiences of a few hundreds at fixed times, and at fixed hours! What if we were to assemble the whole nation on holidays!

And with his accustomed clear-sightedness and power he proceeds to sketch some of the artistic reforms which were to be the basis of the new theatre. In the following lines Diderot saw a vision beyond not only the art of his day, but of our own:

> In order to effect a change in our drama, I ask no more than a broad stage, where, when the subject demanded, the audience might see a wide space with several buildings at a time – the peristyle of a palace, the entrance to a temple – different places where the audience might observe every event of the action; while one section should be hidden for the use of the actors. Such was, or might well have been, the stage on which *The Eumenides* of Æschylus was performed. Shall we ever have anything of the sort on our stage? *There we can never show more than our action, while in nature there are many simultaneous actions, which, if performed at the same time, would intensify the whole, and produce a truly terrible and wondrous effect.* . . . We are waiting for the genius who will combine pantomime with dialogue, mingling dumb-shows with spoken scenes, and render effective the combination; above all, the approach, terrible or comic, to such simultaneous scenes.

Diderot's happy inspiration found a passionate echo in the Shakespearians of the *Sturm und Drangperiode*: Gerstenberg, Herder, and the adolescent Goethe.*

Louis-Sébastien Mercier, an original man, nourished on Shakespeare and the Germans, disciple of Diderot and 'monkey of Jean-Jacques', as he was called, brought together these various theories, and, in formal terms set forth in his *Nouvel essai sur l'Art dramatique* (1773) and the *Nouvel examen de la Tragédie française* (1778), demanded the establishment of a people's theatre, inspired by and intended for the people. He reminded his readers of the mysteries of the Middle Age; and, combining the aesthetic theories of Diderot and the Shakespearians with the moral ideals of Rousseau, he asked for a 'theatre as broad as the universe', which should also be 'a moral spectacle'; for

---

* Herder, in defending Shakespeare in 1773 and holding him up as the ideal dramatist, showed that his plots were not Greek in spirit, but belonged rather to the Middle Age. He said: 'A sea of events, where the moaning waves follow each other; that is Shakespeare. Acts of nature come and go, act and inter-act, no matter how dissimilar they may be; create and re-create, and destroy in turn, in order to realize the ultimate intention of the Creator.'

the first duty of the dramatic poet, he says, 'is to mould the morals and manners of the citizens'. And, practising what he preached, he wrote historical, political, and social plays: *Jean Hennuyer, évêque de Lisieux*, which introduced the figure of an apostle of tolerance at the time of the Massacre of St Bartholomew; *La Mort de Louis XI, roi de France; La Destruction de la Ligue*; and *Philippe II, roi d'Espagne* (1785).

After Mercier, other French writers have taken up the idea of a national theatre, that is, a theatre for the whole nation. Bernardin de Saint-Pierre, in his *Treizième Étude de la Nature*, conjures up an ideal French Shakespeare who should give to the assembled people the great scenes of the *Patrie*, and suggests the subject of *Jeanne d'Arc*. After having traced in a rapid and declamatory style the scene of Jeanne at the stake, he says:

I should like to see this treated by a man of genius after the manner of Shakespeare, who would not have failed, had Jeanne d'Arc been English, to make a great patriotic play out of it; the celebrated shepherdess would have become for us the patroness of war, as Saint Genevieve is of peace. Such a play would be performed only in national crises, in the presence of the people, just as Mahomet's standard is displayed in Constantinople. And I have no doubt that at the sight of her innocence, her services, her misfortunes, and the cruelty of her enemies and horror of her martyrdom, our people could not restrain themselves from crying out: 'War: War against the English!'

In 1789 Marie-Joseph Chénier dedicated his *Charles IX ou l'École des Rois* 'To the French Nation', with these words:

Frenchmen and fellow-citizens: accept the dedication of this patriotic tragedy. I dedicate the work of a free man to a free nation. ... Your scene ought to change with the others that have just changed. A theatre in which there are only petty females and slaves is no longer suited to a nation of men and of citizens. There was one thing lacking to your dramatic poets; it was not genius, and not subjects, but an audience. (15 December 1789.)

And again he says:

The theatre is an agent of public education. ... Without her men of letters, France would stand where Spain stands at this moment. ... We have reached the most important epoch of French history, for the destiny of twenty-five million men is about to be decided. ... Free arts succeed the enslaved arts; the theatre, so long effeminate and abject, will henceforward inspire only a respect of law, love of liberty, hatred of excess, and the execration of tyrants.'*

Mercier's ideas were more directly influential upon Schiller in Germany. He read the Frenchman's books, translated them, and made them his inspiration. It is worthy of note that Mercier, in his *Nouvel Essai*, suggested to Schiller the theme of *Wilhelm Tell*, as Rousseau had suggested *Fiesco*.† And it is highly probable that Mercier suggested certain scenes of *Don Carlos*.‡ Nor must we forget the link that bound the early Revolutionary movement with the man whom the Convention made a French citizen, he who was in a way the great poet of the Revolution, as Beethoven was the great composer: the author of *Die Räuber* (1781–2), of *In Tyrannos* (*Against the Tyrants*), of *Fiesco*, 'a republican tragedy' (1783–4), and of *Don Carlos* (1785), where he says he tried to show 'the spirit of liberty at swords' points with despotism, the shackles of stupidity broken, the prejudices of a thousand years swept away; a nation demanding the rights of man; republican virtues put into practice' – the poet of the *Ode to Joy* (1785), drunk with liberty, heroism, and fraternal love.§

'The theatre,' declared Mercier, 'is the most potent and direct means of strengthening human reason and enlightening the whole nation.'

* *Discours de la liberté du théâtre*, 15 June 1789.
† See Albert Kontz, *Les Drames de la jeunesse de Schiller*, Leroux, 1899.
‡ *Eighth Letter on Don Carlos*, 1788.
§ Goethe kept much further aloof from the Revolutionary spirit, although one can trace its influence in *Egmont* (1788) where the dying hero says: 'People, defend your rights! In order to save what you hold dear, die joyfully. I give you an example!' But the man who preferred injustice to disorder, he who could parody the Revolution in *Der Bürgergeneral* (1793) and *Die Aufgeregten* (1793), was evidently unable to understand art for the people.

And yet, towards the end of his life, he began to have some ideas on the subject. We find traces of them in his *Conversations with Eckermann*.

So thought the Revolution. It appropriated Rousseau's two ideas: popular festivals and education through the theatre. The idea of a People's Theatre was not the exclusive property of any one party, for we find men of opposite and antagonistic creeds united in an effort to establish a popular form of dramatic art. Mirabeau, Talleyrand, Lakanal, David, Marie-Joseph Chénier, Danton, Boissy d'Anglas, Barère, Carnot, Saint-Just, Robespierre, Billaud-Varennes, Prieur, Lindet, Collot d'Herbois, Couthon, Payan, Fourcade, Bouquier, Florian, and many another, defended the cause in words, on paper, and with deeds. Here is a brief summary of certain Revolutionary documents touching on the people's festivals:

In a report dated 11 July 1793, relative to the festival in commemoration of the 10th of August, David suggested that after the ceremony in the Champ-de-Mars – which was to constitute the chief attraction – 'a vast theatre should be erected, where the chief events of our Revolution shall be represented in pantomime.' As a matter of fact, they performed a mimic bombardment of the city of Lille.*

But on the 2nd of August, 1793, the Committee of Public Safety, 'desiring to mould further the sentiments and character of the French into a truer form of republicanism,' proposed a 'regulation of dramatic performances', which

---

'A great dramatic poet, if he is at the same time productive, and is actuated by a strong noble purpose which pervades all his works, may succeed in making the soul of his pieces become the soul of the people. I should think that this was something well worth the trouble. . . . A dramatic poet who knows his vocation should therefore work incessantly at its higher development, in order that his influence on the people may be noble and beneficial.' (1 April 1827.)

And I notice in certain of Goethe's writings, for instance *Wilhelm Meister* (II, III, and following), short descriptions of people's performances. In a mountainous district (Hochdorf) some factory workers have converted a barn into a theatre; there they act a comedy full of movement, but without characters: two rivals abduct a young girl from her guardian, and quarrel over her. A little further on, he described a sort of improvised popular production out-of-doors: a dialogue between a miner and a peasant.

* A fortress was especially erected on the banks of the Seine.

was adopted by the Convention after a speech by Couthon. The Convention decreed that between the 4th of August and the 1st of September – that is, at the time when the festivals celebrating the 10th of August drew to Paris many thousands of people from the provinces – certain theatres, designated by the municipality, should three times a week perform 'republican tragedies', such as *Brutus* (Voltaire), *William Tell* (Lemierre), *Caius Gracchus* (Chénier) . . . one of these performances being given each week at the expense of the Republic.' *

In November, 1793, following up the celebrated discourse by Marie-Joseph Chénier on popular festivals, Fabre d'Eglantine passed a measure providing for *national theatres*, which completed the scheme for popular festivals. A special commission of six members was actually chosen: Romme, David, Fourcroi, Mathieu, Bouquier, and Cloots. On the 11th of Frimaire, Year II (1 December 1793) Bouquier drew up the following resolutions in his *Plan général d'Instruction publique* (section IV: *Du dernier degré d'instruction*):

Article I. Theatres . . . and festivals . . . are a part of the 'second degree' of public instruction.
Article II. In order to facilitate this movement . . . the Convention declares that all former churches and ecclesiastical edifices which are at present empty shall belong to the Communes.

On the 4th of Pluviôse, Year II (23 January 1794) the Convention, under the presidency of Vadier, divided the sum of 100,000 livres among the twenty theatres of Paris which,

according to the decree of 2 August have each given four performances for and by the people.

On the 12th of Pluviôse of the same year (31 January 1794) the Committee of General Surety recommended to the directors of the various theatres of Paris

* The first of these popular performances was given 6 August at the *Théâtre de la République*. *Brutus* was the play, and the announcement bore the inscription: *By and for the People*.

that they make their theatres schools of manners and decency ...
adding to their patriotic plays ... others in which individual
virtues should be set forth in all its grandeur.

Boissy d'Anglas, in a written appeal* to the Convention
and the Committee of Instruction, dated the 25th of
Pluviôse (13 February), asked that

plays should be made the vehicle of public appreciation, and that
through them the prestige of the great men who had fallen should
be emphasized, by showing their great deeds, which ought to be
preserved for posterity. ... In considering the theatre as one of the
properest instruments for furthering the development of society
and rendering men more virtuous and more enlightened, you will,
I am sure, not allow it to become solely an object of financial
speculation, but make it a national enterprise. ... Let this be one
of the principal aims of your public service. ... In this way you will
be opening up a path along which the human mind can pursue its
way to even greater heights than heretofore ... and offer the
people an ever new source of instruction and pleasure, and form
the national character as you wish.

All these ideas for a national theatre which should be a
source of instruction were combined on the 20th of Ventôse,
Year II (10 March 1794) in a decree of the Committee of
Public Safety, which is the true constitution and basis of the
People's Theatre.

The Committee, which was that day composed of Saint-
Just, Couthon, Carnot, Barère, Prieur, Lindet and Collot
d'Herbois, decreed that

the old Théâtre-Français shall be solely devoted to performances given by
and for the people at certain times every month. The building shall bear the
following inscription on its façade: PEOPLE'S THEATRE. The troupes
of actors already established in the various theatres of Paris shall be
requisitioned in turn for performances to be given three times each decade.
The repertory of plays to be performed at the People's Theatre must be sub-

* Quelques idées sur les arts, sur la nécessité de les encourager, sur les institutions qui peuvent en assurer le perfectionnement et sur divers établissements
nécessaires à l'enseignement public, addressées à la Convention nationale et au
Comité d'instruction publique, par Boissy d'Anglas, député du département de
l'Ardèche.

*mitted to and passed by the Committee. Each municipality is commanded
to organize productions which are to be given free to the people every ten
years.*

The Committee of Public Safety realized that the transformation of the old *Théâtre-Français* for the purpose of
giving popular performances was only temporary. The
founders of the People's Theatre were right in thinking that
there were obstacles, probably unsurmountable, to the
establishment of a new form of dramatic art in an old
building, whose material form, audiences, and traditions
would always stand in the way of the development of a new
art. And so they endeavoured to find a new architectural
structure.

On the 5th of Floréal, Year II (24 April 1794), the Committee of Public Safety 'called upon the artists of the
Republic to assist in turning the Opera (now the *Théâtre de
la Porte Saint-Martin*) into a covered arena, where the
triumphs of the Republic and national festivals might be
held'; and on the 25th of Floréal (14 May) Robespierre,
Billaud, Prieur, Barère and Collot signed a decree for the
conversion of the Place de la Révolution (now the Place de
la Concorde) 'into a circus, open on all sides and intended
to be used for the national festivals'.

The mere founding of the People's Theatre was not sufficient: it had to have plays. The Committee, composed of
Robespierre, Couthon, Carnot, Billaud, Lindet, Prieur,
Barère and Collot, appealed to the poets on the 27th of
Floréal to 'celebrate the principal events of the Revolution
and compose republican plays'. But the Committee was too
busy with other things – the struggle against the counter-
revolution, and with the kings – to be able to devote its
undivided attention to 'the regeneration of dramatic art'.
It gave over this difficult task to the Committee of Public
Instruction on the 18th of Prairial (6 June 1794).

The Commission, of which the energetic and intelligent
Joseph Payan was the soul, set to work in earnest. On the
5th of Messidor (23 June 1794) it published a circular under
the title of *Spectacles*, addressed to the directors and managers

of plays, the municipal authorities, dramatists, etc. In this pamphlet, written in a declamatory and incorrect style, but burning with generous ambition, Payan declared war not only on the speculation indulged in by authors and directors, and on the scandalous immorality and huge profits of theatrical enterprise, but against the sluggish spirit of the times, and the servile condition of art.

The theatres are still encumbered with the rubbish of the old régime, feeble copies of the masters, wherein art and taste are set at naught, of ideas and interests which are nothing to us, and of customs and manners foreign to us. We must sweep this chaotic mass out of our theatres. . . . We must clear the stage, and allow reason to enter and speak the language of liberty, throw flowers on the graves of martyrs, sing of heroism and virtue, and inspire love of law and the *Patrie*.

The Commission appealed to all enlightened men: artists, directors and patriotic writers. 'Think of the tremendous moral influence to be exerted by plays. We must erect a great public school wherein taste and virtue shall be equally respected.' This was not an attempt, as has been said, to sacrifice art to politics. On the contrary, Payan, in the name of the Commission, vigorously protested against the mutilations made in the texts of certain plays by the Hébertistes, saying that the 'first laws to be respected in plays are the laws of good taste and good sense'. The grandeur of his conception of a popular art is even more strikingly evident in a decree of the 11th of Messidor, Year II (29 June 1794), wherein he pitilessly criticizes not the anti-republican plays, *but the republican plays* written for the *Festival to the Supreme Being*, which degraded the subject by their mediocrity.

There are many dramatists on the alert to detect the current of the fashion; they know the costumes and the colours of the season; they know to the day when to put on one's red bonnet, and when to take off. Their genius has laid siege to and conquered a whole city, while our brave Republicans have barely opened the breach. . . . Hence the corruption of taste and the degeneration of art. While genius meditates and casts her conceptions into bronze, mediocrity, cowering beneath the aegis of liberty, bears off the laurels of the moment, and gathers without an effort the flowers of an ephemeral success. . . . Let us inspire our young literary men with the idea that the road to immortality is a difficult one, and that if they wish to offer the French people works as imperishable as their glory, they must avoid mere barren profusion and unmerited success, for these kill talent and cause genius to dissipate itself with a few fugitive sparks shot into a night of smoke; hasty attempts to snatch the wreath of victory, made according to a fixed formula, can only result in the degradation of the work and the worker. The Commission deeply regrets that it is forced to point out the first steps along the path of good taste and true beauty by means of severe lessons, but since it assumes the greatest interest in the arts, the regeneration of which is in its hands . . . it feels it is responsible to the nation, to literature, to itself, to the poet, the historian, the genius, and should be guilty of gross neglect should it fail to direct the energies of genius. Let the young author, therefore, fearlessly measure the whole extent of the field before him . . . he must invariably avoid the line of least resistance in thinking, and shun mediocrity in every form. The writer who instead of lessons offers commonplaces; empty action instead of interest; caricatures instead of characters, is of no use to literature, to the moral welfare, and to the State: Plato would have banished him from his Republic.

The superb spirit of this passage shows into what hands art was then confided. Unfortunately the writers were not equal to the task: Payan himself was unable to write the work he announced in his decree of the 29th of June, on the regeneration of the theatre. He was swept away on the 10th of Thermidor (28 July) in the whirlwind which took with it, besides Robespierre and Saint-Just, the very genius of the Revolution. It is regrettable to have to confess that the artists of the time, especially the writers, could in no way be compared with the Revolutionary chiefs. This was especially true of the writers, for painting at least had its David, and music Méhul, Lesueur, Gossec, Chérubini – and the *Marseillaise*. This mediocrity grieved the Committee, and called forth bitter words from Robespierre and Saint-Just. 'Men of letters in general,' said Robespierre in his speech of the 18th of Floréal (7 May 1794), 'have dishonoured themselves in this Revolution and to the everlasting shame of their minds the people's reason has taken the first place.' As has been shown by Eugène Maron* and Eugène Despois,† the year 1793 marks the beginning of the extraordinary developments of the *vaudeville*.

But I understand: all the heroism of the nation had been flung into the battlefield, the assembly, and the riot. Who would have been such a dilettante as to write while the others were fighting? Cowards were the only ones who cultivated the arts. But is it not too bad to think that that sublime tempest passed away without leaving the trace of a work which shall live through the centuries?

Fifty years later one man sounded the echo of those first blasts. Michelet, who has transmitted to us not only the story of those heroic times, but the very soul, for it was in him; Michelet, who wrote the history of the Revolution like a man who had really lived through it, carries on, as it were instinctively, the tradition of the People's Theatre. He expounded his ideas to his students with his customary eloquence:

You must all march at the head of the people. Give them that glorious instruction which was the whole education of the cities of antiquity: a theatre truly of the people. On the stage of that theatre give them their own legends, and show them their own deeds. Nourish the people with the people. ... The theatre is the most potent agent in education and goes far to establish closer relations between man and man; it is, I think, the fairest hope of our national regeneration. I mean a theatre universally of the people, echoing every thought of the people, and extending to every hamlet. ... Before I die I wish to see a spirit of national fraternity in the theatre ... a drama simple and vigorous played throughout the countryside, where the energy of talent, the creative power which lies in the heart, and the youthful imagination of an entirely new people shall do away with mere physical adjuncts, sumptuous stage-settings and costumes, without which the feeble dramatists of this outworn age cannot take a step. ... What is the theatre? It means the resigning of oneself, the abdication of egotism and aggrandizement in order to assume a better role. Ah, how much we

* *Histoire littéraire de la Convention.*
† *Le Vandalisme révolutionnaire.*

need this! . . . Come, I beg you, come and find your souls again in the people's theatre, in the people themselves.*

Michelet suggested certain subjects from our national epic literature which lent themselves to treatment in people's plays: *Jeanne d'Arc, La Tour d'Auvérgne, Austerlitz*; above all, *Les Miracles de la Révolution*.

It was through Michelet that the artistic ideals of the Revolution and the thinkers of the eighteenth century have come down to those of us who are endeavouring to found a People's Theatre.

* Michelet: *L'Etudiant* (lecture-course of 1847–8).

The Theatre Can Belong to Our Century

ERWIN PISCATOR

To what century does the 'modern' theatre belong? It is housed in last century's opera house. In the busiest theatrical centre of the Western World, 'modern' theatre, in rented buildings, is crowded into the byways while the film palaces flourish prominently.

A film palace in Radio City is the symbol of the people's theatre today. When audiences go into this vast building they find a magic wonderland, complete on a one-dimensional screen. Modern science and technology are freeing the visual imagination. Using all the technical devices supplied by research, the film can cover earth and sky, and dwell under the sea. It can project its message into every corner of the house, reaching those farthest from the screen, 'hitting home' with close-ups or with the increased power of voice, music and sound effects.

But when present-day audiences attend a stage play, they find the stage set with scenes and actors on the same unimaginative scale used since the proscenium box-stage emerged from the sixteenth century renaissance theatre. At most we have musical-comedy splendour on that stage. So little have the old forms changed in a new world! How then can the substance and poetry of our drama help but lag behind our changing ways of life? The last important invention for the theatre was the turntable, first used in the 1850s. And used today for musical comedies! The closed-in stage of naturalism, boxing its little domestic dramas, remains almost immovable. It will not expand, turn, open; it will not be budged. In this rigid frame our dramatists must set a time of storm and change, fall of dynasties, revolutions! Everything has been changed by new techniques; the waging of wars, our behaviour, even our thinking. Everything but the stage! Even Shakespeare, using several

471

different parts of a stage to base a world on, unbound by time and place – even he seems more revolutionary today in his use of the stage than do our modern directors. He has more in common with this century than they!

Research in sound holds out unimaginable possibilities in the use of music and voice effects in the theatre. Film projections, the colour organ, the interchange on stage between light and 'film light', complete motorization of the stage – through these, and how many other, innovations modern creative science can supplant the ancient peep-show. And what would happen if it were to introduce a wholly new architecture, making the stage a *play-machine*, a wonder-world, an arena for battling ideas, perhaps even setting the audience on a turntable, dynamically bursting the static illusion of the present stage? I do not say that new techniques will be the saviour of the theatre. I merely say that they can express new dramatic contents by liberating the creative forces of playwrights, directors and actors.

Pressed by the need for new forms with which to express new ideas, Meyerhold tried to overcome the old static stage by forcing acrobatic movement on his actors. Instead of freeing his stage, he forced his actors into a system of bio-mechanics that often distorted his expression of ideas. Suppose an actor in the Meyerhold theatre had to deliver a long monologue while ascending a staircase. Mere physical limitations would prohibit natural movement; therefore, Meyerhold imposed on the performer a series of contortions to fit the movement of the staircase.

We, however, must learn to fit the staircase to the movement as it were, by overcoming the limitations of the proscenium box-stage. We must become the free artists who can use the physical properties of the stage even as a painter freely mixes colour on his palette. In such a way we would use treadmill, turntable, sunken stage raised and lowered for changing levels, moving escalator, motorized bridges, elevators. Film and television would be used in combination with the stage, for stage close-ups. Imagine the other fields, both psychological and epic, such combinations would open! Contrasts between the conscious, spoken thought and subconscious thought could be revealed. Monologues could be visualized; the inner colloquy could be externalized, the actor talking to his own screen image. Asides made visible, motives traced to their sources – all this could be done by contrasting new over-dimensional material (by means of projections referring to the outside world) with human material (the actors on the stage, the actual scene). Film could be used as atmosphere for fantasy, or as moving background, or as chorus: interpreting, prophesying, philosophizing.

This is but an indication of the wholly new theatre which is possible – a theatre that would really belong to our century. Drama can once more be made to function in the lives of great numbers of people, as did the Greek theatre. Once again it can be a place of fascination through exemplification of truth. The education of audiences, optically trained by films, can be used to tremendous advantage. As the background for drama is enlarged, history and our times can be brought to make a drama as epic as our best novels and even as the events in our newspapers. Abstract symbolism, which creates a theatre for the few, could give way before the onrush of illuminating and thrilling expanded new-type realism. Artists, their fantasy and their intelligence given fresh inspiration, and their rightful audiences restored to them would then develop a great modern theatre. Does this seem a dream? Vision has often created reality.

Alexis de Tocqueville

ALEXIS DE TOCQUEVILLE, 1805–59, wrote what still stands, perhaps, as the finest single book about the United States, *Democracy in America* (1835). His chapter on the drama and democracy, here reproduced, is not at all definitive, but it is infinitely suggestive. It leads to discussion of every conceivable aspect of the topic. The author's viewpoint is to be compared with that of Yeats (p. 327 above) and Rolland (p. 455 above).

Some Observations on the Drama amongst Democratic Nations

ALEXIS DE TOCQUEVILLE

Translated by Henry Reeve and revised, 1862, by Francis Bowen

WHEN the revolution which subverts the social and political state of an aristocratic people begins to penetrate into literature, it generally first manifests itself in the drama, and it always remains conspicuous there.

The spectator of a dramatic piece is, to a certain extent, taken by surprise by the impression it conveys. He has no time to refer to his memory or to consult those more able to judge than himself. It does not occur to him to resist the new literary tendencies which begin to be felt by him; he yields to them before he knows what they are.

Authors are very prompt in discovering which way the taste of the public is thus secretly inclined. They shape their productions accordingly; and the literature of the stage, after having served to indicate the approaching literary revolution, speedily completes its accomplishment. If you would judge beforehand of the literature of a people which is lapsing into democracy, study its dramatic productions.

The literature of the stage, moreover, even amongst aristocratic nations, constitutes the most democratic part of their literature. No kind of literary gratification is so much within the reach of the multitude as that which is derived from theatrical representations. Neither preparation nor study is required to enjoy them: they lay hold on you in the midst of your prejudices and your ignorance. When the yet untutored love of the pleasures of the mind begins to affect a class of the community, it instantly draws them to the stage. The theatres of aristocratic nations have always been filled with spectators not belonging to the aristocracy. At the theatre alone the higher ranks mix with the middle and the lower classes; there alone do the former consent to listen to the opinion of the latter, or at least to allow them to give an opinion at all. At the theatre, men of cultivation and of literary attainments have always had more difficulty than elsewhere in making their taste prevail over that of the people, and in preventing themselves from being carried away by the latter. The pit has frequently made laws for the boxes.

If it be difficult for an aristocracy to prevent the people from getting the upper hand in the theatre, it will readily be understood that the people will be supreme there when democratic principles have crept into the laws and manners – when ranks are intermixed – when minds as well as fortunes are brought more nearly together – and when the upper class has lost, with its hereditary wealth, its power, its precedents, and its leisure. The tastes and propensities natural to democratic nations in respect to literature, will therefore first be discernible in the drama, and it may be foreseen that they will break out there with vehemence. In written productions, the literary canons of aristocracy will be gently, gradually, and, so to speak, legally modified; at the theatre they will be riotously overthrown.

The drama brings out most of the good qualities, and almost all the defects, inherent in democratic literature. Democratic peoples hold erudition very cheap, and care but little for what occurred at Rome and Athens; they want to hear something which concerns themselves, and the delineation of the present age is what they demand. When the heroes and the manners of antiquity are frequently brought upon the stage, and dramatic authors faithfully observe the rules of antiquated precedent, that is enough to warrant a conclusion that the democratic classes have not yet got the upper hand in the theatres.

Racine makes a very humble apology in the preface to the Britannicus for having disposed of Junia amongst the Vestals, who, according to Aulus Gellius he says, 'admitted no one below six years of age nor above ten'. We may be sure that he would neither have accused himself of the offence, nor defended himself from censure, if he had written for our contemporaries.

A fact of this kind not only illustrates the state of literature at the time when it occurred, but also that of society itself. A democratic stage does not prove that the nation is in a state of democracy, for, as we have just seen, even in aristocracies it may happen that democratic tastes affect the drama; but when the spirit of aristocracy reigns exclusively on the stage, the fact irrefragably demonstrates that the whole of society is aristocratic; and it may be boldly inferred that the same lettered and learned class which sways the dramatic writers commands the people and governs the country.

The refined tastes and the arrogant bearing of an aristocracy (when it manages the stage) will rarely fail to lead it to make a kind of selection in human nature. Some of the conditions of society claim its chief interest; and the scenes which delineate their manners are preferred upon the stage. Certain virtues, and even certain vices are thought more particularly to deserve to figure there; and they are applauded whilst all others are excluded. Upon the stage, as well as elsewhere, an aristocratic audience will only meet personages of quality, and share the emotions of kings. The same thing applies to style: an aristocracy is apt to impose upon dramatic authors certain modes of expression which give the key in which everything is to be delivered. By these means the stage frequently comes to delineate only one side of man, or sometimes even to represent what is not to be met with in human nature at all – to rise above nature and to go beyond it.

In democratic communities the spectators have no such partialities, and they rarely display any such antipathies: they like to see upon the stage that medley of conditions, of feelings, and of opinions, which occurs before their eyes. The drama becomes more striking, more common, and more true. Sometimes, however, those who write for the stage in democracies also transgress the bounds of human nature, but it is on a different side from their predecessors. By seeking to represent in minute detail the little singularities of the moment and the peculiar characteristics of certain personages, they forget to portray the general features of the race.

When the democratic classes rule the stage, they introduce as much licence in the manner of treating subjects as in the choice of them. As the love of the drama is, of all literary tastes, that which is most natural to democratic nations, the number of authors and of spectators, as well as of theatrical representations, is constantly increasing amongst these communities. Such a multitude, composed of elements so different and scattered in so many different places, cannot acknowledge the same rules or submit to the same laws. No concurrence is possible amongst judges so numerous, who know not when they may meet again; and therefore each pronounces his own sentence on the piece. If the effect of democracy is generally to question the authority of all literary rules and conventions, on the stage it abolishes them altogether, and puts in their place nothing but the whim of each author and of each public.

The drama also displays in an especial manner the truth of what I have said before in speaking more generally of style and art in democratic literature. In reading the criticisms which were occasioned by the dramatic productions of the age of Louis XIV, one is surprised to remark the great stress which the public laid on the probability of the plot, and the importance which was attached to the perfect consistency of the characters, and to their doing nothing which could not be easily explained and understood. The value which was set upon the forms of language at that period, and the paltry strife about words with which dramatic authors were assailed, are no less surprising. It would seem that the men of the age of Louis XIV attached very exaggerated importance to those details, which may be perceived in the study, but which escape attention on the stage. For, after all, the principal object of a dramatic piece is to be performed, and its chief merit is to affect the audience. But the audience and the readers in that age were the same: on quitting the theatre they called up the author for judgement to their own firesides.

In democracies, dramatic pieces are listened to, but not read. Most of those who frequent the amusements of the stage do not go there to seek the pleasures of the mind, but the keen emotions of the heart. They do not expect to hear a fine literary work, but to see a play; and provided the author writes the language of his country correctly enough to be understood, and that his characters excite curiosity and awaken sympathy, the audience are satisfied. They ask no more of fiction, and immediately return to real life. Accuracy of style is therefore less required, because the attentive observance of its rules is less perceptible on the stage.

As for the probability of the plot, it is incompatible with perpetual novelty, surprise, and rapidity of invention. It is therefore neglected, and the public excuses the neglect. You may be sure that if you succeed in bringing your audience into the presence of something that affects them, they will not care by what road you brought them there: and they will never reproach you for having excited their emotions in spite of dramatic rules.

The Americans, when they go to the theatre, very broadly display all the different propensities which I have here described, but it must be acknowledged that as yet a very small number of them go to the theatre at all. Although playgoers and plays have prodigiously increased in the United States in the last forty years, the population indulge in this kind of amusement only with the greatest reserve. This is attributable to peculiar causes, which the reader is already acquainted with, and of which a few words will suffice to remind him.

The Puritans who founded the American republics not only were enemies to amusements, but they professed an especial abhorrence for the stage. They considered it as an abominable pastime; and as long as their principles prevailed with undivided sway, scenic performances were wholly unknown amongst them. These opinions of the first fathers of the colony have left very deep marks on the minds of their descendants.

The extreme regularity of habits and the great strictness of manners which are observable in the United States have as yet opposed additional obstacles to the growth of dramatic art. There are no dramatic subjects in a country which has witnessed no great political catastrophes and in which love invariably leads by a straight and easy road to matrimony. People who spend every day in the week in making money, and the Sunday in going to church, have nothing to invite the Muse of Comedy.

A single fact suffices to show that the stage is not very popular in the United States. The Americans, whose laws allow of the utmost freedom, and even licence of language in all other respects, have nevertheless subjected their dramatic authors to a sort of censorship. Theatrical performances can only take place by permission of the municipal authorities. This may serve to show how much communities are like individuals; they surrender themselves unscrupulously to their ruling passions, and afterwards take the greatest care not to yield too much to the vehemence of tastes which they do not possess.

No portion of literature is connected by closer or more numerous ties with the present condition of society than the drama. The drama of one period can never be suited to the following age if in the interval an important revolution has changed the manners and the laws of the nation.

The great authors of a preceding age may be read; but pieces written for a different public will not be followed. The dramatic authors of the past live only in books. The traditional taste of certain individuals, vanity, fashion, or the genius of an actor may sustain or resuscitate for a time the aristocratic drama amongst a democracy; but it will speedily fall away of itself – not overthrown, but abandoned.

This book came out forty years ago. Some critics at that time said it had no future, but it did in fact find a market and hold on to it, not only in the UK and the US but in Australia and around the globe. Saddam Hussein's ministry of information brought out an Arabic translation.

Its detractors pointed out what purposes it did NOT serve. It did not, for example, establish that there was a single entity called Modern Theatre which subscribed to a single theory. It was really just a book of theorizing about a theatre which was modern in the sense that it happened not long ago. The theories were diverse and even in conflict, as befits a world less and less totalitarian, more and more pluralistic.

My colleague Irving Wardle, then of *The Times*, thought most of my contributors regarded theatre, not as art, much less as entertainment, but as an instrument of salvation, social or religious. Now, I myself had devoted a whole essay entitled 'More Than a Play?' to combat that notion and claim that a play must first of all be a play. But I could hardly buck the fact that, in the past hundred years, the champions of a New Theatre had always seen that theatre as a Cause and that Cause as in some sense, however metaphorical, salvationist, redemptive. Indeed the figure of *one* hundred years is too modest. The sense that theatre has a *mission* to modern society can be traced back at least to Lessing and Schiller.

So much for the general tenor of this volume. I had also to confront what every anthologist confronts: criticism of his particular choices. Had I omitted all the writers people most wished to read? Here I must refer that present reader back to the Preface on page 9, but let me add a thought or two, and even qualify what I said about one of the writers, Richard Wagner, on page 281. To study modern theatre in any depth, one does have to read Wagner's own works, and I would revise the present volume to include an excerpt, if any excerpt of less than, say, fifty pages could give an adequate impression of his view of things. Wagner is totally omitted at this point only because, to grasp what he is after, you have to read him at great length. The same is true, incidentally, of his friend and enemy, Friedrich Nietzsche. At least one drama anthology on my shelves contains a few pages from the latter's *Birth of Tragedy*. Students, I have found, cannot make head or tail of them, and I don't blame such students. In fact, *The Birth of Tragedy* will not reveal its more interesting meanings until you have read, not only the whole book, but other works by Nietzsche and indeed works by Richard Wagner which he cites.

The points I am making would apply, *mutatis mutandis*, to other authors, the main thing being that children should be taught at an early age that 'real books' are more important than collections of excerpts. So am I writing myself, as an anthologist, out of business? That will be for the book-buyer – or the teacher who assigns student reading – to decide. I am putting the present anthology back on the market in this 21st century because it has already proved itself to be more than just another bundle of snippets and has no less interest for readers in 2008 than it had in 1968.

Thumbing through a few other anthologies in my library, I get the impression that their editors are trying to replace the books they are drawing on, suggesting to their readers, 'everything you really need is *here*; you won't need to read all those formidable tomes by A and B and C and D, because all the wit and wisdom is encapsulated for you *here* – and anything that might not be clear can be explained by your teacher in class.' I have dealt with some of the fallacies involved on pages 12 and 13 above, and need only add that teachers who use anthologies in this way are hostile to reading: they wish to reduce reading to a minimum, as if it were something to be got out of the way, while we proceed to ... well, what? I will not bother to answer this query because my own anthologizing is founded on a quite different presumption, namely, that reading – the habit of intensive reading, whatever may happen on screens large or small – remains at the centre, not only of our schooling when young, but of our lives as auto-didacts later. (For do we not all become auto-didacts when we stop going to class but do continue to learn?)

The justification for the present book is not (a) that it tells you all you need to know about theory or theatre or (b) that it sums up all that its contributors had to say. Its Preface states, and I now confirm, that it is an introduction and it only introduces. Let me add (if indeed it is an addition and was not implicit from the start): the book should generate thought. The late I. A. Richards had a formula that fits my case: 'A book is a machine to think with.' This contrasts neatly with the vain hope of many today that some super-machine will do their thinking for them.

E.B.

Index of Persons and Works

PENGUIN MODERN CLASSICS

EQUUS
PETER SHAFFER

A seventeen-year-old boy, Alan, is brought to a psychiatric hospital because he has blinded several horses with a hoof pick. A psychiatrist, Dysart, works to 'normalize' the boy, all the while feeling that though he makes the boy 'safe' for society, he is taking away from him his wonder and sexual vitality – both of which are missing in the doctor's own personal life.

'A very important play' *The New York Times*

'Sensationally good' *Guardian*

PENGUIN MODERN CLASSICS

AMADEUS
PETER SHAFFER

When Peter Shaffer's *Amadeus* opened at the National Theatre in November 1979, it was enthusiastically received by audiences and critics alike. The play explores the rivalry between Wolfgang Amadeus Mozart and Antonio Salieri, the Court Composer for the Emperor of Austria in the late eighteenth century.

'A marvellously engrossing and often amusing costume-thriller, a feast for the eye and the ear' *Observer*

'Glorious … *Amadeus* may be a play inspired by music and death, but it fills the theatre with that mocking, heavenly silence that is the overwhelming terror of life' *The New York Times*

PENGUIN MODERN CLASSICS

THE ROYAL HUNT OF THE SUN
PETER SHAFFER

In the rich, humid air of sixteenth-century Peru, Atahuallpa, the Sun-God King, meets Pizarro the Conquistador, representative of the Spanish Empire at its most insatiable. While the Inca King is convinced of his own immortality, the Spaniard is cynical and greedy, leading to a collision of power and authority. Soon both men are locked in a struggle for survival; one of them must die and the survivor must face mortality, and the terrible truth of the world he lives in. Moving and atmospheric, *The Royal Hunt of the Sun* is an unforgettable drama of pride, empire and the conquest of bodies and souls.

'Tremendous, admirable, profound, enduring' Bernard Levin

Penguin Modern Classics

CAT ON A HOT TIN ROOF AND OTHER PLAYS
TENNESSEE WILLIAMS

CAT ON A HOT TIN ROOF/ THE MILK TRAIN DOESN'T STOP HERE
ANY MORE/ THE NIGHT OF THE IGUANA

'Tennessee will live as long as drama itself ... he is, quite simply, indispensable'
Peter Shaffer

As mirrors of his emotional and imaginative life, the plays of Tennessee Williams
explore the darker side of human nature and are haunted by the pervasive theme of
loneliness that is humanity's inescapable destiny.

Cat on a Hot Tin Roof, one of his masterpieces, seethes with the family tensions,
suppressed sexuality and the less-than-secret whisper of scandal that lie beneath
the civilized veneer of the American South. *The Milk Train Doesn't Stop Here Any
More* is a passionate examination of a woman's life as she recounts her memoirs in
the face of death. In *The Night of the Iguana*, a group of diverse people are thrown
together in an isolated Mexican hotel, all imprisoned in their own way.

Penguin Modern Classics

THE ROSE TATTOO AND OTHER PLAYS
TENNESSEE WILLIAMS

THE ROSE TATTOO/ CAMINO REAL/ ORPHEUS DESCENDING

'A wild, poetic, earthy and hilarious story of a woman's bereavement and her sensual reawakening' *Sunday Times* on *The Rose Tattoo*

In these three exotic, steamy dramas, Tennessee Williams portrays loss, faded lives and passionate affairs.

The Rose Tattoo is set in a bustling Sicilian-American community, where newly widowed Serafina is paralysed by grief. But when she has her romantic illusions about her dead husband shattered, she rediscovers her true nature as a fiery prima donna, in a life-affirming celebration of love and sex. Tennessee Williams explored a new 'wild and unrestricted' theatrical form in *Camino Real*, a colourful tropical fantasy which was described by *The New York Times* as 'a play of genuinely poetic vision'. *Orpheus Descending*, however, takes us into the familiar dark territory of Williams's Deep South: the corrupt hell of a small, brutal township, where a forbidden and tragic love affair sparks horrific violence.

PENGUIN MODERN CLASSICS

OUR TOWN AND OTHER PLAYS

OUR TOWN/ THE SKIN OF OUR TEETH/THE MATCHMAKER

THORNTON WILDER

'A wizard, a magus, a waver of wands who summons up shapes from chaos and conjures worlds out of clouds, all in an instant' *Washington Post*

Finding the theatre in the 1920s lacking in bite and conviction, Thornton Wilder set out to bring back realism and to celebrate the innocent, simple and religious. Yet he also tried to endow the individual experience with cosmic significance, and *Our Town* is both an affectionate portrait of American life and 'an attempt to find a value above all price for the smallest events in our daily life'. *The Skin of Our Teeth* deals with human survival in a 'comic strip' way, and *The Matchmaker* is a hilarious farce which urges rebellion against all the constraints that deny a rich, full life.

PENGUIN MODERN CLASSICS

THE CRUCIBLE
ARTHUR MILLER

'One of a handful of great plays that will both survive the twentieth century and bear witness to it' John Peter, *Sunday Times*

Arthur Miller's classic parable of mass hysteria draws a chilling parallel between the Salem witch-hunt of 1692 – 'one of the strangest and most awful chapters in human history' – and the McCarthyism which gripped America in the 1950s. The story of how the small community of Salem is stirred to madness by superstition, paranoia and malice, culminating in a violent climax, is a savage attack on the evils of mindless persecution and the terrifying power of false accusations.

PENGUIN MODERN CLASSICS

RHINOCEROS, THE CHAIRS, THE LESSON
EUGÈNE IONESCO

'It's not a certain society that seems ridiculous to me, it's mankind'

These three great plays by one of the founding fathers of the Theatre of the Absurd are alive and kicking with tragedy and humour, bleakness and farce. In *Rhinoceros* we are shown the innate brutality of people when everyone, except for Berenger, turns into clumsy, unthinking rhinoceroses. *The Chairs* depicts the futile struggle of two old people to convey the meaning of life to the rest of humanity, while *The Lesson* is a chilling, but anarchically funny drama of verbal domination. In these three 'antiplays', dream, nonsense and fantasy combine to create an unsettling, bizarre view of society.

'Ionesco's verbal rhythms are subtle and brilliant, creating their own kind of hypnotic tension' Raymond Williams

Rhinoceros Translated by Derek Prouse
The Chairs/The Lesson Translated by Donald Watson

PENGUIN MODERN CLASSICS

CALIGULA AND OTHER PLAYS
ALBERT CAMUS

CALIGULA/ CROSS PURPOSE/ THE JUST/ THE POSSESSED

'Few French writers of this century have been more versatile or more influential than Camus' *The Times*

Camus' four philosophical dramas illustrate the shift in his perception of the human condition. *Caligula* reveals some aspects of the existential notion of 'the absurd' by portraying an emperor so monstrous that in his search for freedom he destroys gods, men and himself. *Cross Purpose* portrays a universe in which cruel, inexplicable things happen to innocent and evil people alike. By the time of the overtly political plays, *The Just* and *The Possessed*, Camus dramatizes action and revolt in the name of liberty.

With an Introduction by John Cruikshank

WINNER OF THE NOBEL PRIZE FOR LITERATURE